SUPERMAN

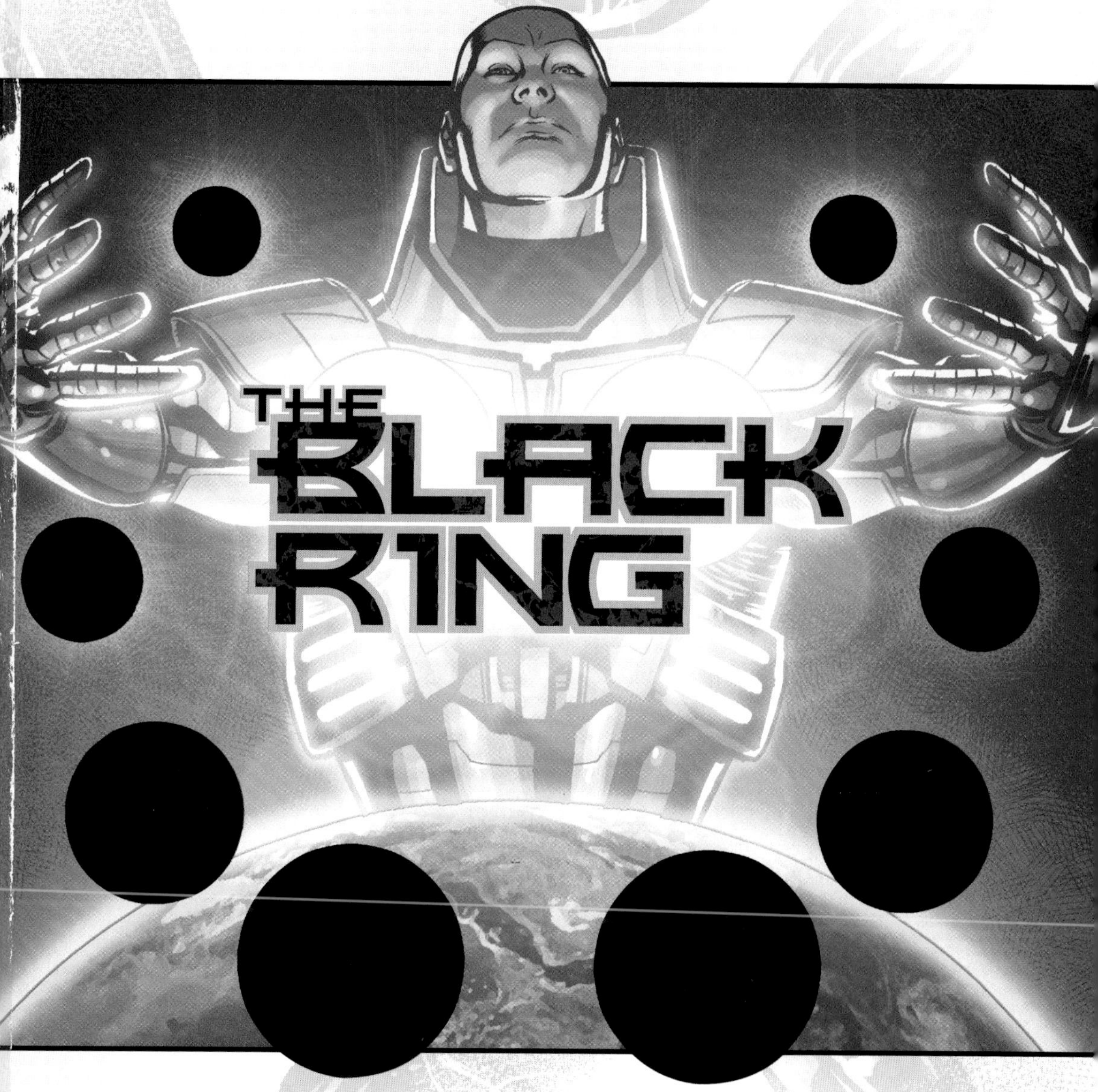
THE
BLACK
RING

volume one

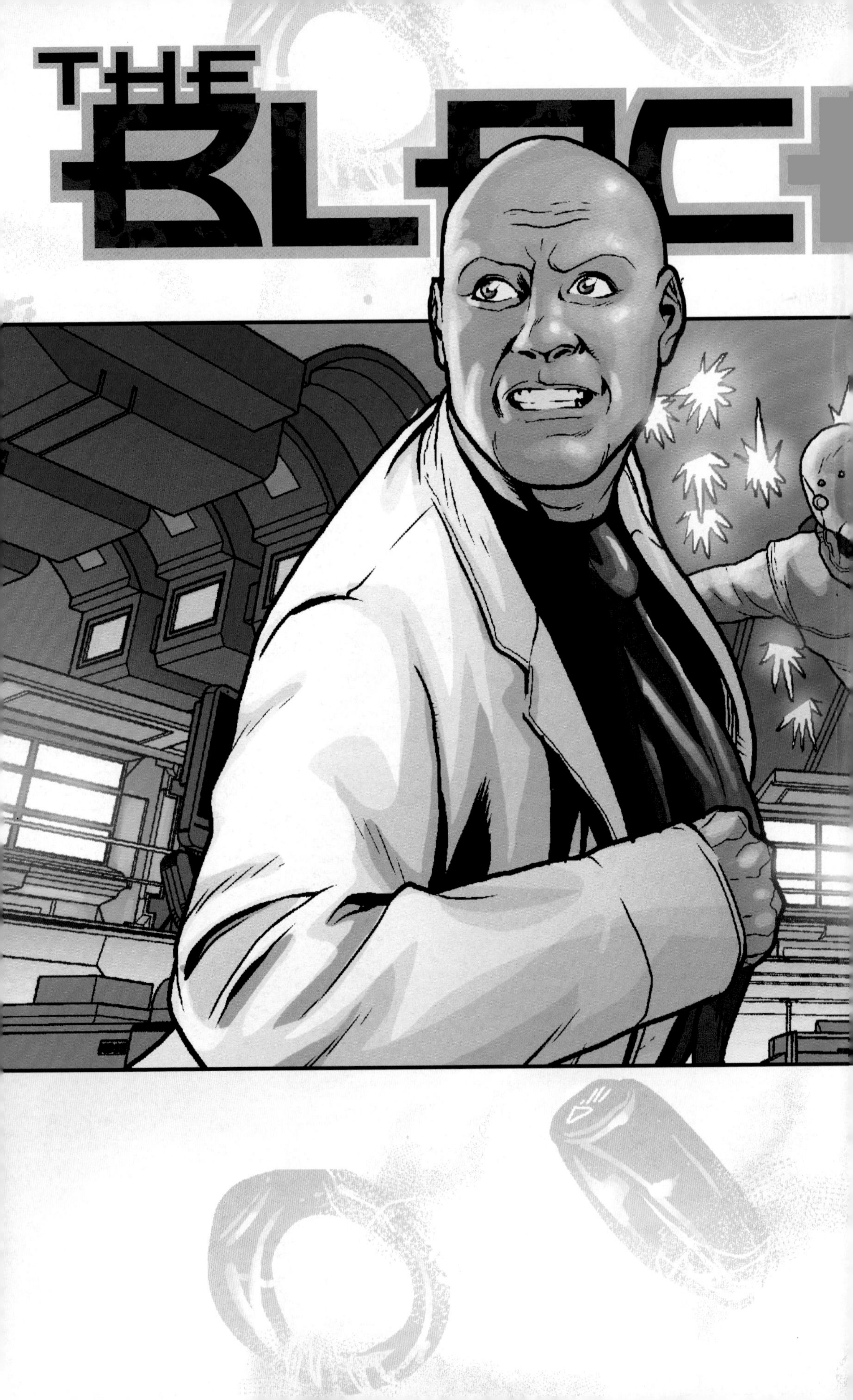
THE

SUPERMAN

K RING

volume one

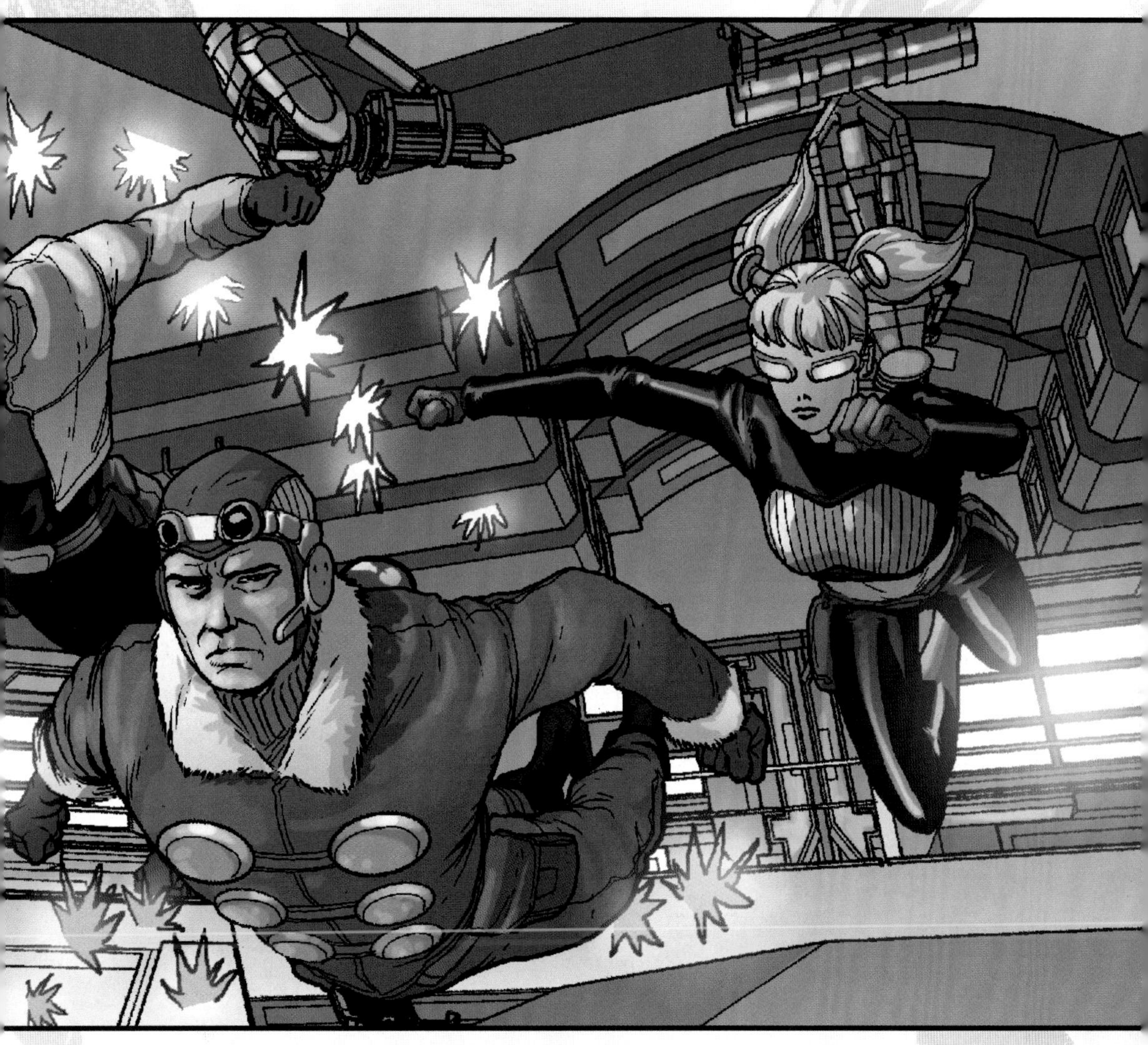

PAUL CORNELL writer **PETE WOODS** artist

CAFU & BIT **PERE PÉREZ** **SEAN CHEN & WAYNE FAUCHER** additional art

BRAD ANDERSON colorist **ROB LEIGH** letterer

Very special thanks to **NEIL GAIMAN**

Superman created by **JERRY SIEGEL & JOE SHUSTER**

Death created by **NEIL GAIMAN & MIKE DRINGENBERG**

MATT IDELSON EDITOR-ORIGINAL SERIES   **WIL MOSS** ASSISTANT EDITOR-ORIGINAL SERIES
BOB HARRAS GROUP EDITOR-COLLECTED EDITIONS   **SEAN MACKIEWICZ** EDITOR   **ROBBIN BROSTERMAN** DESIGN DIRECTOR-BOOKS

DC COMICS

DIANE NELSON PRESIDENT   **DAN DIDIO** AND **JIM LEE** CO-PUBLISHERS
GEOFF JOHNS CHIEF CREATIVE OFFICER   **PATRICK CALDON** EVP-FINANCE AND ADMINISTRATION
JOHN ROOD EVP-SALES, MARKETING AND BUSINESS DEVELOPMENT
AMY GENKINS SVP-BUSINESS AND LEGAL AFFAIRS
STEVE ROTTERDAM SVP-SALES AND MARKETING
JOHN CUNNINGHAM VP-MARKETING
TERRI CUNNINGHAM VP-MANAGING EDITOR
ALISON GILL VP-MANUFACTURING
DAVID HYDE VP-PUBLICITY   **SUE POHJA** VP-BOOK TRADE SALES
ALYSSE SOLL VP-ADVERTISING AND CUSTOM PUBLISHING
BOB WAYNE VP-SALES   **MARK CHIARELLO** ART DIRECTOR

Publication design by Robbie Biederman

SUPERMAN: THE BLACK RING VOLUME ONE

Published by DC Comics. Cover and compilation Copyright © 2011 DC Comics. All Rights Reserved.
Originally published in single magazine form in ACTION COMICS 890-895. Copyright © 2010, 2011 DC Comics.
All Rights Reserved. All characters, their distinctive likenesses and related elements featured in this publication are
trademarks of DC Comics. The stories, characters and incidents featured in this publication are entirely fictional.
DC Comics does not read or accept unsolicited submissions of ideas, stories or artwork.

DC Comics, 1700 Broadway, New York, NY 10019. A Warner Bros. Entertainment Company
Printed by Quad/Graphics, Dubuque, IA, USA. 2/25/11. First printing.
HC ISBN: 978-1-4012-3033-3   SC ISBN: 978-1-4012-3034-0

SUSTAINABLE FORESTRY INITIATIVE

Certified Chain of Custody
Promoting Sustainable
Forest Management
www.sfiprogram.org
Fiber used in this product line meets the sourcing requirements
of the SFI program. www.sfiprogram.org SGS-SFICOC-0130

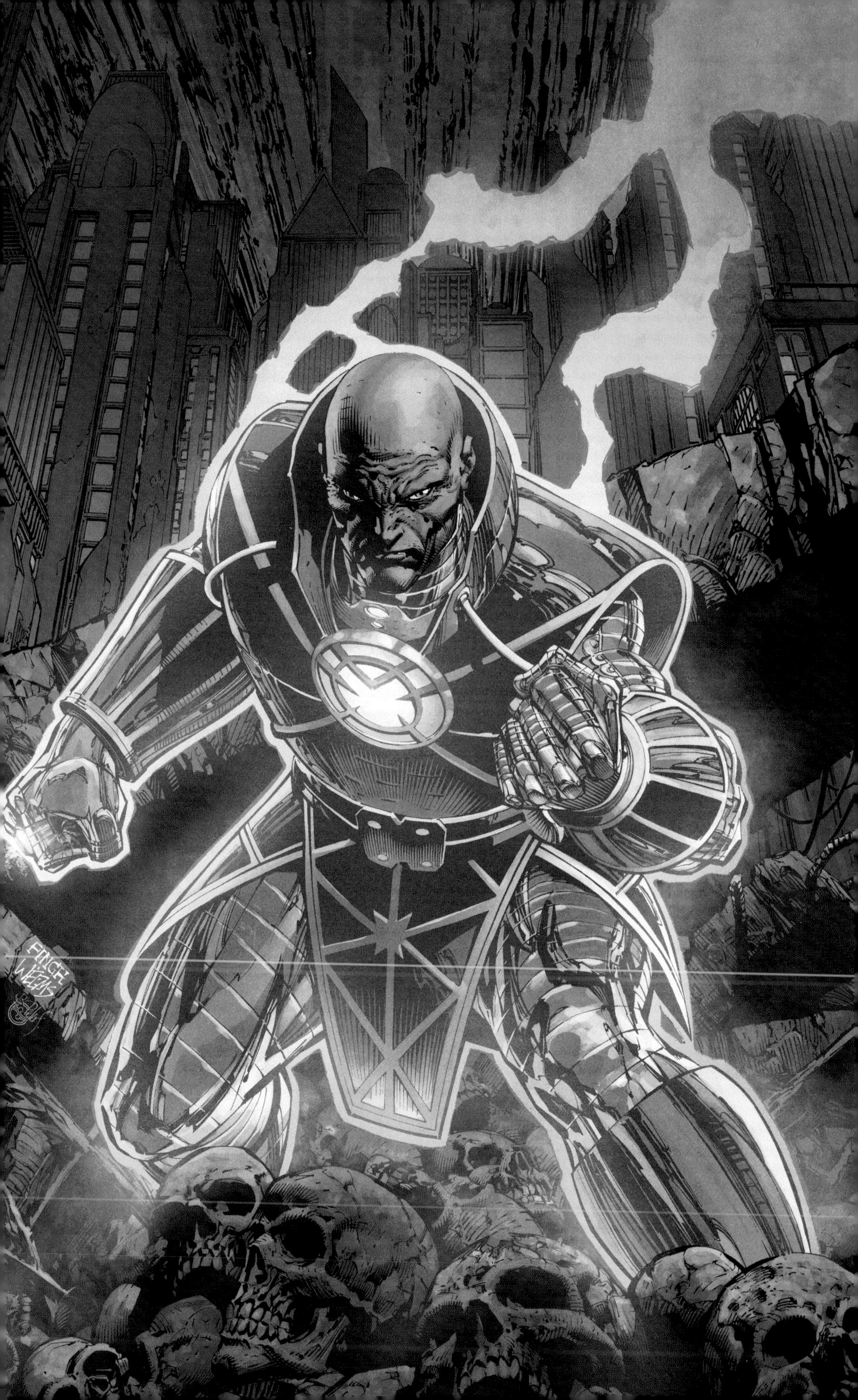
FINCH
WEEMS

THE BLACK RING
part one

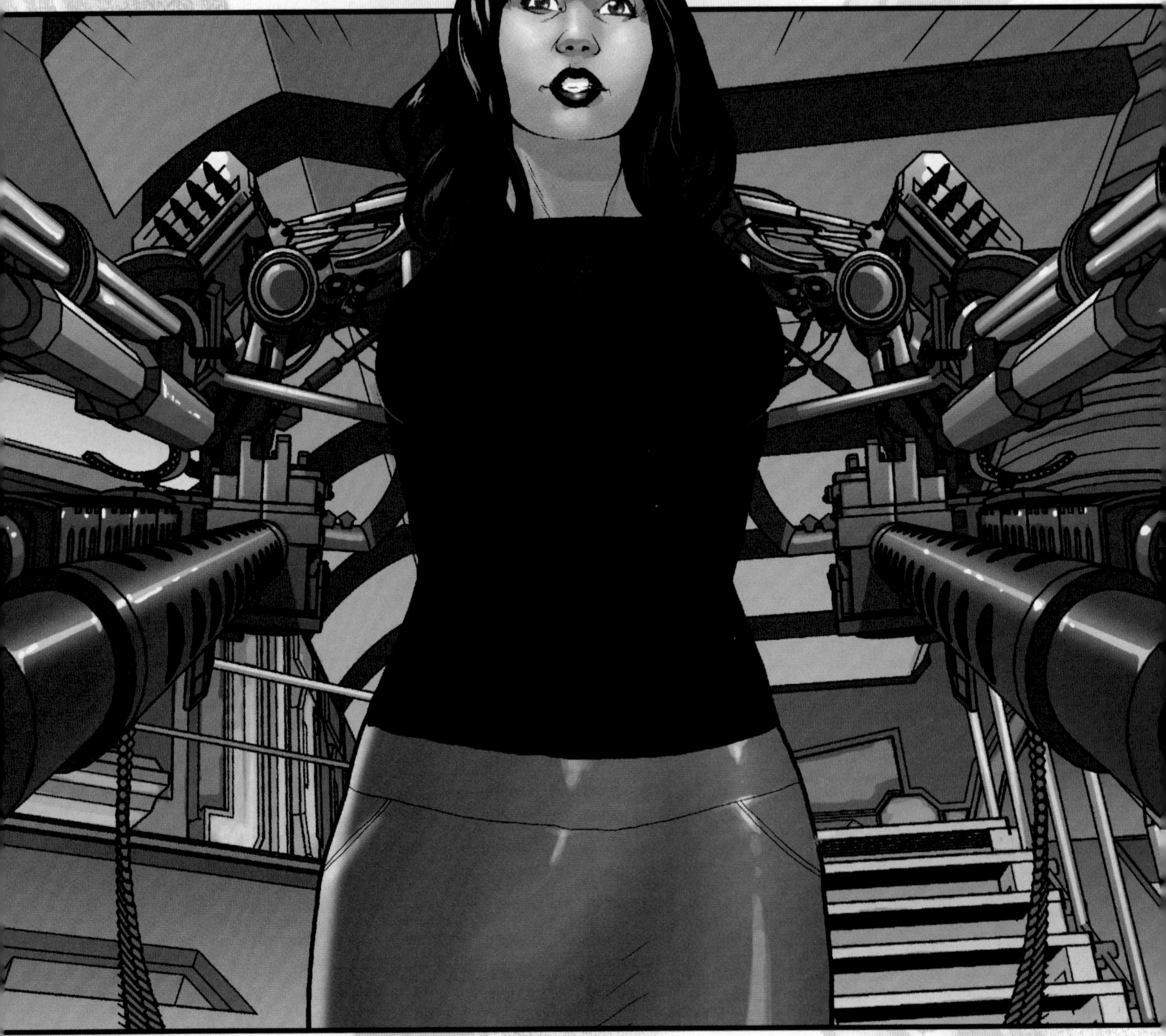

cover by
DAVID **FINCH**, JOE **WEEMS** & PETER **STEIGERWALD**

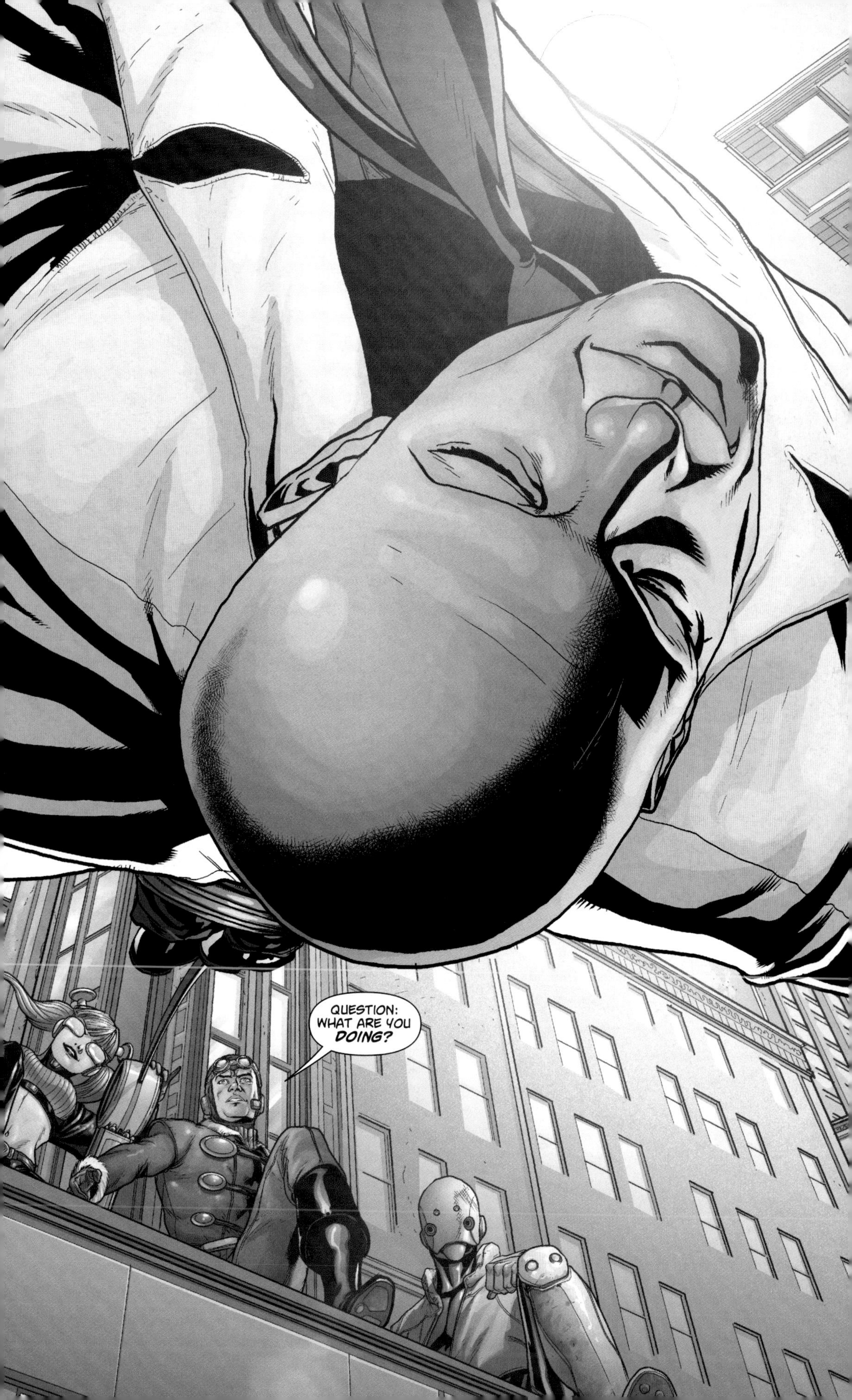
QUESTION: WHAT ARE YOU *DOING?*

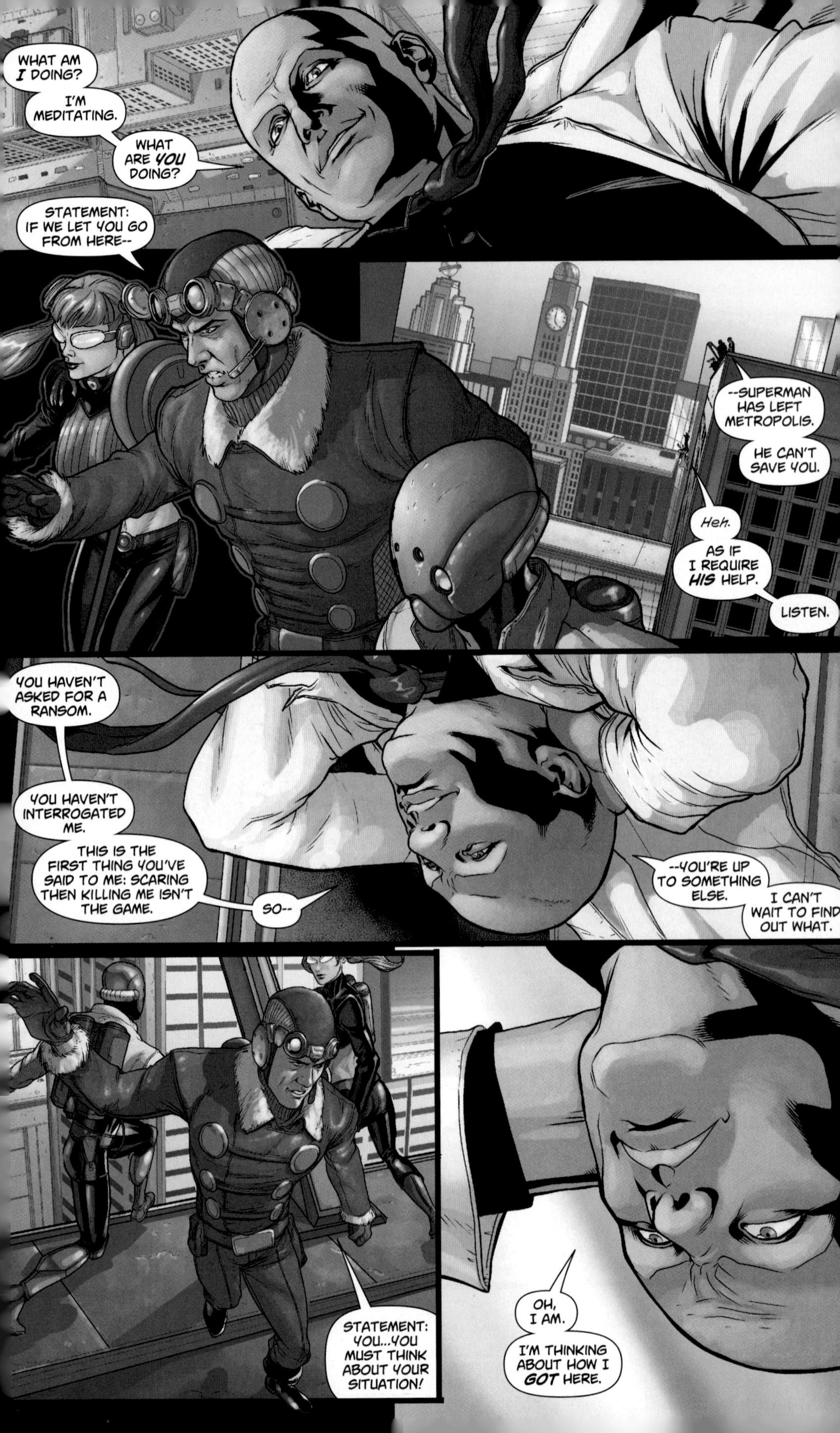
WHAT AM *I* DOING?
I'M MEDITATING.
WHAT ARE ***YOU*** DOING?
STATEMENT: IF WE LET YOU GO FROM HERE--
--SUPERMAN HAS LEFT METROPOLIS.
HE CAN'T SAVE YOU.
Heh.
AS IF I REQUIRE ***HIS*** HELP.
LISTEN.
YOU HAVEN'T ASKED FOR A RANSOM.
YOU HAVEN'T INTERROGATED ME.
THIS IS THE FIRST THING YOU'VE SAID TO ME: SCARING THEN KILLING ME ISN'T THE GAME.
SO--
--YOU'RE UP TO SOMETHING ELSE.
I CAN'T WAIT TO FIND OUT WHAT.
STATEMENT: YOU...YOU MUST THINK ABOUT YOUR SITUATION!
OH, I AM.
I'M THINKING ABOUT HOW I ***GOT*** HERE.

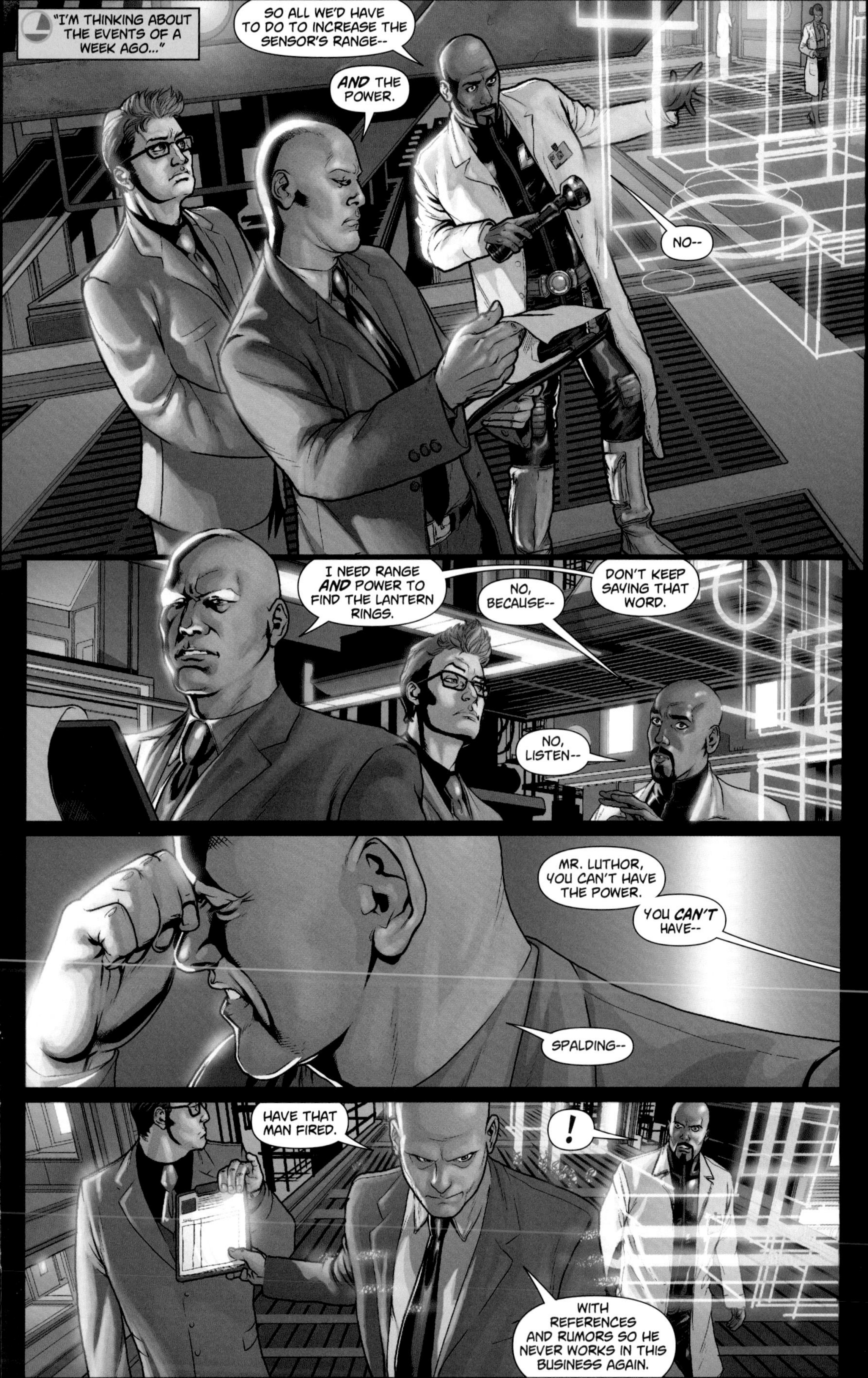
"I'M THINKING ABOUT THE EVENTS OF A WEEK AGO..."
SO ALL WE'D HAVE TO DO TO INCREASE THE SENSOR'S RANGE--
AND THE POWER.
NO--
I NEED RANGE AND POWER TO FIND THE LANTERN RINGS.
NO, BECAUSE--
DON'T KEEP SAYING THAT WORD.
NO, LISTEN--
MR. LUTHOR, YOU CAN'T HAVE THE POWER.
YOU CAN'T HAVE--
SPALDING--
HAVE THAT MAN FIRED.
!
WITH REFERENCES AND RUMORS SO HE NEVER WORKS IN THIS BUSINESS AGAIN.

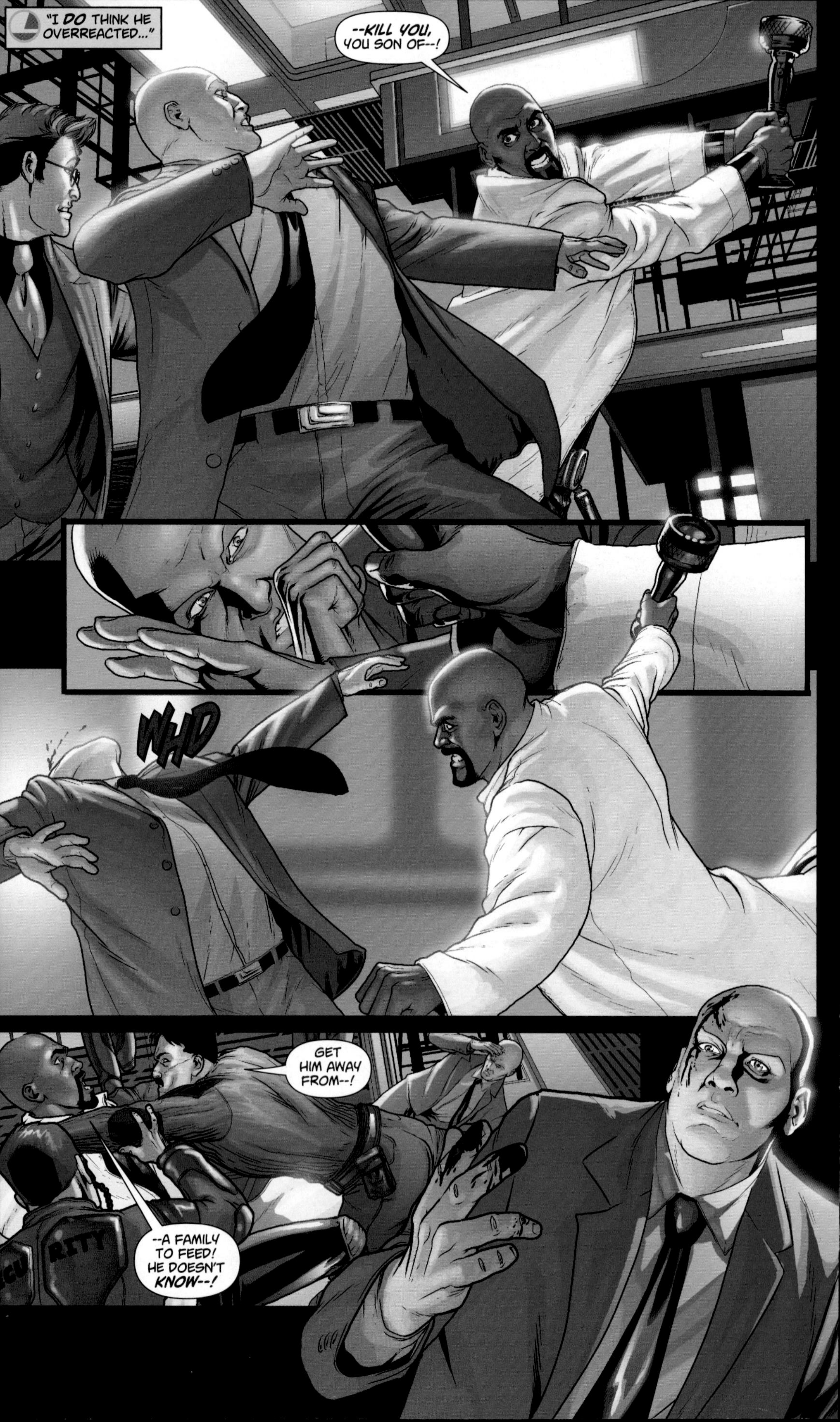
"I DO THINK HE OVERREACTED..."
--KILL YOU, YOU SON OF--!
WHD
GET HIM AWAY FROM--!
--A FAMILY TO FEED! HE DOESN'T KNOW--!

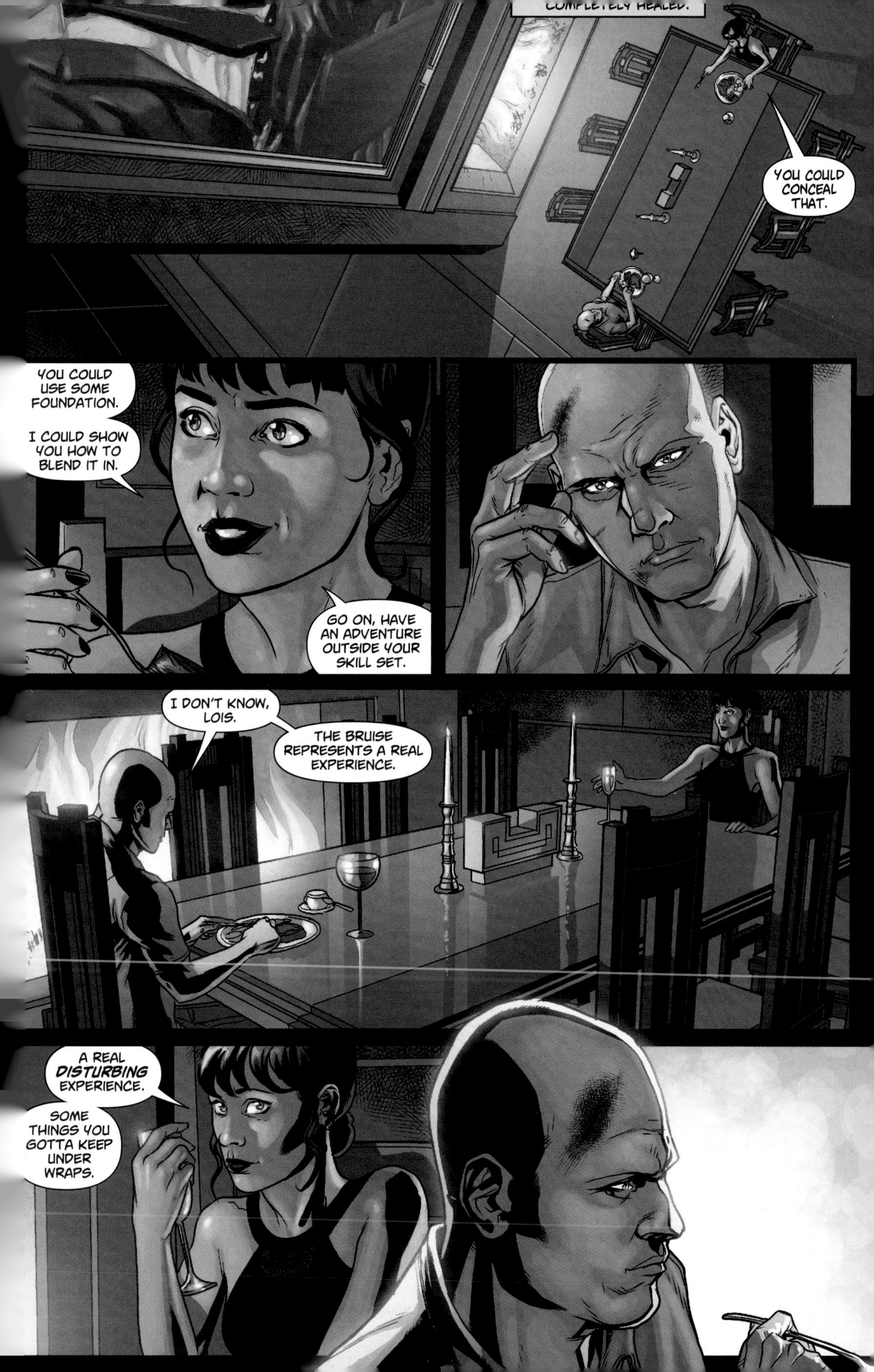
COMPLETELY HEALED.
YOU COULD CONCEAL THAT.
YOU COULD USE SOME FOUNDATION.
I COULD SHOW YOU HOW TO BLEND IT IN.
GO ON, HAVE AN ADVENTURE OUTSIDE YOUR SKILL SET.
I DON'T KNOW, LOIS.
THE BRUISE REPRESENTS A REAL EXPERIENCE.
A REAL *DISTURBING* EXPERIENCE.
SOME THINGS YOU GOTTA KEEP UNDER WRAPS.

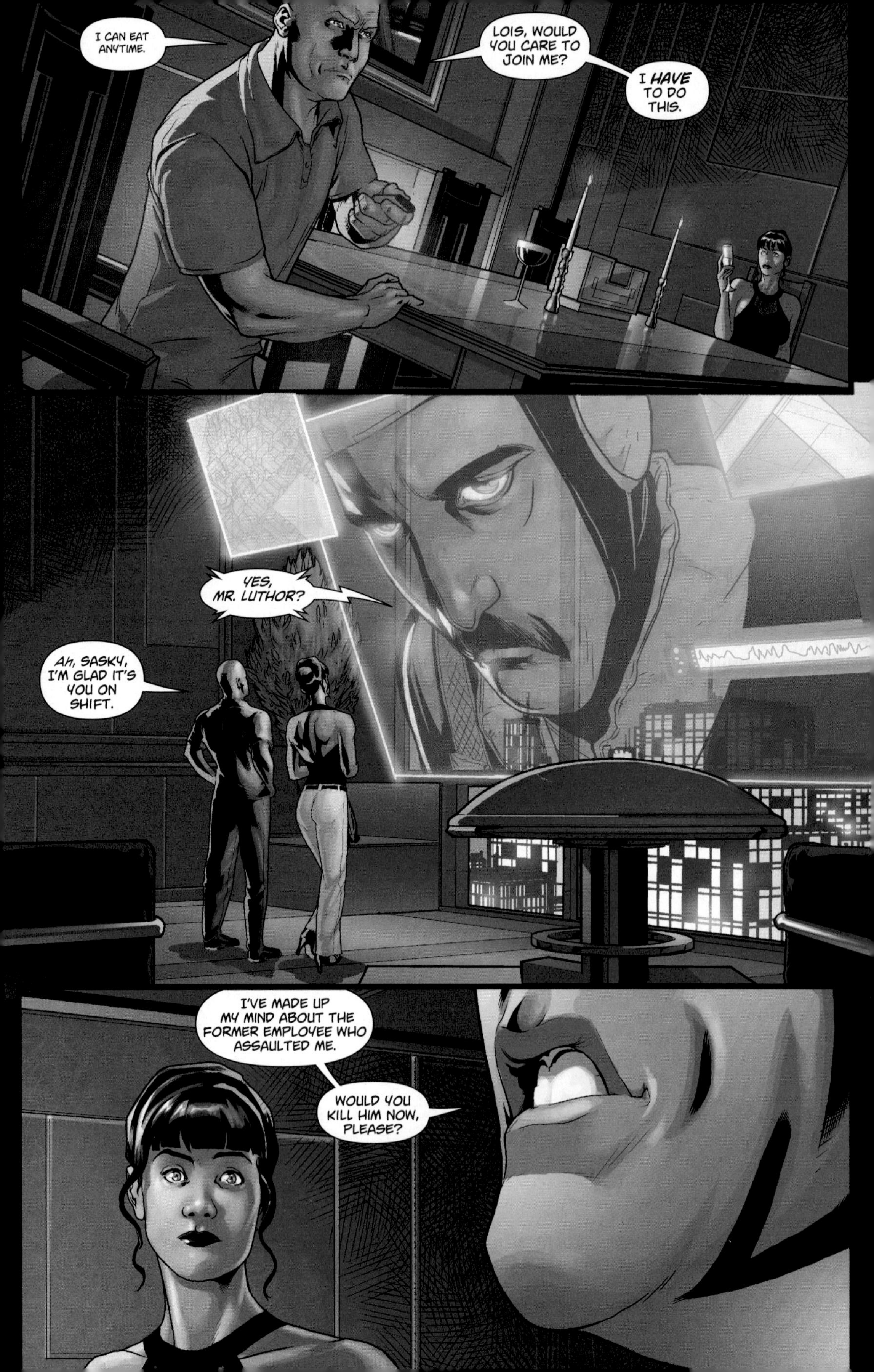
I CAN EAT ANYTIME.
LOIS, WOULD YOU CARE TO JOIN ME?
I HAVE TO DO THIS.
YES, MR. LUTHOR?
Ah, SASKY, I'M GLAD IT'S YOU ON SHIFT.
I'VE MADE UP MY MIND ABOUT THE FORMER EMPLOYEE WHO ASSAULTED ME.
WOULD YOU KILL HIM NOW, PLEASE?

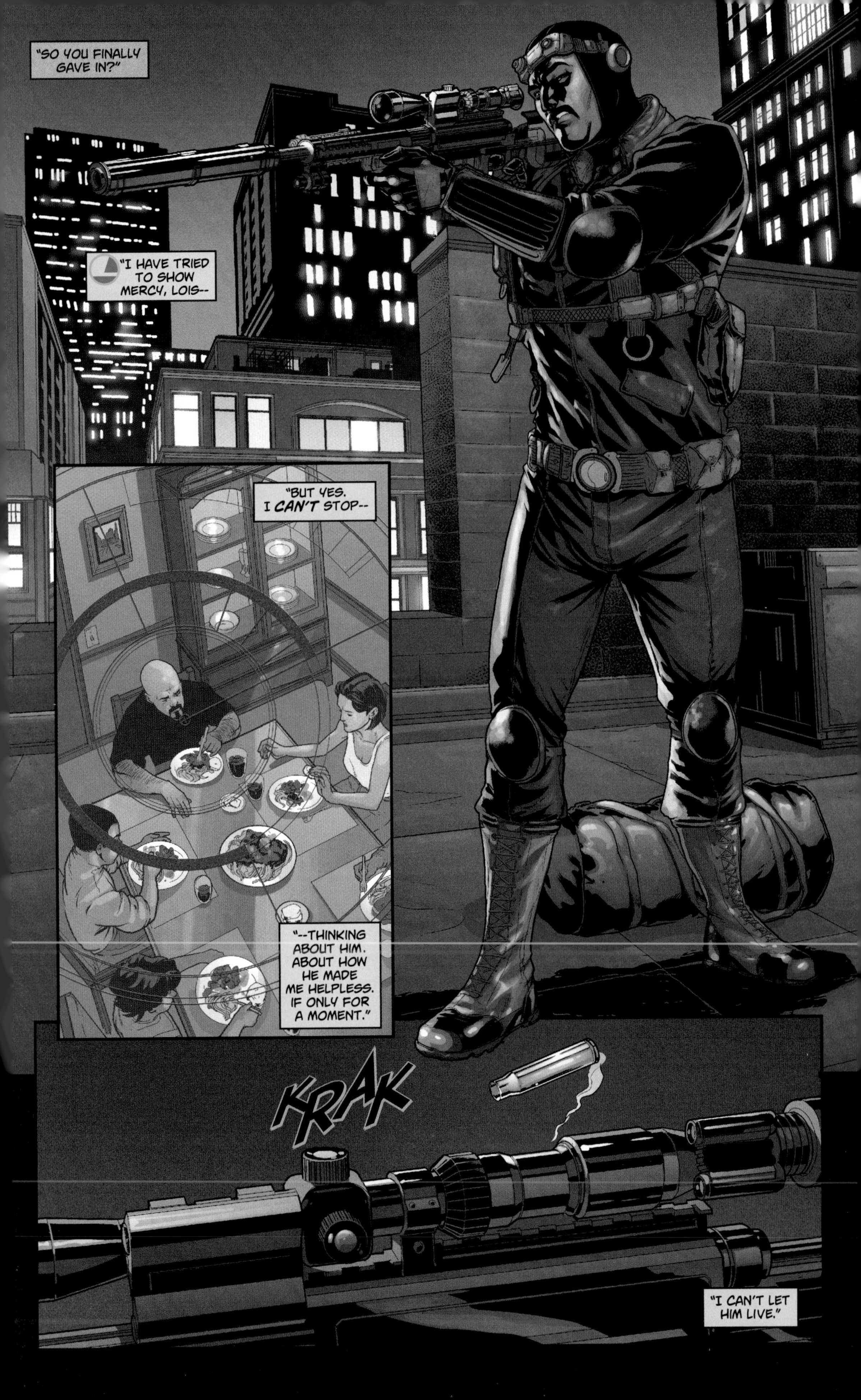
"SO YOU FINALLY GAVE IN?"
"I HAVE TRIED TO SHOW MERCY, LOIS--
"BUT YES. I CAN'T STOP--
"--THINKING ABOUT HIM. ABOUT HOW HE MADE ME HELPLESS. IF ONLY FOR A MOMENT."
KRAK
"I CAN'T LET HIM LIVE."

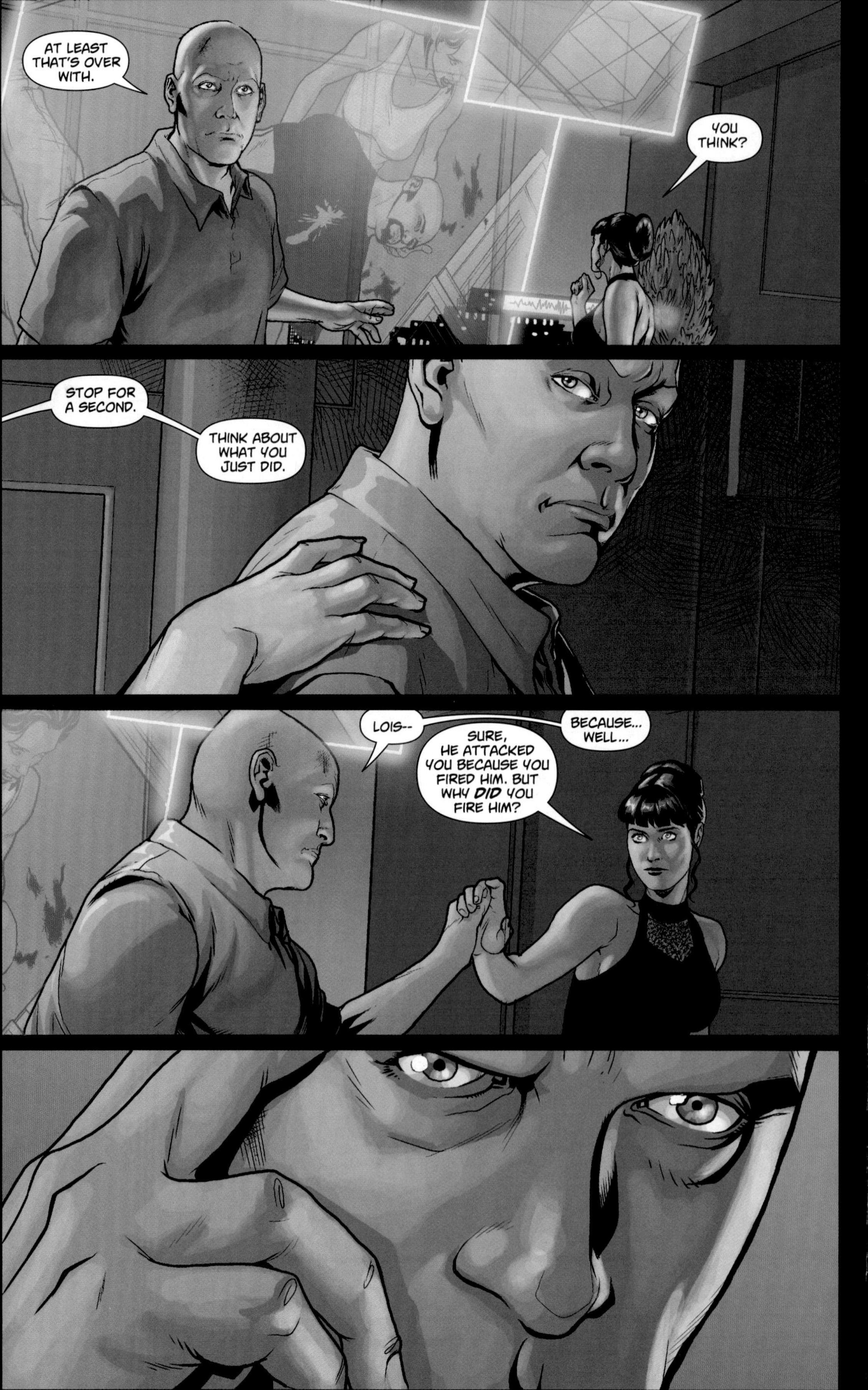
AT LEAST THAT'S OVER WITH.
YOU THINK?
STOP FOR A SECOND.
THINK ABOUT WHAT YOU JUST DID.
LOIS--
BECAUSE... WELL...
SURE, HE ATTACKED YOU BECAUSE YOU FIRED HIM. BUT WHY *DID* YOU FIRE HIM?

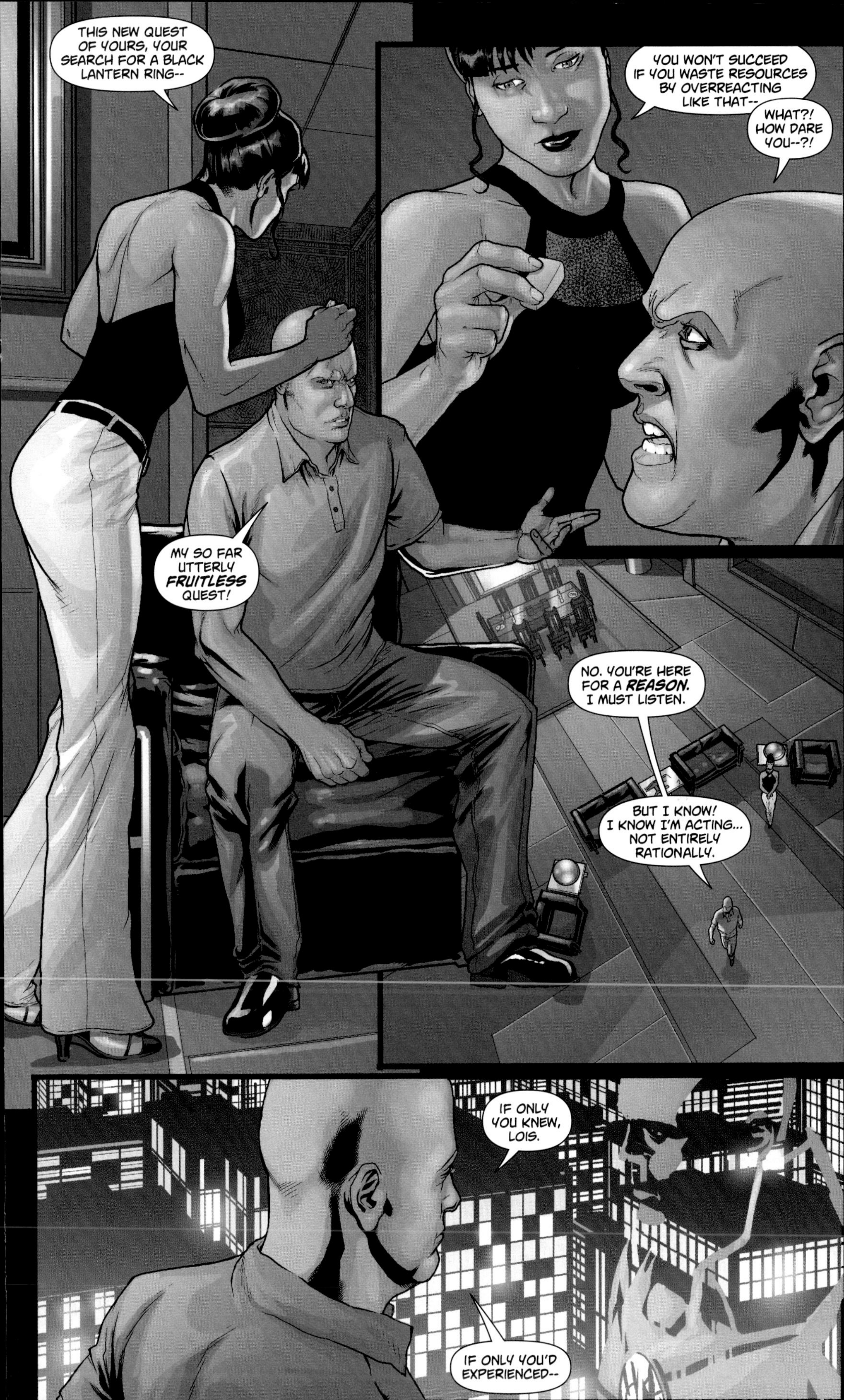
THIS NEW QUEST OF YOURS, YOUR SEARCH FOR A BLACK LANTERN RING--
YOU WON'T SUCCEED IF YOU WASTE RESOURCES BY OVERREACTING LIKE THAT--
WHAT?! HOW DARE YOU--?!
MY SO FAR UTTERLY FRUITLESS QUEST!
NO. YOU'RE HERE FOR A REASON. I MUST LISTEN.
BUT I KNOW! I KNOW I'M ACTING... NOT ENTIRELY RATIONALLY.
IF ONLY YOU KNEW, LOIS.
IF ONLY YOU'D EXPERIENCED--

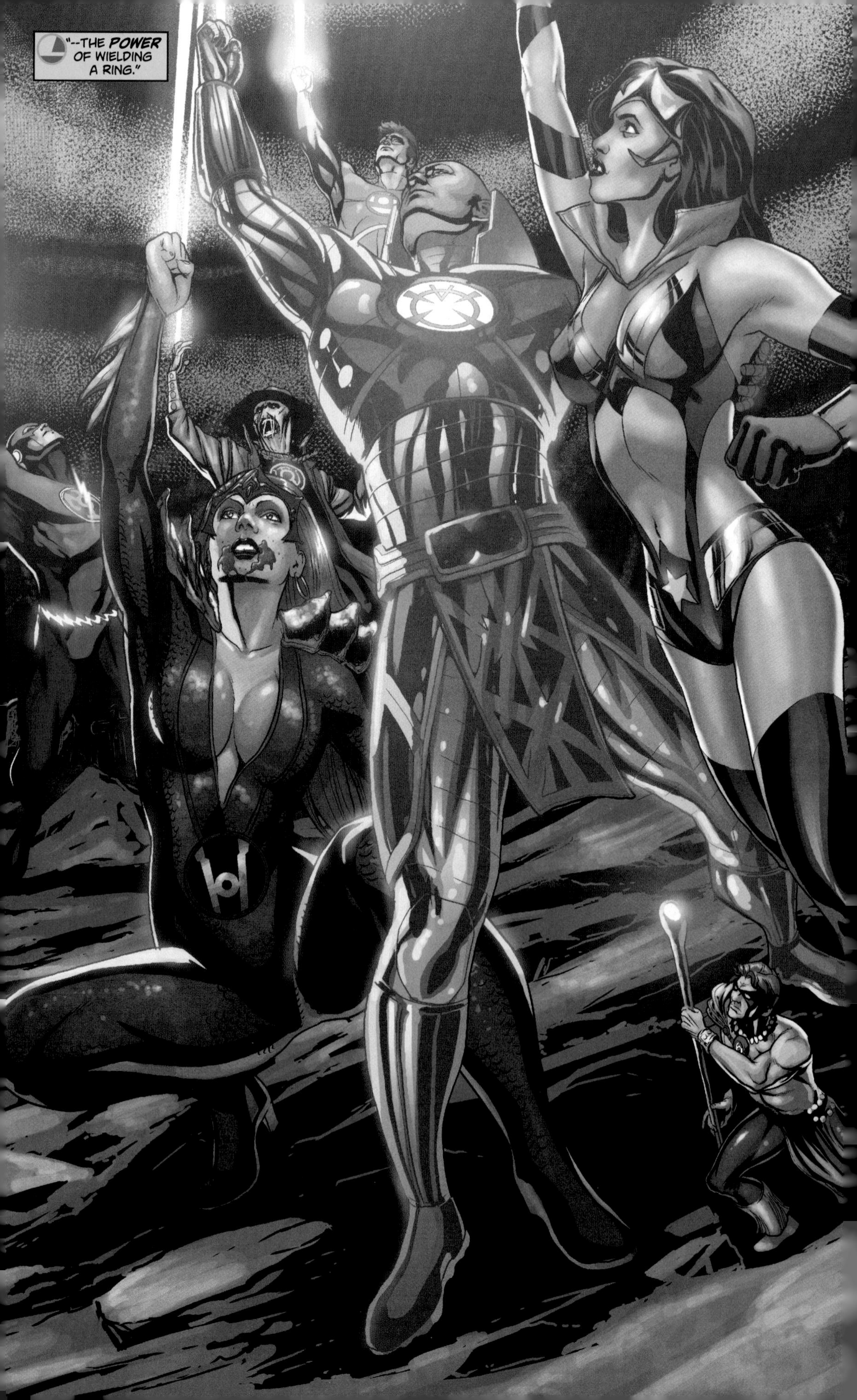
"--THE POWER OF WIELDING A RING."

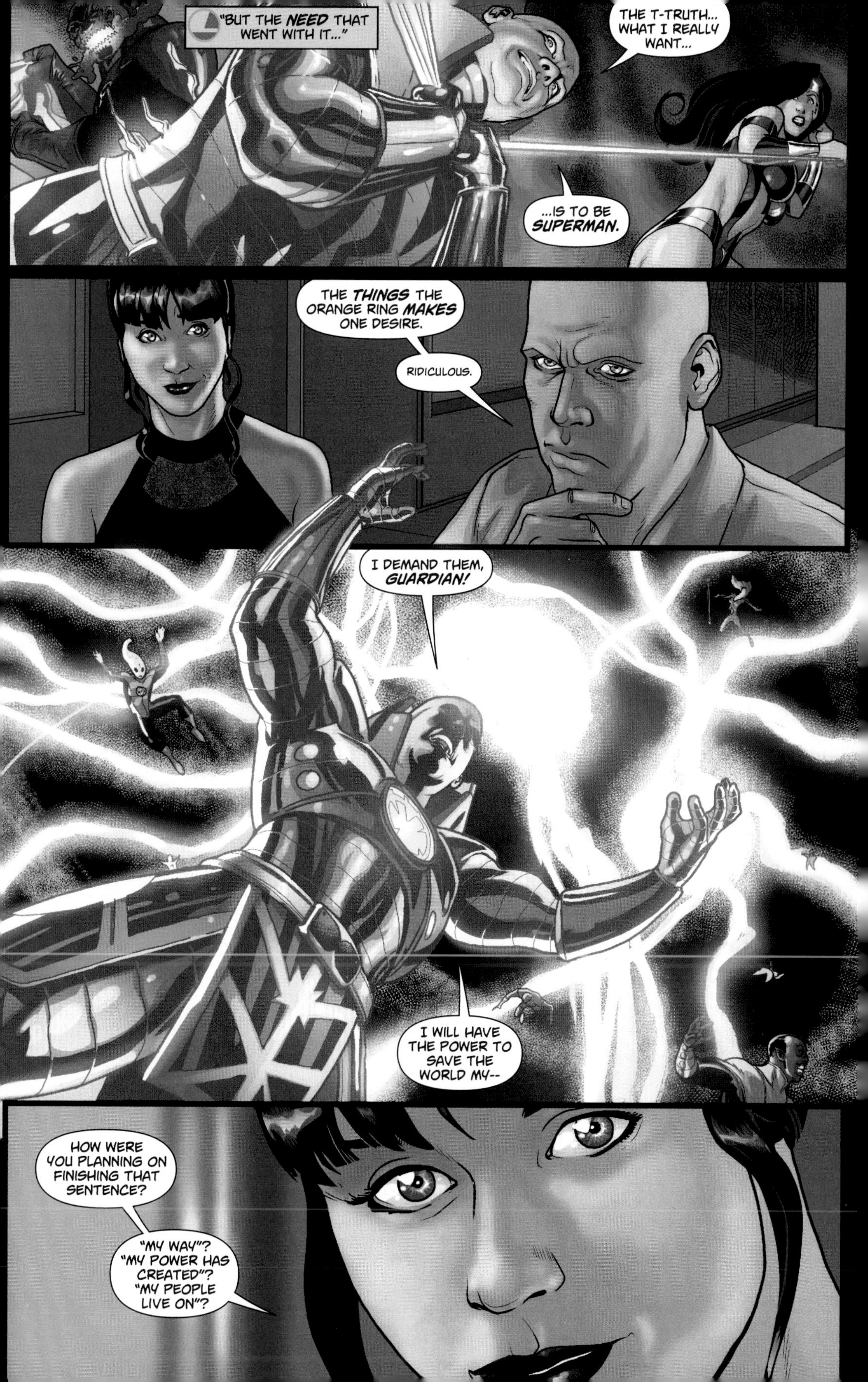
"BUT THE NEED THAT WENT WITH IT..."
THE T-TRUTH... WHAT I REALLY WANT...
...IS TO BE SUPERMAN.
THE THINGS THE ORANGE RING MAKES ONE DESIRE.
RIDICULOUS.
I DEMAND THEM, GUARDIAN!
I WILL HAVE THE POWER TO SAVE THE WORLD MY--
HOW WERE YOU PLANNING ON FINISHING THAT SENTENCE?
"MY WAY"? "MY POWER HAS CREATED"? "MY PEOPLE LIVE ON"?

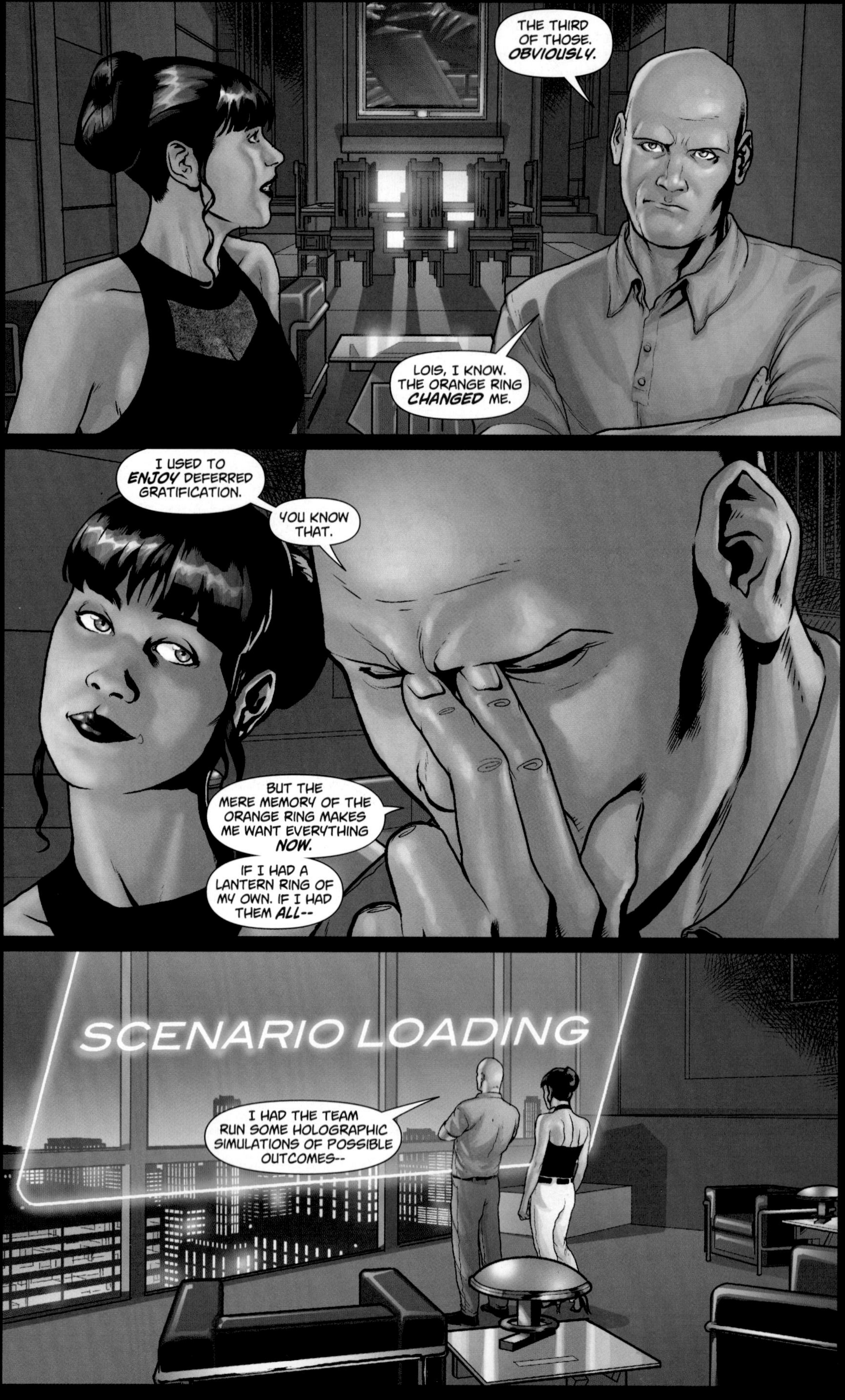
THE THIRD OF THOSE. OBVIOUSLY.
LOIS, I KNOW. THE ORANGE RING CHANGED ME.
I USED TO ENJOY DEFERRED GRATIFICATION.
YOU KNOW THAT.
BUT THE MERE MEMORY OF THE ORANGE RING MAKES ME WANT EVERYTHING NOW.
IF I HAD A LANTERN RING OF MY OWN. IF I HAD THEM ALL--
SCENARIO LOADING
I HAD THE TEAM RUN SOME HOLOGRAPHIC SIMULATIONS OF POSSIBLE OUTCOMES--

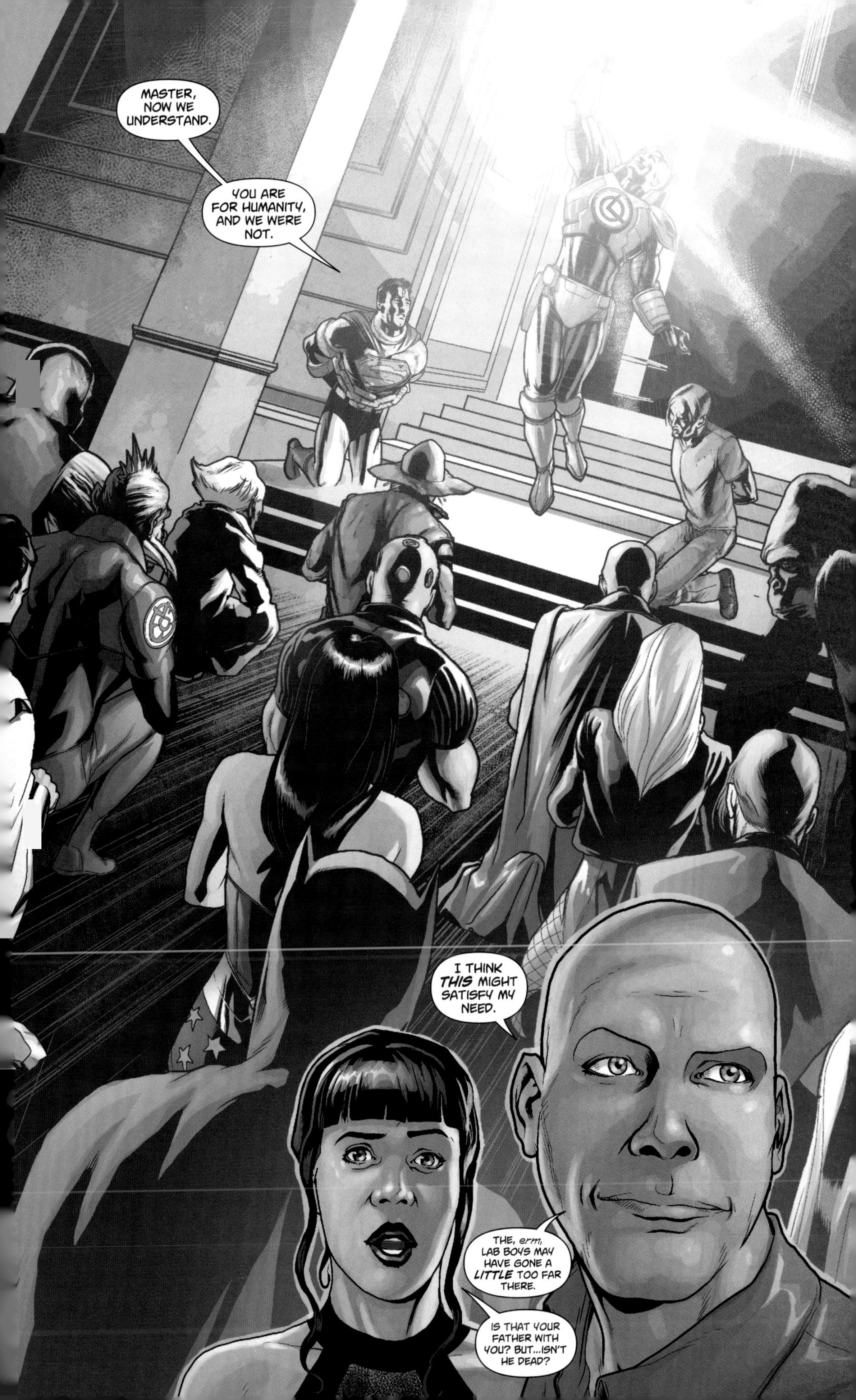
MASTER, NOW WE UNDERSTAND.
YOU ARE FOR HUMANITY, AND WE WERE NOT.
I THINK *THIS* MIGHT SATISFY MY NEED.
THE, *erm*, LAB BOYS MAY HAVE GONE A *LITTLE* TOO FAR THERE.
IS THAT YOUR FATHER WITH YOU? BUT...ISN'T HE DEAD?

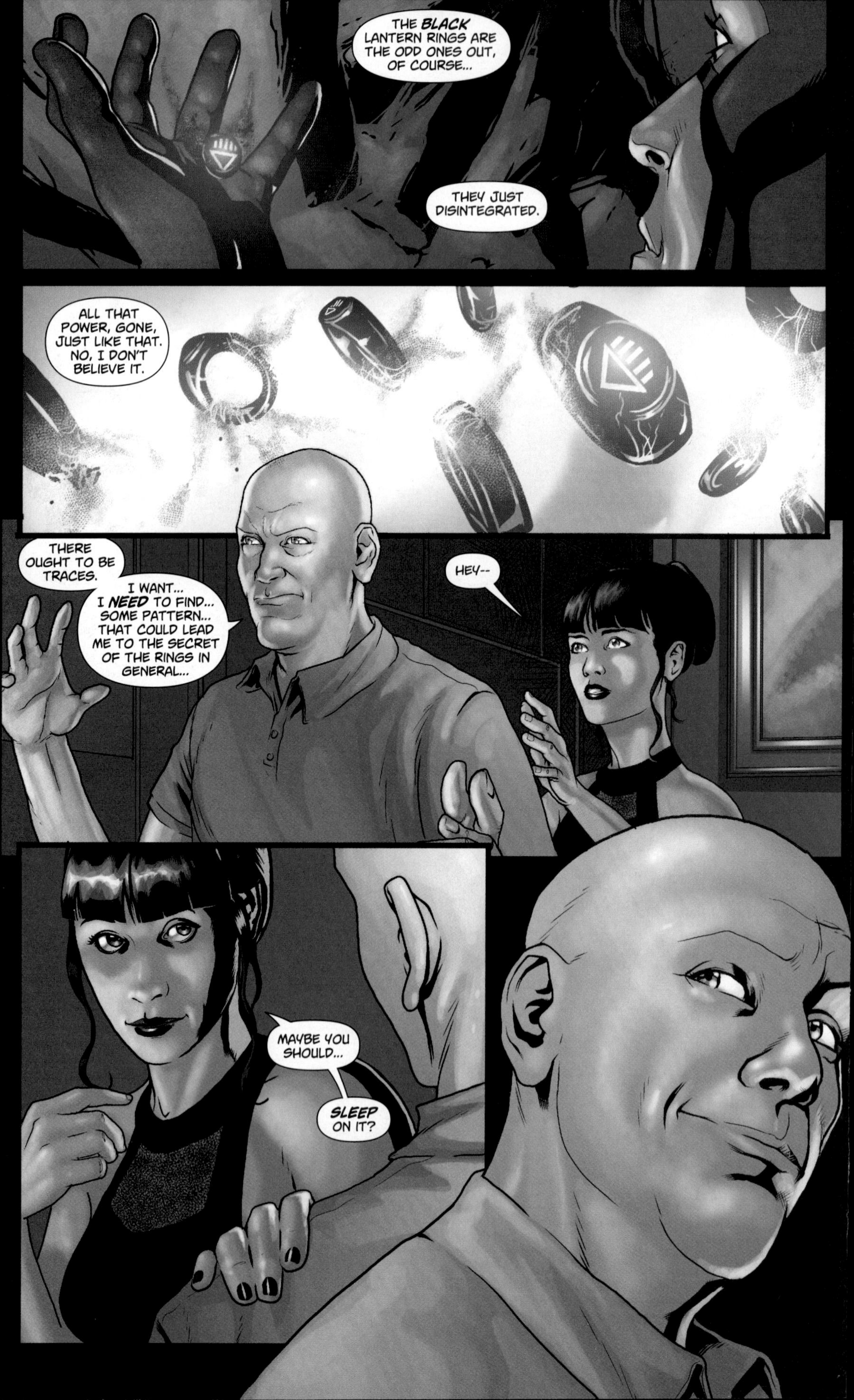
THE BLACK LANTERN RINGS ARE THE ODD ONES OUT, OF COURSE...
THEY JUST DISINTEGRATED.
ALL THAT POWER, GONE, JUST LIKE THAT. NO, I DON'T BELIEVE IT.
THERE OUGHT TO BE TRACES.
I WANT... I NEED TO FIND... SOME PATTERN... THAT COULD LEAD ME TO THE SECRET OF THE RINGS IN GENERAL...
HEY--
MAYBE YOU SHOULD...
SLEEP ON IT?

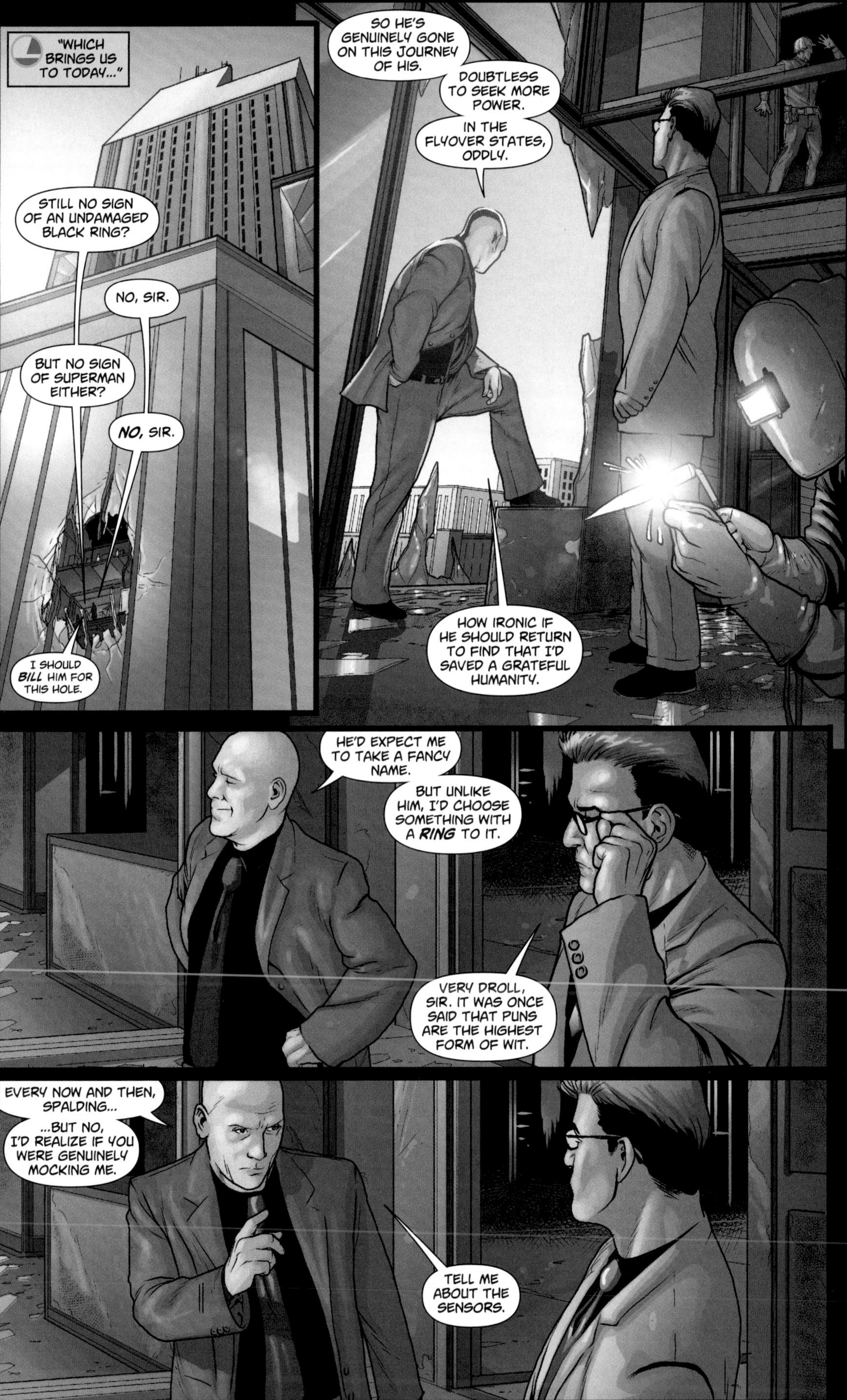
"WHICH BRINGS US TO TODAY..."
STILL NO SIGN OF AN UNDAMAGED BLACK RING?
NO, SIR.
BUT NO SIGN OF SUPERMAN EITHER?
NO, SIR.
I SHOULD BILL HIM FOR THIS HOLE.
SO HE'S GENUINELY GONE ON THIS JOURNEY OF HIS.
DOUBTLESS TO SEEK MORE POWER.
IN THE FLYOVER STATES, ODDLY.
HOW IRONIC IF HE SHOULD RETURN TO FIND THAT I'D SAVED A GRATEFUL HUMANITY.
HE'D EXPECT ME TO TAKE A FANCY NAME.
BUT UNLIKE HIM, I'D CHOOSE SOMETHING WITH A RING TO IT.
VERY DROLL, SIR. IT WAS ONCE SAID THAT PUNS ARE THE HIGHEST FORM OF WIT.
EVERY NOW AND THEN, SPALDING...
...BUT NO, I'D REALIZE IF YOU WERE GENUINELY MOCKING ME.
TELL ME ABOUT THE SENSORS.

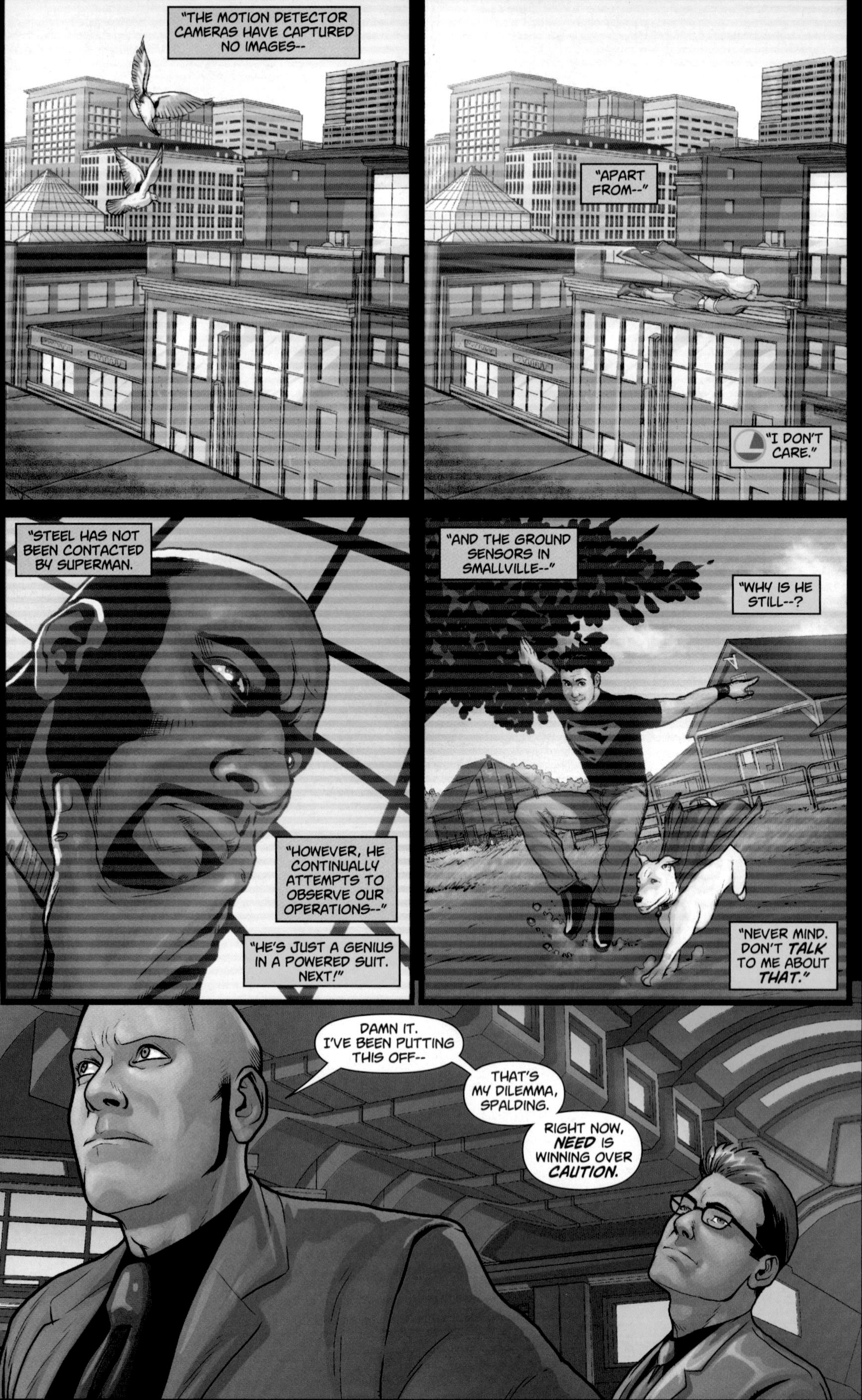

"THE MOTION DETECTOR CAMERAS HAVE CAPTURED NO IMAGES--
"APART FROM--"
"I DON'T CARE."
"STEEL HAS NOT BEEN CONTACTED BY SUPERMAN.
"HOWEVER, HE CONTINUALLY ATTEMPTS TO OBSERVE OUR OPERATIONS--"
"HE'S JUST A GENIUS IN A POWERED SUIT. NEXT!"
"AND THE GROUND SENSORS IN SMALLVILLE--"
"WHY IS HE STILL--?
"NEVER MIND. DON'T TALK TO ME ABOUT THAT."
DAMN IT. I'VE BEEN PUTTING THIS OFF--
THAT'S MY DILEMMA, SPALDING.
RIGHT NOW, NEED IS WINNING OVER CAUTION.

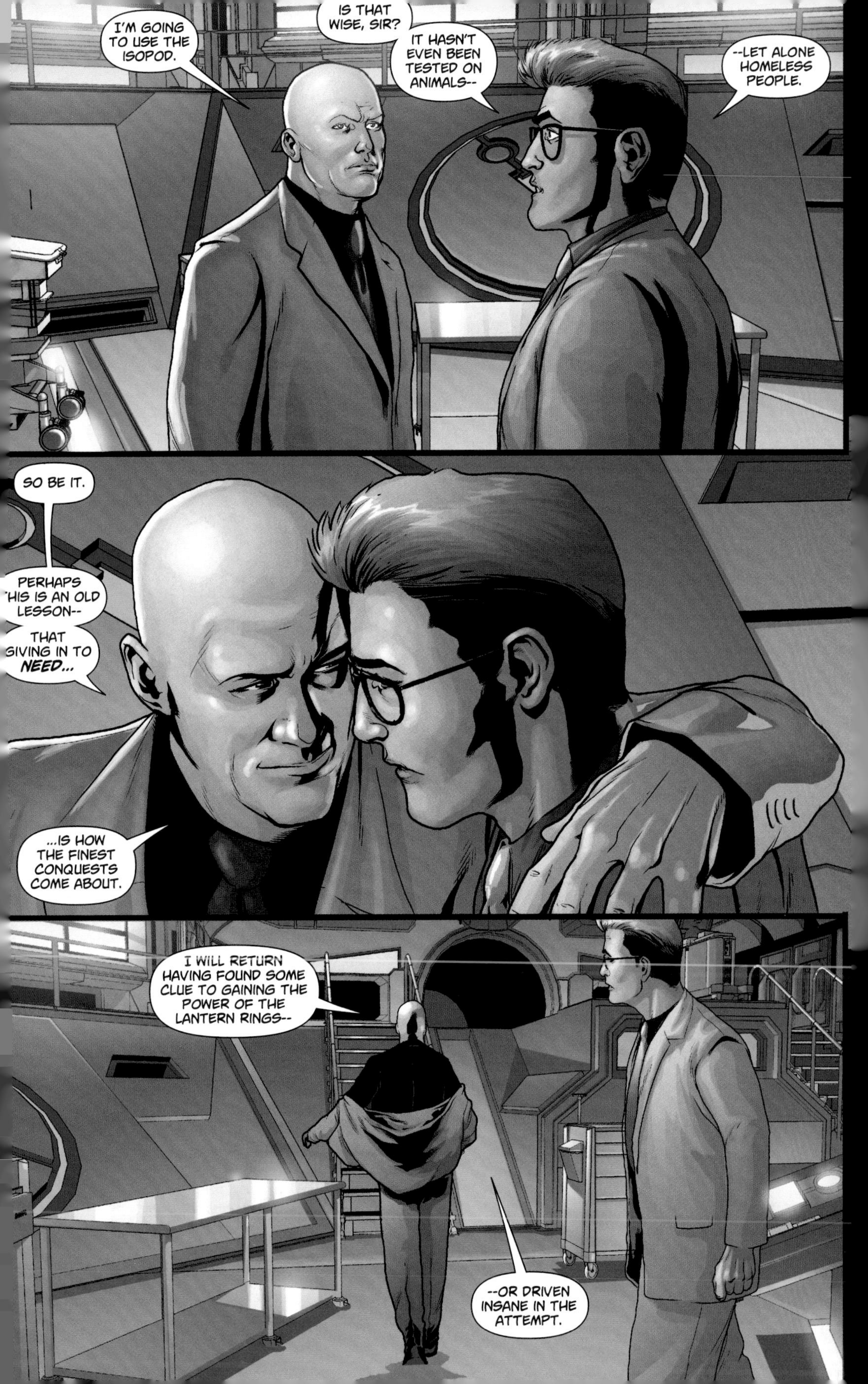
I'M GOING TO USE THE ISOPOD.
IS THAT WISE, SIR?
IT HASN'T EVEN BEEN TESTED ON ANIMALS--
--LET ALONE HOMELESS PEOPLE.
SO BE IT.
PERHAPS THIS IS AN OLD LESSON--
THAT GIVING IN TO NEED...
...IS HOW THE FINEST CONQUESTS COME ABOUT.
I WILL RETURN HAVING FOUND SOME CLUE TO GAINING THE POWER OF THE LANTERN RINGS--
--OR DRIVEN INSANE IN THE ATTEMPT.

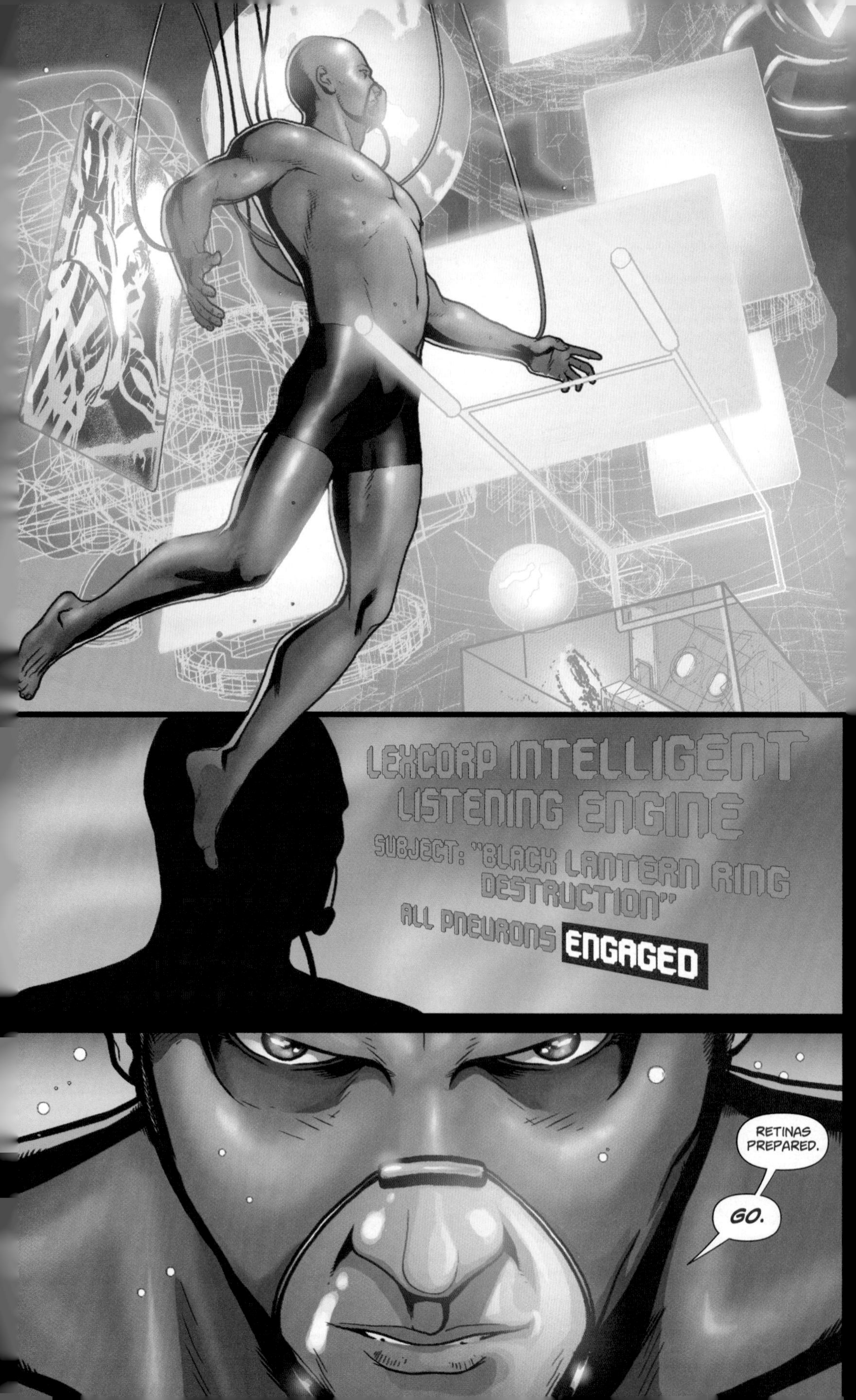
LEXCORP INTELLIGENT LISTENING ENGINE
SUBJECT: "BLACK LANTERN RING DESTRUCTION"
ALL PNEURONS ENGAGED
RETINAS PREPARED.
GO.

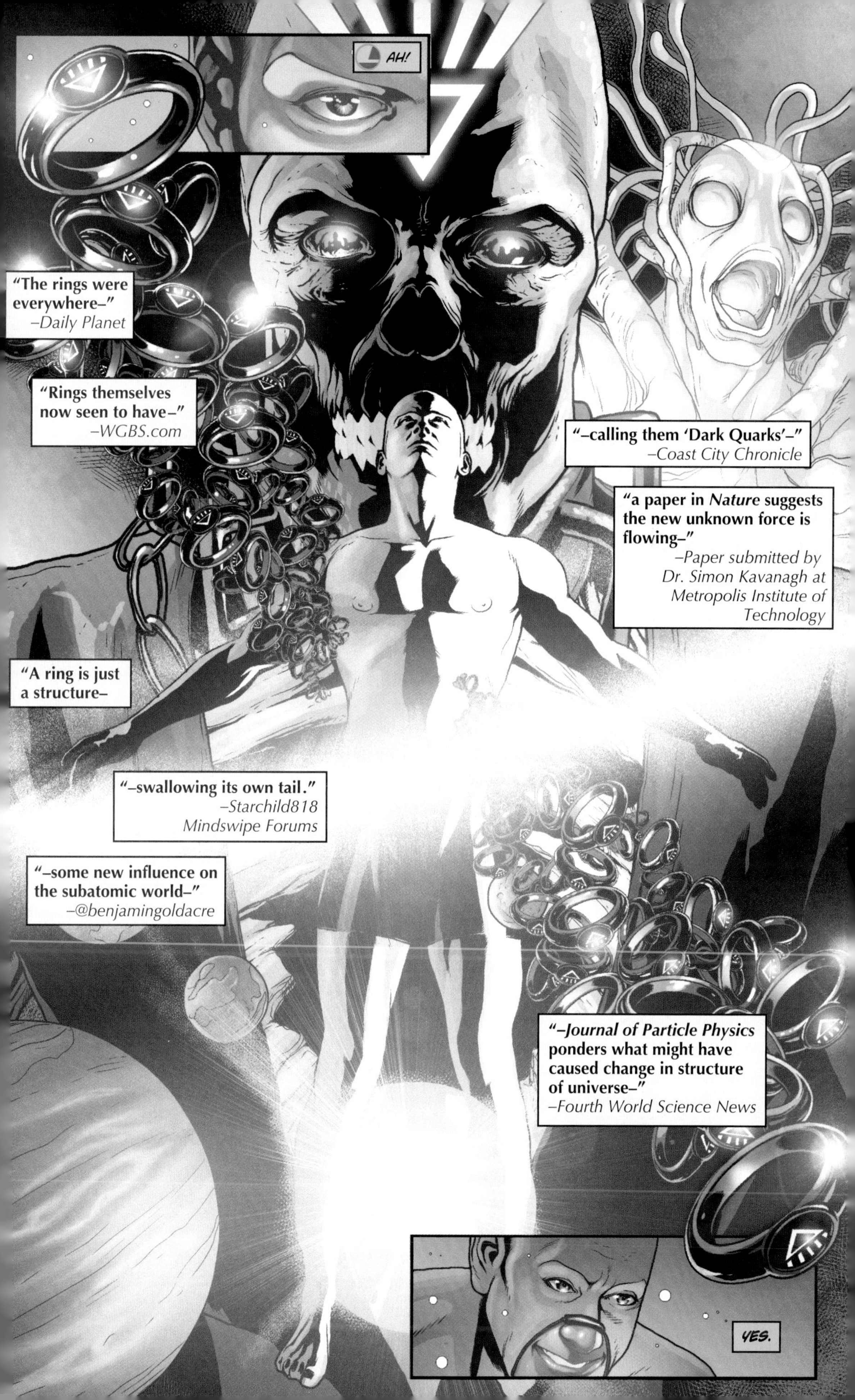
AH!
"The rings were everywhere–" –Daily Planet
"Rings themselves now seen to have–" –WGBS.com
"–calling them 'Dark Quarks'–" –Coast City Chronicle
"a paper in Nature suggests the new unknown force is flowing–" –Paper submitted by Dr. Simon Kavanagh at Metropolis Institute of Technology
"A ring is just a structure–
"–swallowing its own tail." –Starchild818 Mindswipe Forums
"–some new influence on the subatomic world–" –@benjamingoldacre
"–Journal of Particle Physics ponders what might have caused change in structure of universe–" –Fourth World Science News
YES.

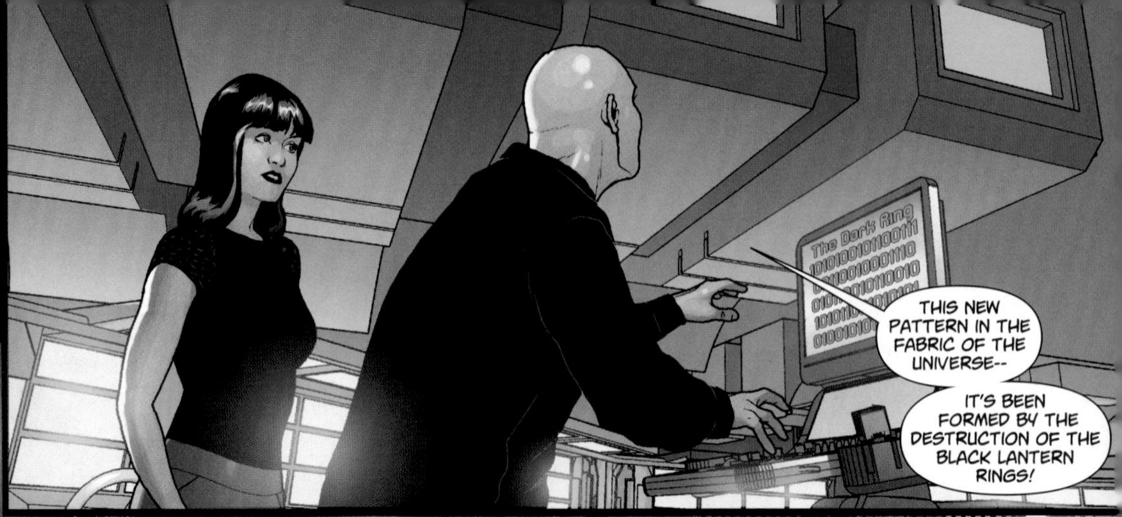

The Dark Ring
THIS NEW PATTERN IN THE FABRIC OF THE UNIVERSE--
IT'S BEEN FORMED BY THE DESTRUCTION OF THE BLACK LANTERN RINGS!

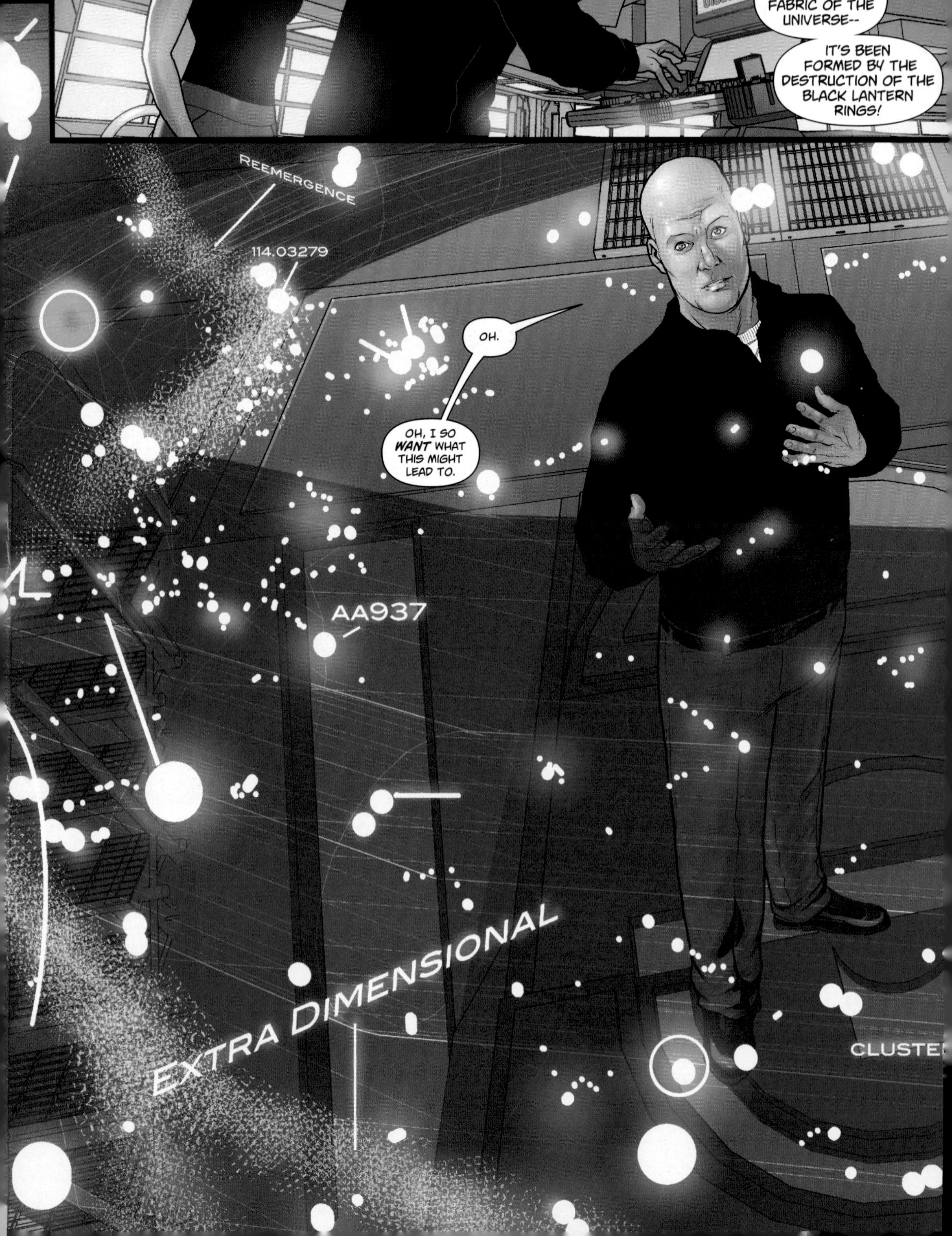

REEMERGENCE
114.03279
OH.
OH, I SO **WANT** WHAT THIS MIGHT LEAD TO.
AA937
EXTRA DIMENSIONAL
CLUSTE

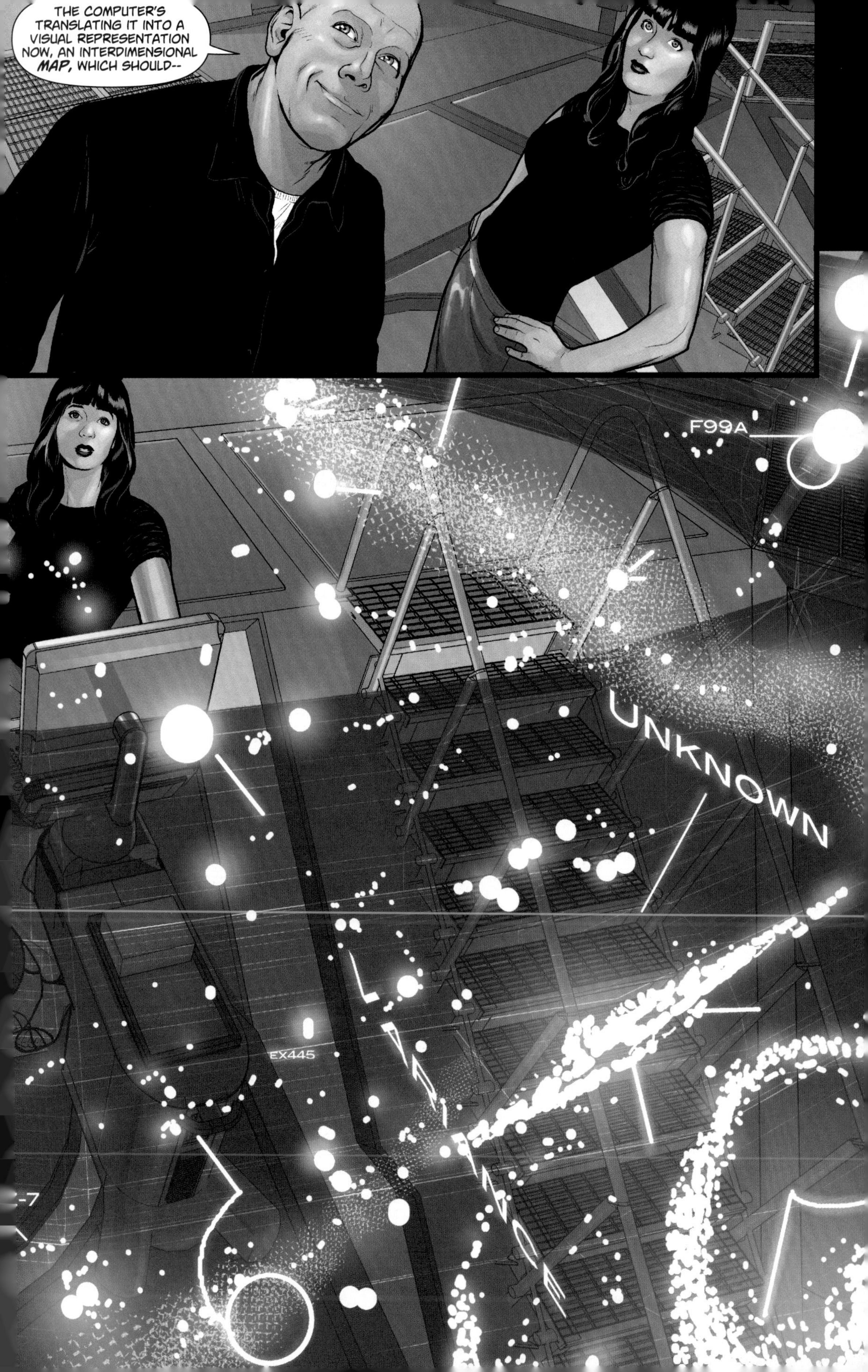
THE COMPUTER'S TRANSLATING IT INTO A VISUAL REPRESENTATION NOW, AN INTERDIMENSIONAL MAP, WHICH SHOULD--
F99A
UNKNOWN
EX445

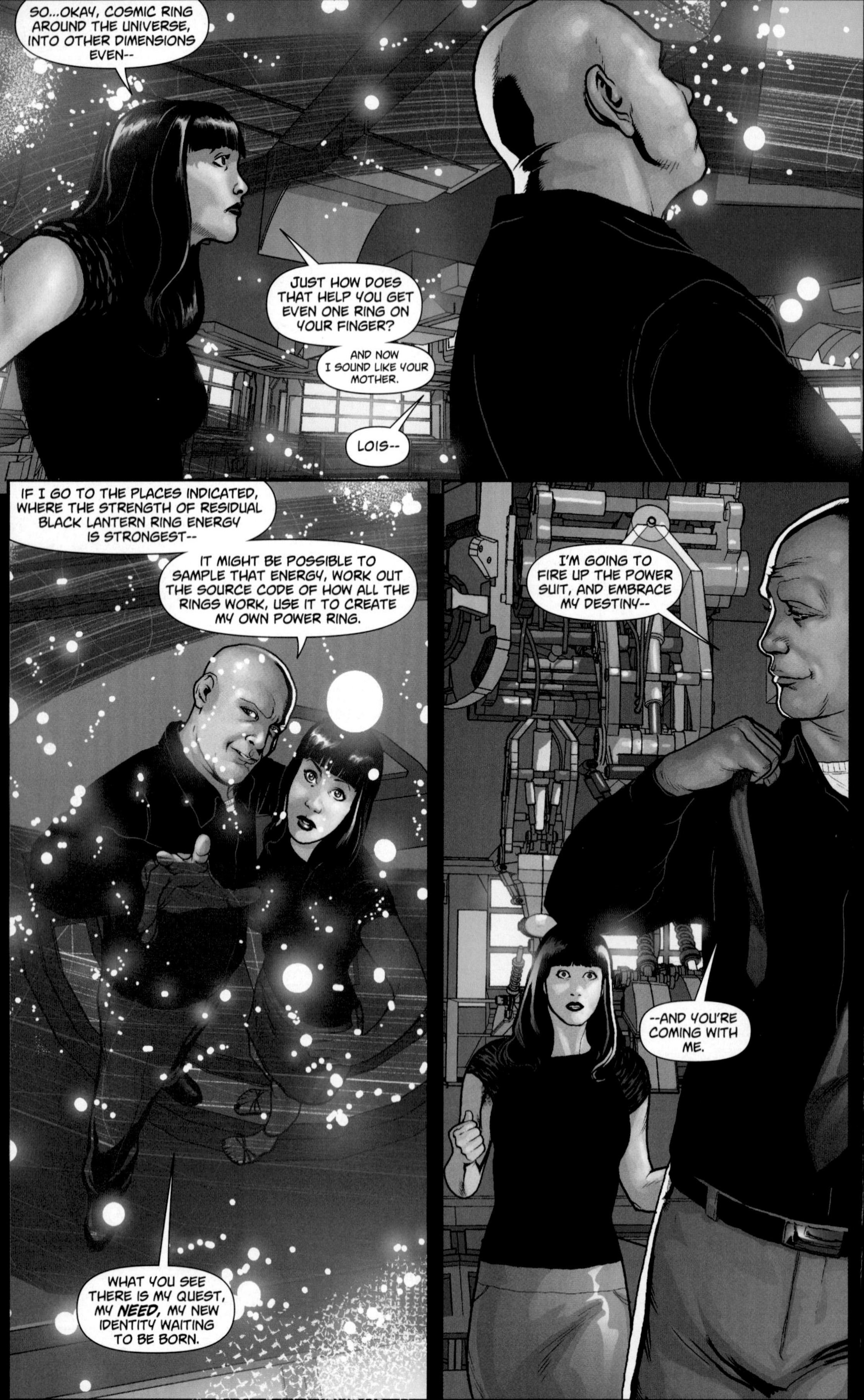
SO...OKAY, COSMIC RING AROUND THE UNIVERSE, INTO OTHER DIMENSIONS EVEN--
JUST HOW DOES THAT HELP YOU GET EVEN ONE RING ON YOUR FINGER?
AND NOW I SOUND LIKE YOUR MOTHER.
LOIS--
IF I GO TO THE PLACES INDICATED, WHERE THE STRENGTH OF RESIDUAL BLACK LANTERN RING ENERGY IS STRONGEST--
IT MIGHT BE POSSIBLE TO SAMPLE THAT ENERGY, WORK OUT THE SOURCE CODE OF HOW ALL THE RINGS WORK, USE IT TO CREATE MY OWN POWER RING.
WHAT YOU SEE THERE IS MY QUEST, MY ***NEED,*** MY NEW IDENTITY WAITING TO BE BORN.
I'M GOING TO FIRE UP THE POWER SUIT, AND EMBRACE MY DESTINY--
--AND YOU'RE COMING WITH ME.

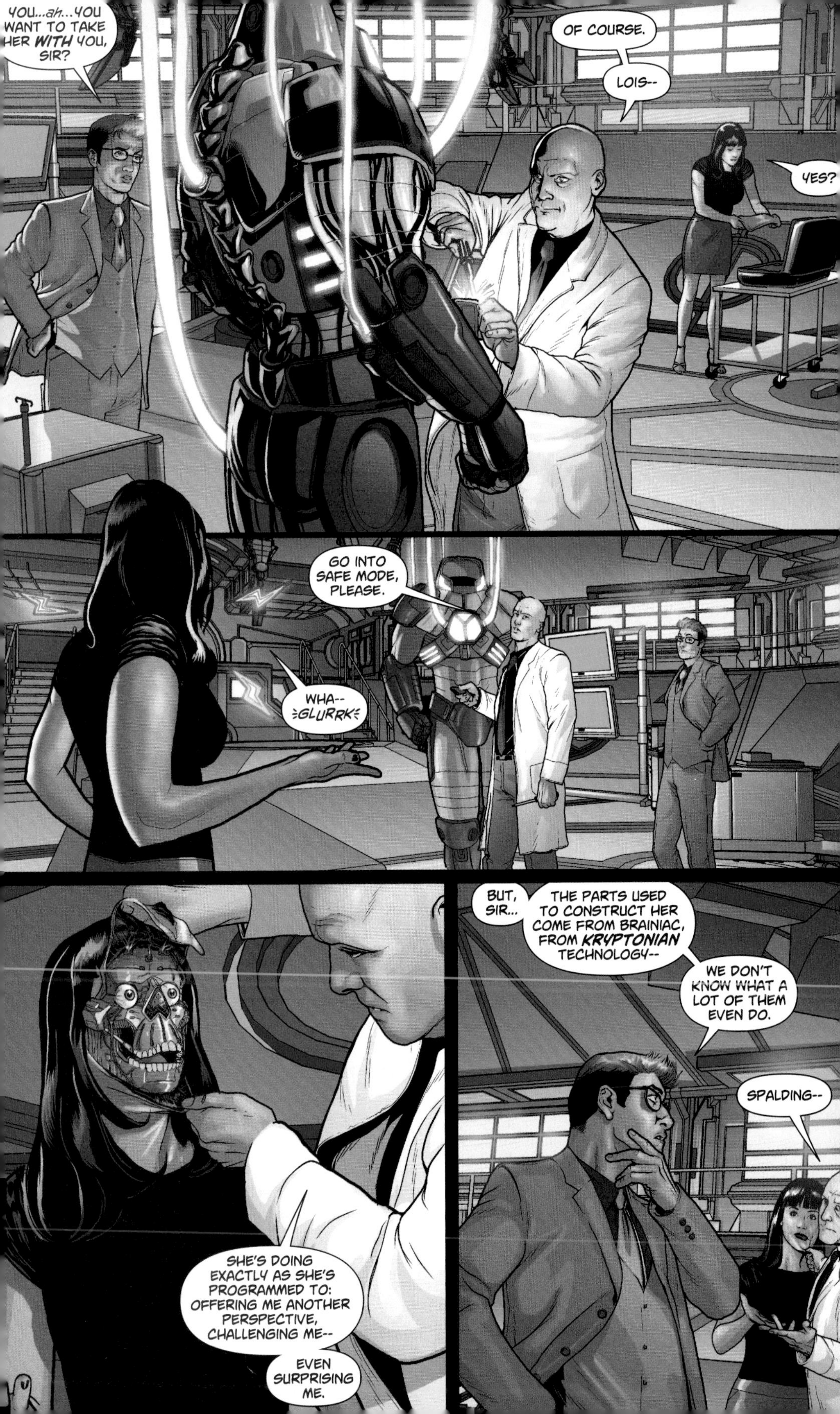
YOU...ah...YOU WANT TO TAKE HER WITH YOU, SIR?
OF COURSE.
LOIS--
YES?
GO INTO SAFE MODE, PLEASE.
WHA-- GLURRK
BUT, SIR...
THE PARTS USED TO CONSTRUCT HER COME FROM BRAINIAC, FROM KRYPTONIAN TECHNOLOGY--
WE DON'T KNOW WHAT A LOT OF THEM EVEN DO.
SPALDING--
SHE'S DOING EXACTLY AS SHE'S PROGRAMMED TO: OFFERING ME ANOTHER PERSPECTIVE, CHALLENGING ME--
EVEN SURPRISING ME.

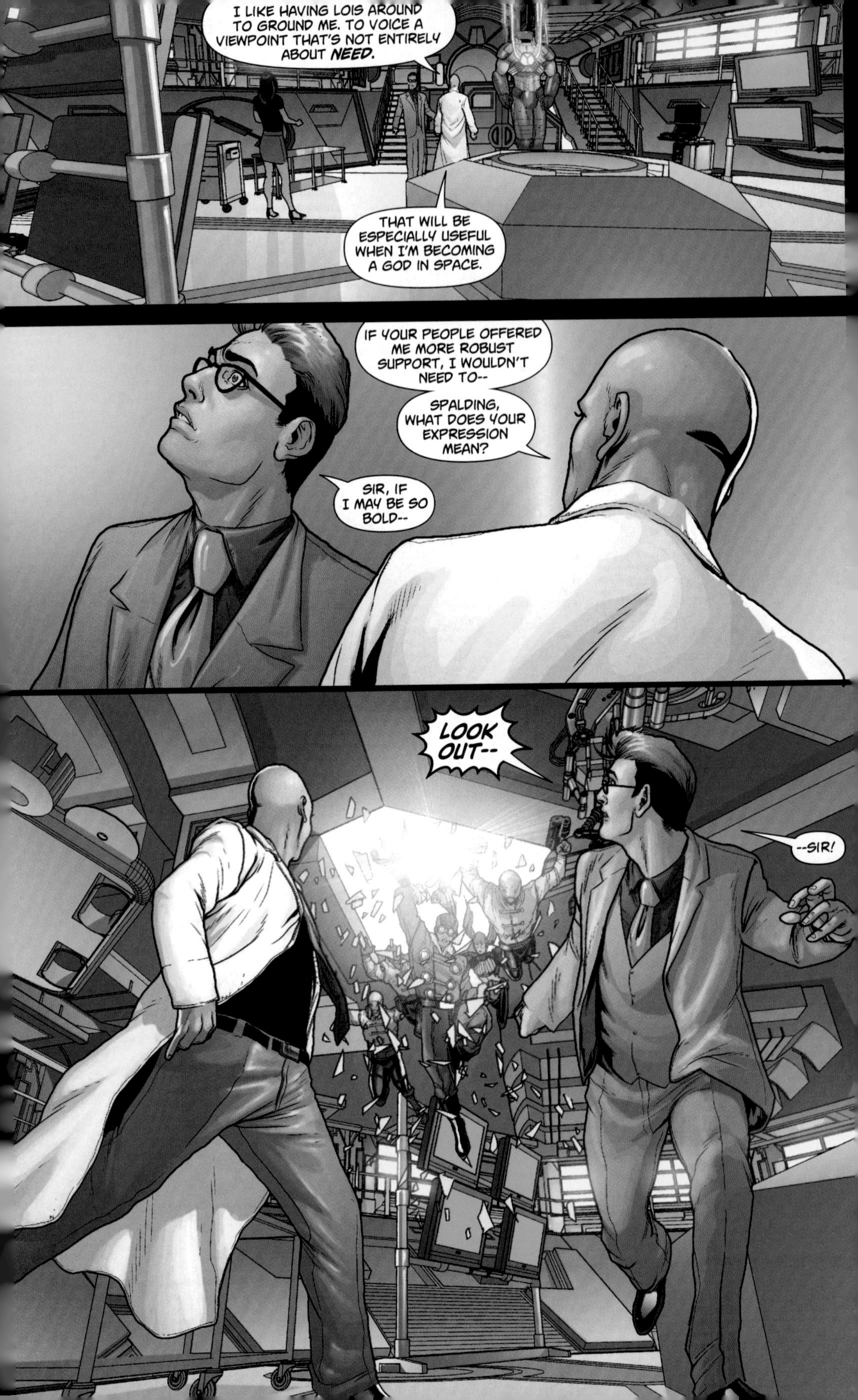
I LIKE HAVING LOIS AROUND TO GROUND ME. TO VOICE A VIEWPOINT THAT'S NOT ENTIRELY ABOUT *NEED*.
THAT WILL BE ESPECIALLY USEFUL WHEN I'M BECOMING A GOD IN SPACE.
IF YOUR PEOPLE OFFERED ME MORE ROBUST SUPPORT, I WOULDN'T NEED TO--
SPALDING, WHAT DOES YOUR EXPRESSION MEAN?
SIR, IF I MAY BE SO BOLD--
LOOK OUT--
--SIR!

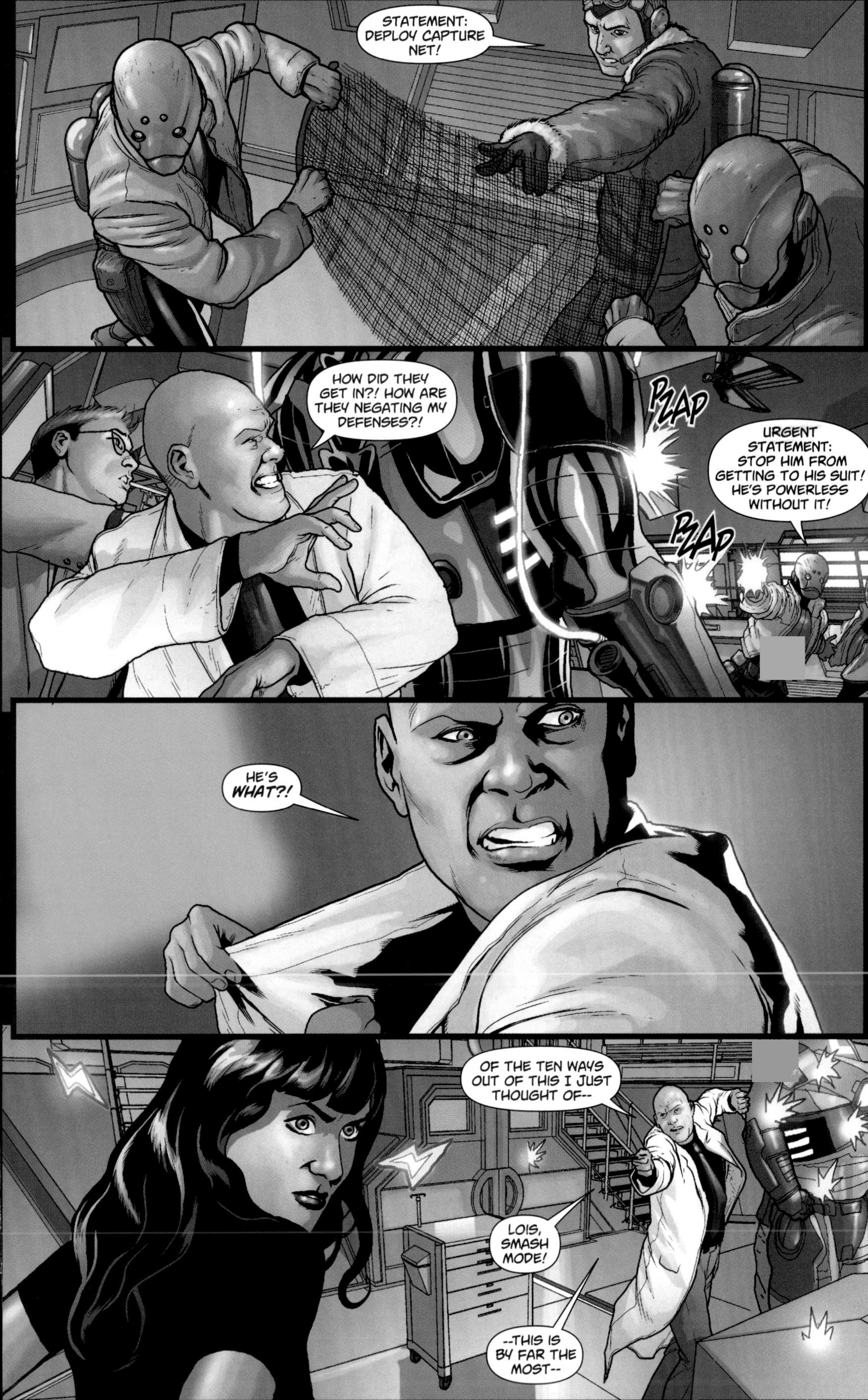
STATEMENT: DEPLOY CAPTURE NET!
HOW DID THEY GET IN?! HOW ARE THEY NEGATING MY DEFENSES?!
PZZAP
URGENT STATEMENT: STOP HIM FROM GETTING TO HIS SUIT! HE'S POWERLESS WITHOUT IT!
PZZAP
HE'S WHAT?!
OF THE TEN WAYS OUT OF THIS I JUST THOUGHT OF--
LOIS, SMASH MODE!
--THIS IS BY FAR THE MOST--

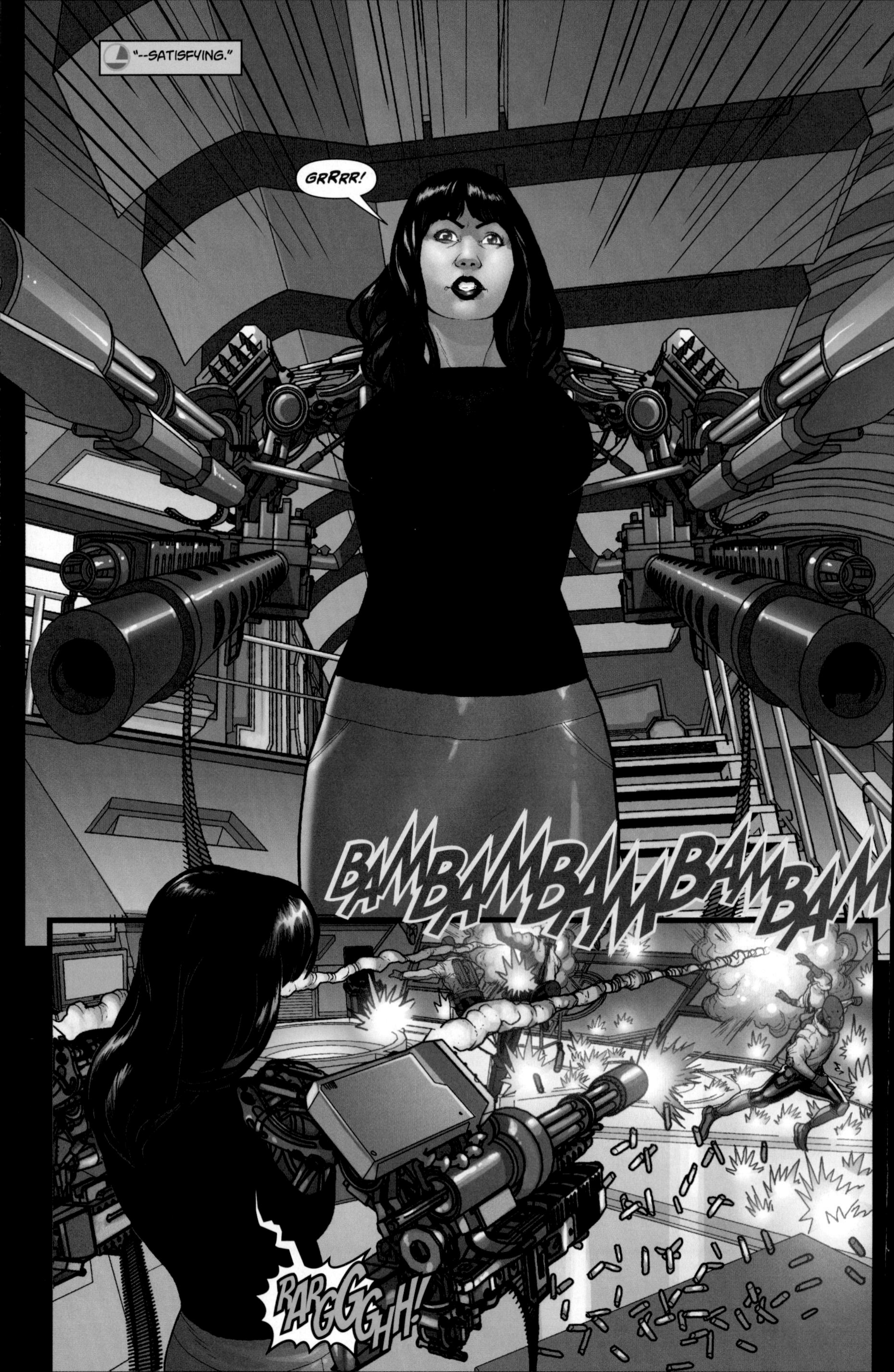
"--SATISFYING."
GRRRR!
BAMBAMBAMBAMBAMBAMBAMBAMBAM
RARGGGHH!

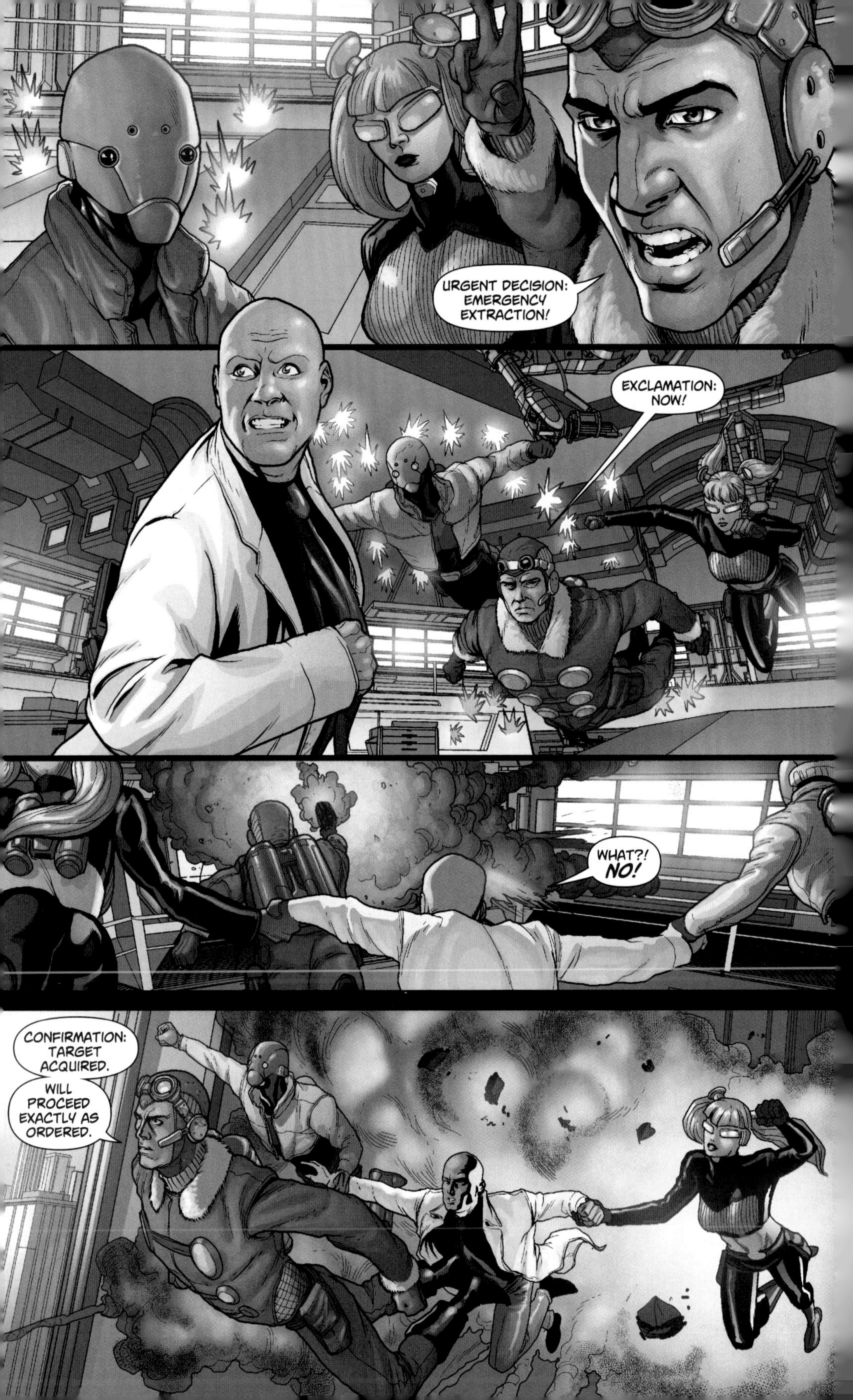
URGENT DECISION: EMERGENCY EXTRACTION!
EXCLAMATION: NOW!
WHAT?! NO!
CONFIRMATION: TARGET ACQUIRED.
WILL PROCEED EXACTLY AS ORDERED.

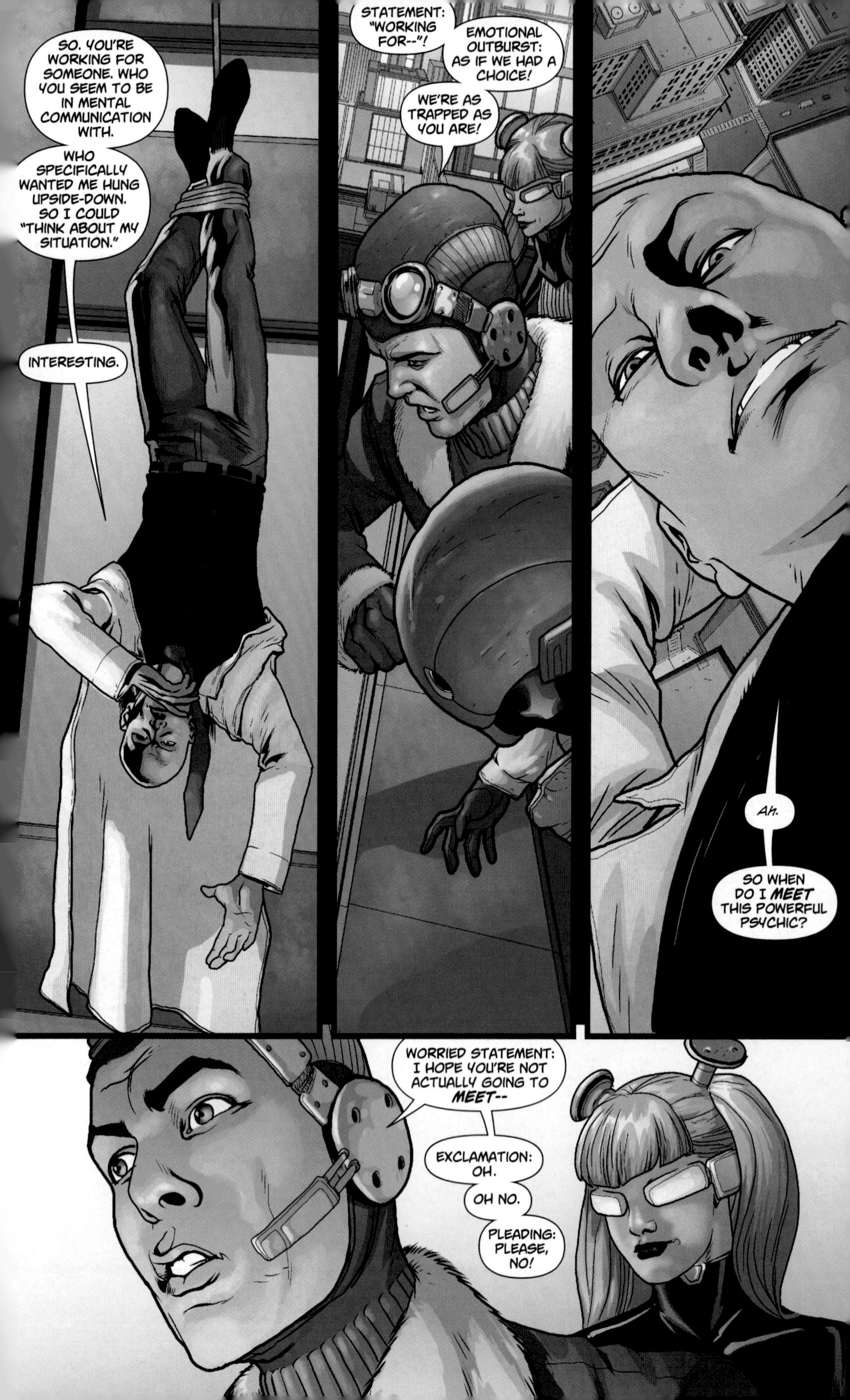
SO. YOU'RE WORKING FOR SOMEONE. WHO YOU SEEM TO BE IN MENTAL COMMUNICATION WITH.
WHO SPECIFICALLY WANTED ME HUNG UPSIDE-DOWN. SO I COULD "THINK ABOUT MY SITUATION."
INTERESTING.
STATEMENT: "WORKING FOR--"!
EMOTIONAL OUTBURST: AS IF WE HAD A CHOICE!
WE'RE AS TRAPPED AS YOU ARE!
Ah.
SO WHEN DO I *MEET* THIS POWERFUL PSYCHIC?
WORRIED STATEMENT: I HOPE YOU'RE NOT ACTUALLY GOING TO *MEET*--
EXCLAMATION: OH.
OH NO.
PLEADING: PLEASE, NO!

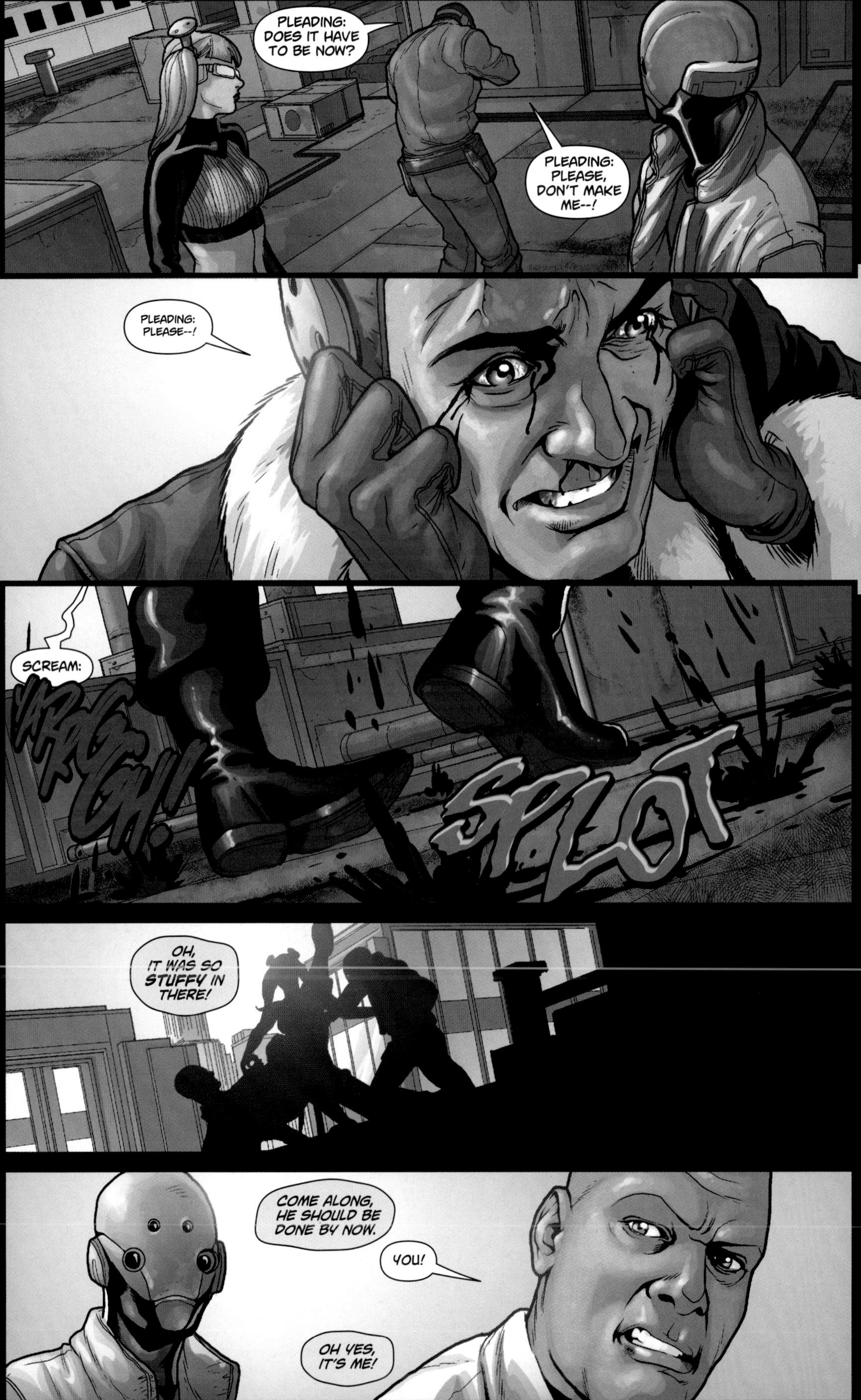
PLEADING: DOES IT HAVE TO BE NOW?
PLEADING: PLEASE, DON'T MAKE ME--!
PLEADING: PLEASE--!
SCREAM:
SPLOT
OH, IT WAS SO STUFFY IN THERE!
COME ALONG, HE SHOULD BE DONE BY NOW.
YOU!
OH YES, IT'S ME!

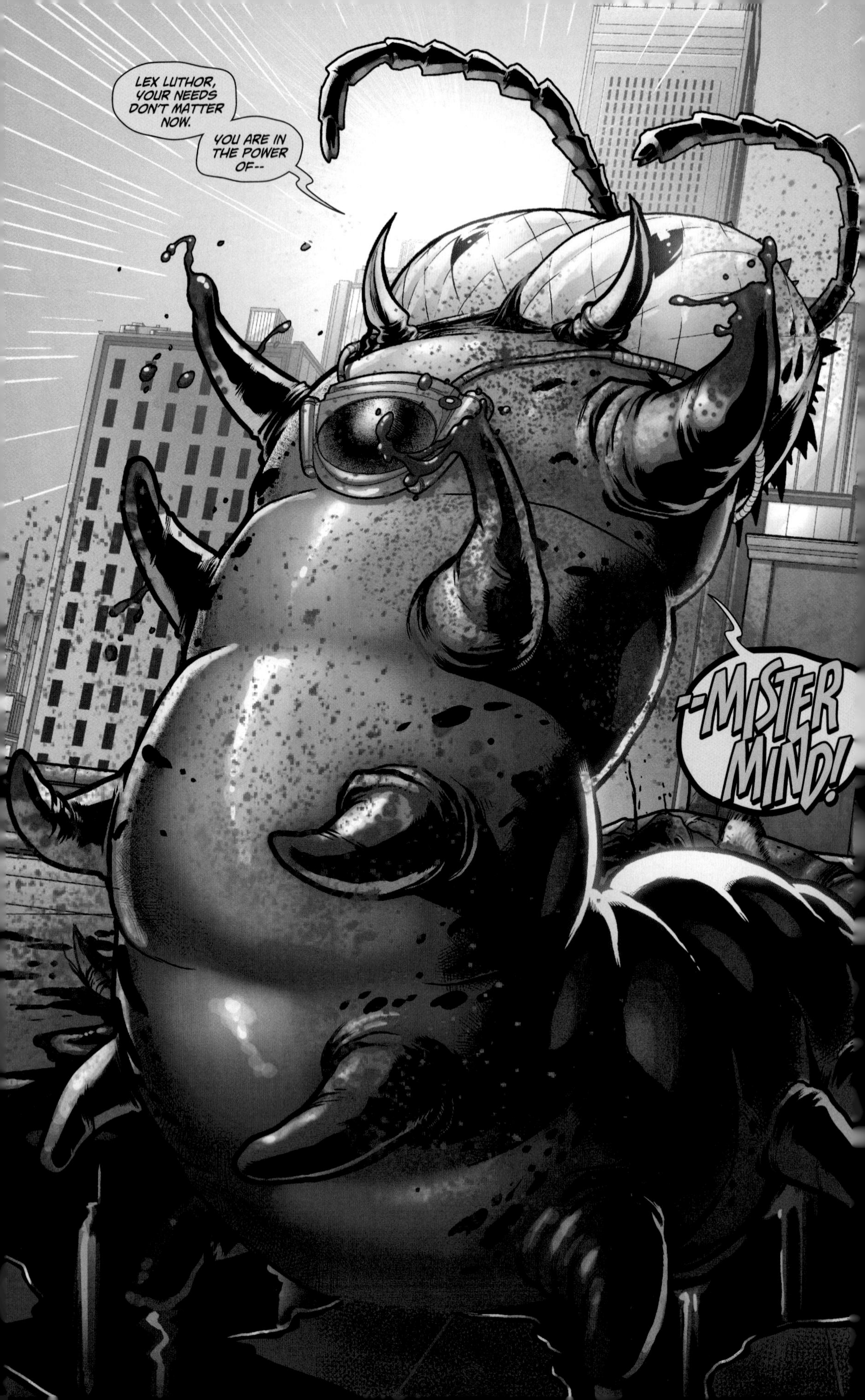
LEX LUTHOR, YOUR NEEDS DON'T MATTER NOW.
YOU ARE IN THE POWER OF--
--MISTER MIND!

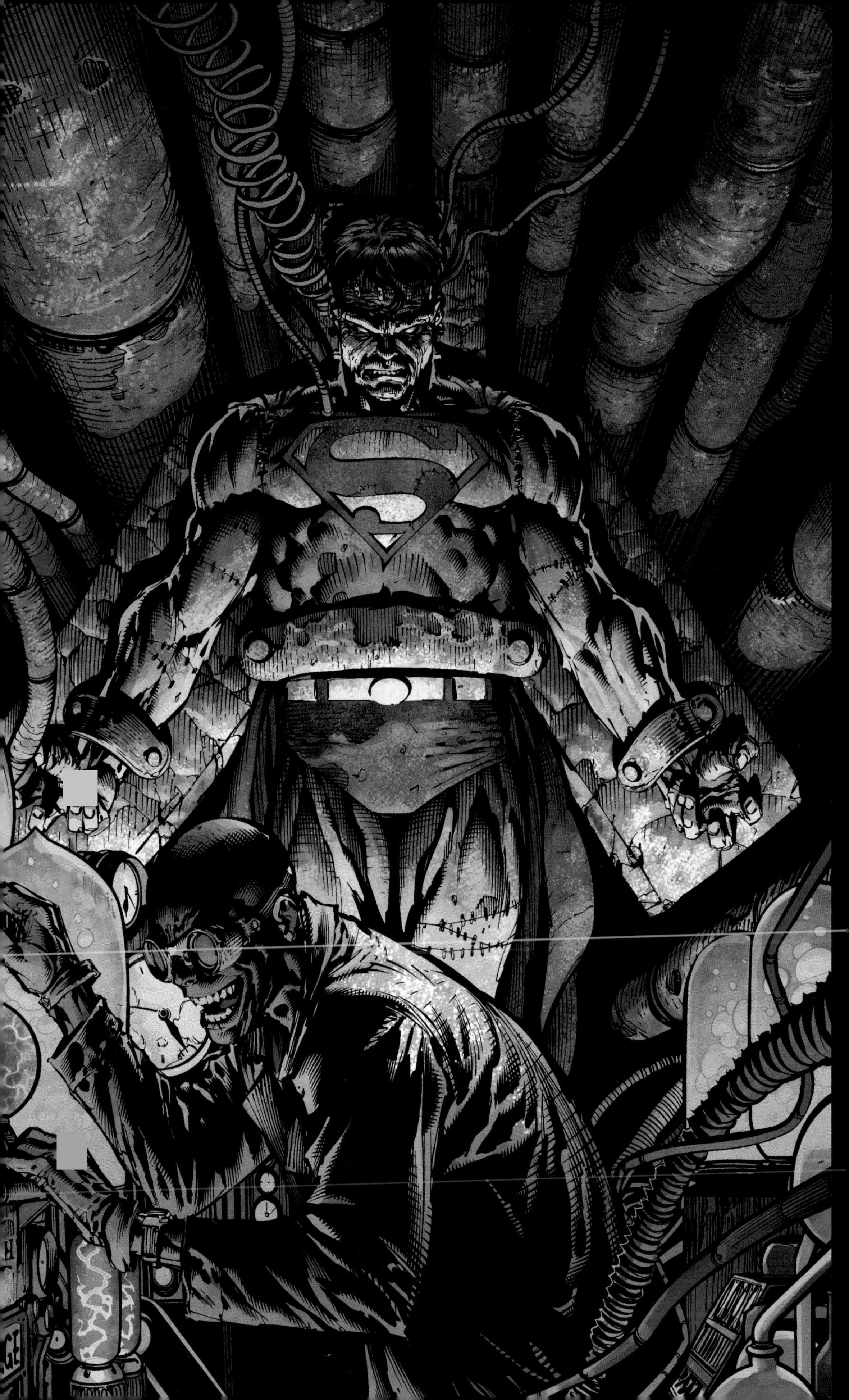

THE BLACK RING
part two

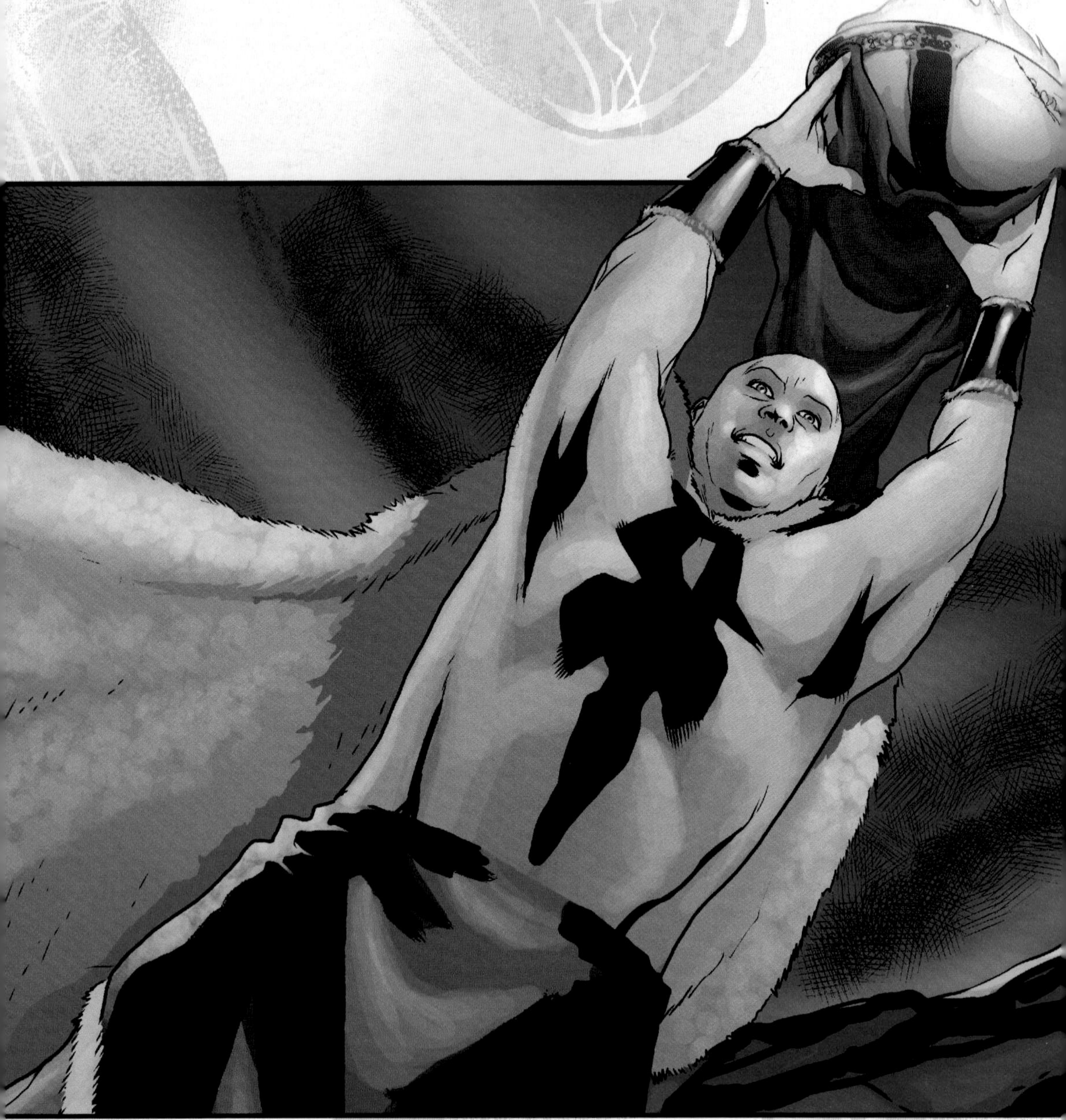

cover by
DAVID **FINCH, BATT** & PETER **STEIGERWALD**

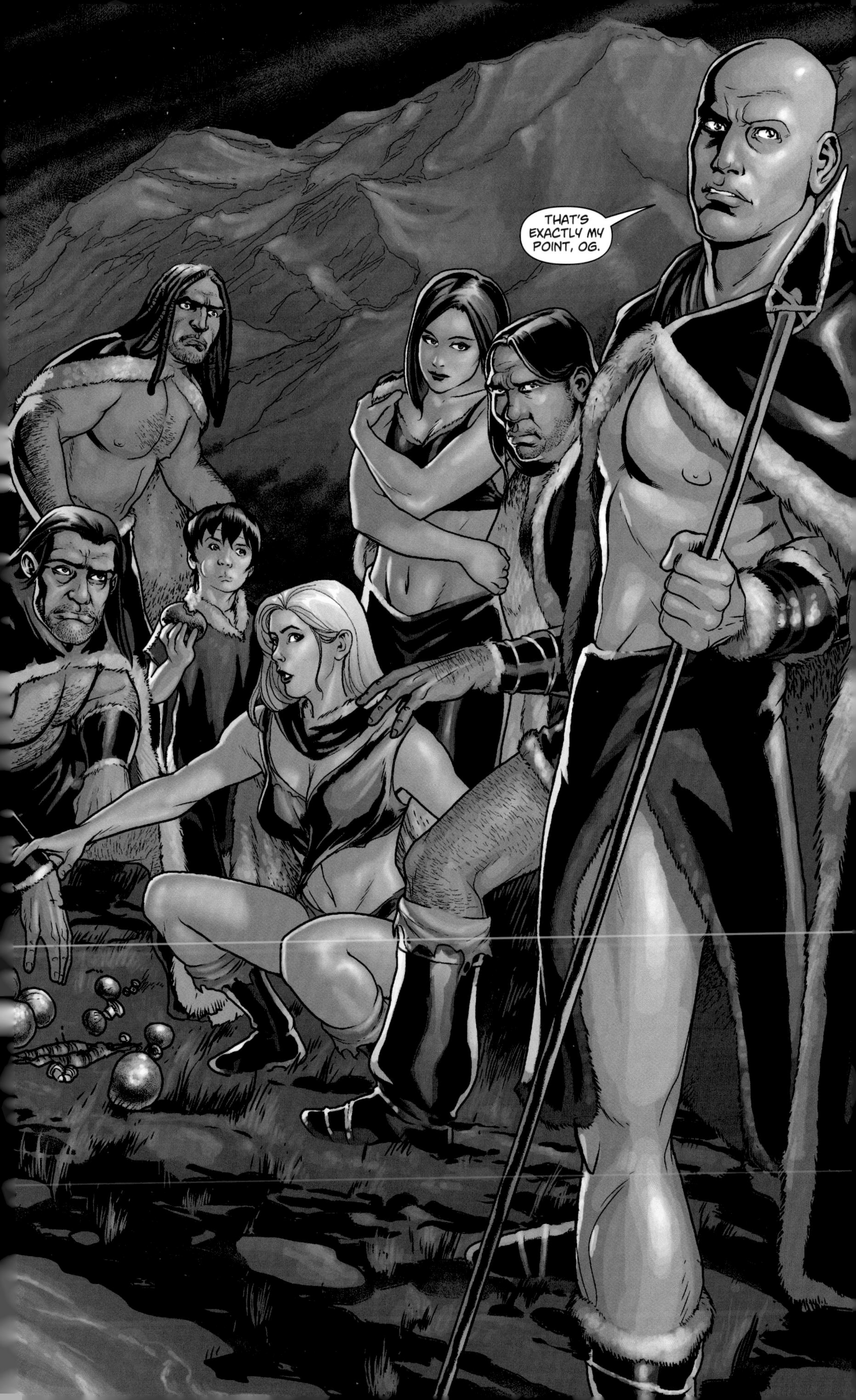
THAT'S EXACTLY MY POINT, OG.

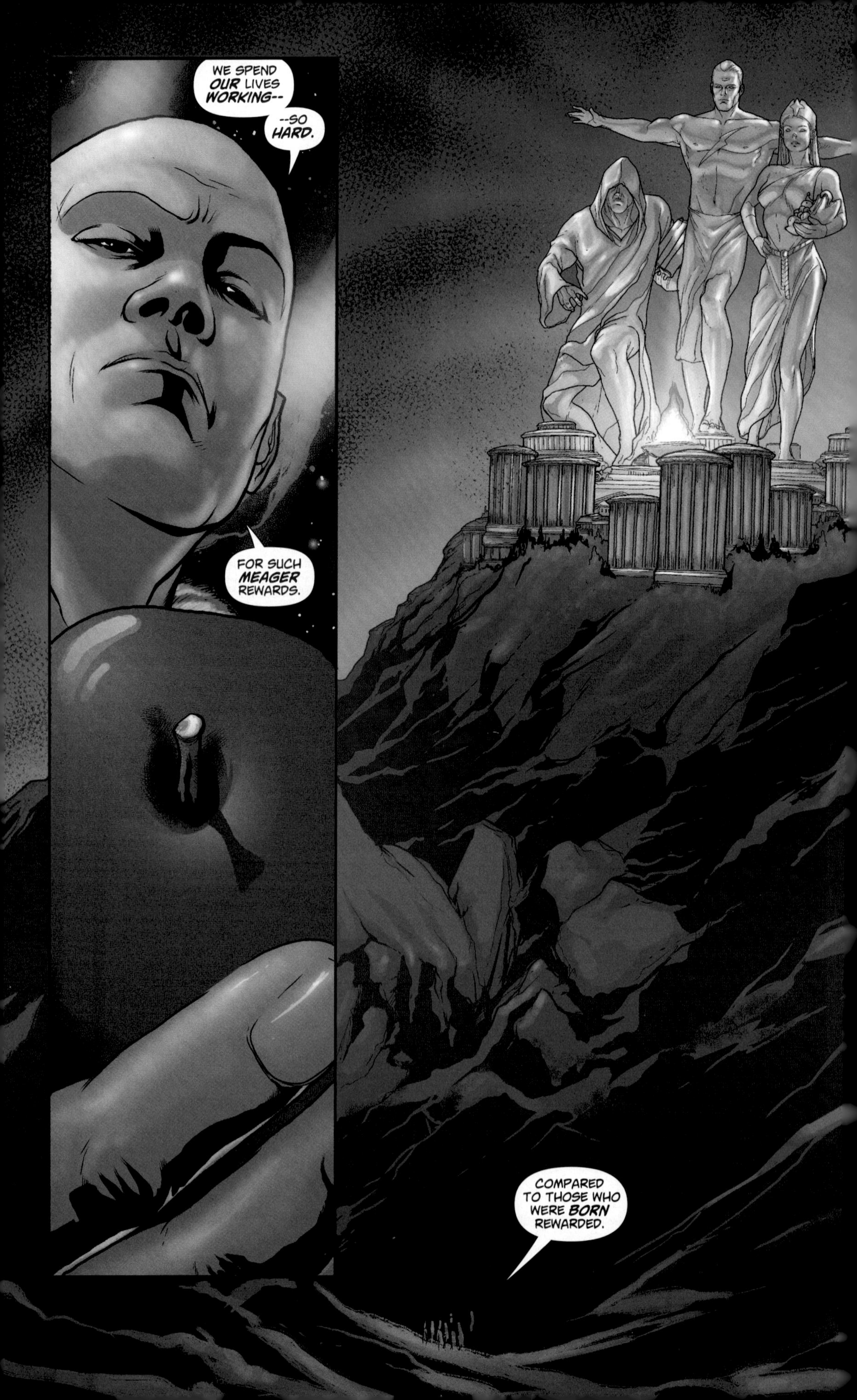
WE SPEND OUR LIVES WORKING--
--SO HARD.
FOR SUCH MEAGER REWARDS.
COMPARED TO THOSE WHO WERE BORN REWARDED.

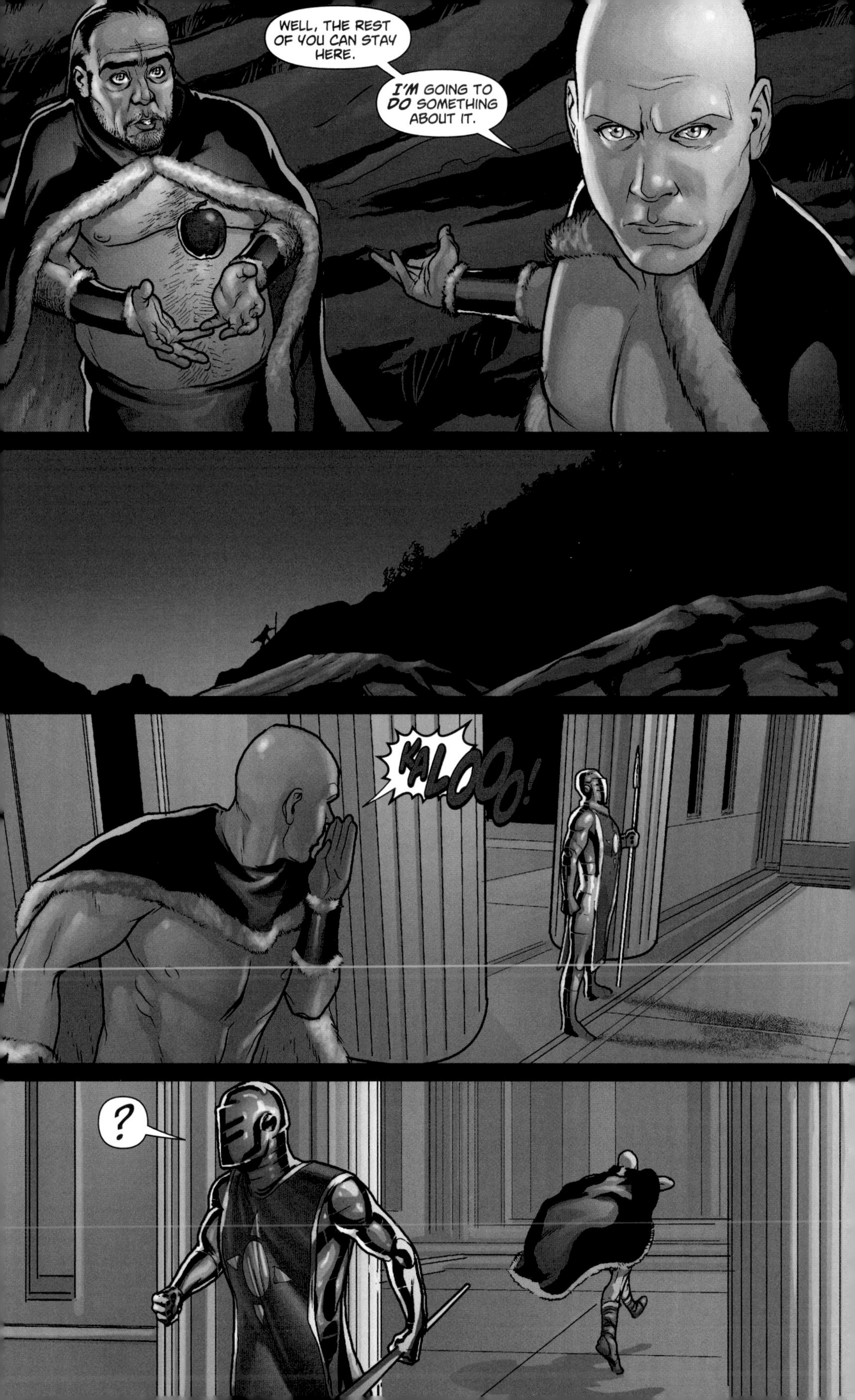
WELL, THE REST OF YOU CAN STAY HERE.
I'M GOING TO DO SOMETHING ABOUT IT.
KALOOO!
?

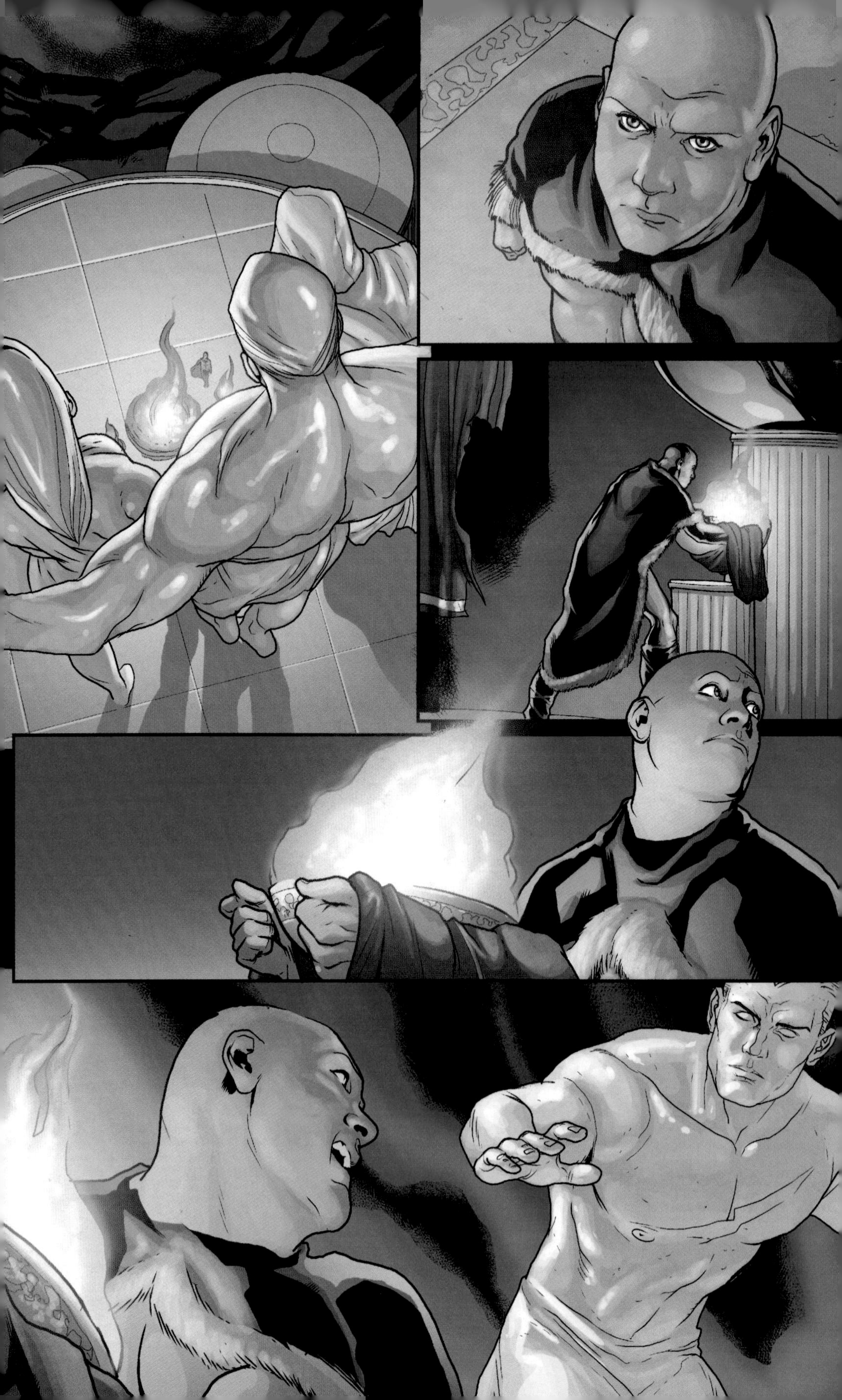

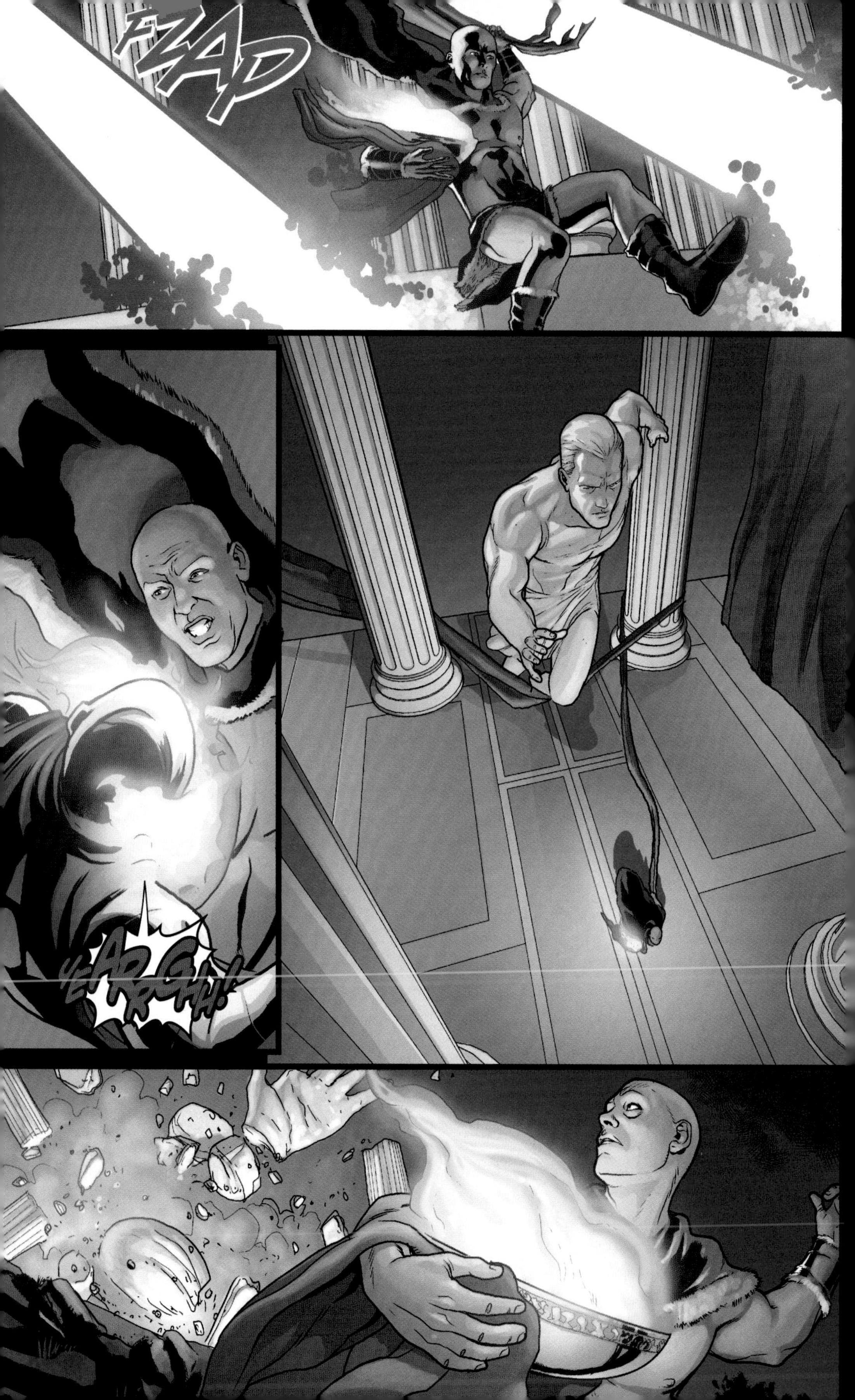
FZAP
YEARRGHH!

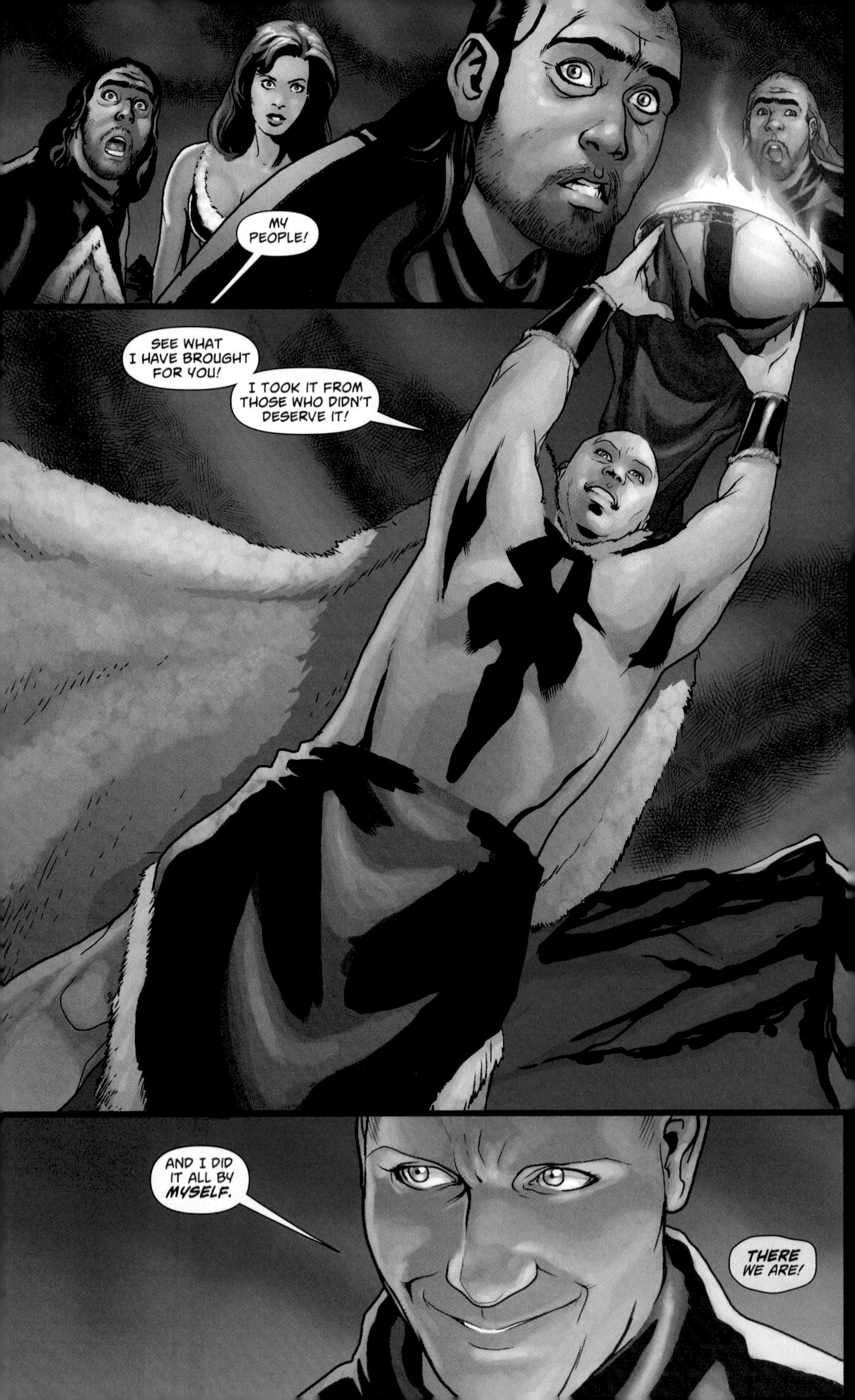
MY PEOPLE!
SEE WHAT I HAVE BROUGHT FOR YOU!
I TOOK IT FROM THOSE WHO DIDN'T DESERVE IT!
AND I DID IT ALL BY MYSELF.
THERE WE ARE!

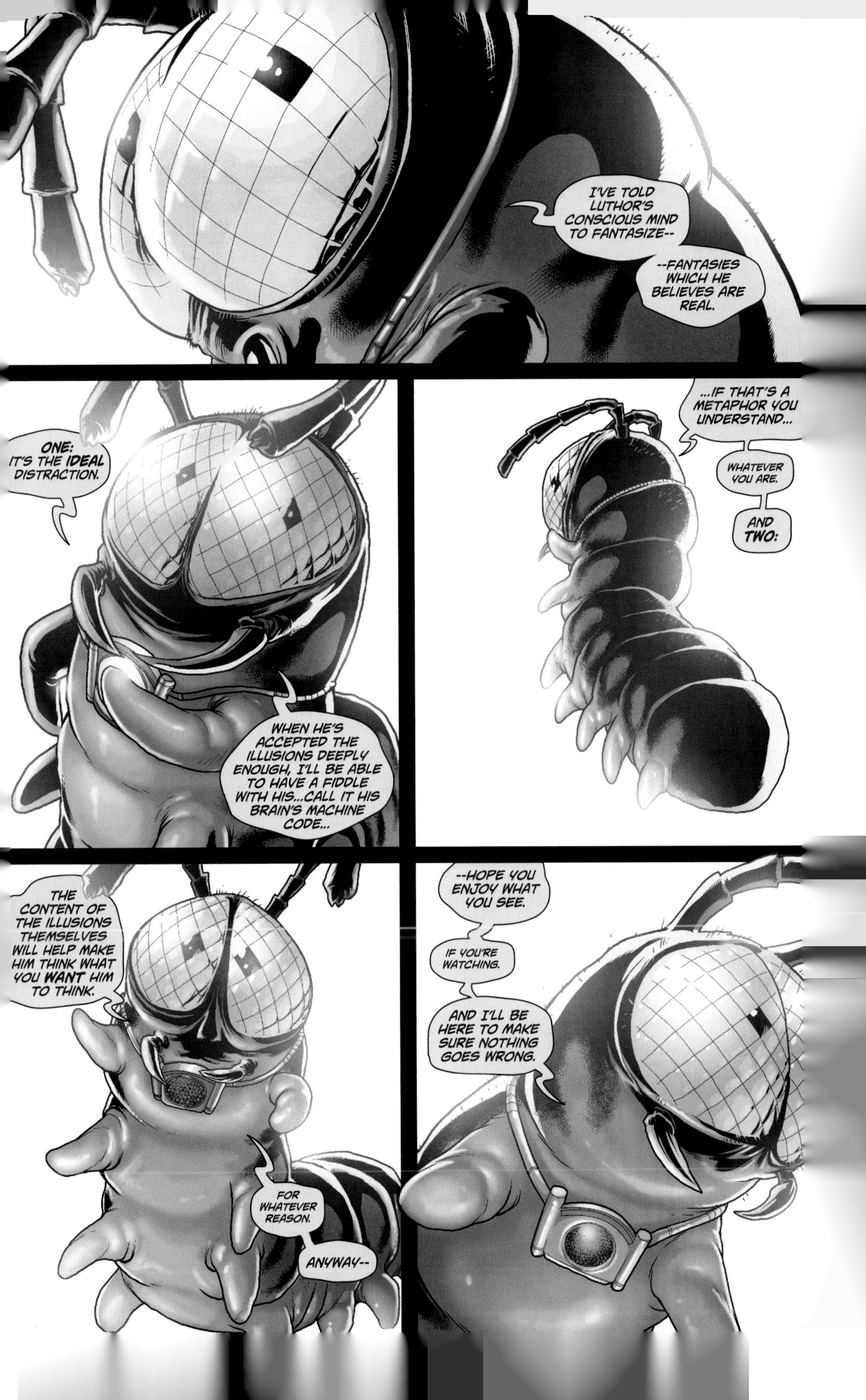
I'VE TOLD LUTHOR'S CONSCIOUS MIND TO FANTASIZE--
--FANTASIES WHICH HE BELIEVES ARE REAL.
ONE: IT'S THE IDEAL DISTRACTION.
WHEN HE'S ACCEPTED THE ILLUSIONS DEEPLY ENOUGH, I'LL BE ABLE TO HAVE A FIDDLE WITH HIS...CALL IT HIS BRAIN'S MACHINE CODE...
...IF THAT'S A METAPHOR YOU UNDERSTAND...
WHATEVER YOU ARE.
AND TWO:
THE CONTENT OF THE ILLUSIONS THEMSELVES WILL HELP MAKE HIM THINK WHAT YOU WANT HIM TO THINK.
FOR WHATEVER REASON.
ANYWAY--
--HOPE YOU ENJOY WHAT YOU SEE.
IF YOU'RE WATCHING.
AND I'LL BE HERE TO MAKE SURE NOTHING GOES WRONG.

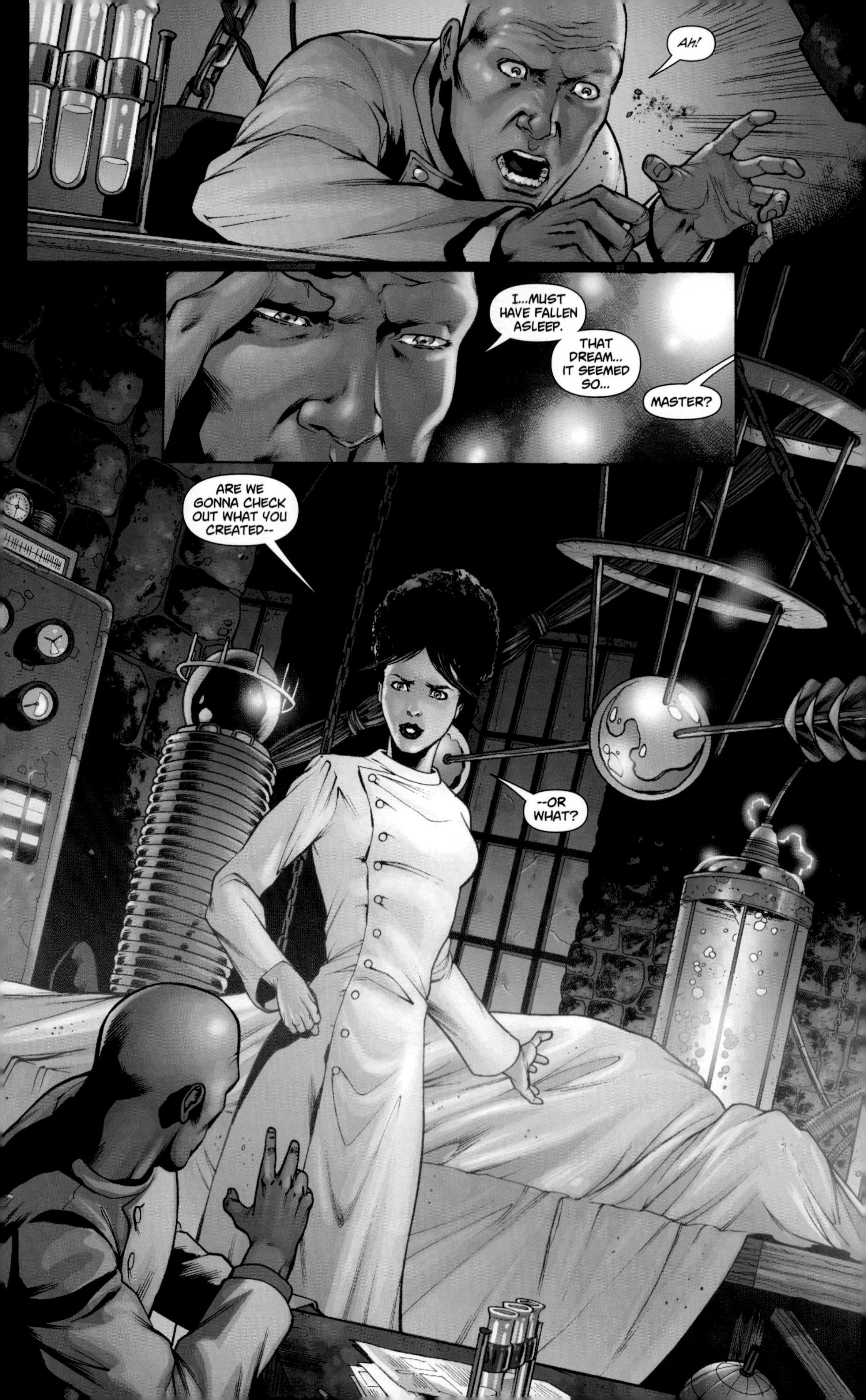
Ah!
I...MUST HAVE FALLEN ASLEEP.
THAT DREAM... IT SEEMED SO...
MASTER?
ARE WE GONNA CHECK OUT WHAT YOU CREATED--
--OR WHAT?

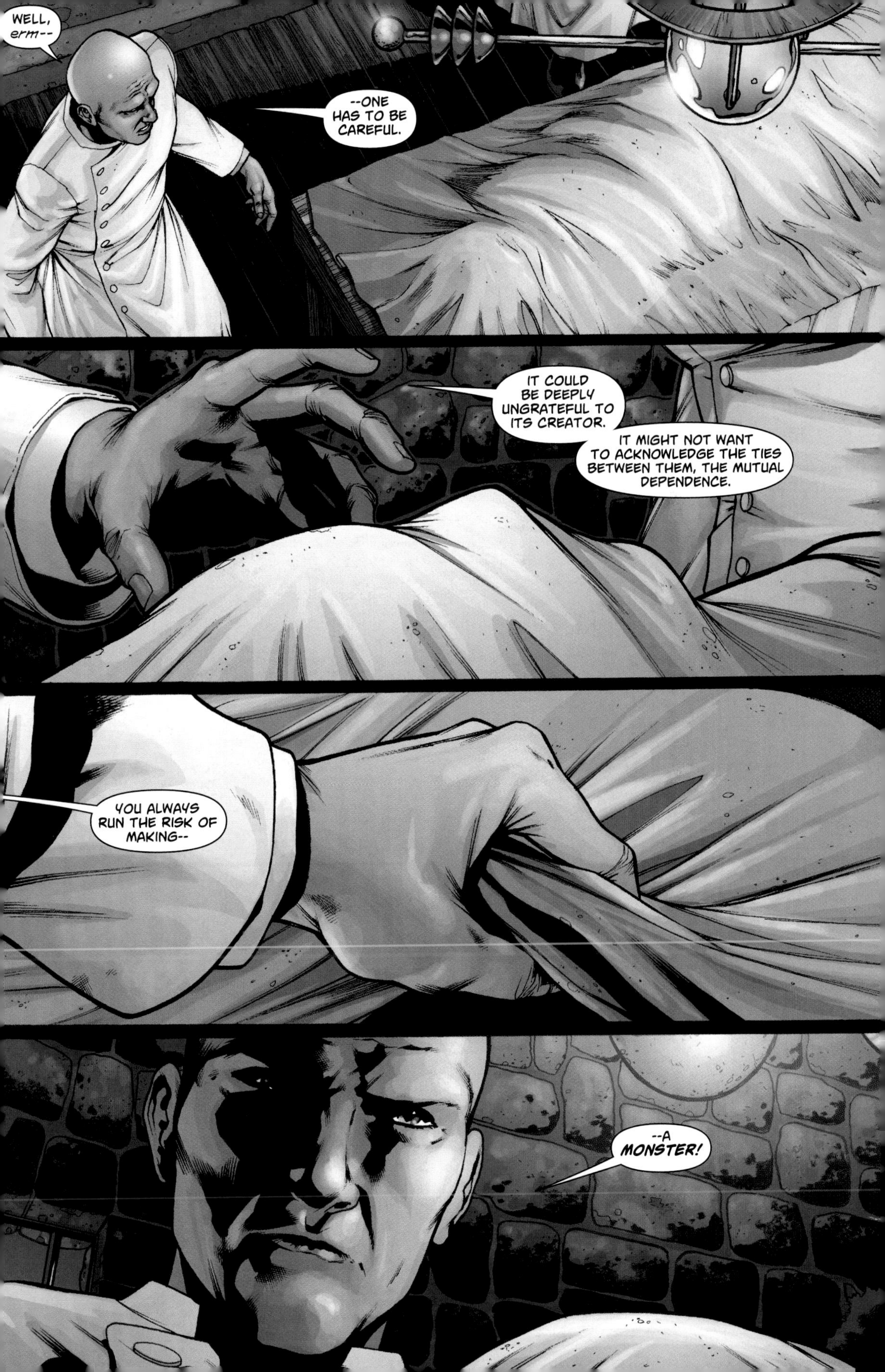
WELL, erm--
--ONE HAS TO BE CAREFUL.
IT COULD BE DEEPLY UNGRATEFUL TO ITS CREATOR.
IT MIGHT NOT WANT TO ACKNOWLEDGE THE TIES BETWEEN THEM, THE MUTUAL DEPENDENCE.
YOU ALWAYS RUN THE RISK OF MAKING--
--A MONSTER!

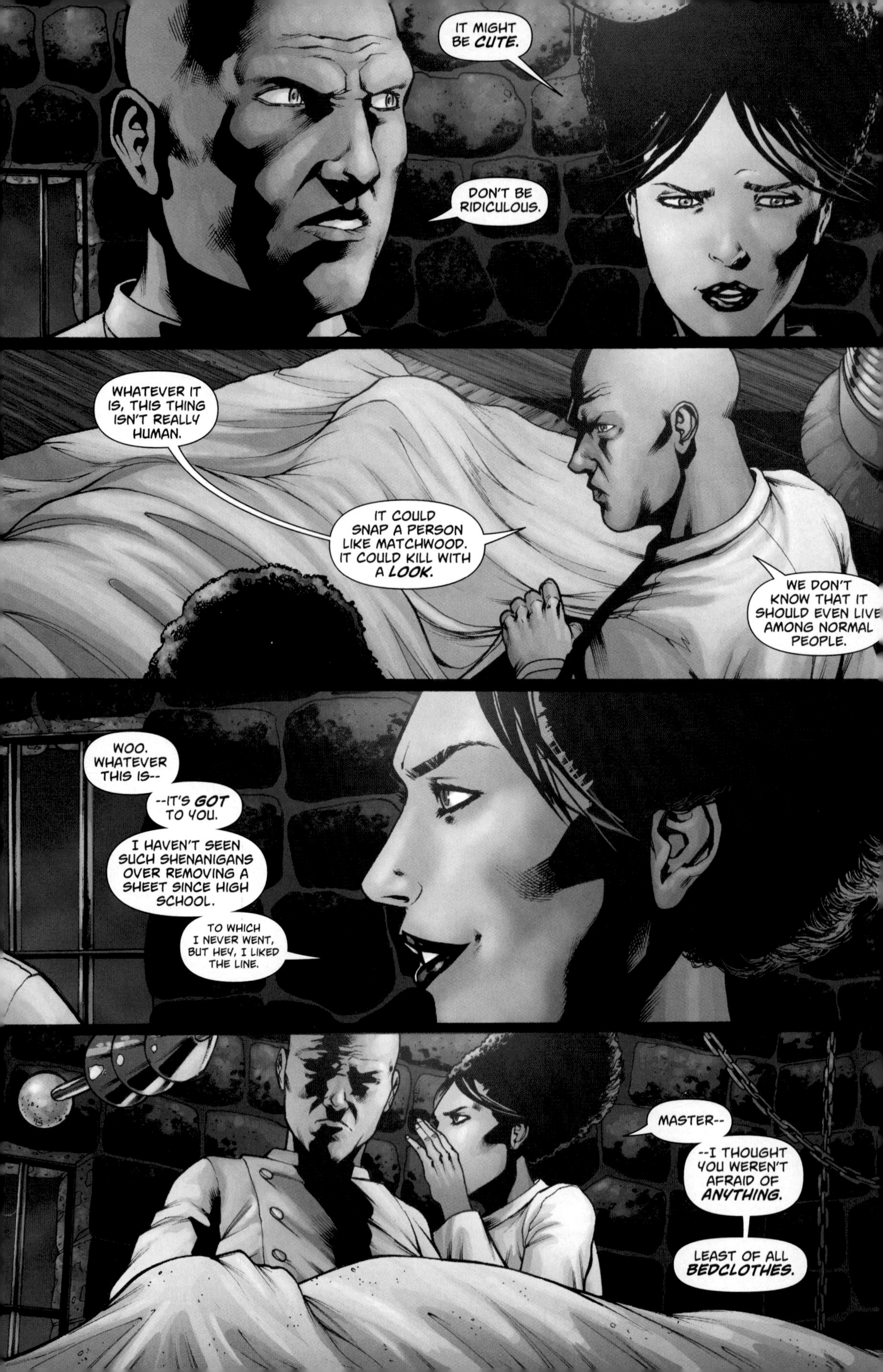
IT MIGHT BE CUTE.
DON'T BE RIDICULOUS.
WHATEVER IT IS, THIS THING ISN'T REALLY HUMAN.
IT COULD SNAP A PERSON LIKE MATCHWOOD. IT COULD KILL WITH A LOOK.
WE DON'T KNOW THAT IT SHOULD EVEN LIVE AMONG NORMAL PEOPLE.
WOO. WHATEVER THIS IS--
--IT'S GOT TO YOU.
I HAVEN'T SEEN SUCH SHENANIGANS OVER REMOVING A SHEET SINCE HIGH SCHOOL.
TO WHICH I NEVER WENT, BUT HEY, I LIKED THE LINE.
MASTER--
--I THOUGHT YOU WEREN'T AFRAID OF ANYTHING.
LEAST OF ALL BEDCLOTHES.

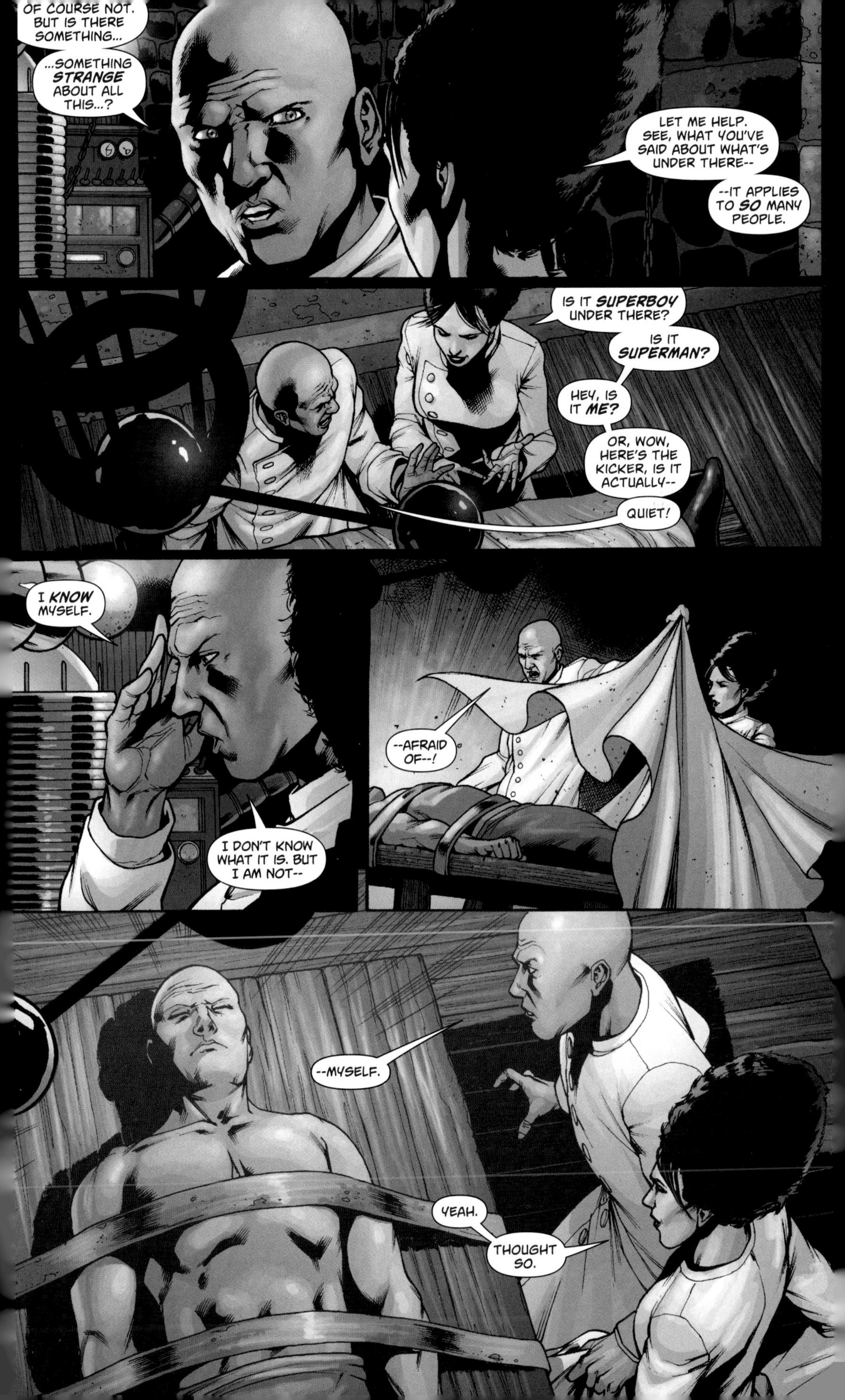
OF COURSE NOT. BUT IS THERE SOMETHING...
...SOMETHING STRANGE ABOUT ALL THIS...?
LET ME HELP. SEE, WHAT YOU'VE SAID ABOUT WHAT'S UNDER THERE--
--IT APPLIES TO SO MANY PEOPLE.
IS IT SUPERBOY UNDER THERE?
IS IT SUPERMAN?
HEY, IS IT ME?
OR, WOW, HERE'S THE KICKER, IS IT ACTUALLY--
QUIET!
I KNOW MYSELF.
I DON'T KNOW WHAT IT IS. BUT I AM NOT--
--AFRAID OF--!
--MYSELF.
YEAH.
THOUGHT SO.

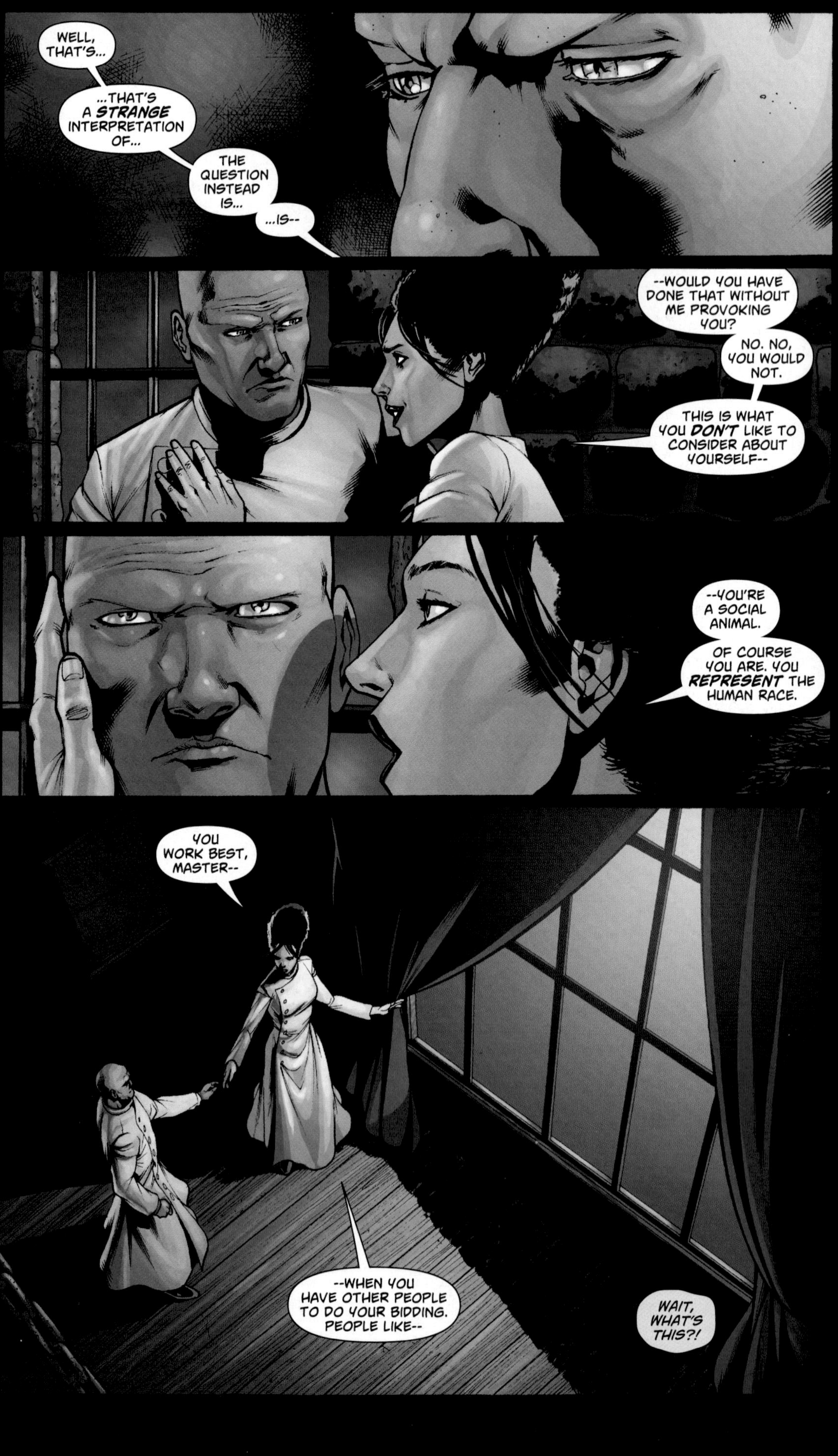
WELL, THAT'S...
...THAT'S A STRANGE INTERPRETATION OF...
THE QUESTION INSTEAD IS...
...IS--
--WOULD YOU HAVE DONE THAT WITHOUT ME PROVOKING YOU?
NO. NO, YOU WOULD NOT.
THIS IS WHAT YOU DON'T LIKE TO CONSIDER ABOUT YOURSELF--
--YOU'RE A SOCIAL ANIMAL.
OF COURSE YOU ARE. YOU REPRESENT THE HUMAN RACE.
YOU WORK BEST, MASTER--
--WHEN YOU HAVE OTHER PEOPLE TO DO YOUR BIDDING. PEOPLE LIKE--
WAIT, WHAT'S THIS?!

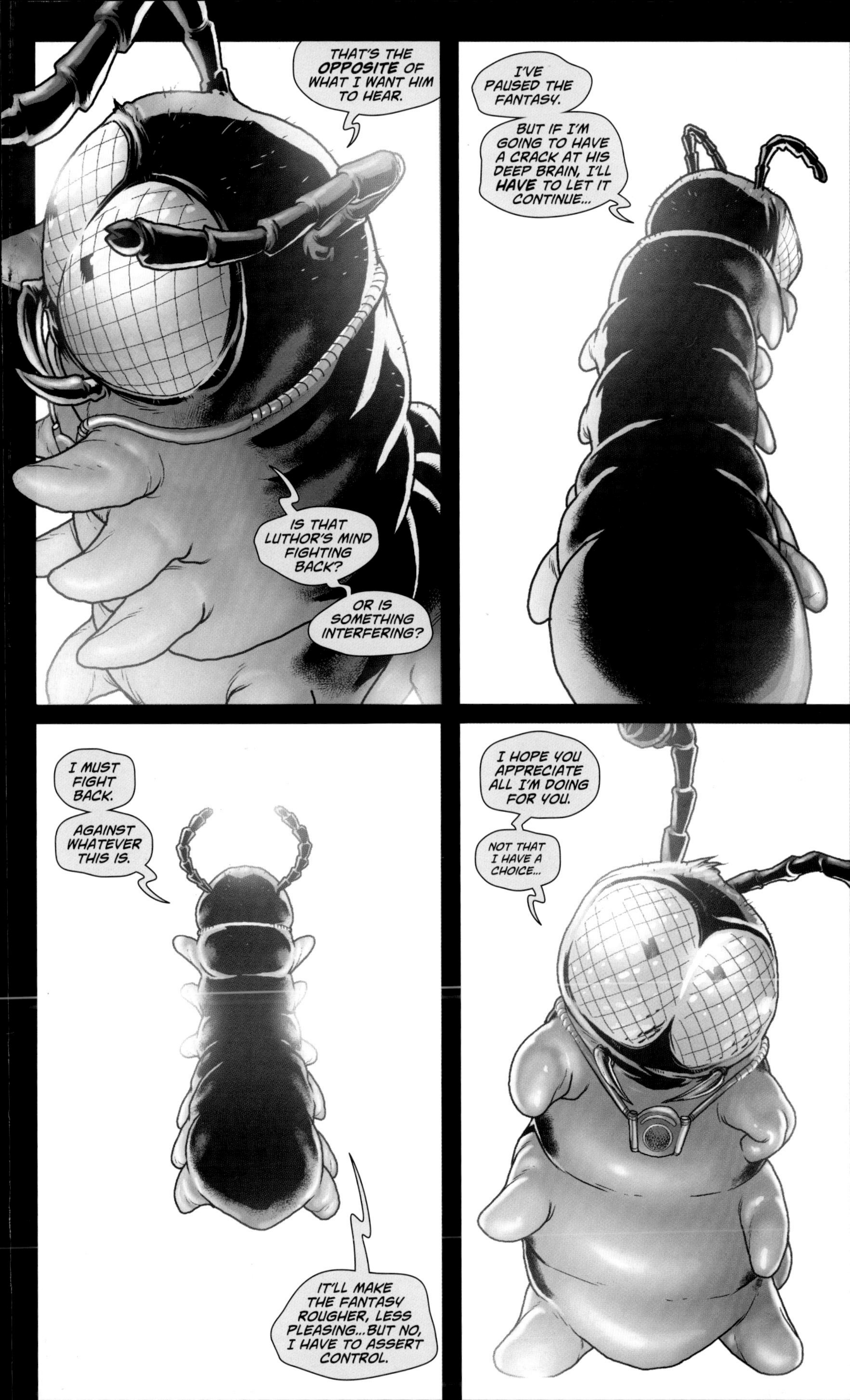
THAT'S THE OPPOSITE OF WHAT I WANT HIM TO HEAR.
IS THAT LUTHOR'S MIND FIGHTING BACK?
OR IS SOMETHING INTERFERING?
I'VE PAUSED THE FANTASY.
BUT IF I'M GOING TO HAVE A CRACK AT HIS DEEP BRAIN, I'LL HAVE TO LET IT CONTINUE...
I MUST FIGHT BACK.
AGAINST WHATEVER THIS IS.
IT'LL MAKE THE FANTASY ROUGHER, LESS PLEASING...BUT NO, I HAVE TO ASSERT CONTROL.
I HOPE YOU APPRECIATE ALL I'M DOING FOR YOU.
NOT THAT I HAVE A CHOICE...

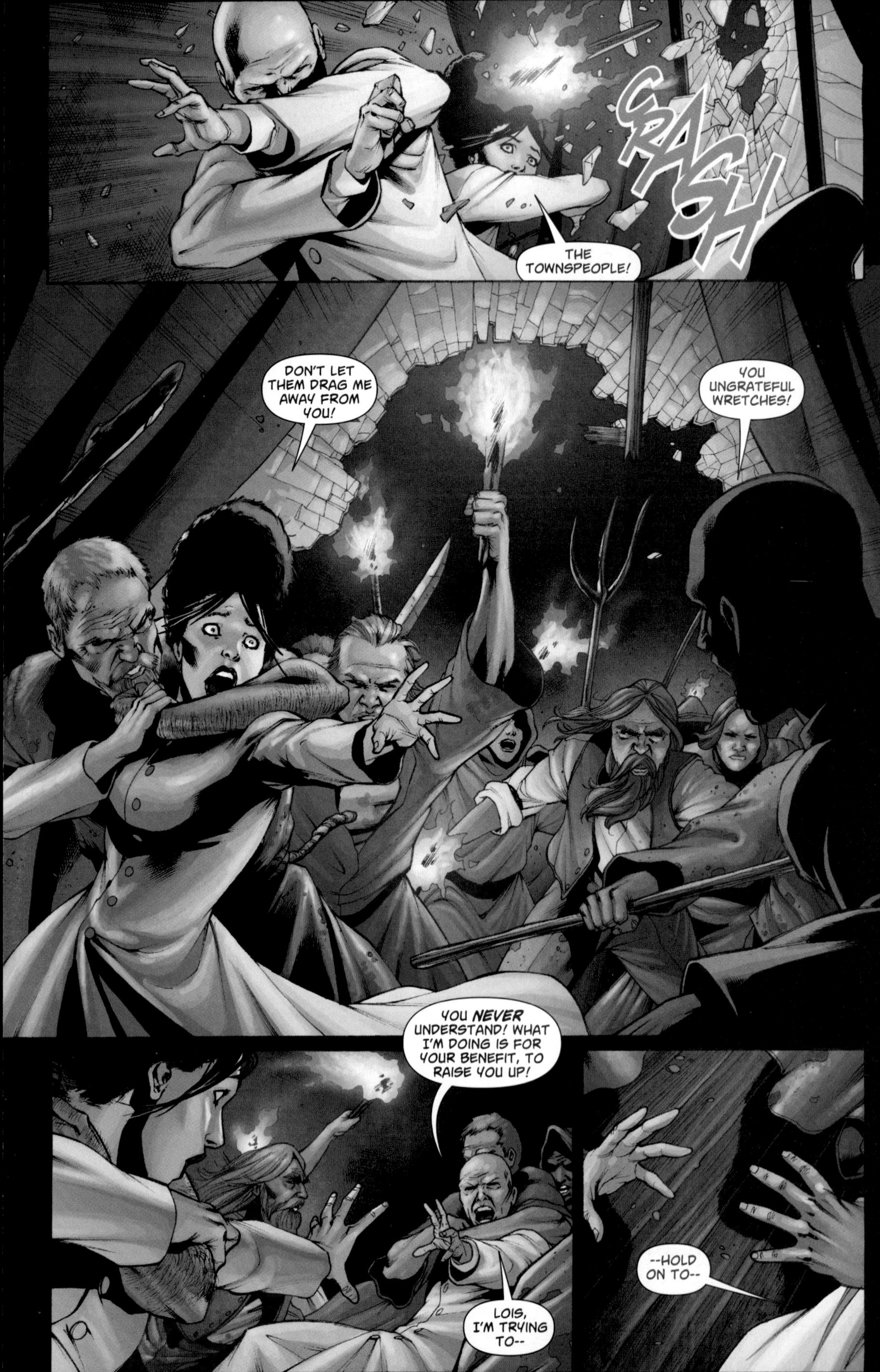
CRASH
THE TOWNSPEOPLE!
DON'T LET THEM DRAG ME AWAY FROM YOU!
YOU UNGRATEFUL WRETCHES!
YOU NEVER UNDERSTAND! WHAT I'M DOING IS FOR YOUR BENEFIT, TO RAISE YOU UP!
LOIS, I'M TRYING TO--
--HOLD ON TO--

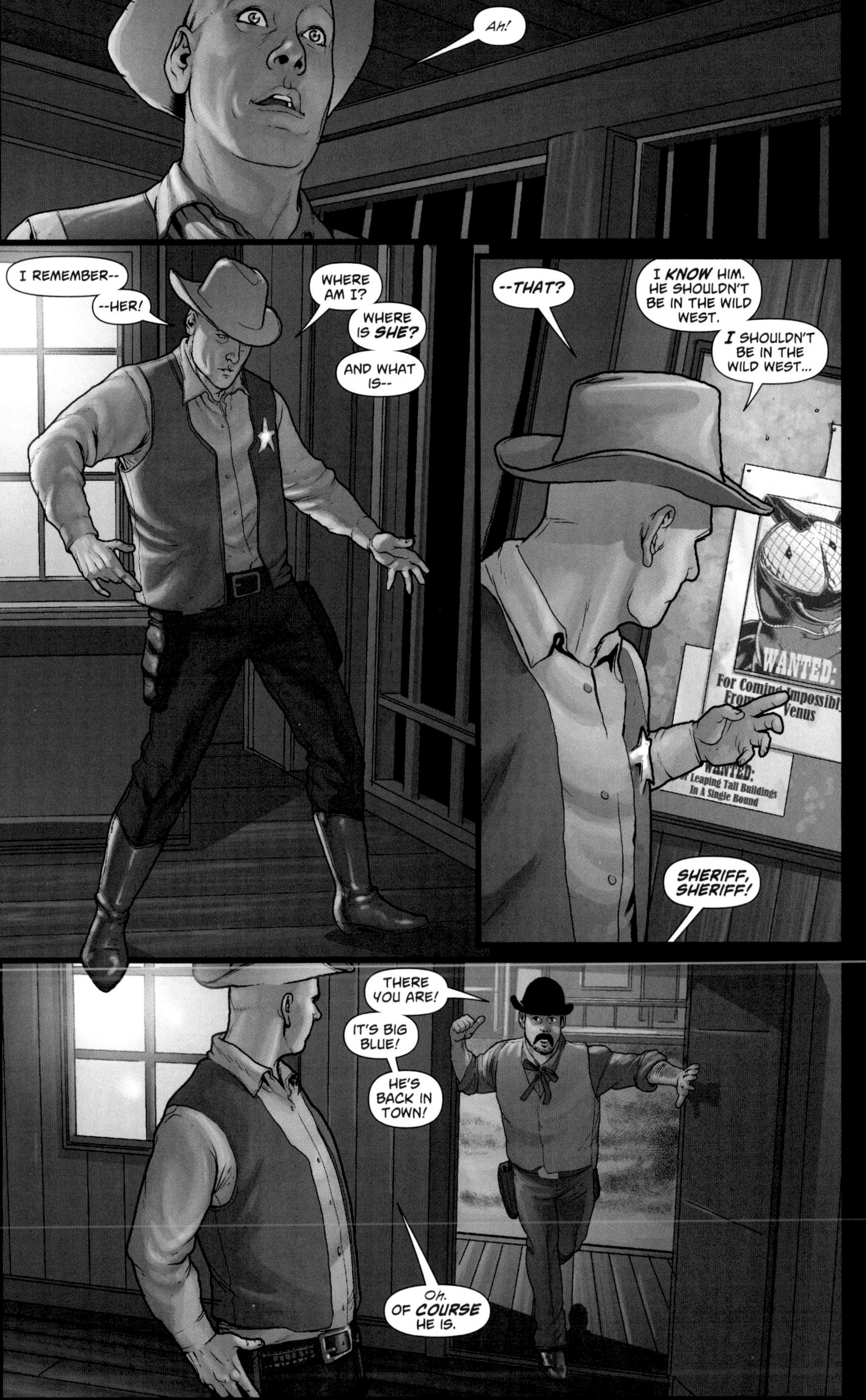
Ah!
I REMEMBER--
--HER!
WHERE AM I?
WHERE IS SHE?
AND WHAT IS--
--THAT?
I KNOW HIM. HE SHOULDN'T BE IN THE WILD WEST.
I SHOULDN'T BE IN THE WILD WEST...
WANTED:
For Coming
Venus
WANTED:
Leaping Tall Buildings In A Single Bound
SHERIFF, SHERIFF!
THERE YOU ARE!
IT'S BIG BLUE!
HE'S BACK IN TOWN!
Oh. OF COURSE HE IS.

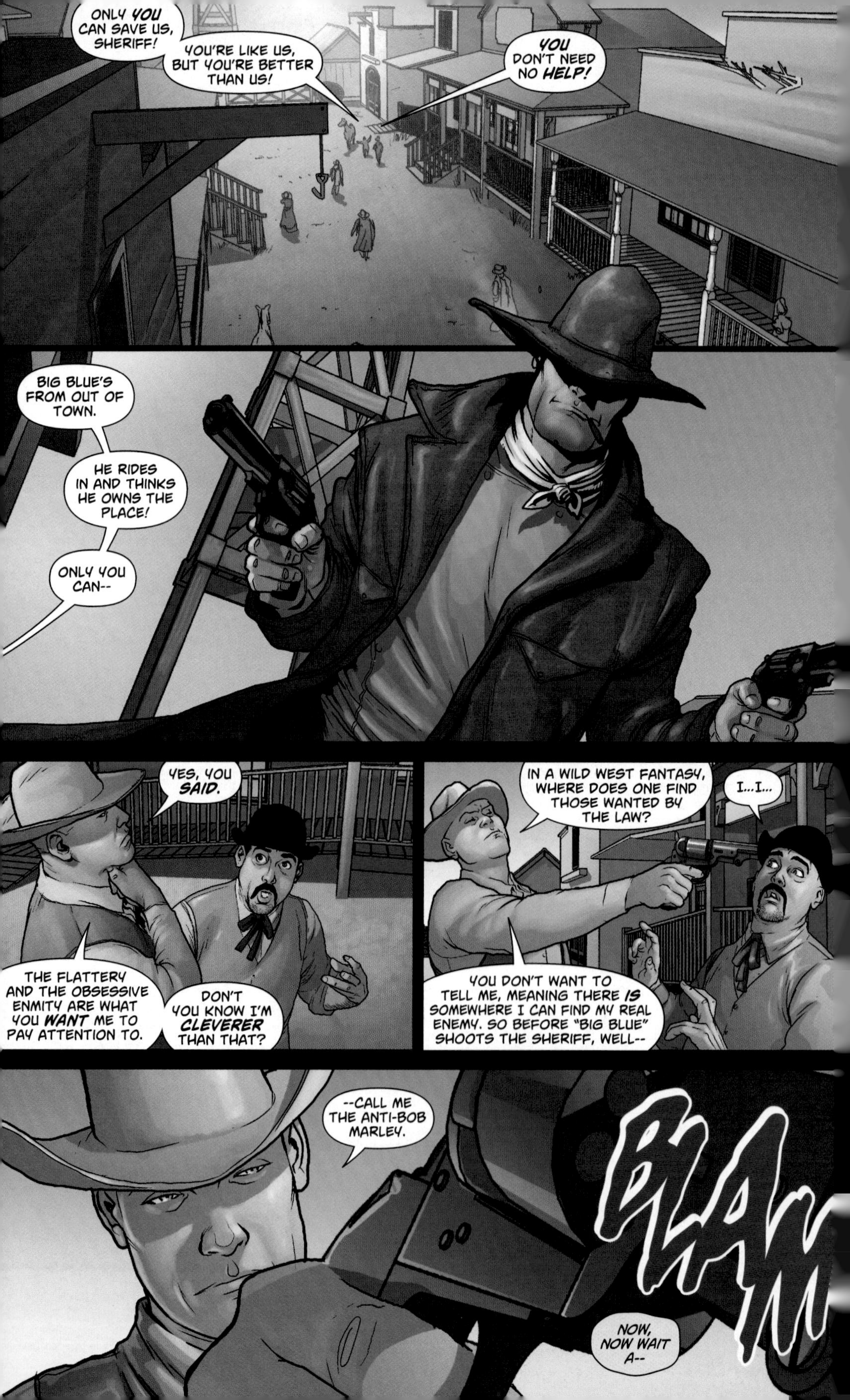

ONLY YOU CAN SAVE US, SHERIFF!
YOU'RE LIKE US, BUT YOU'RE BETTER THAN US!
YOU DON'T NEED NO HELP!
BIG BLUE'S FROM OUT OF TOWN.
HE RIDES IN AND THINKS HE OWNS THE PLACE!
ONLY YOU CAN--
YES, YOU SAID.
THE FLATTERY AND THE OBSESSIVE ENMITY ARE WHAT YOU WANT ME TO PAY ATTENTION TO.
DON'T YOU KNOW I'M CLEVERER THAN THAT?
IN A WILD WEST FANTASY, WHERE DOES ONE FIND THOSE WANTED BY THE LAW?
I...I...
YOU DON'T WANT TO TELL ME, MEANING THERE IS SOMEWHERE I CAN FIND MY REAL ENEMY. SO BEFORE "BIG BLUE" SHOOTS THE SHERIFF, WELL--
--CALL ME THE ANTI-BOB MARLEY.
BLAM
NOW, NOW WAIT A--

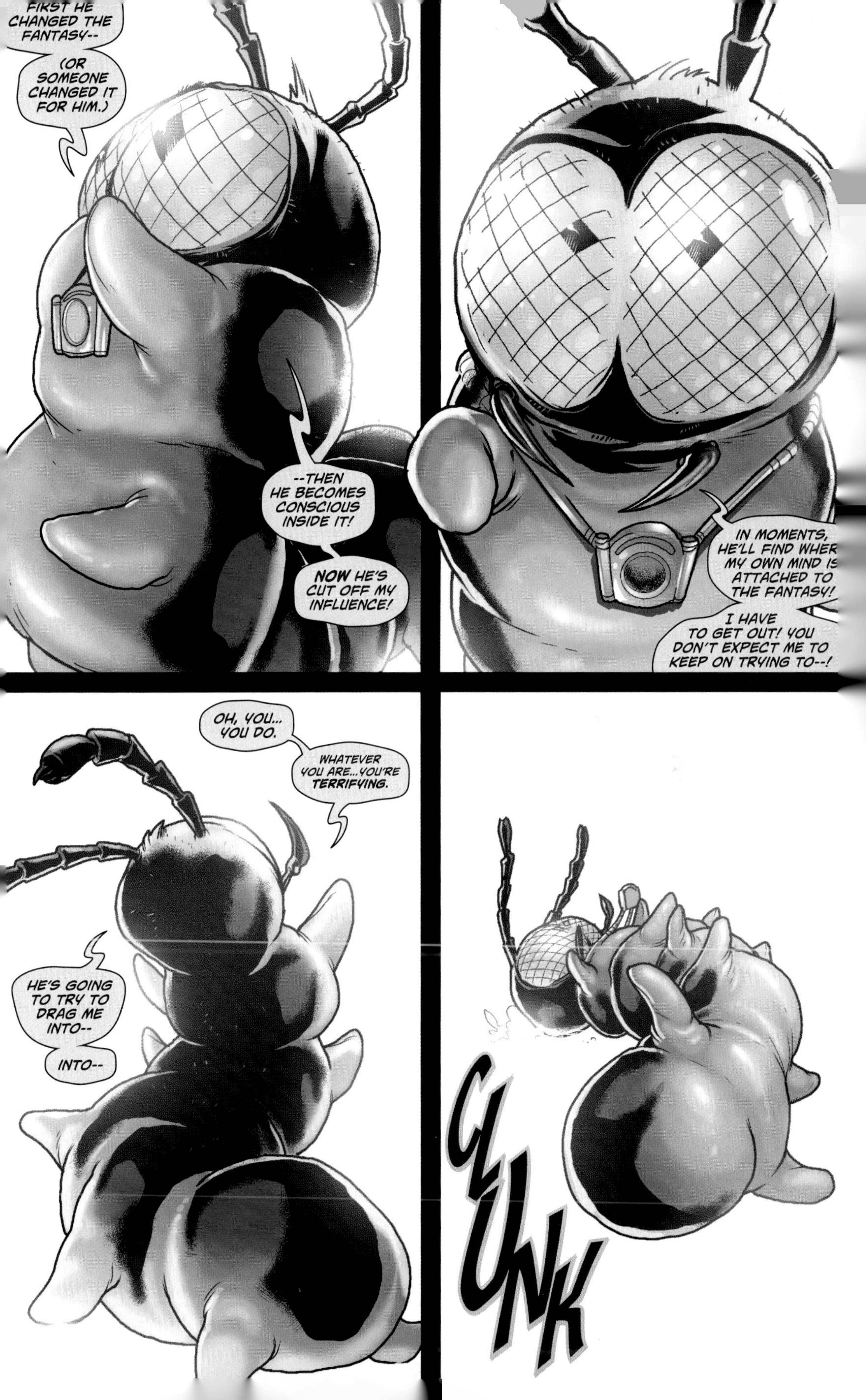
FIRST HE CHANGED THE FANTASY--
(OR SOMEONE CHANGED IT FOR HIM.)
--THEN HE BECOMES CONSCIOUS INSIDE IT!
NOW HE'S CUT OFF MY INFLUENCE!
IN MOMENTS, HE'LL FIND WHER MY OWN MIND IS ATTACHED TO THE FANTASY!
I HAVE TO GET OUT! YOU DON'T EXPECT ME TO KEEP ON TRYING TO--!
OH, YOU... YOU DO.
WHATEVER YOU ARE...YOU'RE TERRIFYING.
HE'S GOING TO TRY TO DRAG ME INTO--
INTO--
CLUNK

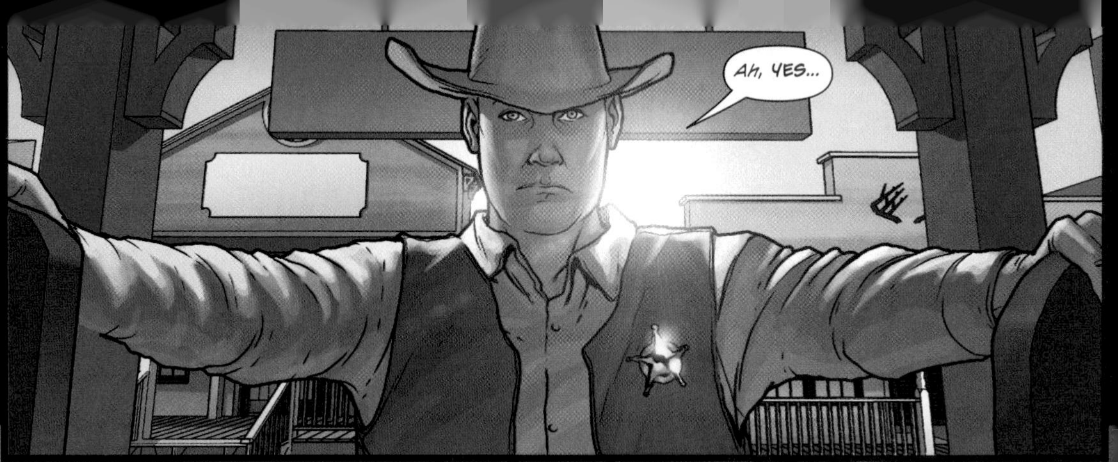
AH, YES...

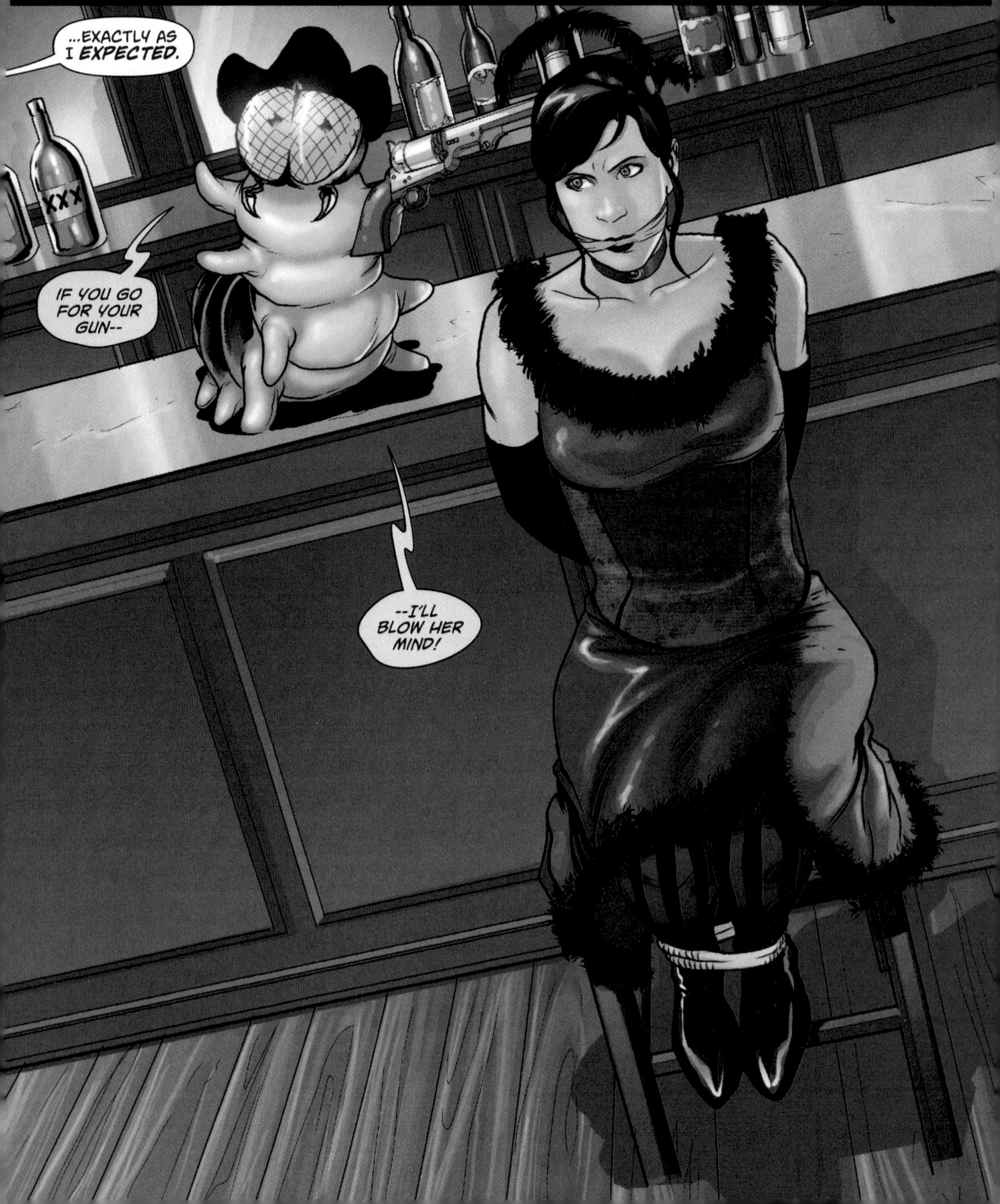
...EXACTLY AS I **EXPECTED.**
IF YOU GO FOR YOUR GUN--
--I'LL BLOW HER MIND!

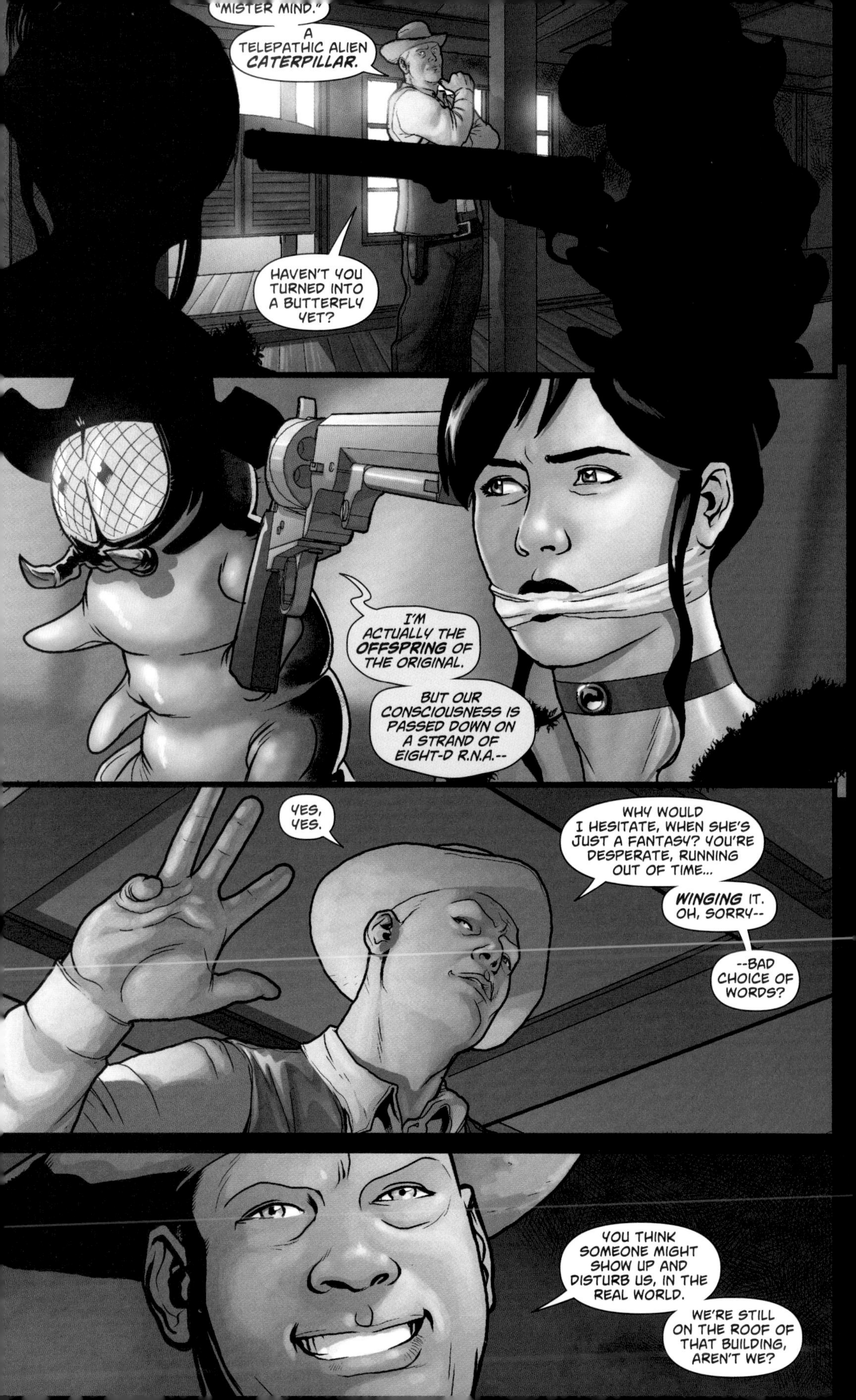
"MISTER MIND."
A TELEPATHIC ALIEN CATERPILLAR.
HAVEN'T YOU TURNED INTO A BUTTERFLY YET?
I'M ACTUALLY THE OFFSPRING OF THE ORIGINAL.
BUT OUR CONSCIOUSNESS IS PASSED DOWN ON A STRAND OF EIGHT-D R.N.A.--
YES, YES.
WHY WOULD I HESITATE, WHEN SHE'S JUST A FANTASY? YOU'RE DESPERATE, RUNNING OUT OF TIME...
WINGING IT. OH, SORRY--
--BAD CHOICE OF WORDS?
YOU THINK SOMEONE MIGHT SHOW UP AND DISTURB US, IN THE REAL WORLD.
WE'RE STILL ON THE ROOF OF THAT BUILDING, AREN'T WE?

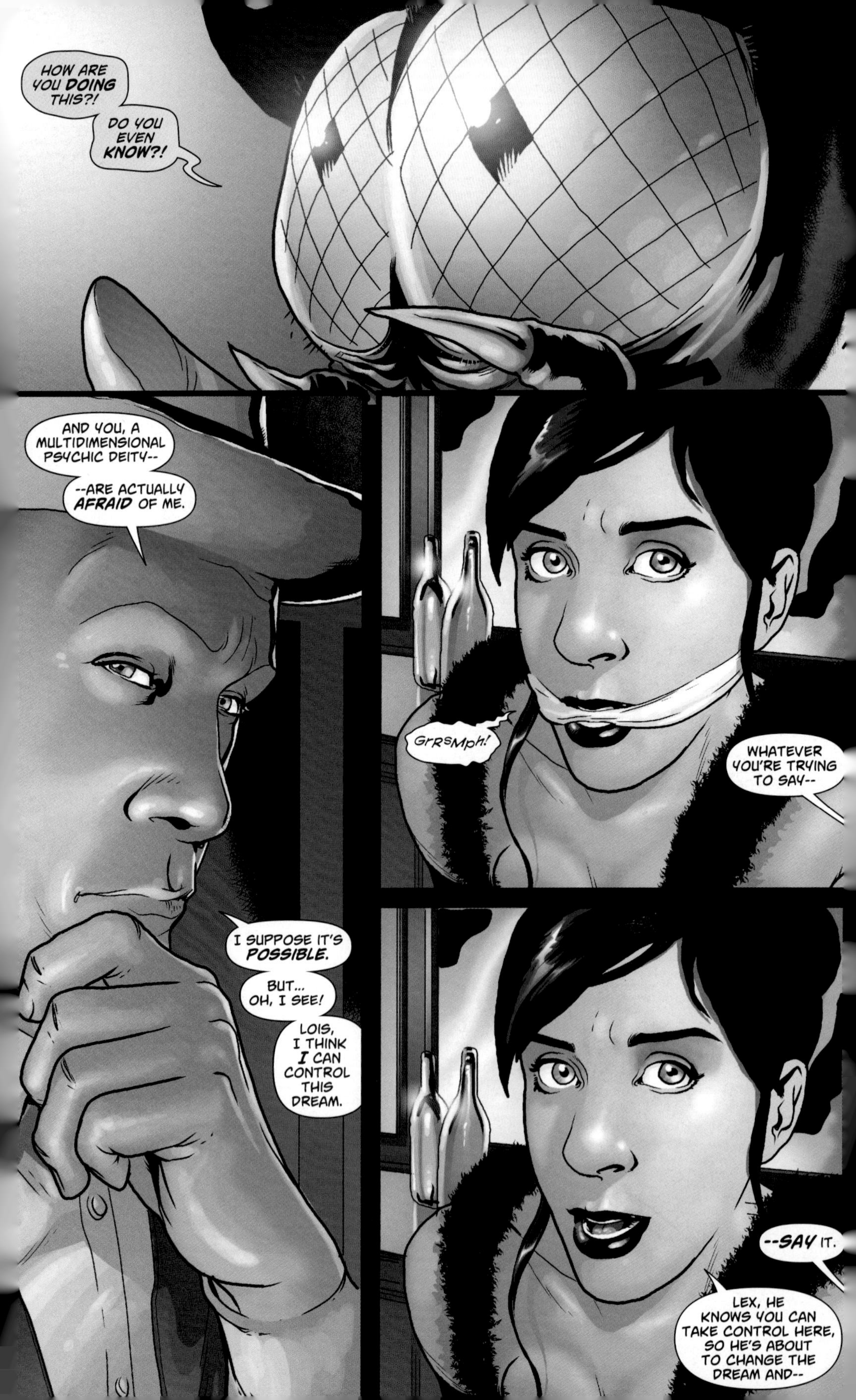
HOW ARE YOU DOING THIS?!
DO YOU EVEN KNOW?!
AND YOU, A MULTIDIMENSIONAL PSYCHIC DEITY--
--ARE ACTUALLY AFRAID OF ME.
GrRSMph!
WHATEVER YOU'RE TRYING TO SAY--
I SUPPOSE IT'S POSSIBLE.
BUT... OH, I SEE!
LOIS, I THINK I CAN CONTROL THIS DREAM.
--SAY IT.
LEX, HE KNOWS YOU CAN TAKE CONTROL HERE, SO HE'S ABOUT TO CHANGE THE DREAM AND--

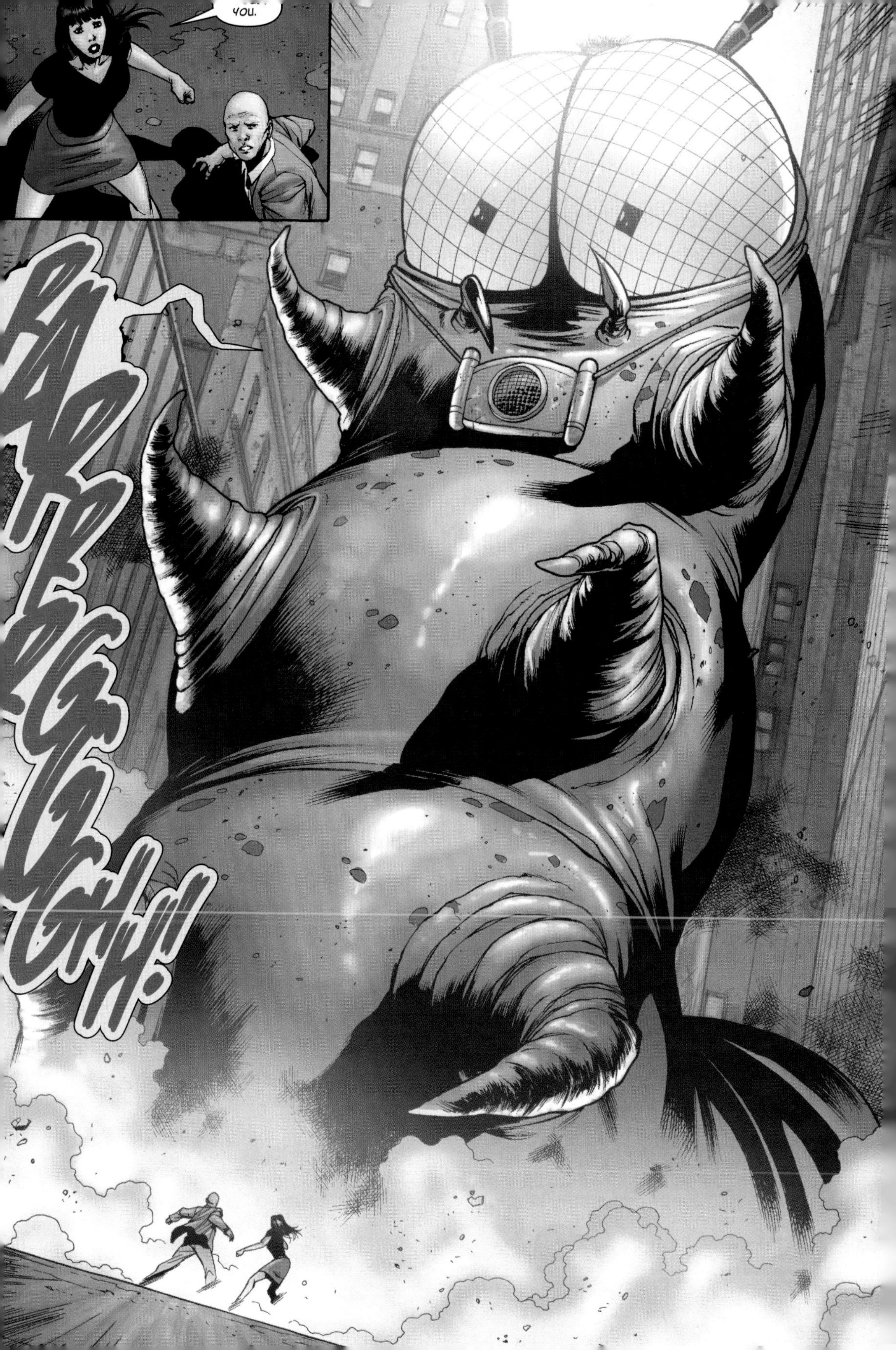
YOU.
RAAARRGGGGH!!

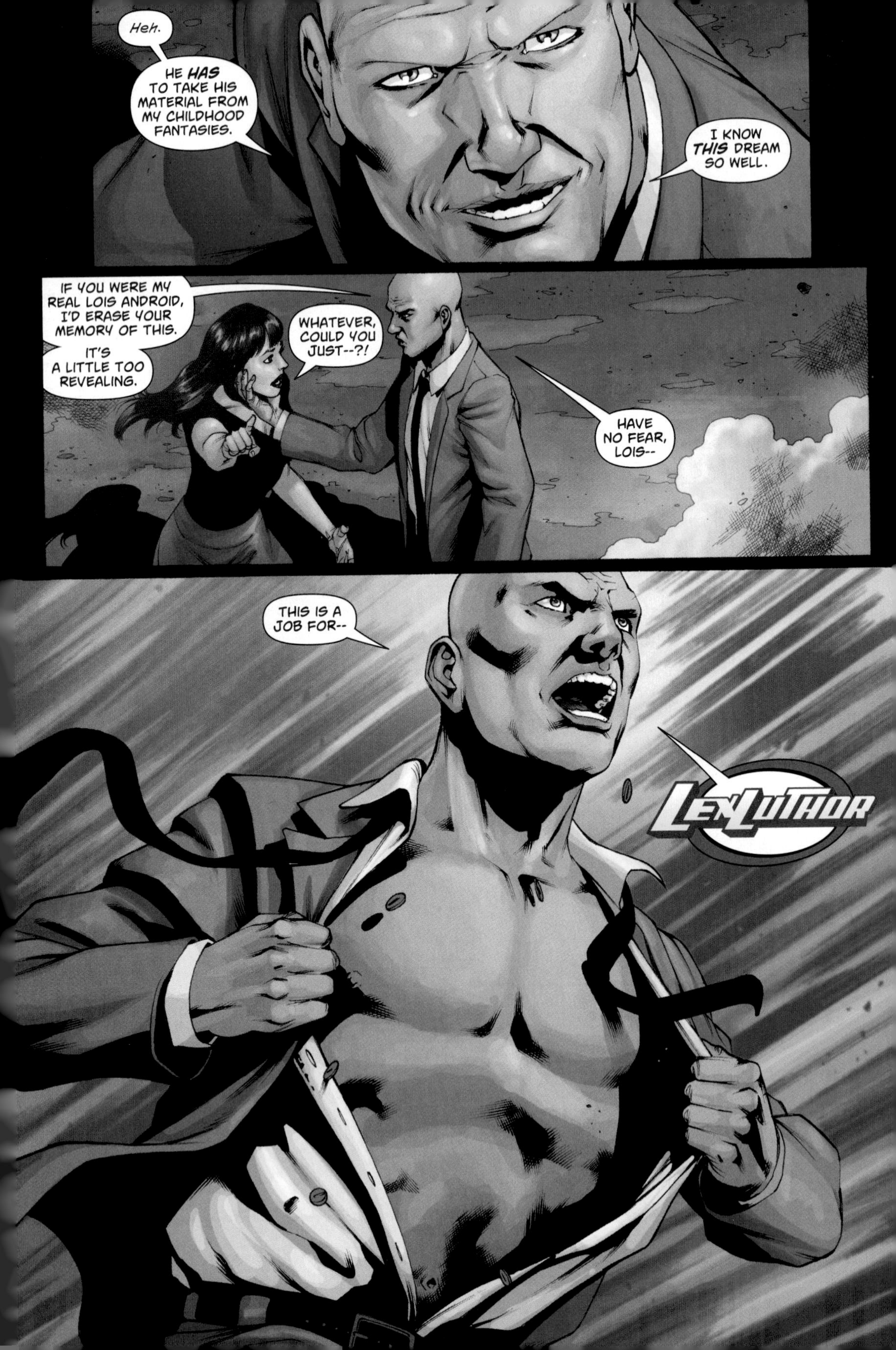

Heh.
HE HAS TO TAKE HIS MATERIAL FROM MY CHILDHOOD FANTASIES.
I KNOW THIS DREAM SO WELL.
IF YOU WERE MY REAL LOIS ANDROID, I'D ERASE YOUR MEMORY OF THIS.
IT'S A LITTLE TOO REVEALING.
WHATEVER, COULD YOU JUST--?!
HAVE NO FEAR, LOIS--
THIS IS A JOB FOR--
LEX LUTHOR

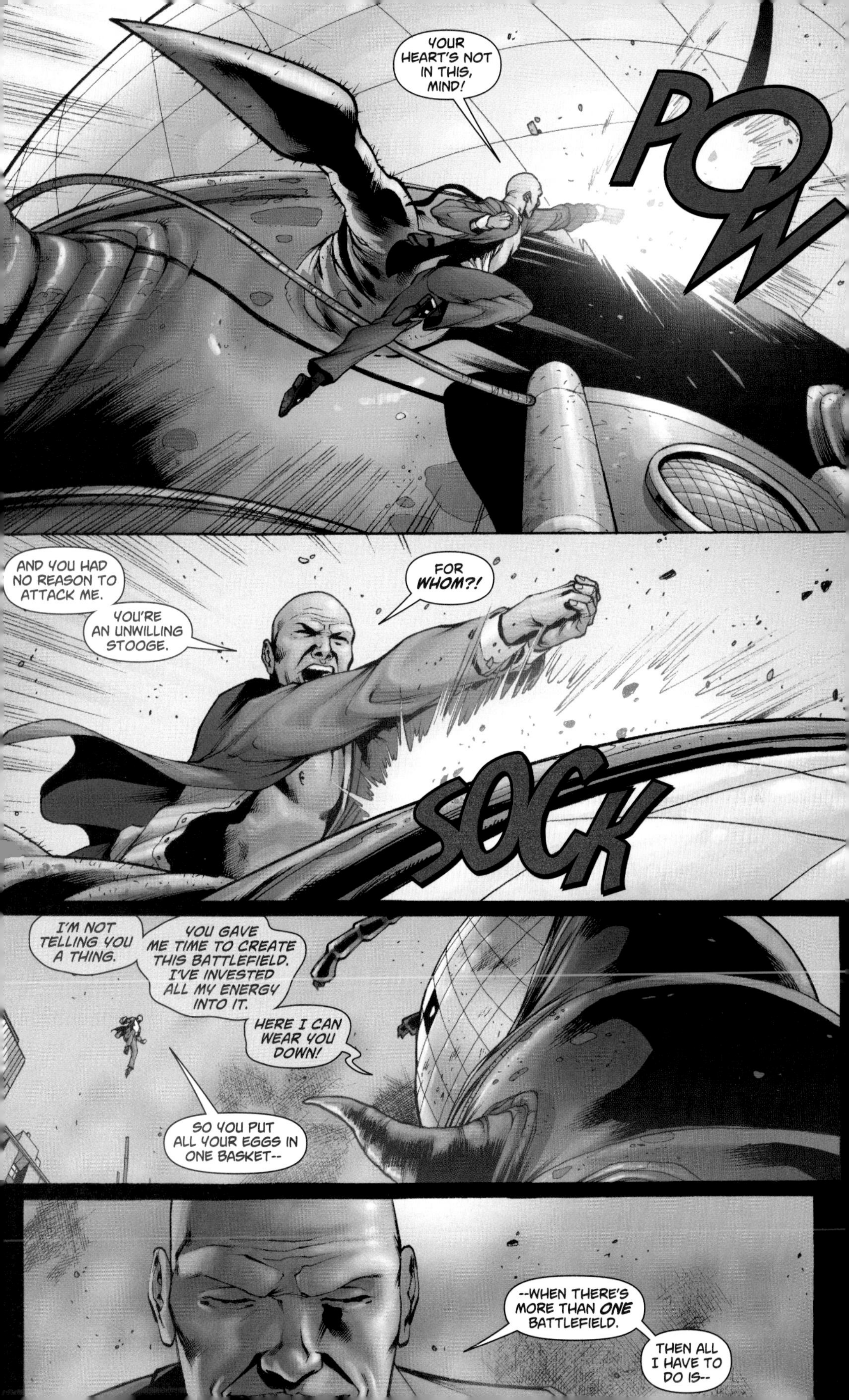
YOUR HEART'S NOT IN THIS, MIND!
POW
AND YOU HAD NO REASON TO ATTACK ME.
YOU'RE AN UNWILLING STOOGE.
FOR *WHOM?!*
SOCK
I'M NOT TELLING YOU A THING.
YOU GAVE ME TIME TO CREATE THIS BATTLEFIELD. I'VE INVESTED ALL MY ENERGY INTO IT.
HERE I CAN WEAR YOU DOWN!
SO YOU PUT ALL YOUR EGGS IN ONE BASKET--
--WHEN THERE'S MORE THAN *ONE* BATTLEFIELD.
THEN ALL I HAVE TO DO IS--

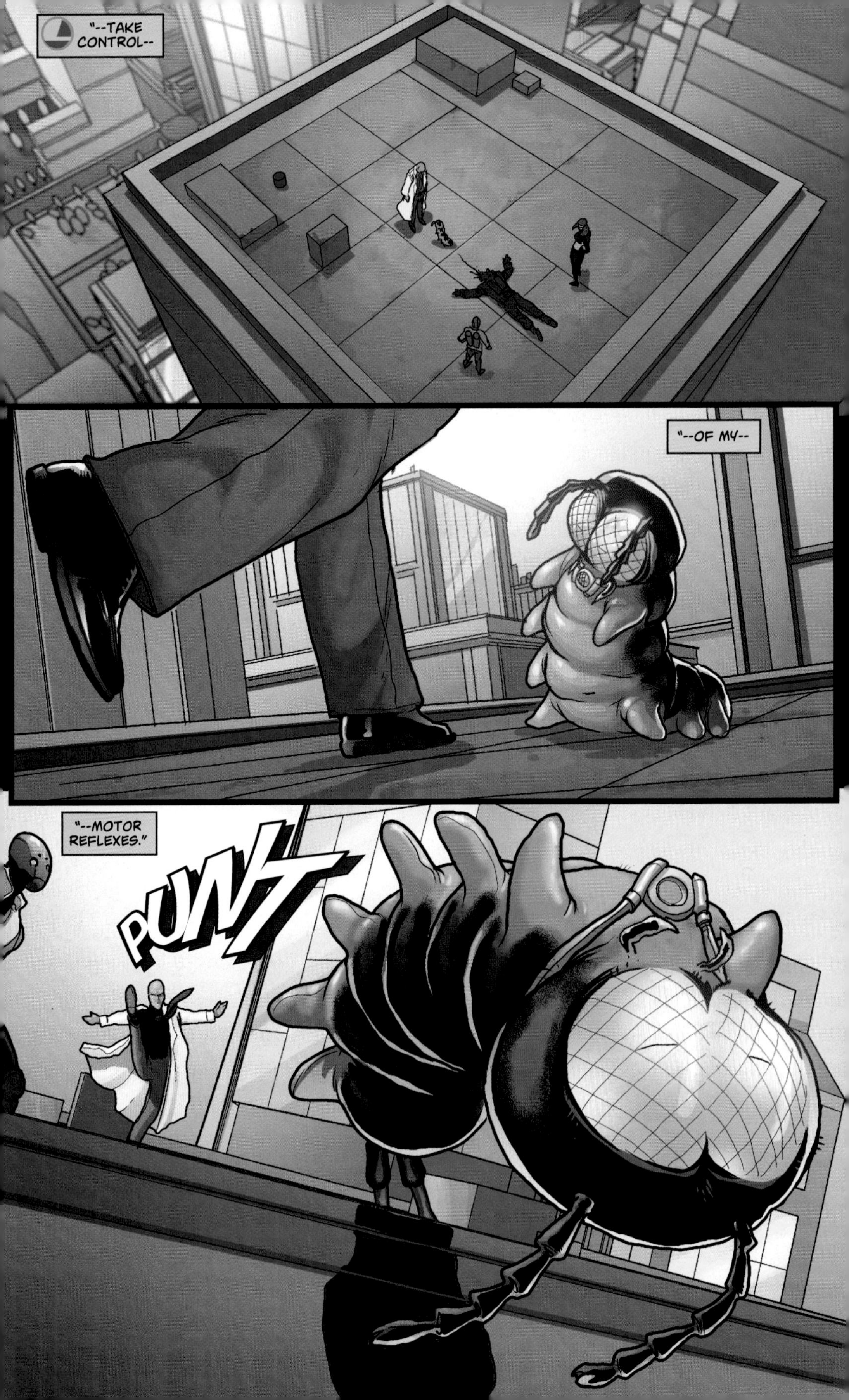
"--TAKE CONTROL--
"--OF MY--
"--MOTOR REFLEXES."
PUNT

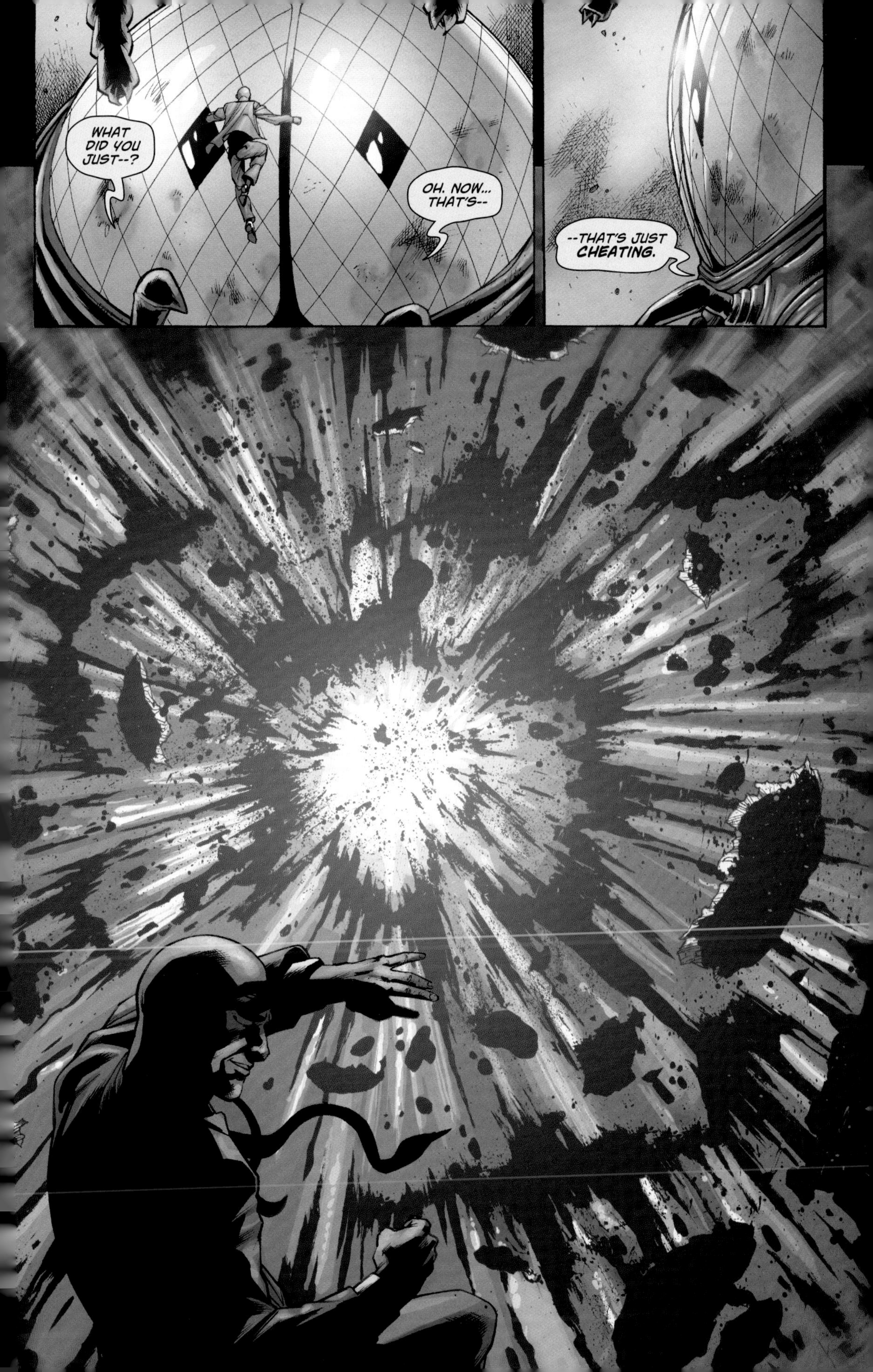
WHAT DID YOU JUST--?
OH. NOW... THAT'S--
--THAT'S JUST CHEATING.

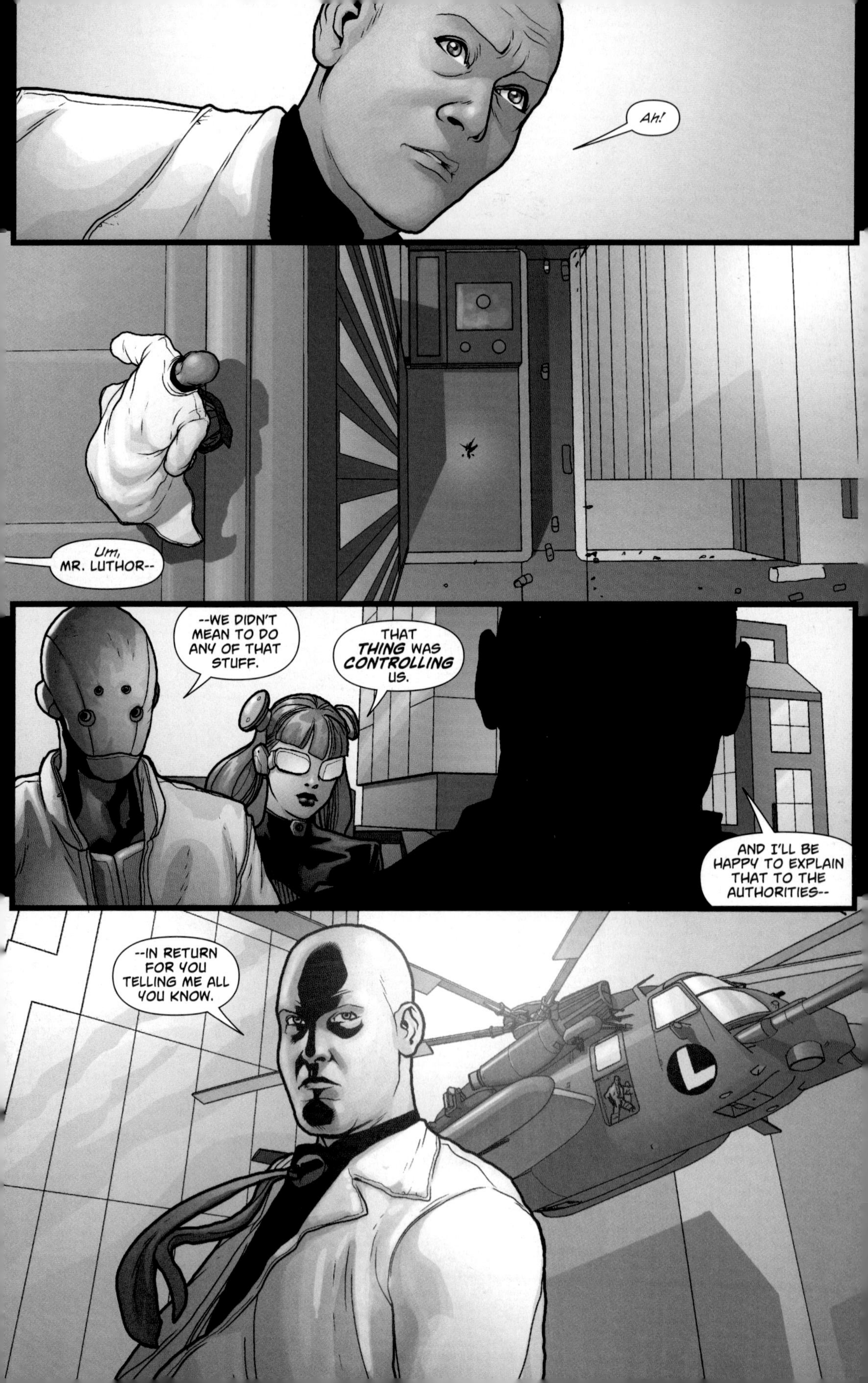
Ah!
Um, MR. LUTHOR--
--WE DIDN'T MEAN TO DO ANY OF THAT STUFF.
THAT THING WAS CONTROLLING US.
AND I'LL BE HAPPY TO EXPLAIN THAT TO THE AUTHORITIES--
--IN RETURN FOR YOU TELLING ME ALL YOU KNOW.

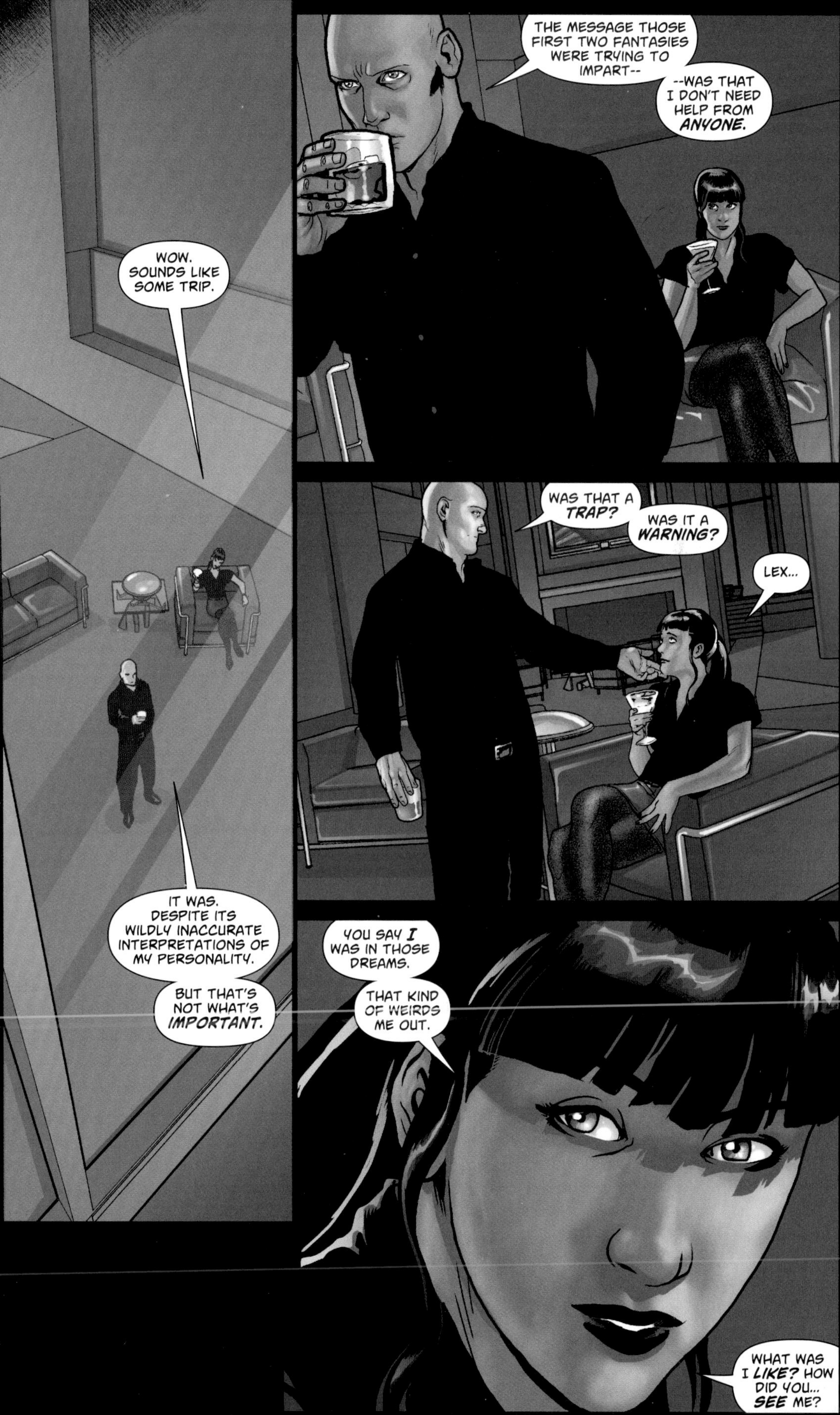
WOW. SOUNDS LIKE SOME TRIP.
IT WAS. DESPITE ITS WILDLY INACCURATE INTERPRETATIONS OF MY PERSONALITY.
BUT THAT'S NOT WHAT'S IMPORTANT.
THE MESSAGE THOSE FIRST TWO FANTASIES WERE TRYING TO IMPART--
--WAS THAT I DON'T NEED HELP FROM ANYONE.
WAS THAT A TRAP?
WAS IT A WARNING?
LEX...
YOU SAY I WAS IN THOSE DREAMS.
THAT KIND OF WEIRDS ME OUT.
WHAT WAS I LIKE? HOW DID YOU... SEE ME?

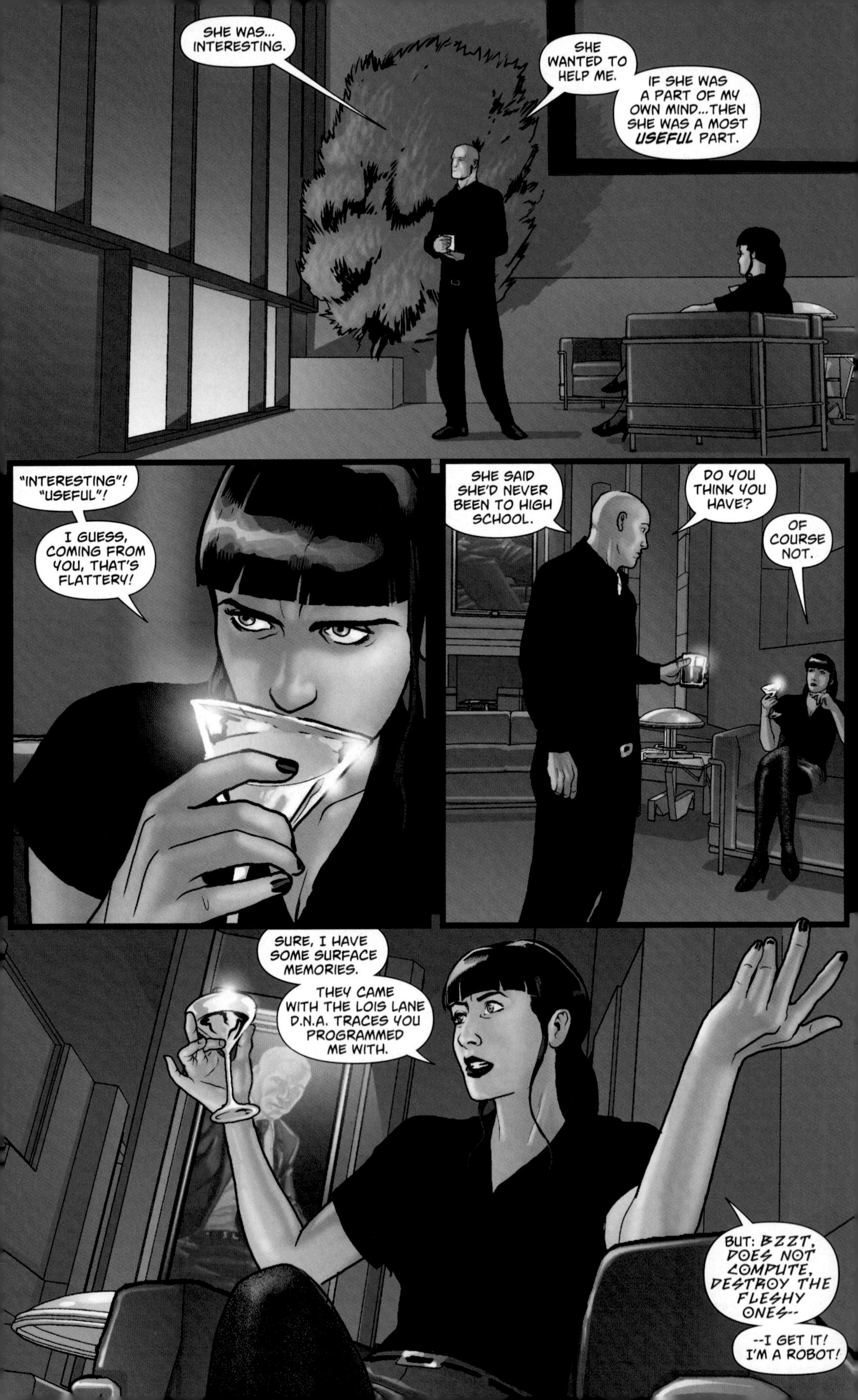
SHE WAS... INTERESTING.
SHE WANTED TO HELP ME.
IF SHE WAS A PART OF MY OWN MIND...THEN SHE WAS A MOST USEFUL PART.
"INTERESTING"! "USEFUL"!
I GUESS, COMING FROM YOU, THAT'S FLATTERY!
SHE SAID SHE'D NEVER BEEN TO HIGH SCHOOL.
DO YOU THINK YOU HAVE?
OF COURSE NOT.
SURE, I HAVE SOME SURFACE MEMORIES.
THEY CAME WITH THE LOIS LANE D.N.A. TRACES YOU PROGRAMMED ME WITH.
BUT: BZZT, DOES NOT COMPUTE, DESTROY THE FLESHY ONES--
--I GET IT! I'M A ROBOT!

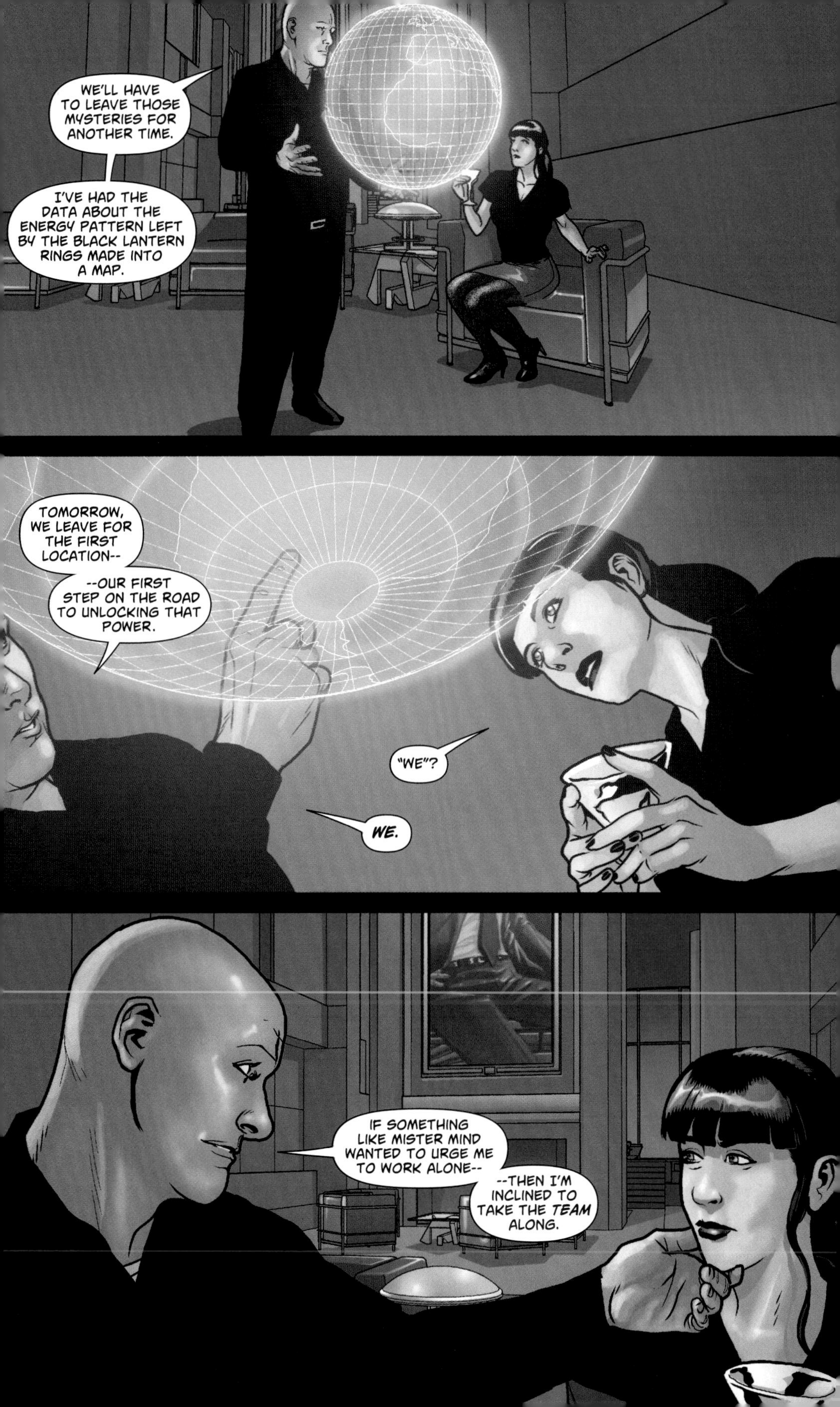
WE'LL HAVE TO LEAVE THOSE MYSTERIES FOR ANOTHER TIME.
I'VE HAD THE DATA ABOUT THE ENERGY PATTERN LEFT BY THE BLACK LANTERN RINGS MADE INTO A MAP.
TOMORROW, WE LEAVE FOR THE FIRST LOCATION--
--OUR FIRST STEP ON THE ROAD TO UNLOCKING THAT POWER.
"WE"?
WE.
IF SOMETHING LIKE MISTER MIND WANTED TO URGE ME TO WORK ALONE--
--THEN I'M INCLINED TO TAKE THE *TEAM* ALONG.

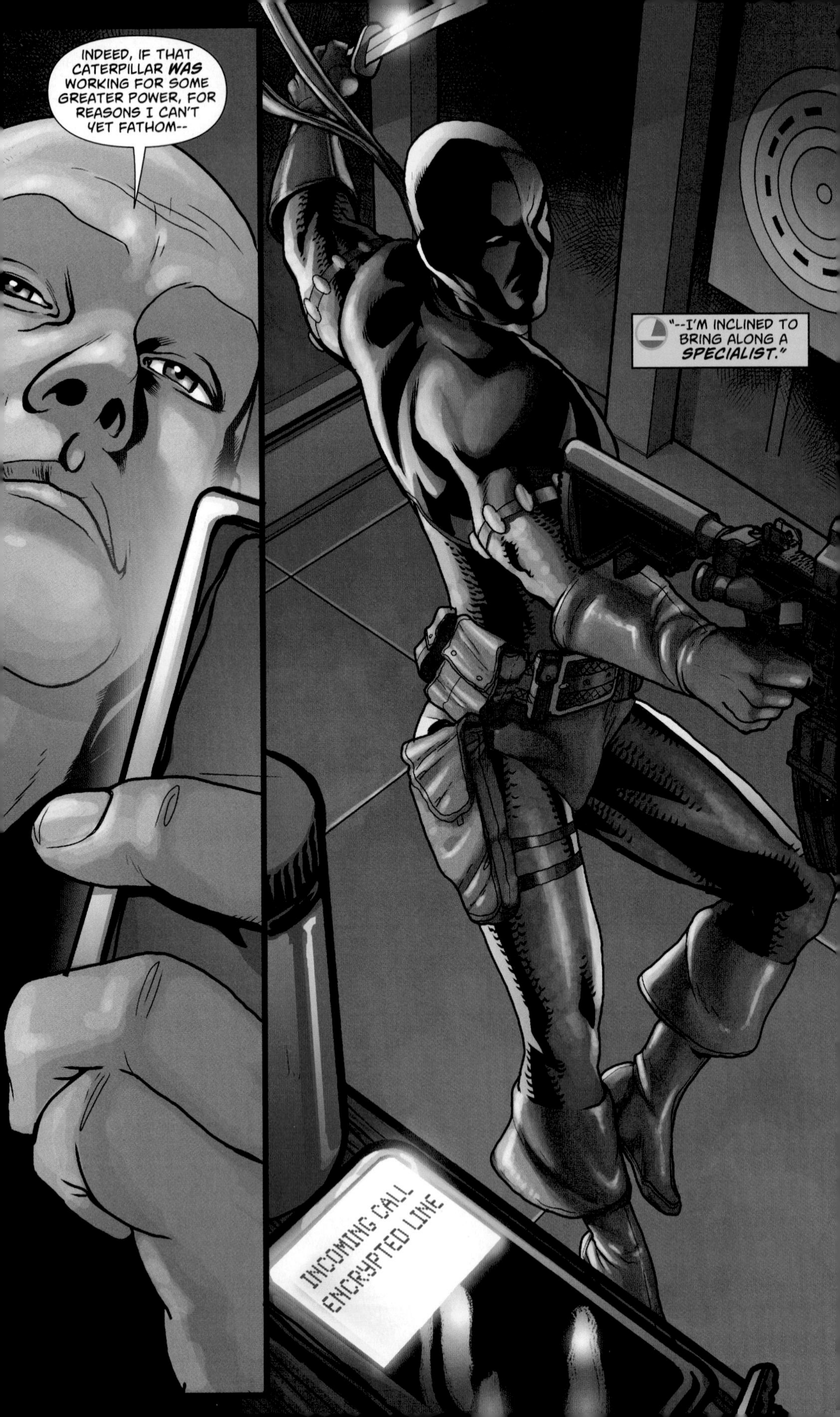
INDEED, IF THAT CATERPILLAR WAS WORKING FOR SOME GREATER POWER, FOR REASONS I CAN'T YET FATHOM--
"--I'M INCLINED TO BRING ALONG A SPECIALIST."
INCOMING CALL ENCRYPTED LINE

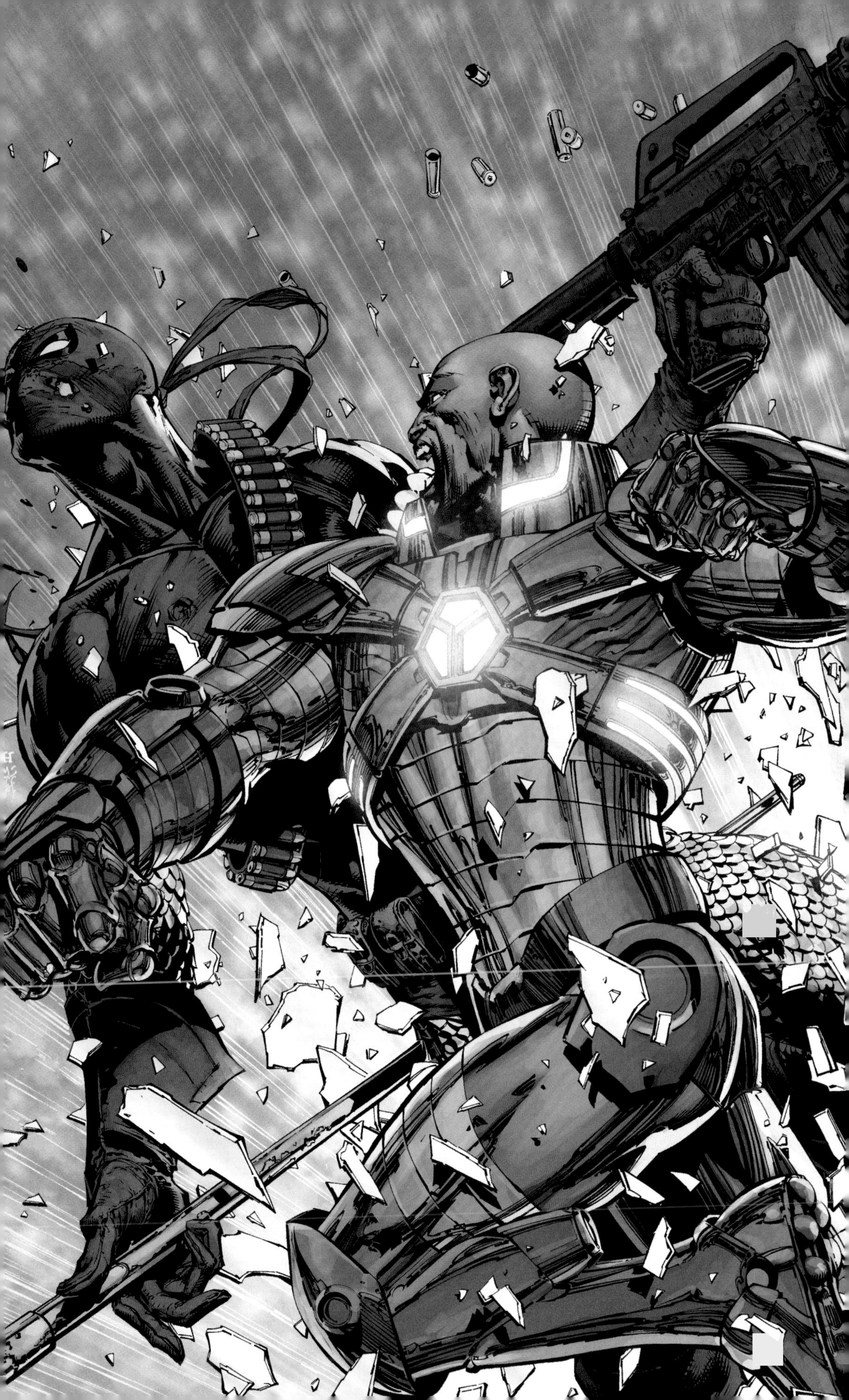

THE BLACK RING

part three

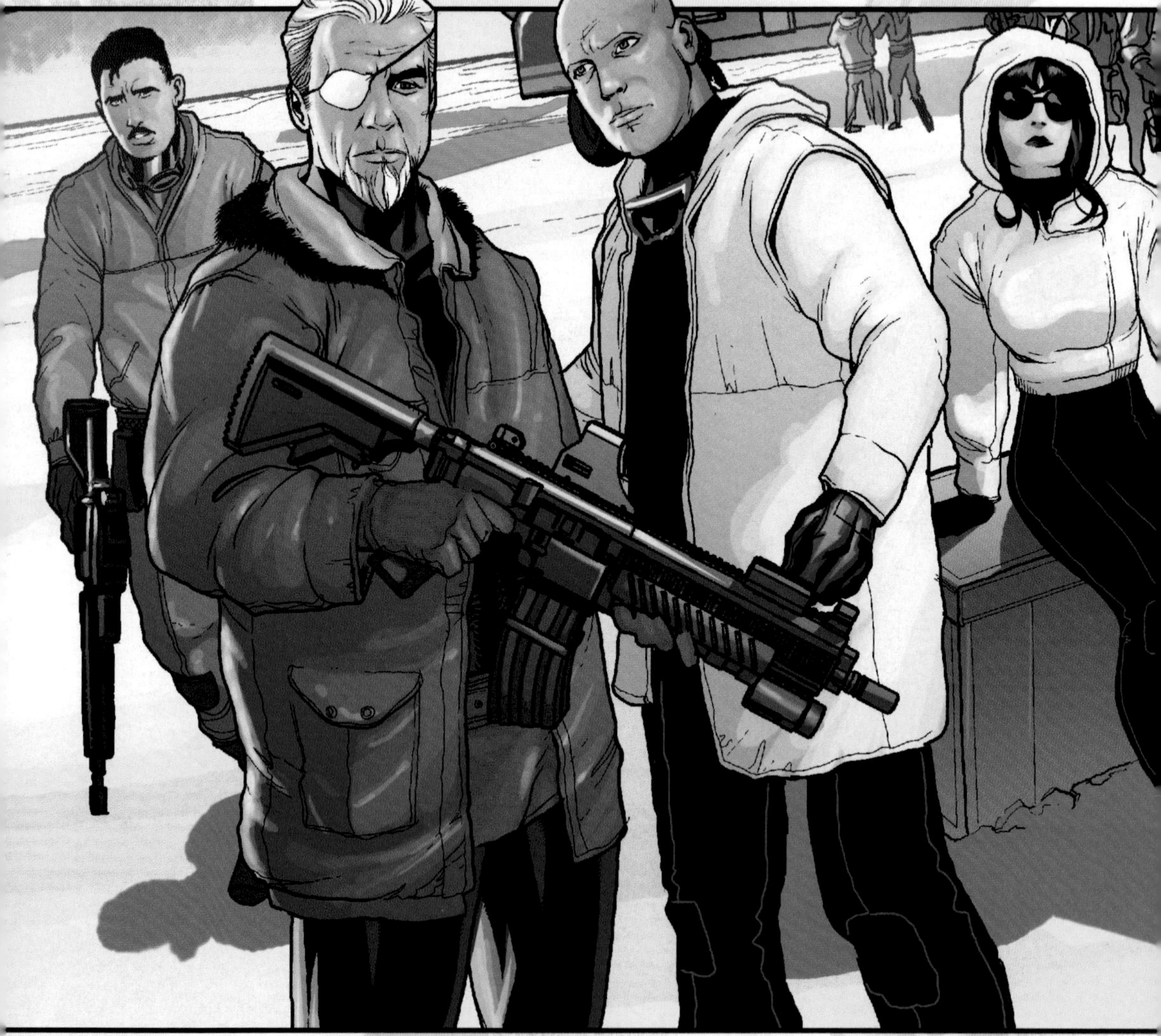

cover by

DAVID **FINCH**, JOE **WEEMS** & PETER **STEIGERWALD**

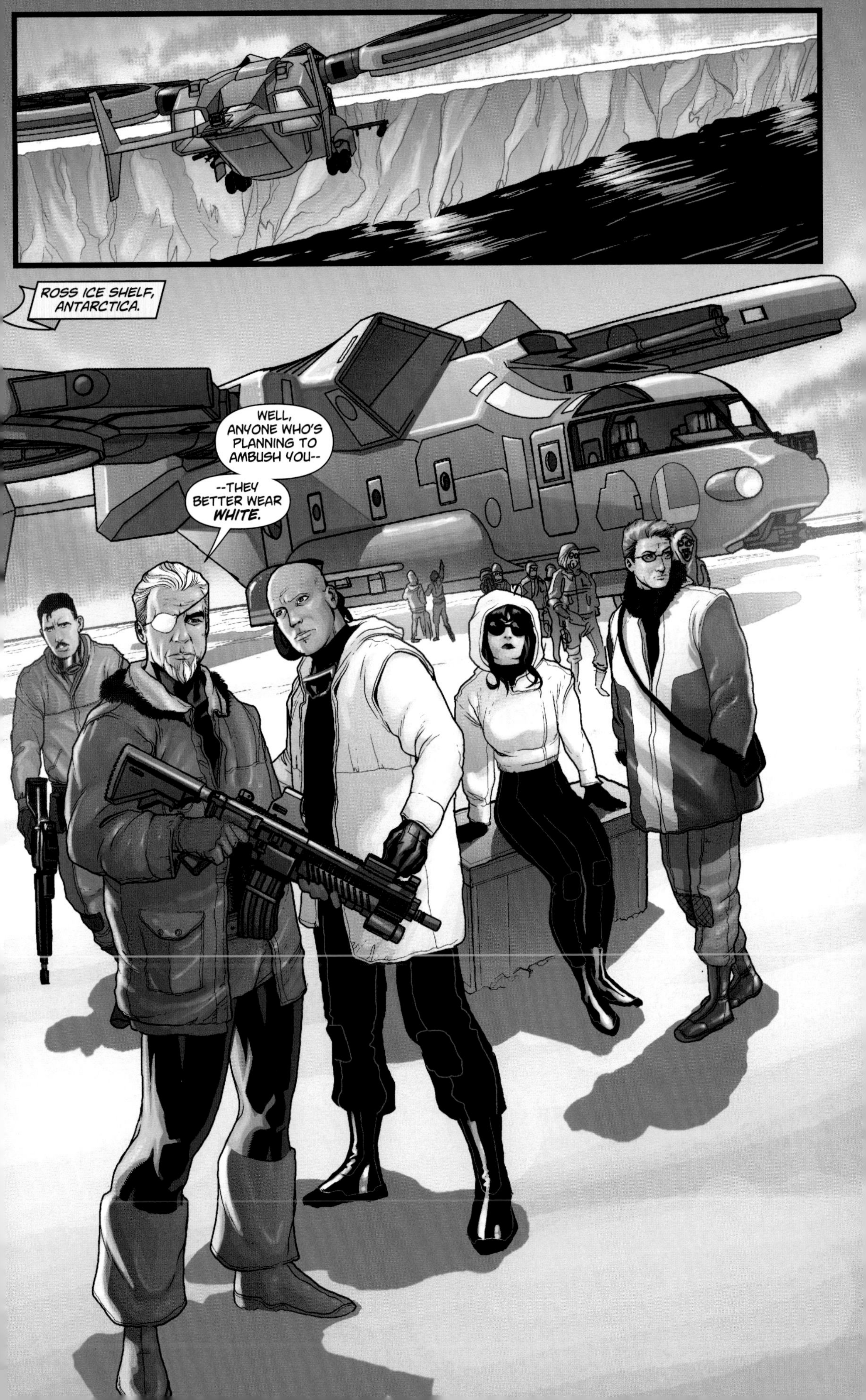
ROSS ICE SHELF, ANTARCTICA.
WELL, ANYONE WHO'S PLANNING TO AMBUSH YOU--
--THEY BETTER WEAR WHITE.

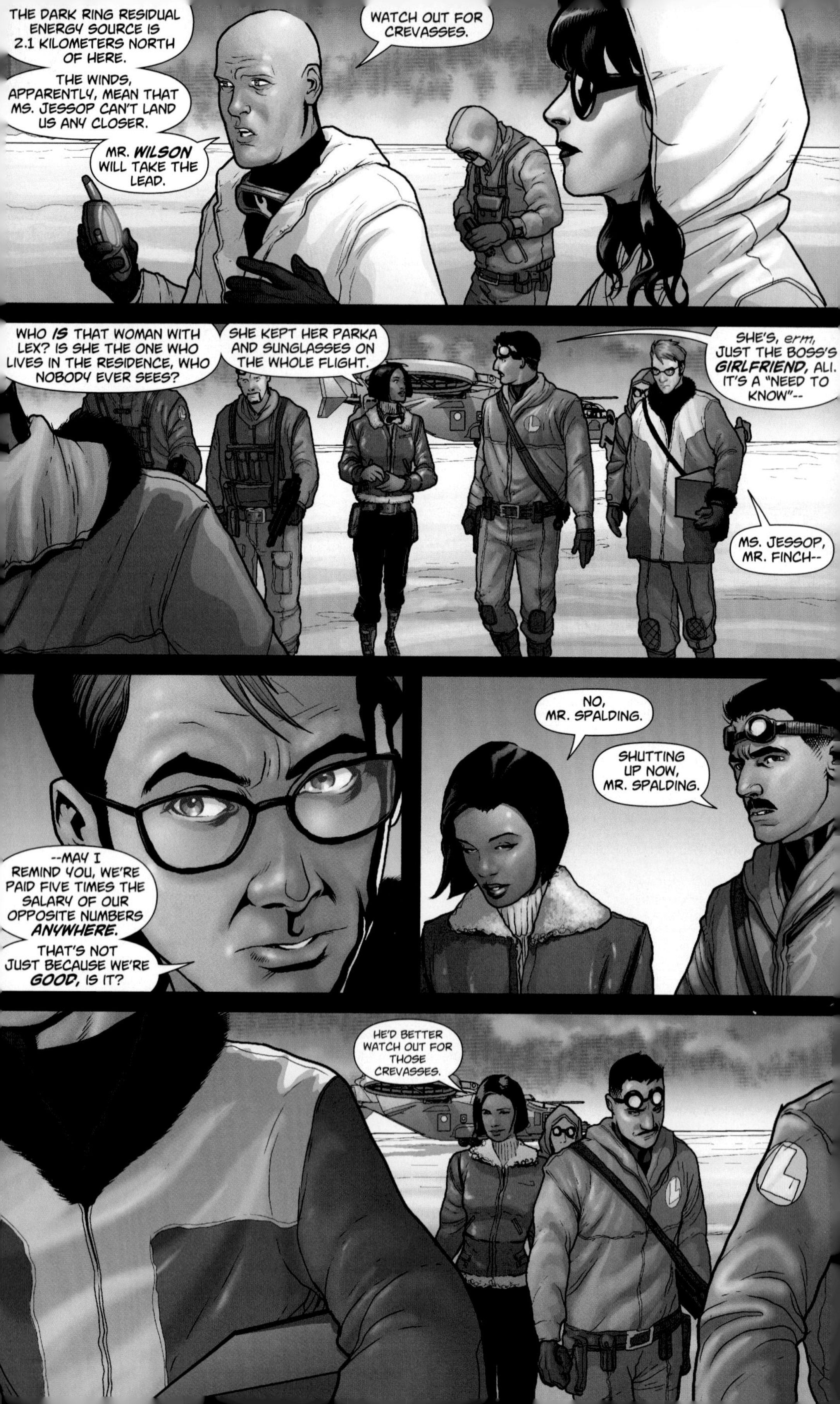
THE DARK RING RESIDUAL ENERGY SOURCE IS 2.1 KILOMETERS NORTH OF HERE.
THE WINDS, APPARENTLY, MEAN THAT MS. JESSOP CAN'T LAND US ANY CLOSER.
MR. WILSON WILL TAKE THE LEAD.
WATCH OUT FOR CREVASSES.
WHO IS THAT WOMAN WITH LEX? IS SHE THE ONE WHO LIVES IN THE RESIDENCE, WHO NOBODY EVER SEES?
SHE KEPT HER PARKA AND SUNGLASSES ON THE WHOLE FLIGHT.
SHE'S, erm, JUST THE BOSS'S GIRLFRIEND, ALI. IT'S A "NEED TO KNOW"--
MS. JESSOP, MR. FINCH--
--MAY I REMIND YOU, WE'RE PAID FIVE TIMES THE SALARY OF OUR OPPOSITE NUMBERS ANYWHERE.
THAT'S NOT JUST BECAUSE WE'RE GOOD, IS IT?
NO, MR. SPALDING.
SHUTTING UP NOW, MR. SPALDING.
HE'D BETTER WATCH OUT FOR THOSE CREVASSES.

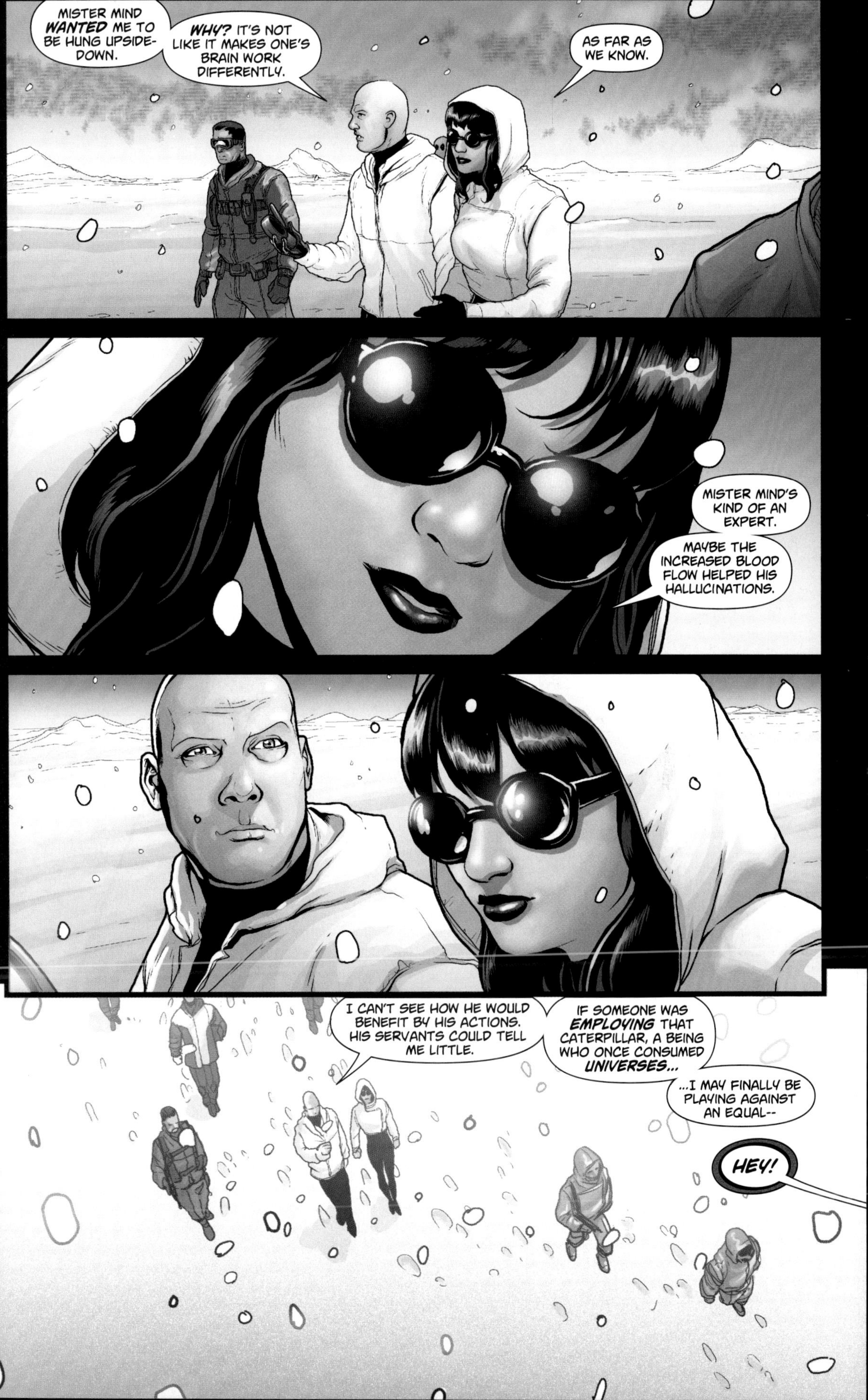
MISTER MIND WANTED ME TO BE HUNG UPSIDE-DOWN.
WHY? IT'S NOT LIKE IT MAKES ONE'S BRAIN WORK DIFFERENTLY.
AS FAR AS WE KNOW.
MISTER MIND'S KIND OF AN EXPERT.
MAYBE THE INCREASED BLOOD FLOW HELPED HIS HALLUCINATIONS.
I CAN'T SEE HOW HE WOULD BENEFIT BY HIS ACTIONS. HIS SERVANTS COULD TELL ME LITTLE.
IF SOMEONE WAS EMPLOYING THAT CATERPILLAR, A BEING WHO ONCE CONSUMED UNIVERSES...
...I MAY FINALLY BE PLAYING AGAINST AN EQUAL--
HEY!

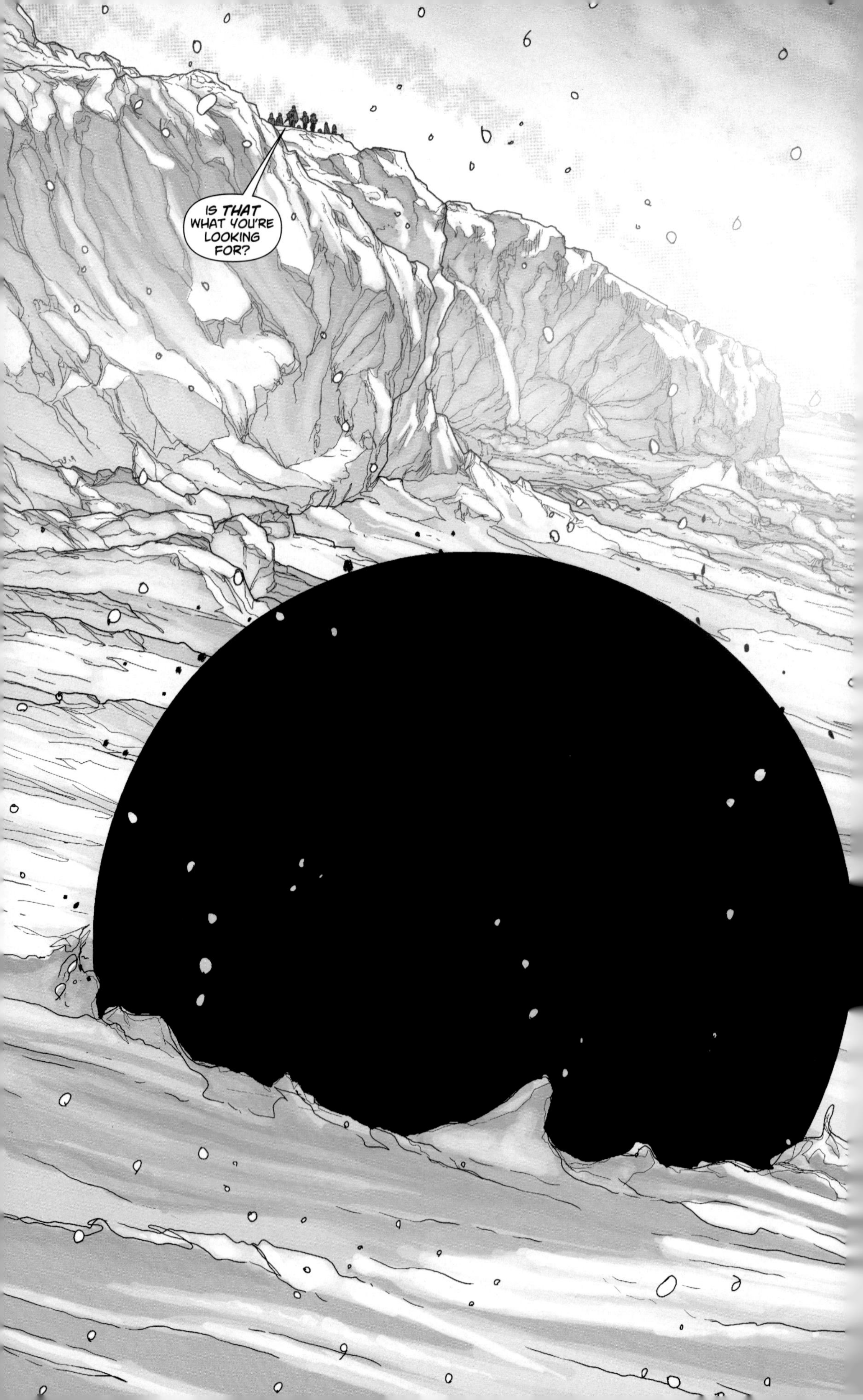
IS THAT WHAT YOU'RE LOOKING FOR?

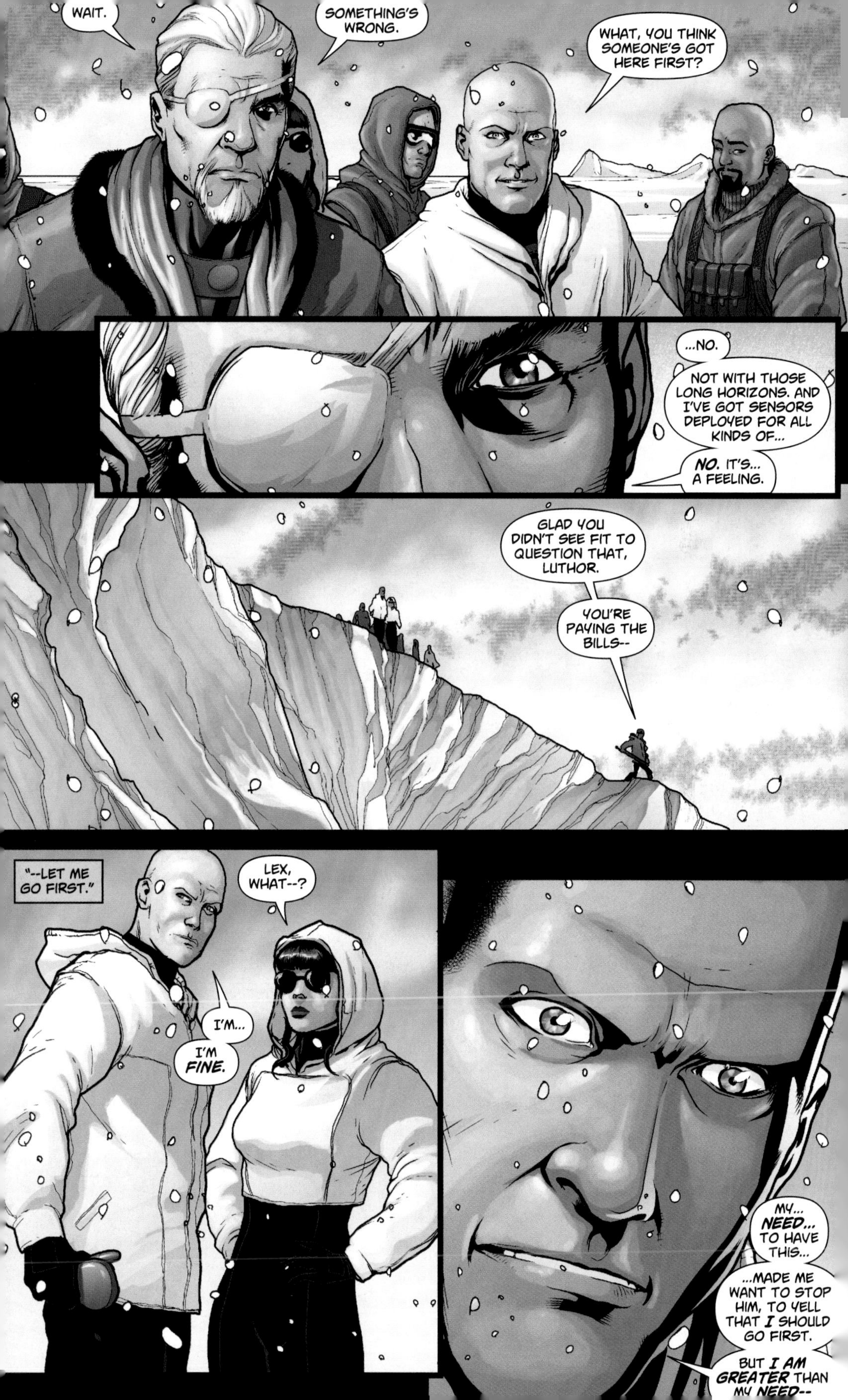
WAIT.
SOMETHING'S WRONG.
WHAT, YOU THINK SOMEONE'S GOT HERE FIRST?
...NO.
NOT WITH THOSE LONG HORIZONS. AND I'VE GOT SENSORS DEPLOYED FOR ALL KINDS OF...
NO. IT'S... A FEELING.
GLAD YOU DIDN'T SEE FIT TO QUESTION THAT, LUTHOR.
YOU'RE PAYING THE BILLS--
"--LET ME GO FIRST."
LEX, WHAT--?
I'M...
I'M FINE.
MY... NEED... TO HAVE THIS...
...MADE ME WANT TO STOP HIM, TO YELL THAT I SHOULD GO FIRST.
BUT I AM GREATER THAN MY NEED--

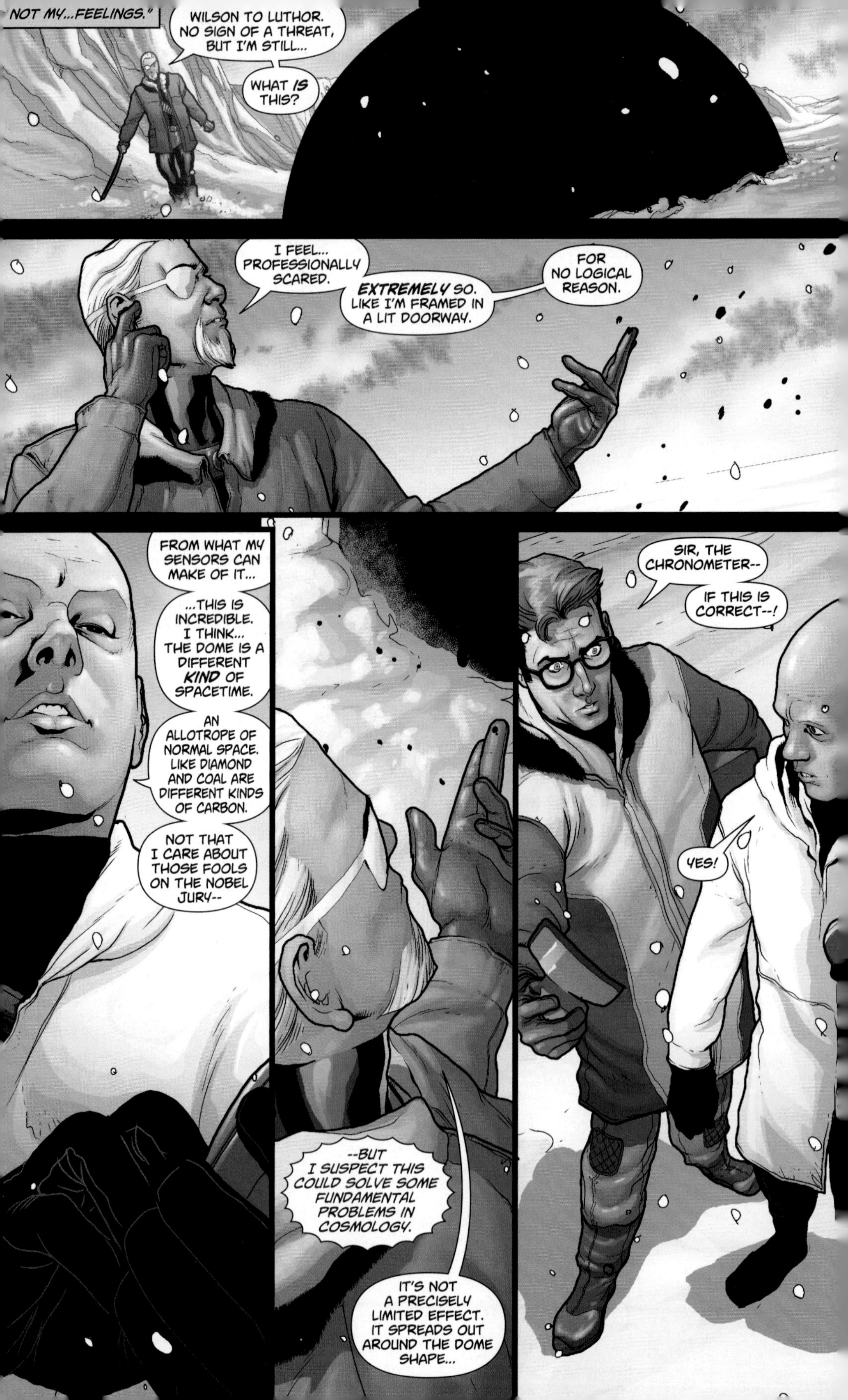
NOT MY...FEELINGS."
WILSON TO LUTHOR. NO SIGN OF A THREAT, BUT I'M STILL...
WHAT IS THIS?
I FEEL... PROFESSIONALLY SCARED.
EXTREMELY SO. LIKE I'M FRAMED IN A LIT DOORWAY.
FOR NO LOGICAL REASON.
FROM WHAT MY SENSORS CAN MAKE OF IT...
...THIS IS INCREDIBLE. I THINK... THE DOME IS A DIFFERENT KIND OF SPACETIME.
AN ALLOTROPE OF NORMAL SPACE. LIKE DIAMOND AND COAL ARE DIFFERENT KINDS OF CARBON.
NOT THAT I CARE ABOUT THOSE FOOLS ON THE NOBEL JURY--
--BUT I SUSPECT THIS COULD SOLVE SOME FUNDAMENTAL PROBLEMS IN COSMOLOGY.
IT'S NOT A PRECISELY LIMITED EFFECT. IT SPREADS OUT AROUND THE DOME SHAPE...
SIR, THE CHRONOMETER--
IF THIS IS CORRECT--!
YES!

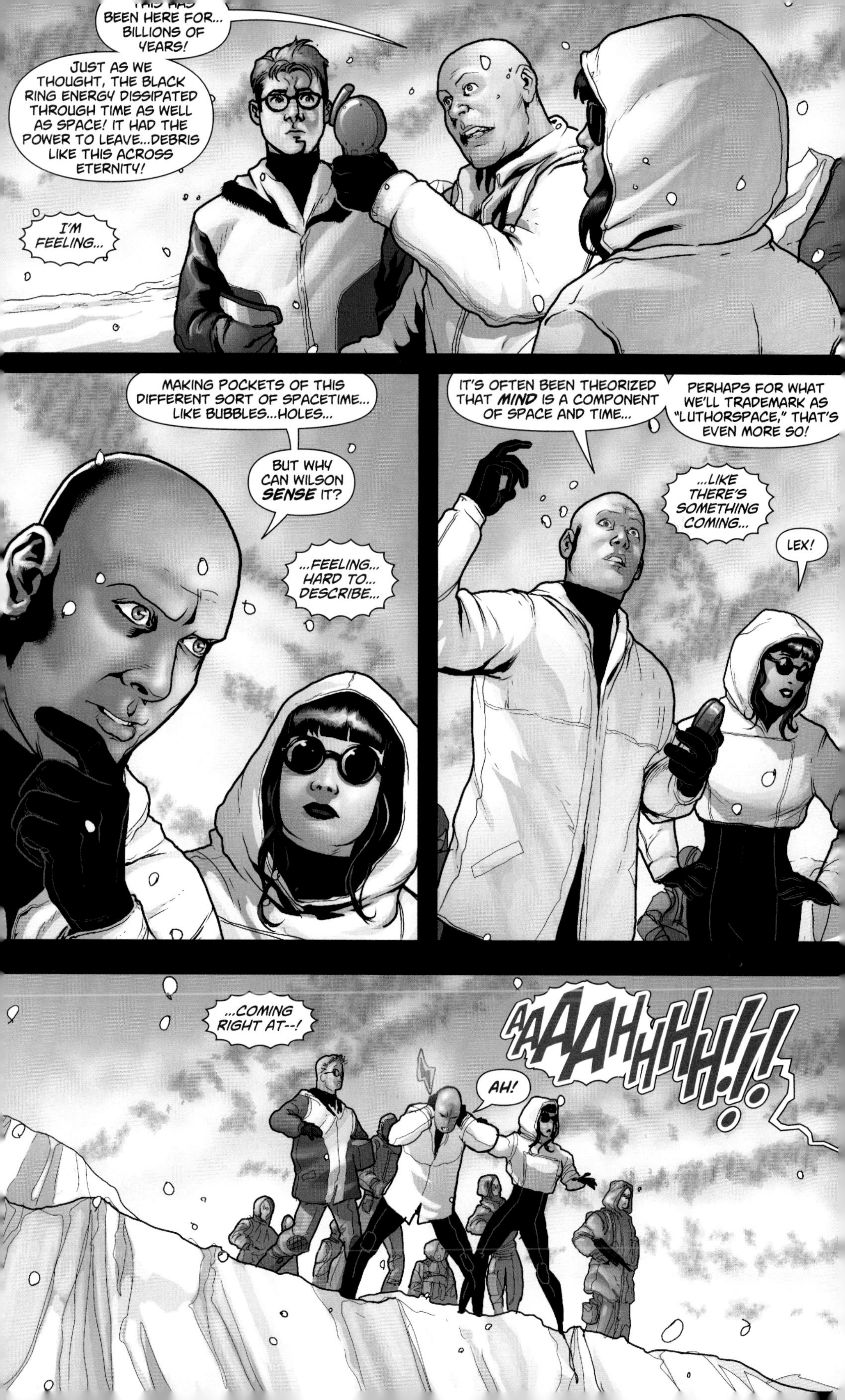
THIS HAS BEEN HERE FOR... BILLIONS OF YEARS!
JUST AS WE THOUGHT, THE BLACK RING ENERGY DISSIPATED THROUGH TIME AS WELL AS SPACE! IT HAD THE POWER TO LEAVE...DEBRIS LIKE THIS ACROSS ETERNITY!
I'M FEELING...
MAKING POCKETS OF THIS DIFFERENT SORT OF SPACETIME... LIKE BUBBLES...HOLES...
BUT WHY CAN WILSON SENSE IT?
...FEELING... HARD TO... DESCRIBE...
IT'S OFTEN BEEN THEORIZED THAT MIND IS A COMPONENT OF SPACE AND TIME...
PERHAPS FOR WHAT WE'LL TRADEMARK AS "LUTHORSPACE," THAT'S EVEN MORE SO!
...LIKE THERE'S SOMETHING COMING...
LEX!
...COMING RIGHT AT--!
AAAAHHHHH!!!
AH!

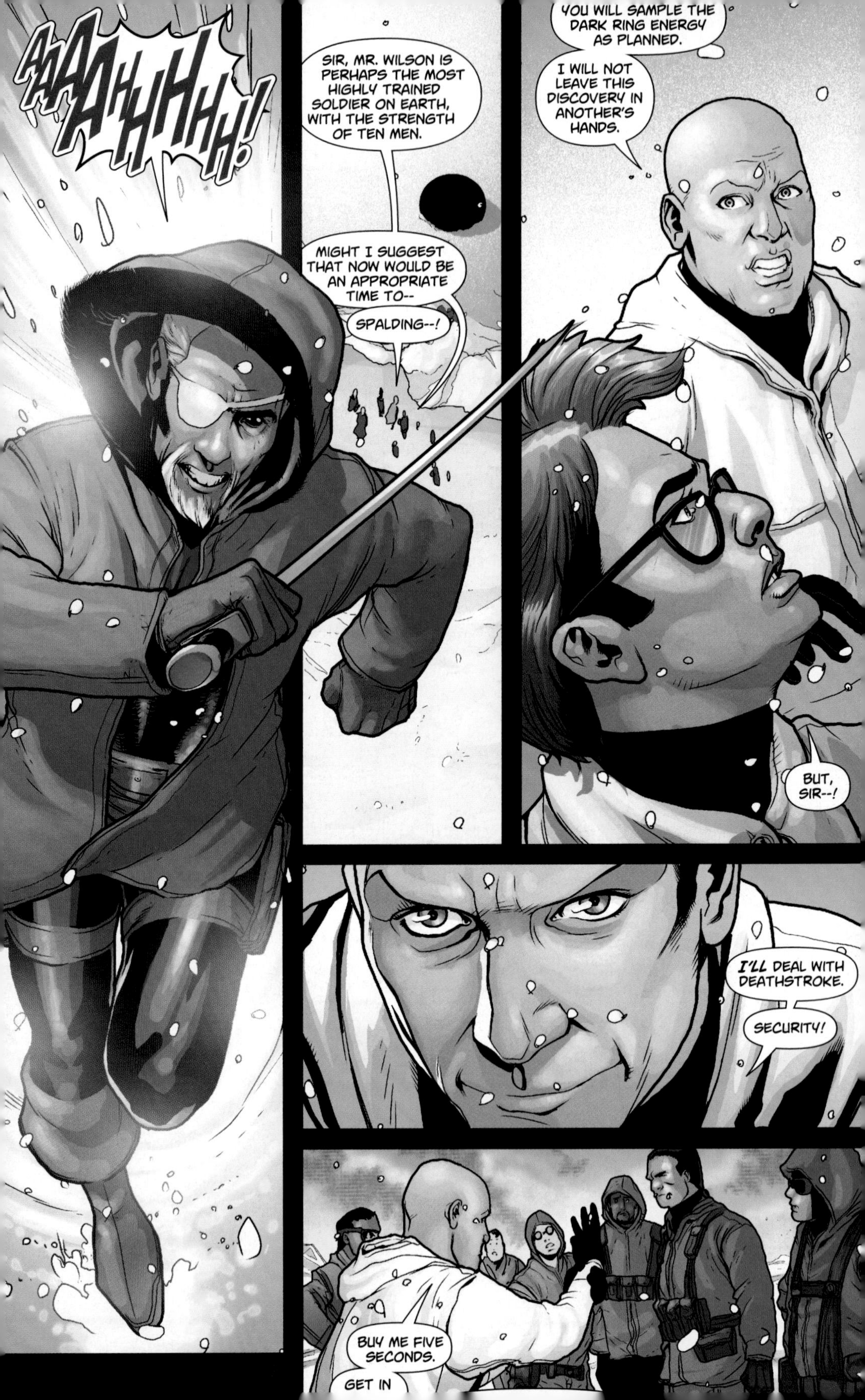
AAAAHHHHH!
SIR, MR. WILSON IS PERHAPS THE MOST HIGHLY TRAINED SOLDIER ON EARTH, WITH THE STRENGTH OF TEN MEN.
MIGHT I SUGGEST THAT NOW WOULD BE AN APPROPRIATE TIME TO--
SPALDING--!
YOU WILL SAMPLE THE DARK RING ENERGY AS PLANNED.
I WILL NOT LEAVE THIS DISCOVERY IN ANOTHER'S HANDS.
BUT, SIR--!
I'LL DEAL WITH DEATHSTROKE.
SECURITY!
BUY ME FIVE SECONDS.
GET IN

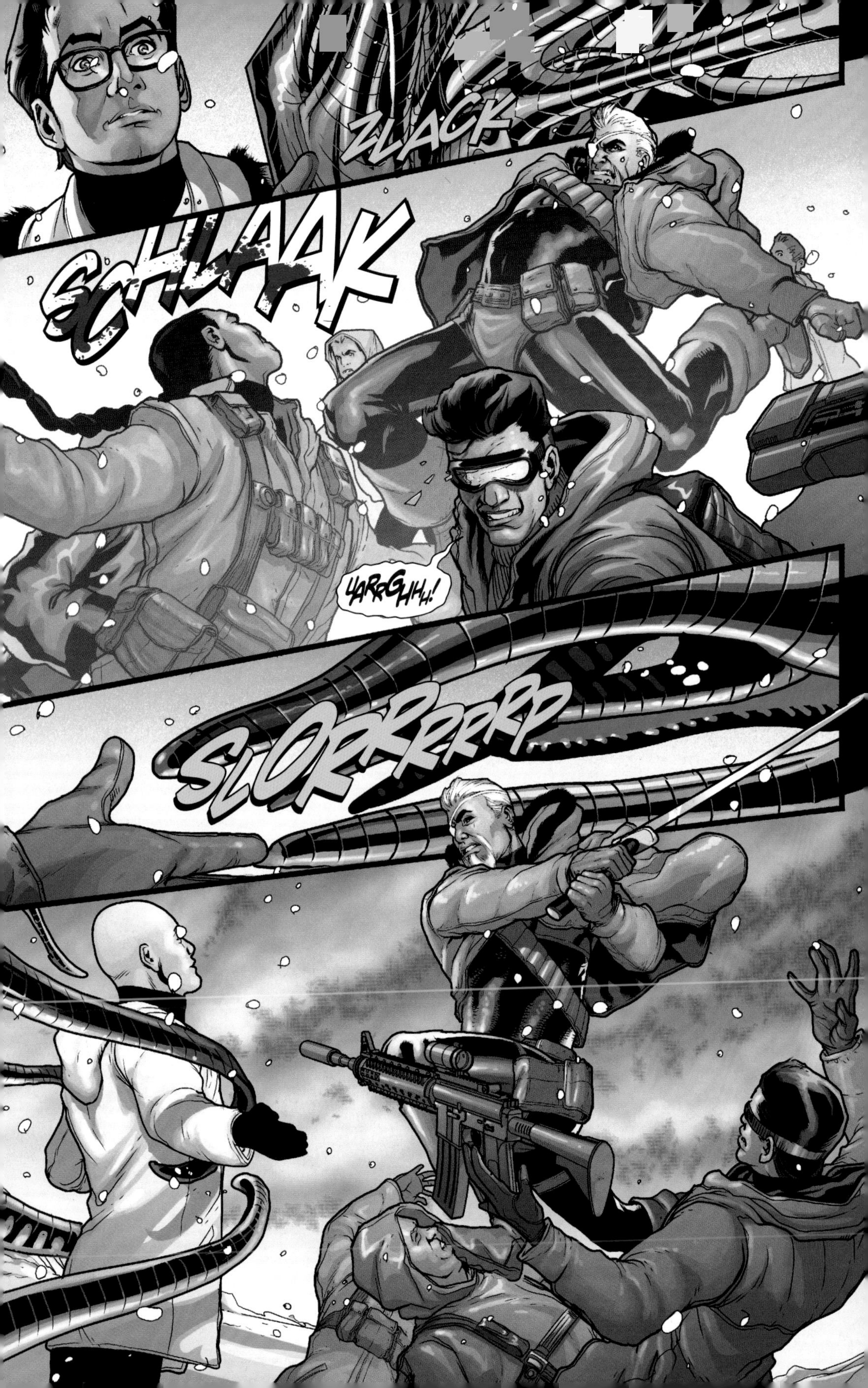
ZLACK
SCHLAAK
UARRGHHH!
SLORRRRRP

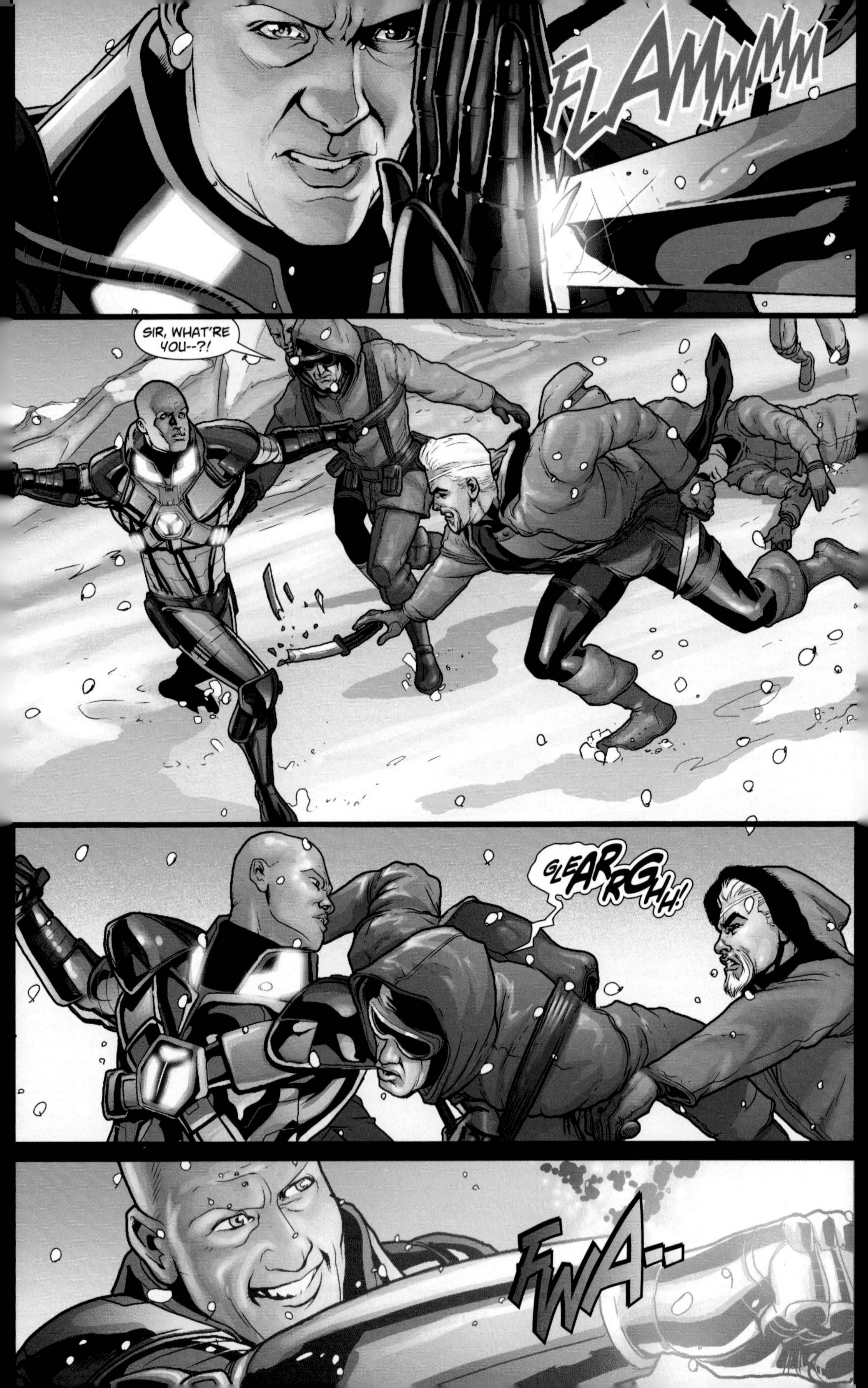
FLAMMMMM
SIR, WHAT'RE YOU--?!
GLEARRRGHH!
FWA--

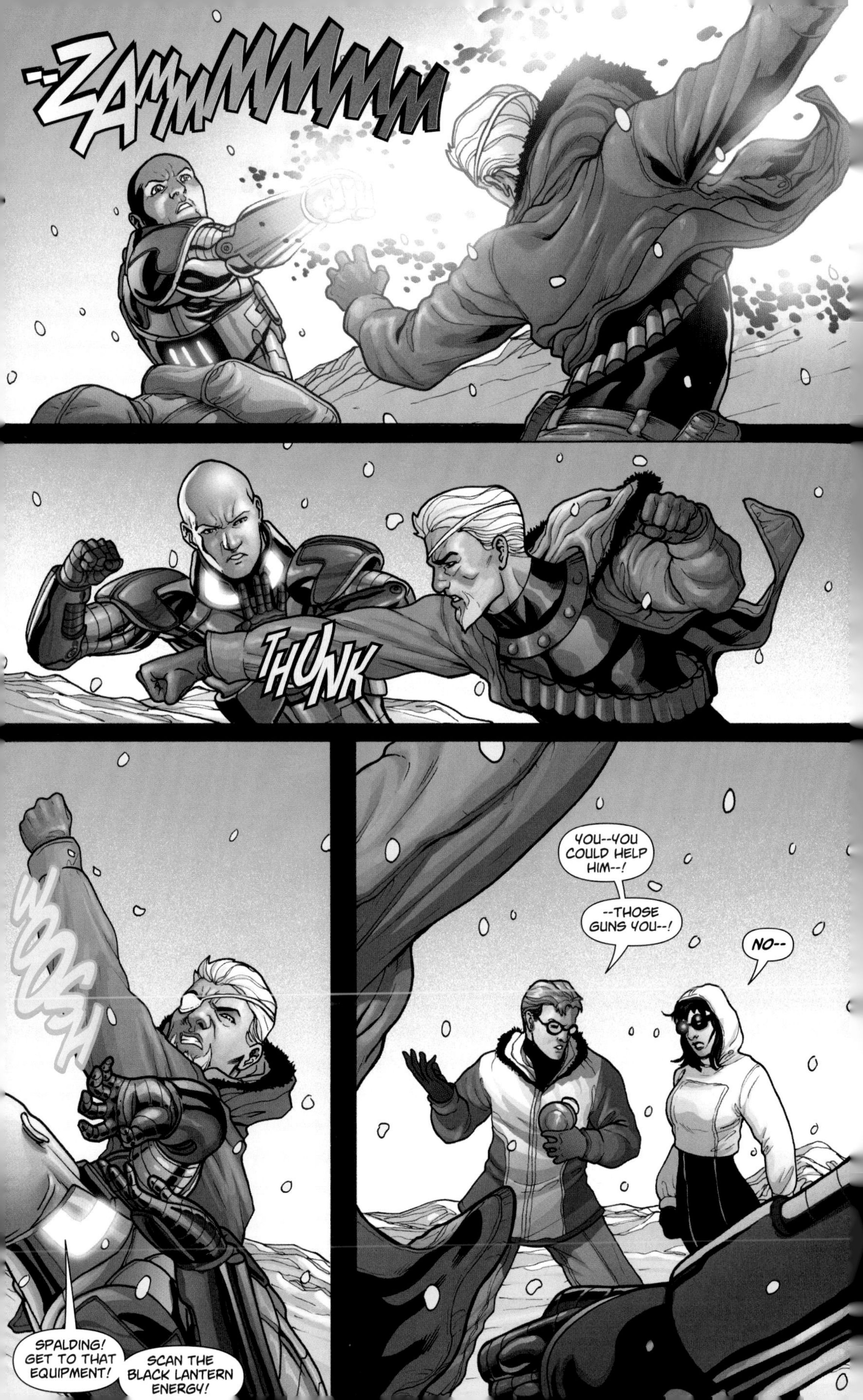
--ZAMMMMMMM
THUNK
SPALDING! GET TO THAT EQUIPMENT!
SCAN THE BLACK LANTERN ENERGY!
YOU--YOU COULD HELP HIM--!
--THOSE GUNS YOU--!
NO--

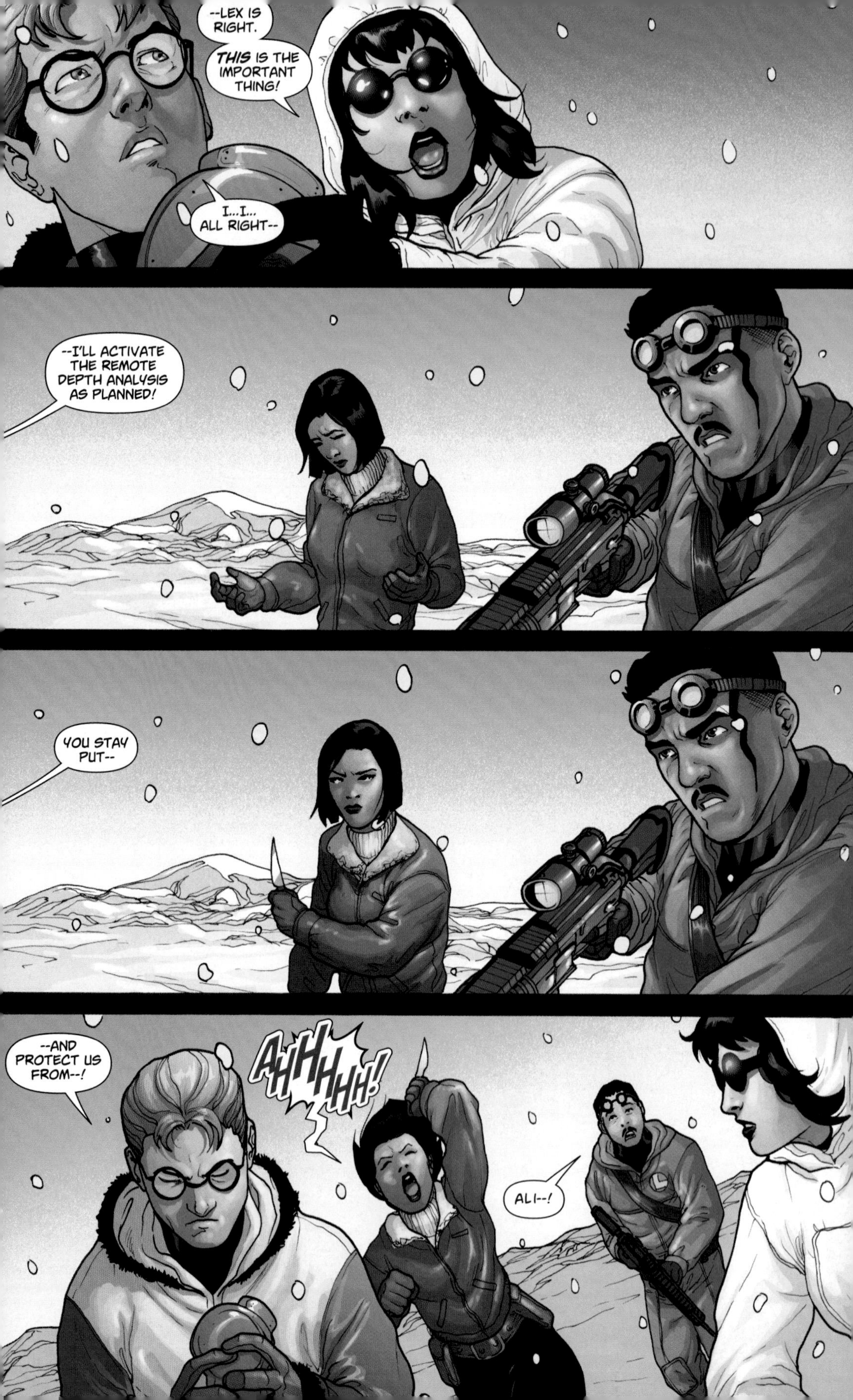
--LEX IS RIGHT.
THIS IS THE IMPORTANT THING!
I...I... ALL RIGHT--
--I'LL ACTIVATE THE REMOTE DEPTH ANALYSIS AS PLANNED!
YOU STAY PUT--
--AND PROTECT US FROM--!
AHHHHHH!
ALI--!

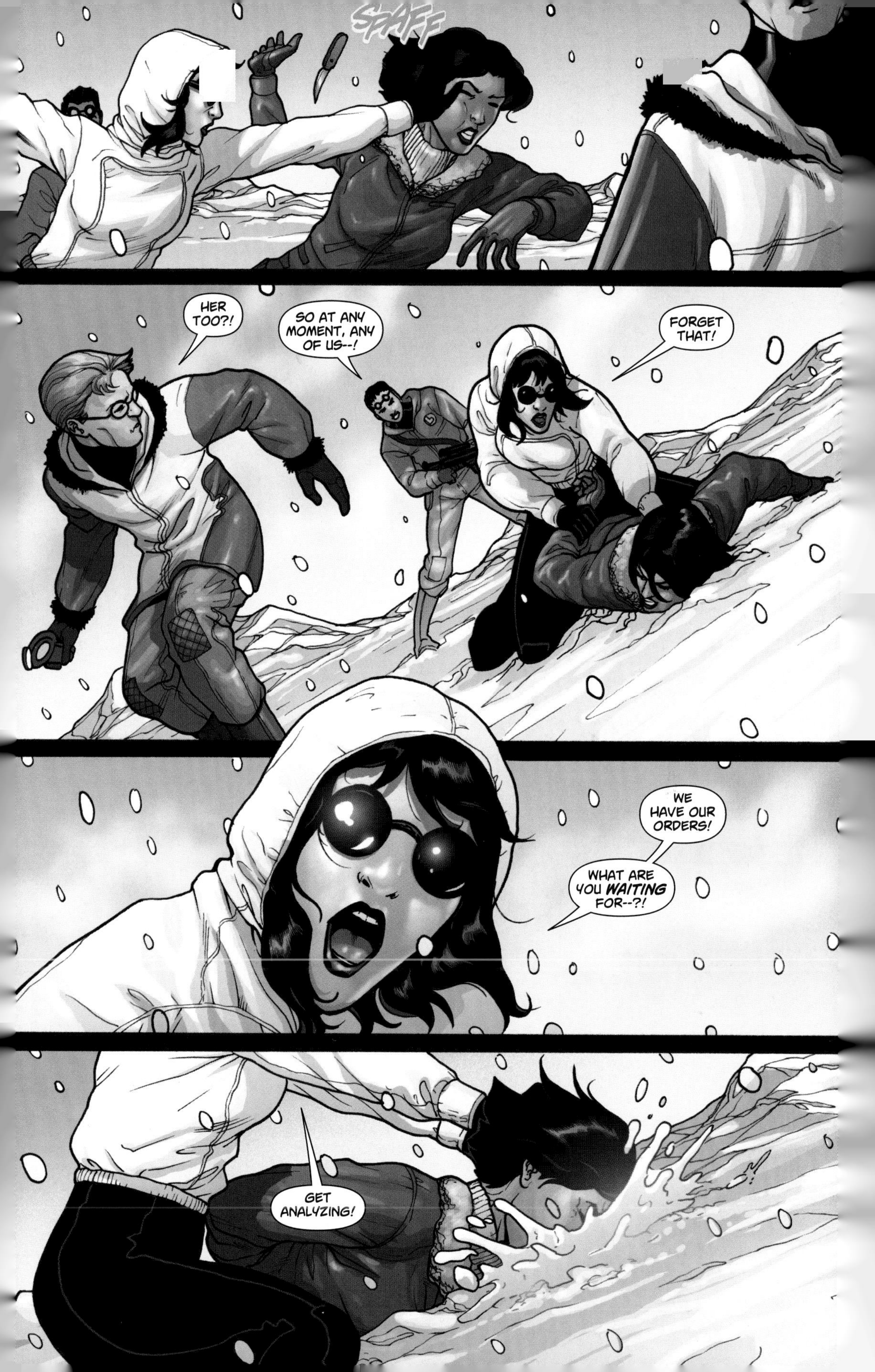
SPAFF
HER TOO?!
SO AT ANY MOMENT, ANY OF US--!
FORGET THAT!
WE HAVE OUR ORDERS!
WHAT ARE YOU *WAITING* FOR--?!
GET ANALYZING!

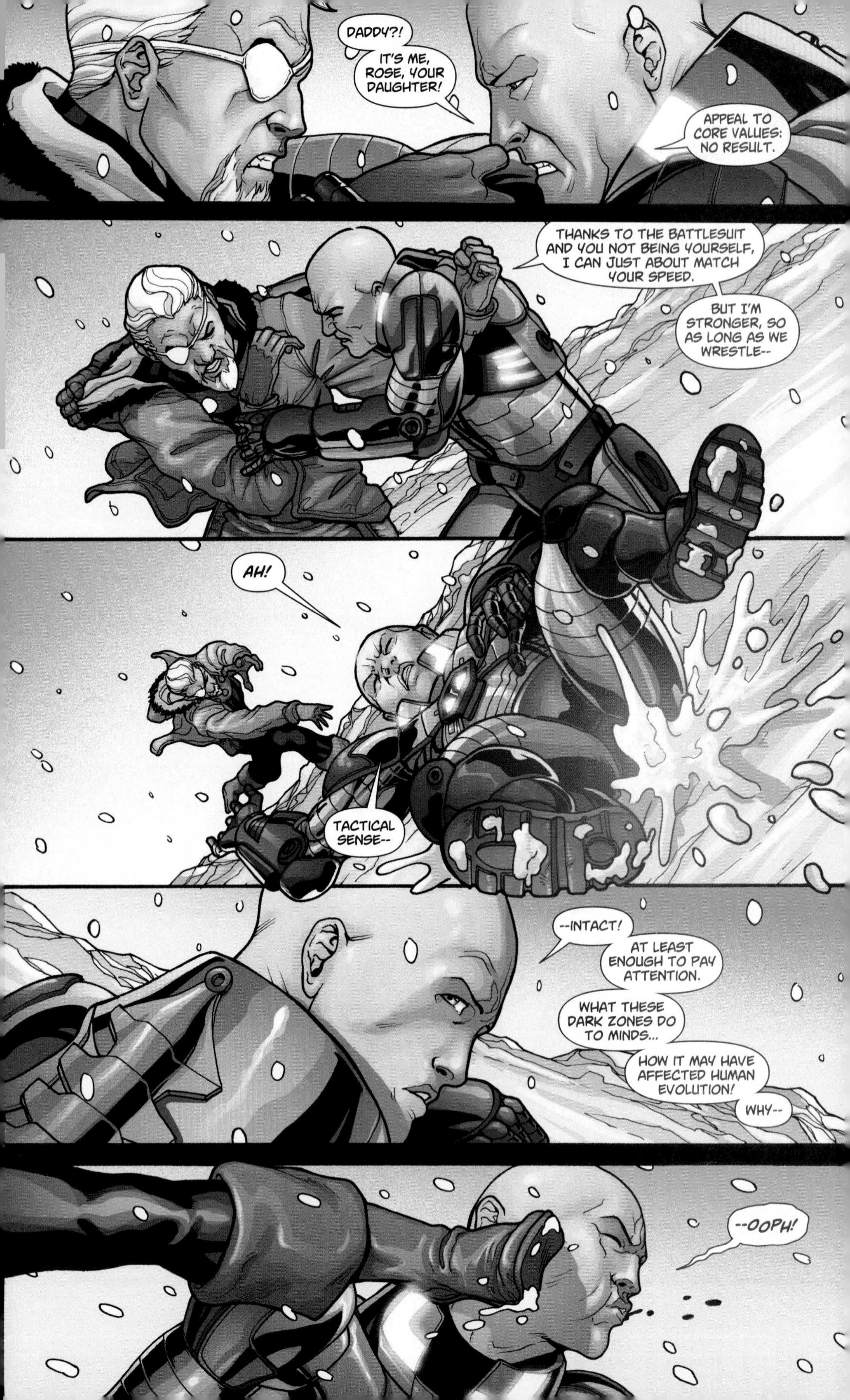
DADDY?!
IT'S ME, ROSE, YOUR DAUGHTER!
APPEAL TO CORE VALUES: NO RESULT.
THANKS TO THE BATTLESUIT AND YOU NOT BEING YOURSELF, I CAN JUST ABOUT MATCH YOUR SPEED.
BUT I'M STRONGER, SO AS LONG AS WE WRESTLE--
AH!
TACTICAL SENSE--
--INTACT!
AT LEAST ENOUGH TO PAY ATTENTION.
WHAT THESE DARK ZONES DO TO MINDS...
HOW IT MAY HAVE AFFECTED HUMAN EVOLUTION!
WHY--
--OOPH!

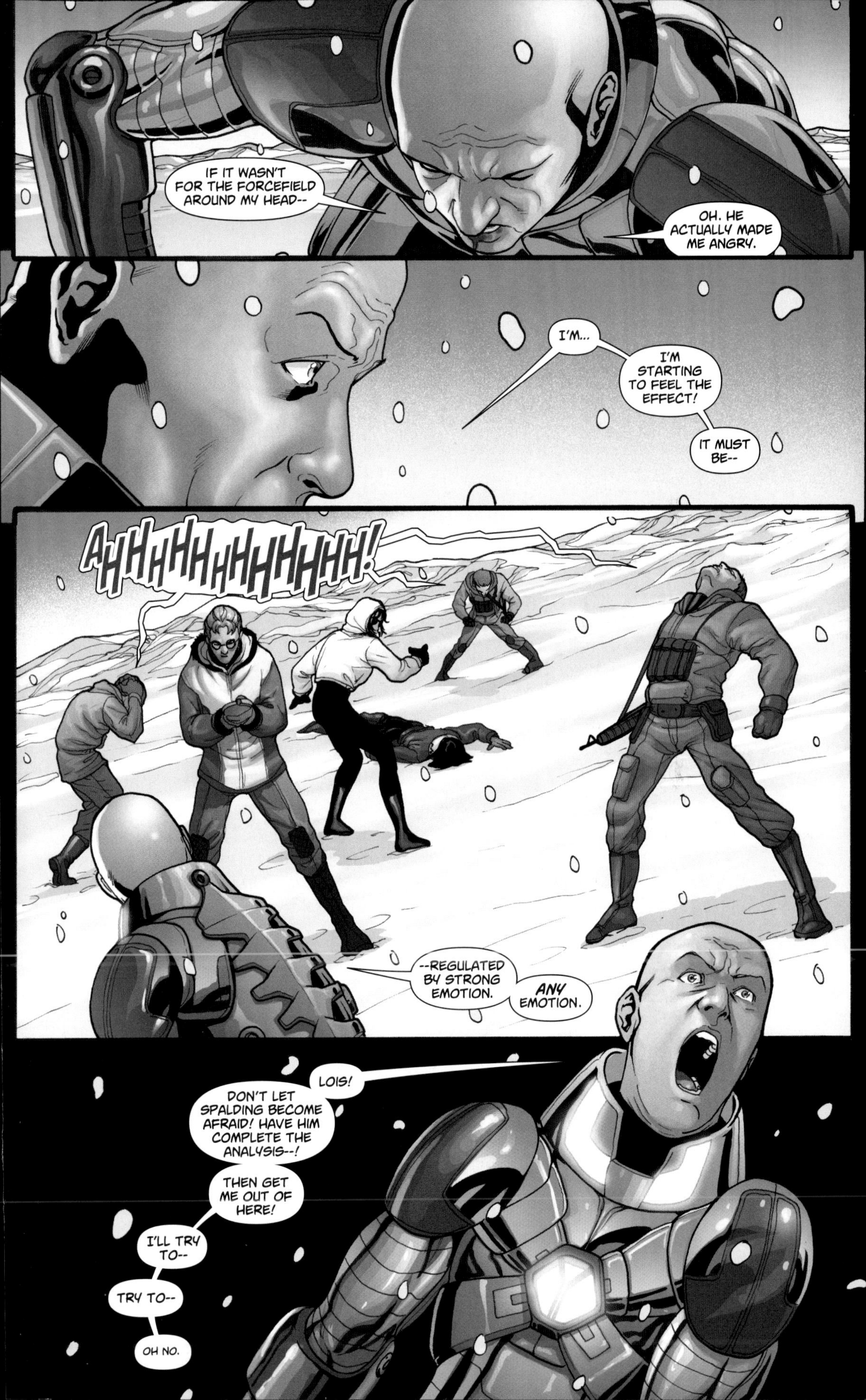
IF IT WASN'T FOR THE FORCEFIELD AROUND MY HEAD--
OH. HE ACTUALLY MADE ME ANGRY.
I'M...
I'M STARTING TO FEEL THE EFFECT!
IT MUST BE--
AHHHHHHHHHHHHH!
--REGULATED BY STRONG EMOTION.
ANY EMOTION.
LOIS!
DON'T LET SPALDING BECOME AFRAID! HAVE HIM COMPLETE THE ANALYSIS--!
THEN GET ME OUT OF HERE!
I'LL TRY TO--
TRY TO--
OH NO.

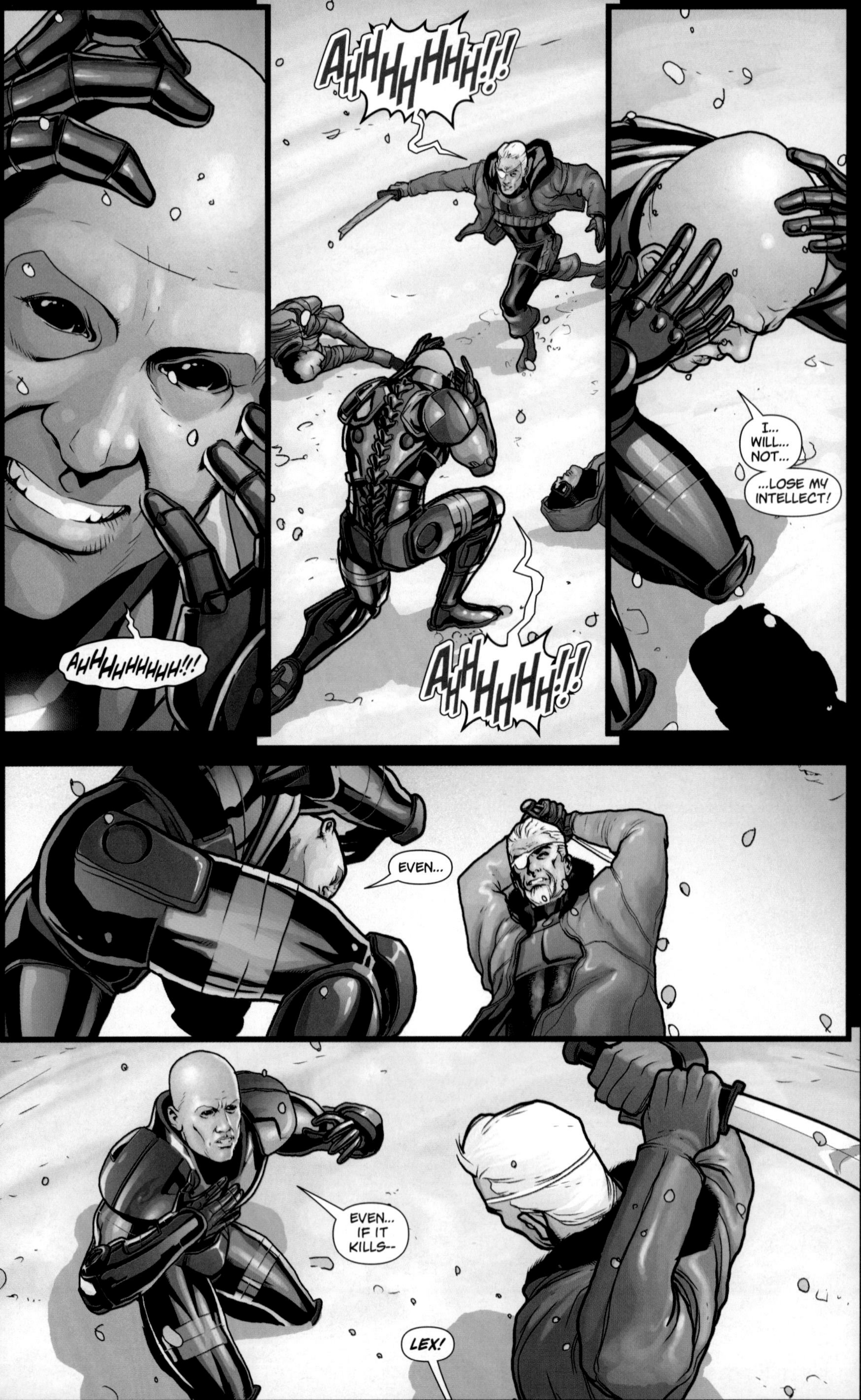
AHHHHHHHHH!!!
AHHHHHHH!!!
AHHHHHH!!!
I... WILL... NOT...
...LOSE MY INTELLECT!
EVEN...
EVEN... IF IT KILLS--
LEX!

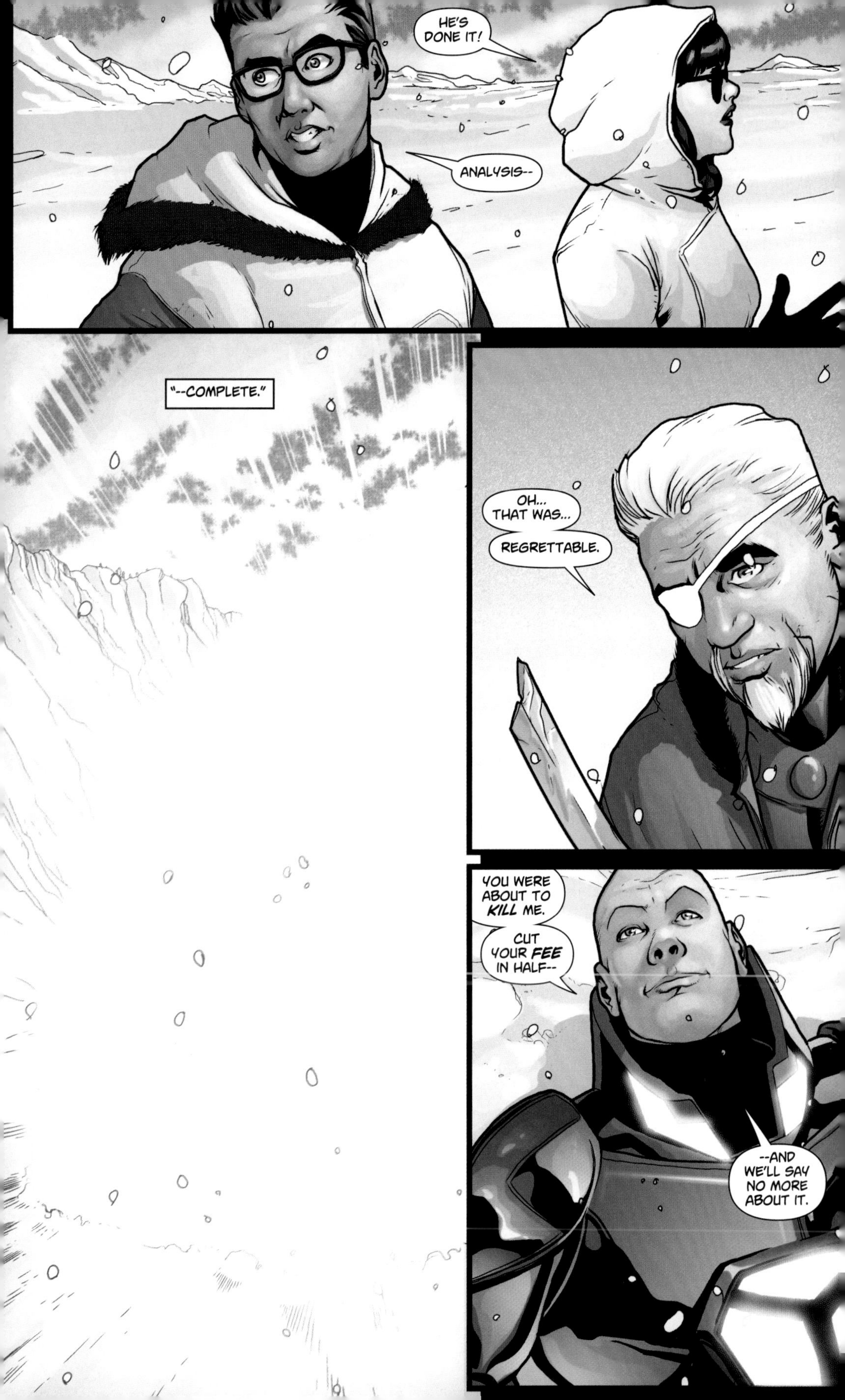
HE'S DONE IT!
ANALYSIS--
"--COMPLETE."
OH... THAT WAS...
REGRETTABLE.
YOU WERE ABOUT TO KILL ME.
CUT YOUR FEE IN HALF--
--AND WE'LL SAY NO MORE ABOUT IT.

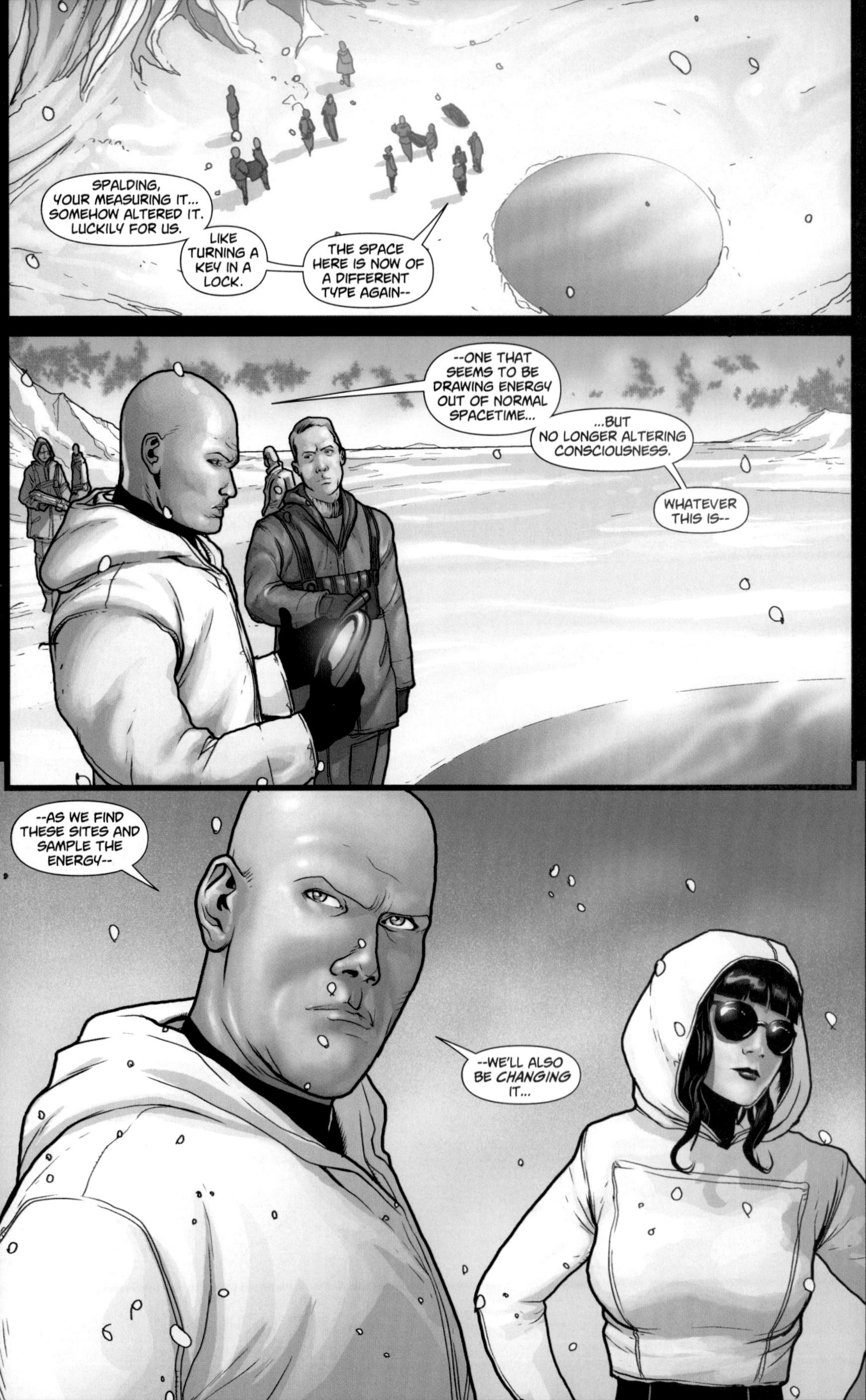
SPALDING, YOUR MEASURING IT... SOMEHOW ALTERED IT. LUCKILY FOR US.
LIKE TURNING A KEY IN A LOCK.
THE SPACE HERE IS NOW OF A DIFFERENT TYPE AGAIN--
--ONE THAT SEEMS TO BE DRAWING ENERGY OUT OF NORMAL SPACETIME...
...BUT NO LONGER ALTERING CONSCIOUSNESS.
WHATEVER THIS IS--
--AS WE FIND THESE SITES AND SAMPLE THE ENERGY--
--WE'LL ALSO BE *CHANGING* IT...

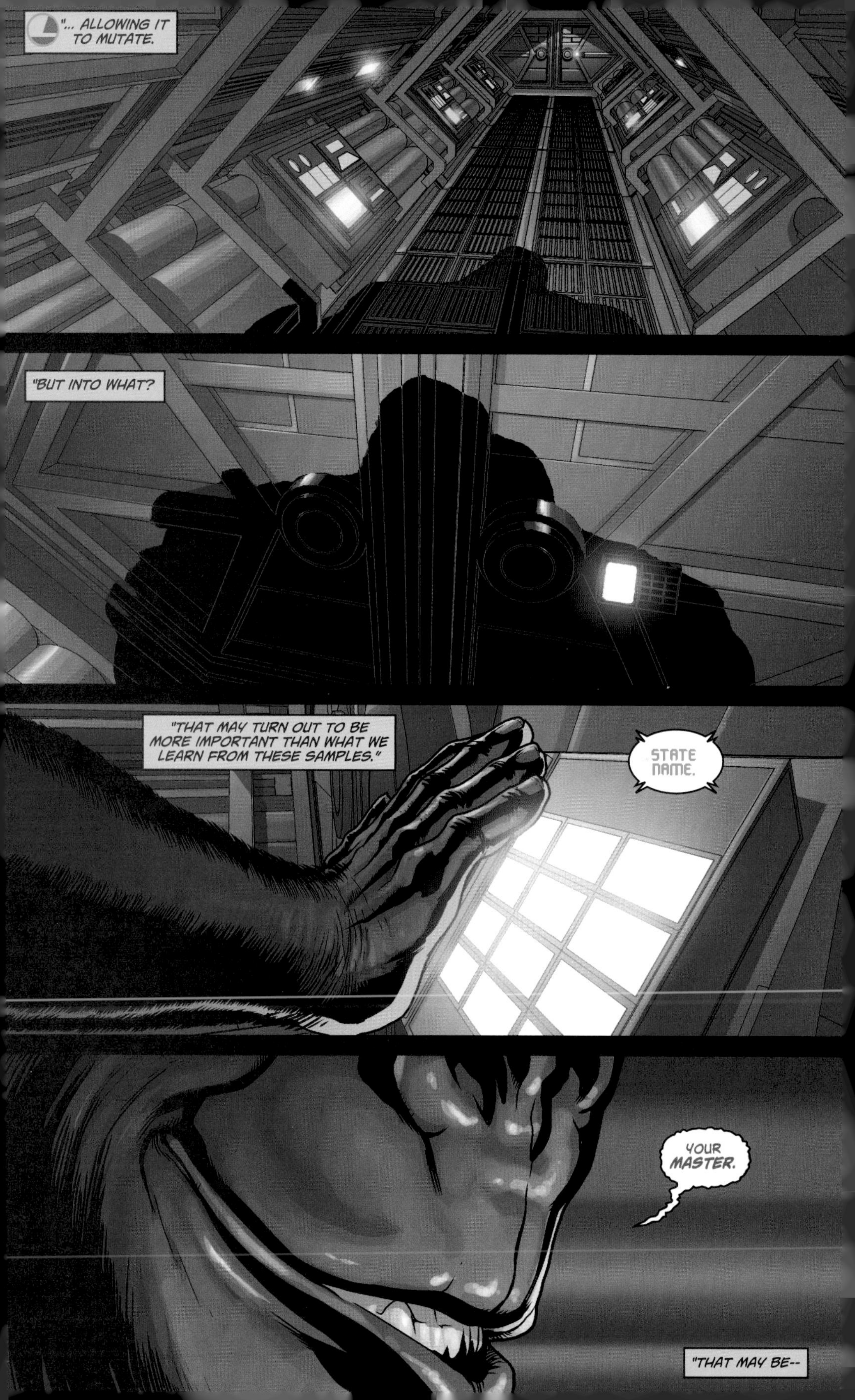
"... ALLOWING IT TO MUTATE.
"BUT INTO WHAT?
"THAT MAY TURN OUT TO BE MORE IMPORTANT THAN WHAT WE LEARN FROM THESE SAMPLES."
STATE NAME.
YOUR MASTER.
"THAT MAY BE--

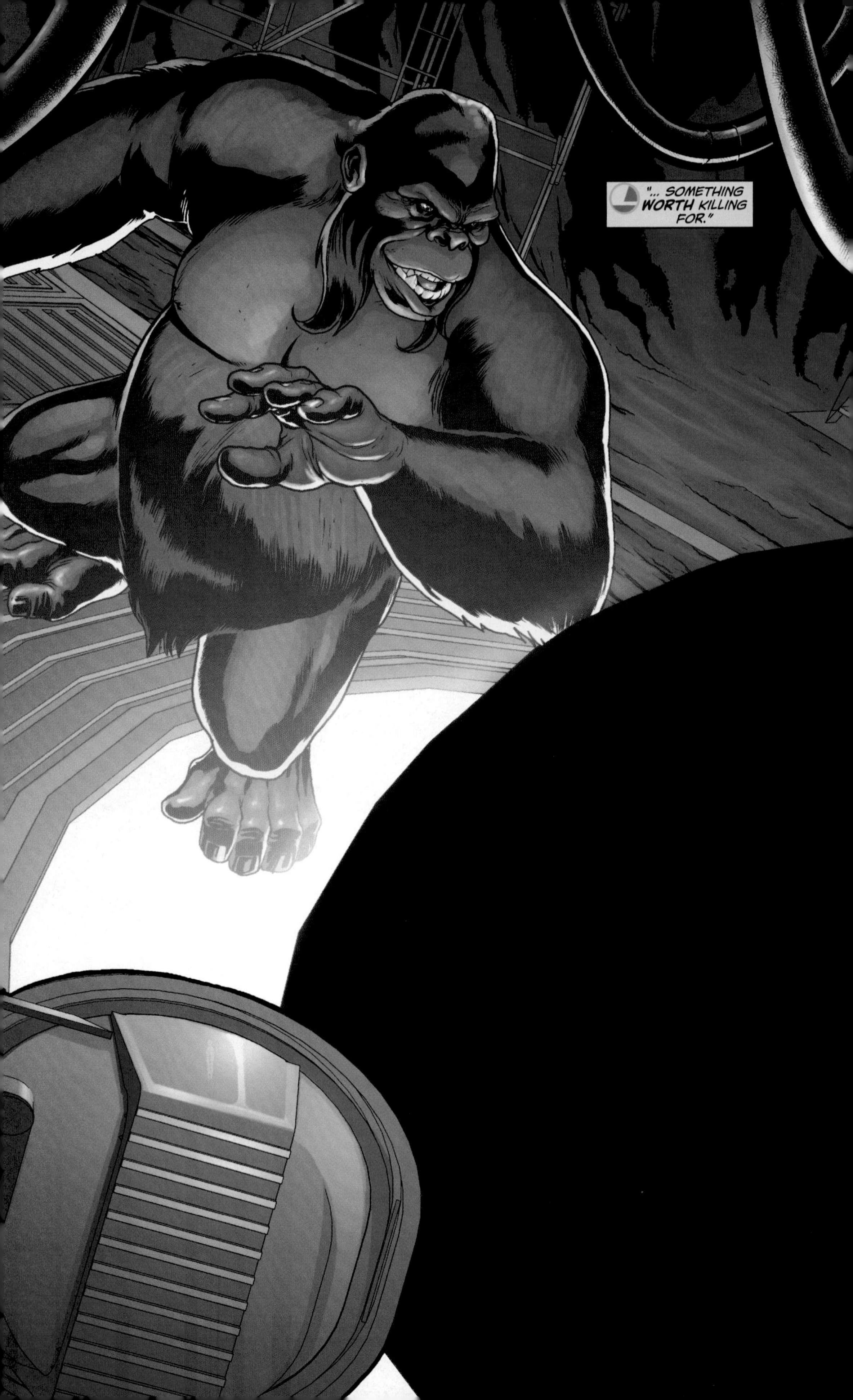
"... SOMETHING WORTH KILLING FOR."

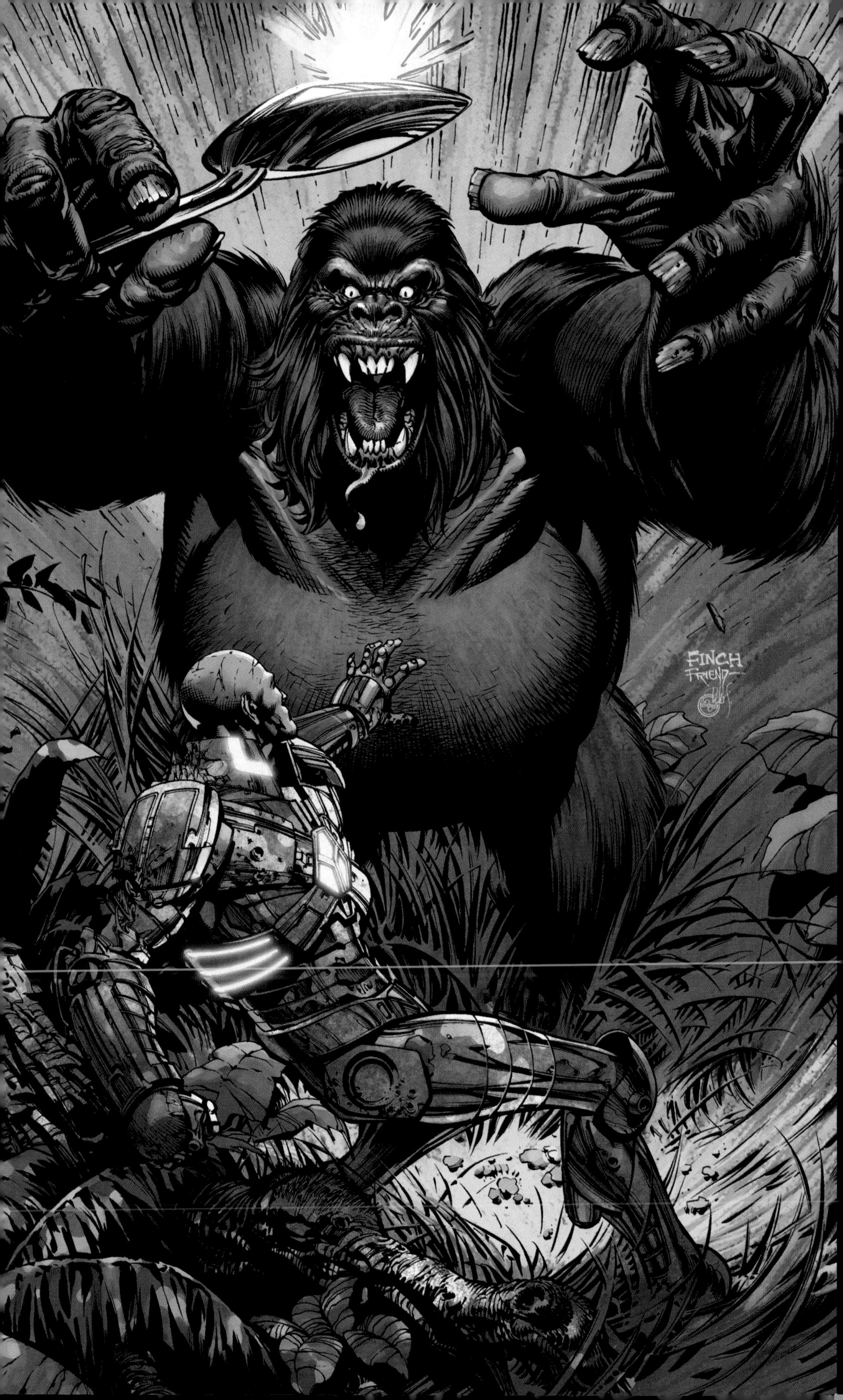
FINCH
FRIEND

THE BLACK RING
part four

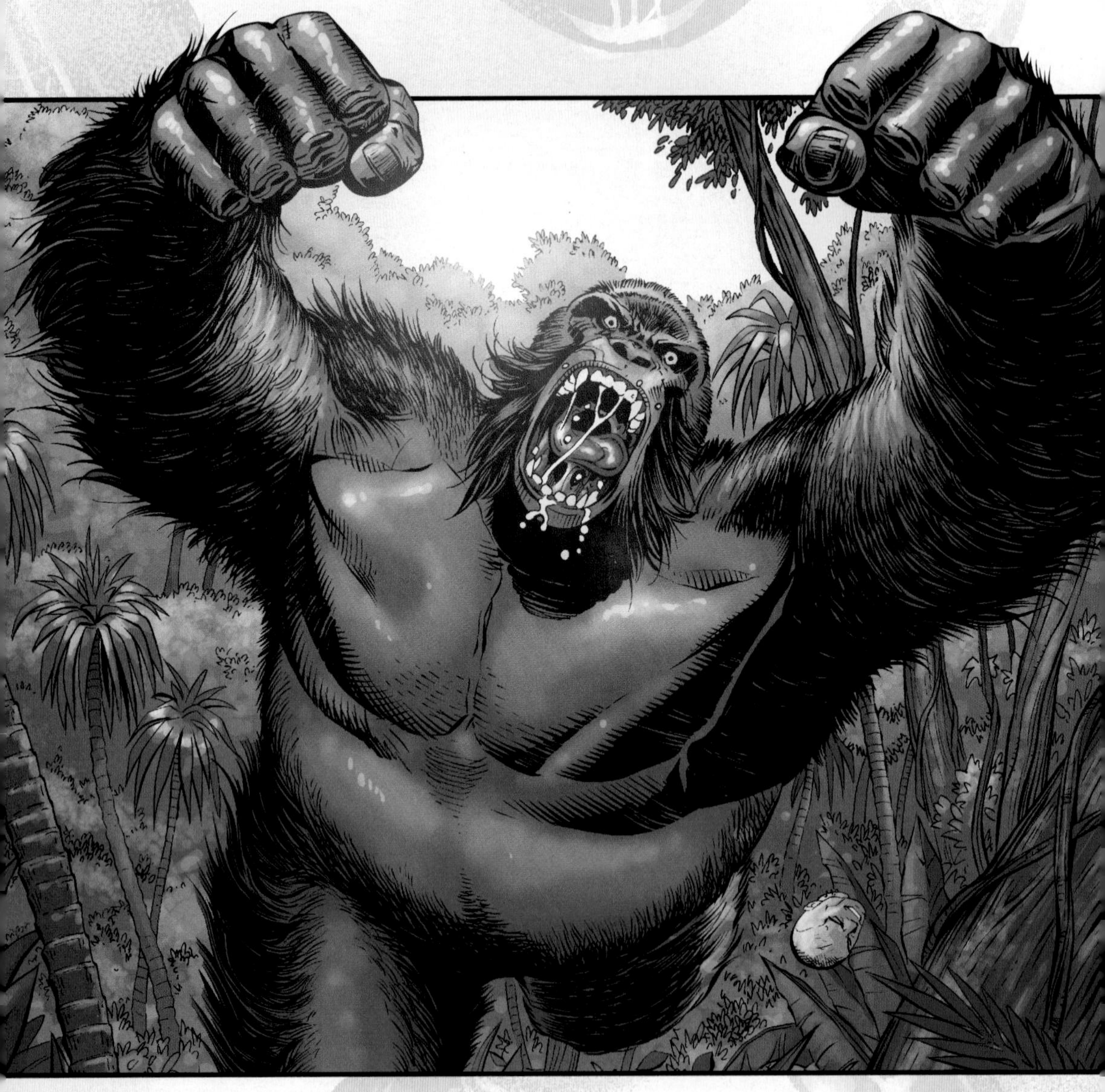

cover by
DAVID **FINCH**, RICHARD **FRIEND** & PETER **STEIGERWALD**

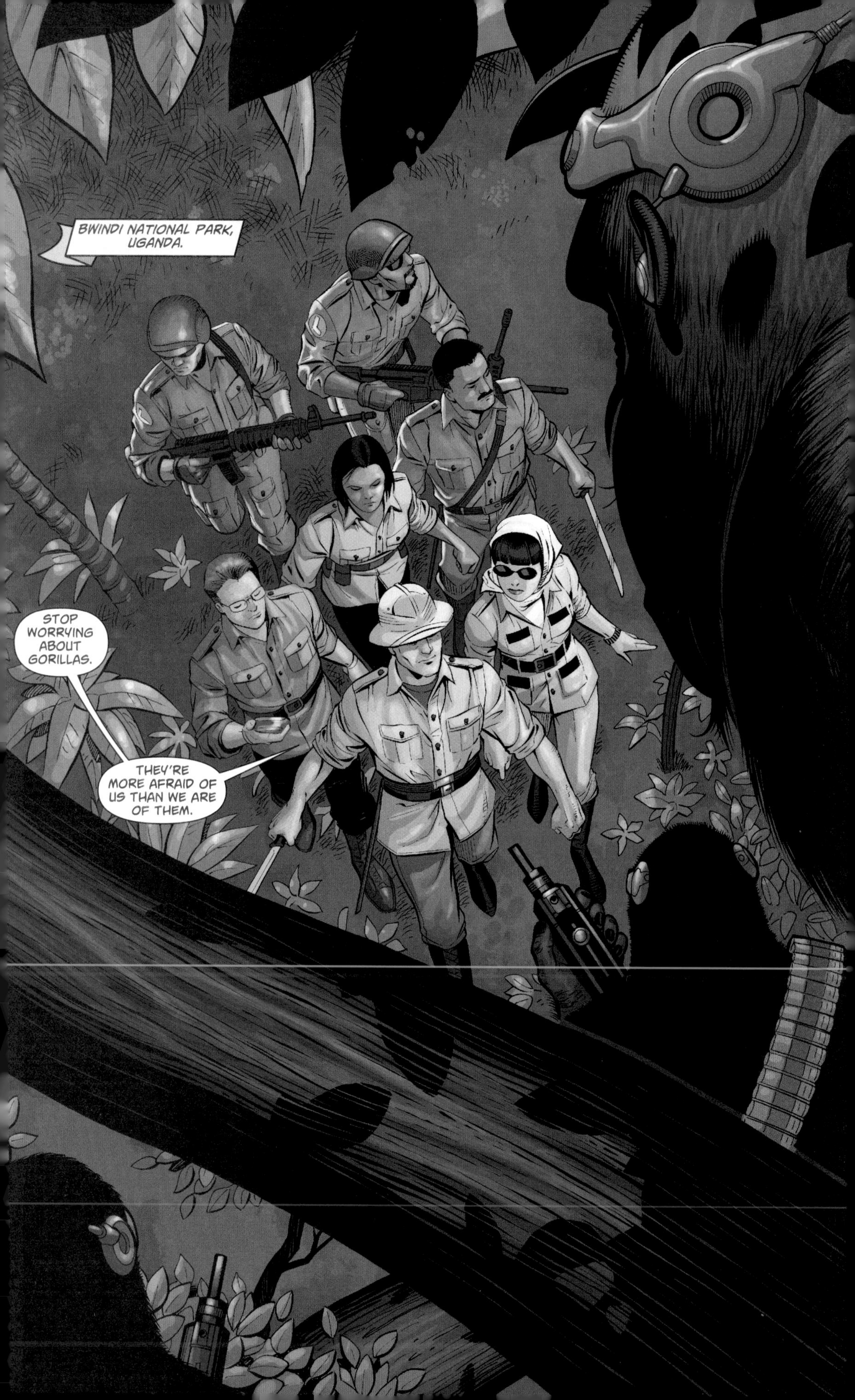
BWINDI NATIONAL PARK, UGANDA.
STOP WORRYING ABOUT GORILLAS.
THEY'RE MORE AFRAID OF US THAN WE ARE OF THEM.

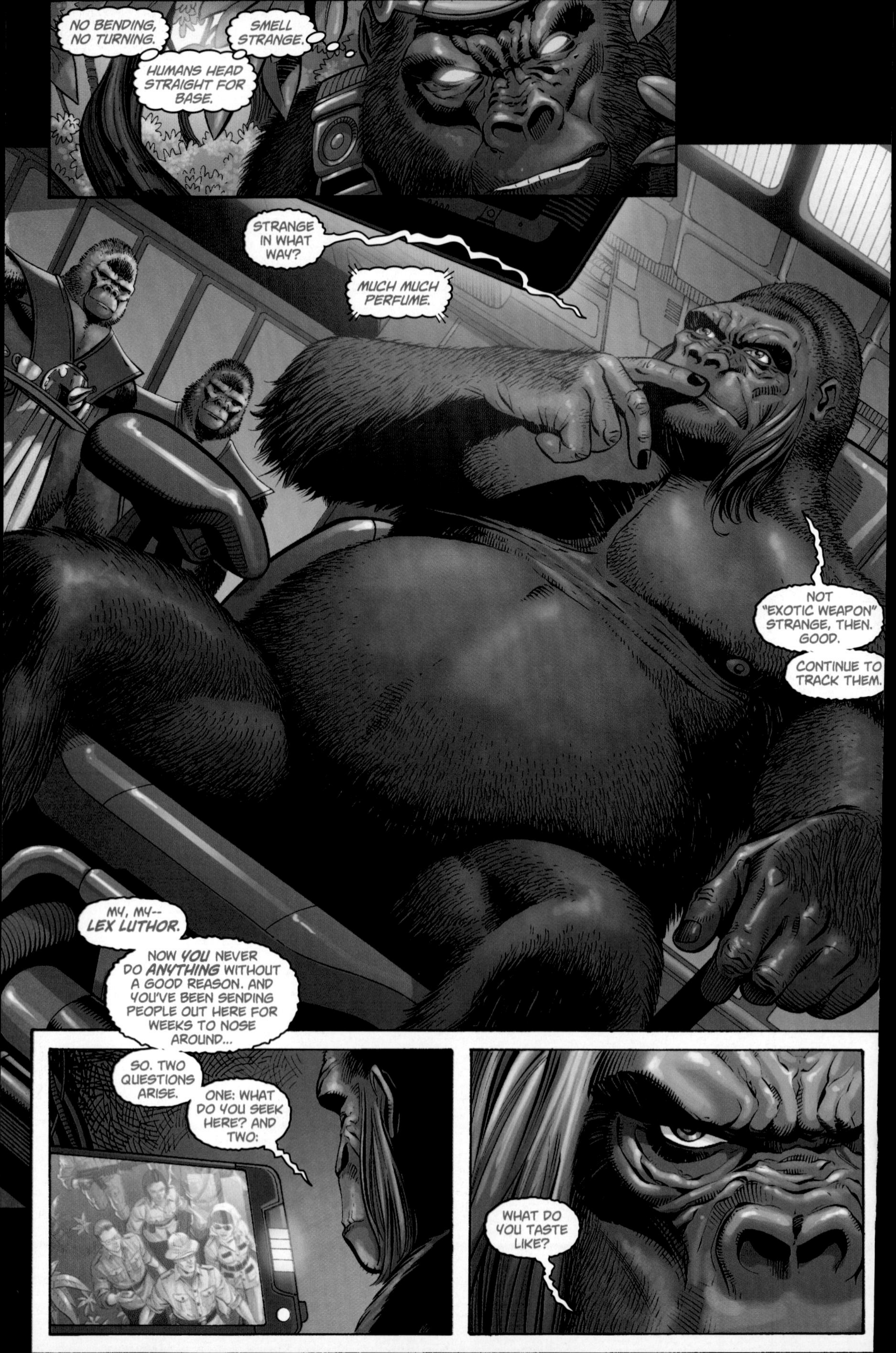
NO BENDING, NO TURNING.
SMELL STRANGE.
HUMANS HEAD STRAIGHT FOR BASE.
STRANGE IN WHAT WAY?
MUCH MUCH PERFUME.
NOT "EXOTIC WEAPON" STRANGE, THEN. GOOD.
CONTINUE TO TRACK THEM.
MY, MY-- LEX LUTHOR.
NOW YOU NEVER DO ANYTHING WITHOUT A GOOD REASON. AND YOU'VE BEEN SENDING PEOPLE OUT HERE FOR WEEKS TO NOSE AROUND...
SO. TWO QUESTIONS ARISE.
ONE: WHAT DO YOU SEEK HERE? AND TWO:
WHAT DO YOU TASTE LIKE?

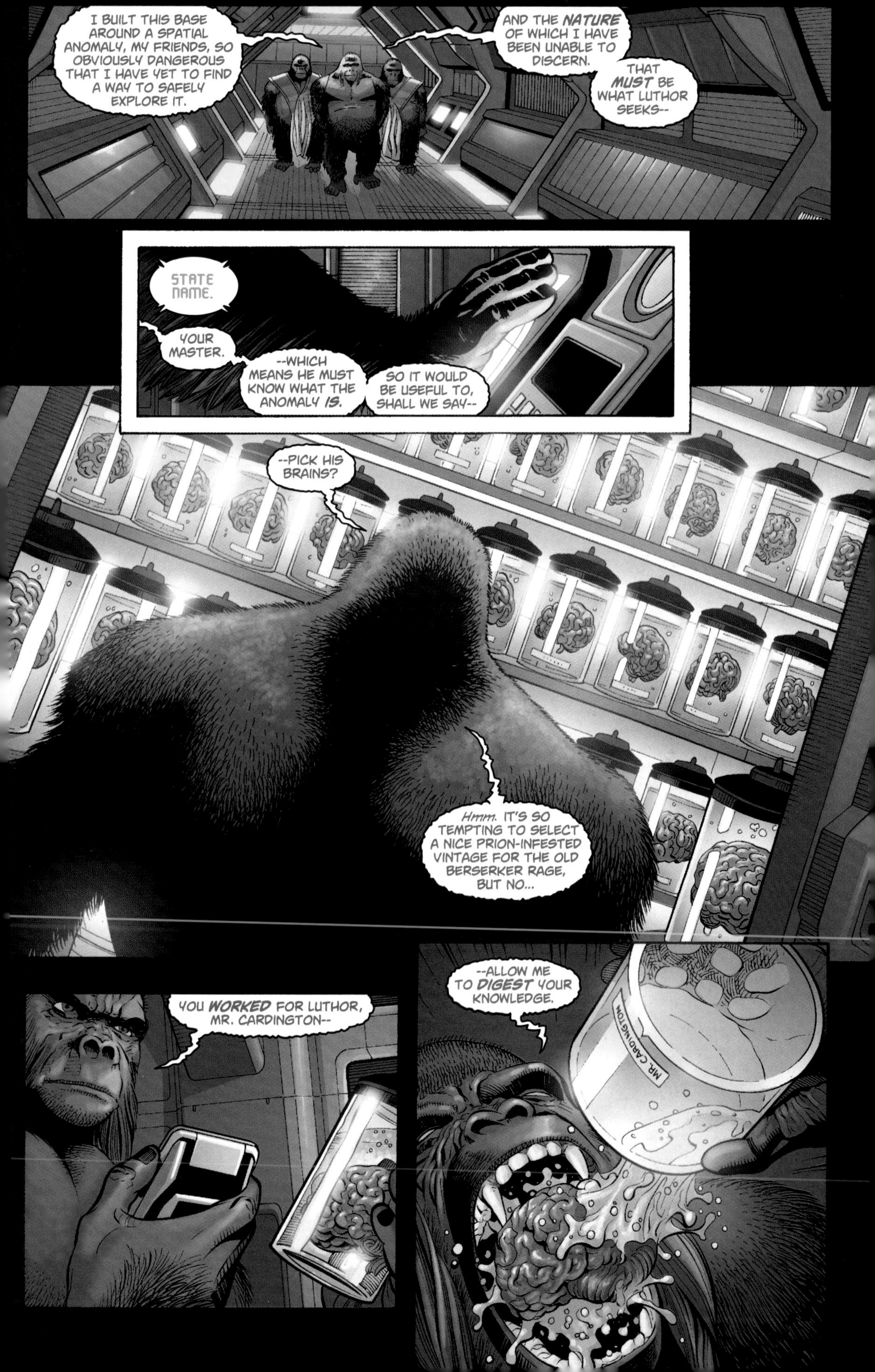

I BUILT THIS BASE AROUND A SPATIAL ANOMALY, MY FRIENDS, SO OBVIOUSLY DANGEROUS THAT I HAVE YET TO FIND A WAY TO SAFELY EXPLORE IT.
AND THE NATURE OF WHICH I HAVE BEEN UNABLE TO DISCERN.
THAT MUST BE WHAT LUTHOR SEEKS--
STATE NAME.
YOUR MASTER.
--WHICH MEANS HE MUST KNOW WHAT THE ANOMALY IS.
SO IT WOULD BE USEFUL TO, SHALL WE SAY--
--PICK HIS BRAINS?
Hmm. IT'S SO TEMPTING TO SELECT A NICE PRION-INFESTED VINTAGE FOR THE OLD BERSERKER RAGE, BUT NO...
YOU WORKED FOR LUTHOR, MR. CARDINGTON--
--ALLOW ME TO DIGEST YOUR KNOWLEDGE.
MR. CARDINGTON

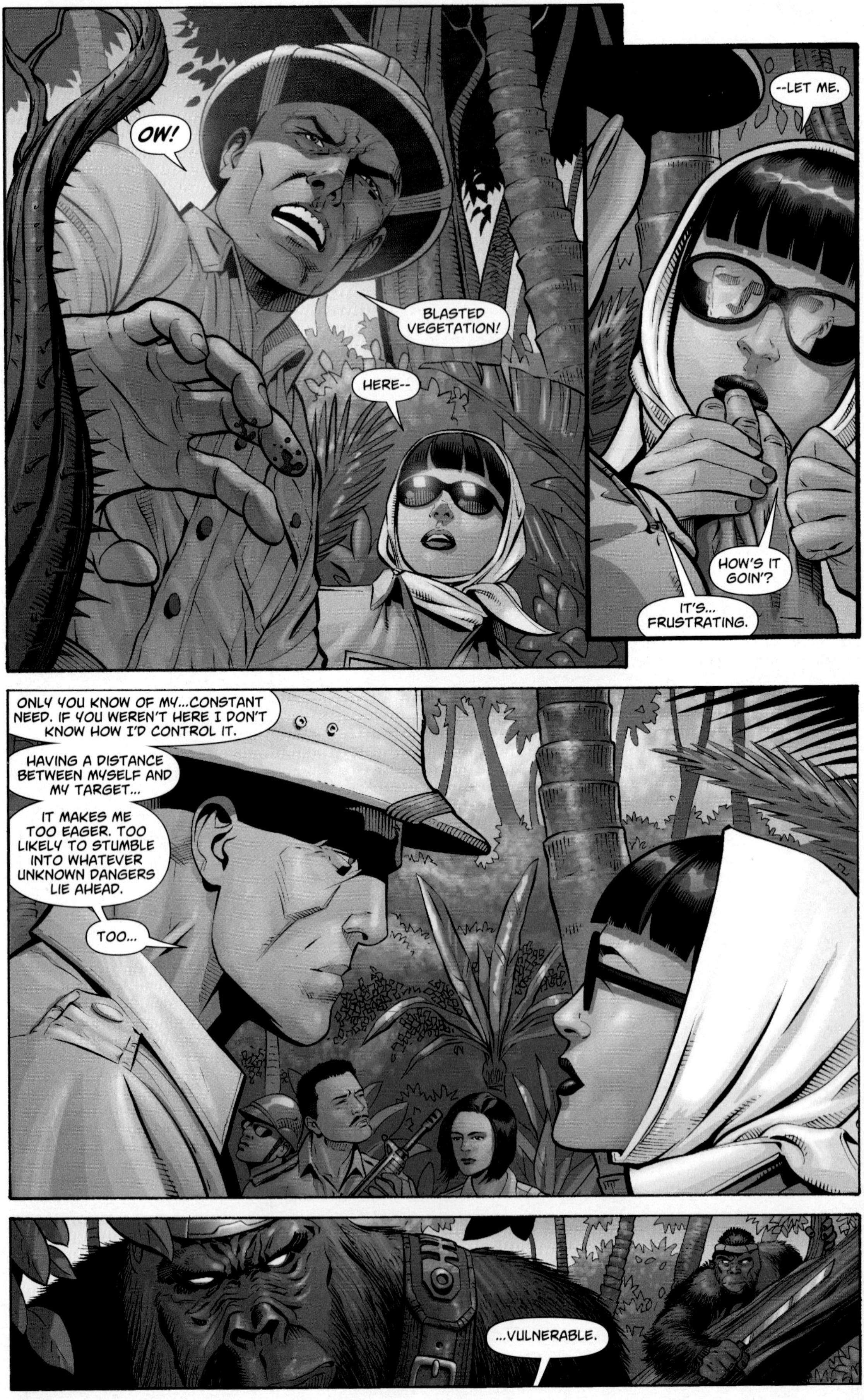
OW!
BLASTED VEGETATION!
HERE--
--LET ME.
HOW'S IT GOIN'?
IT'S... FRUSTRATING.
ONLY YOU KNOW OF MY...CONSTANT NEED. IF YOU WEREN'T HERE I DON'T KNOW HOW I'D CONTROL IT.
HAVING A DISTANCE BETWEEN MYSELF AND MY TARGET...
IT MAKES ME TOO EAGER. TOO LIKELY TO STUMBLE INTO WHATEVER UNKNOWN DANGERS LIE AHEAD.
TOO...
...VULNERABLE.

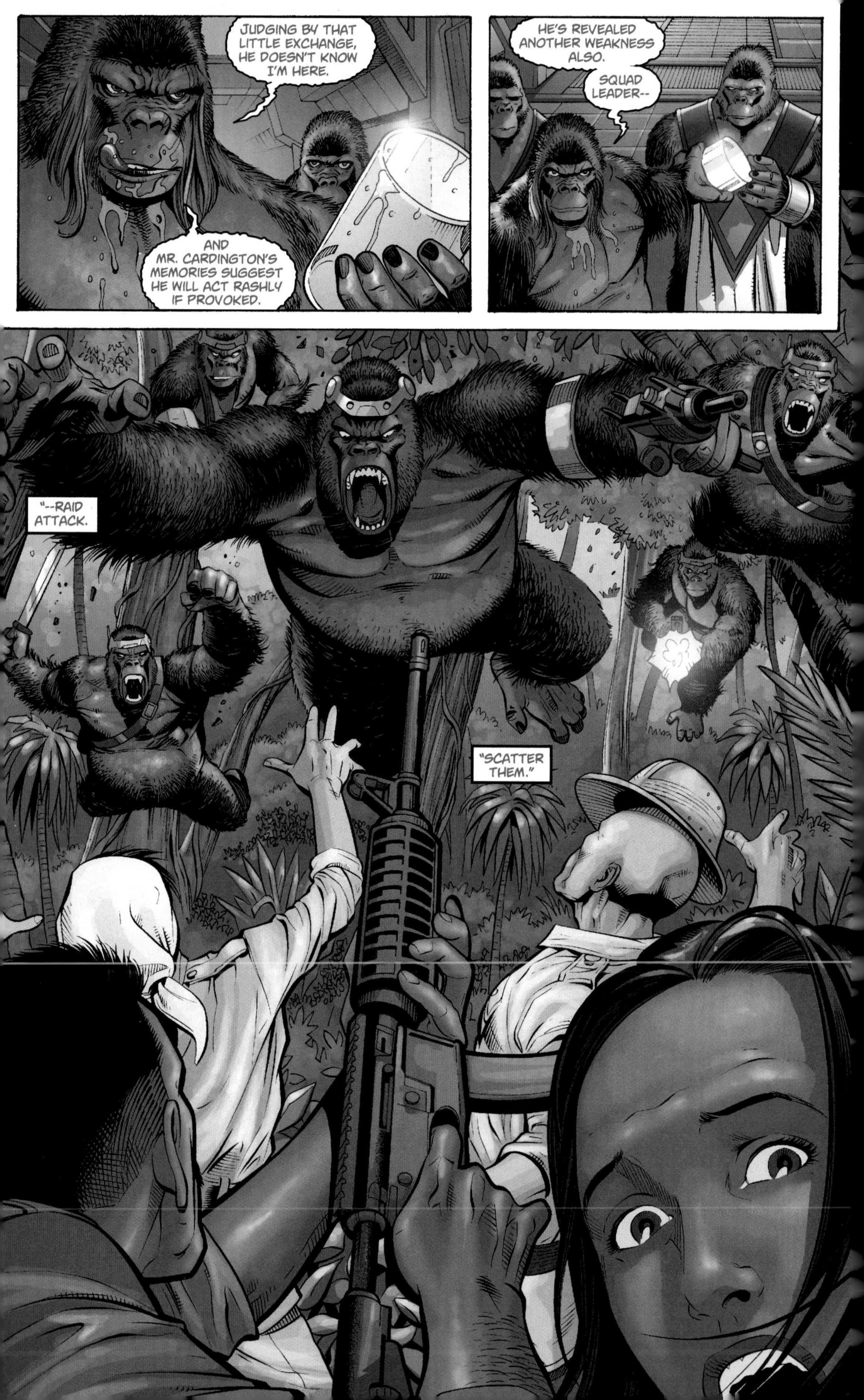
JUDGING BY THAT LITTLE EXCHANGE, HE DOESN'T KNOW I'M HERE.
AND MR. CARDINGTON'S MEMORIES SUGGEST HE WILL ACT RASHLY IF PROVOKED.
HE'S REVEALED ANOTHER WEAKNESS ALSO.
SQUAD LEADER--
"--RAID ATTACK.
"SCATTER THEM."

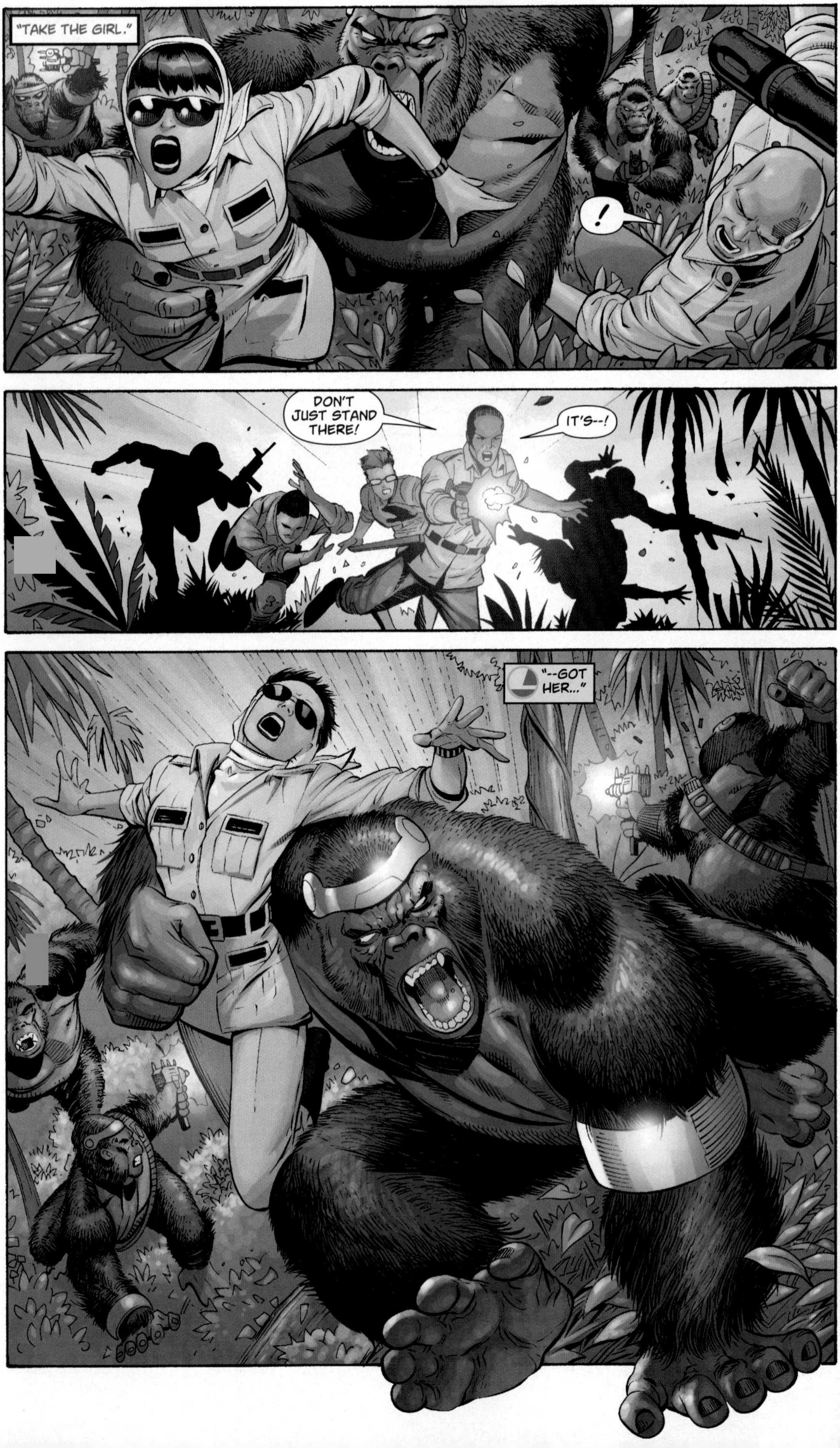
"TAKE THE GIRL."
!
DON'T JUST STAND THERE!
IT'S--!
"--GOT HER..."

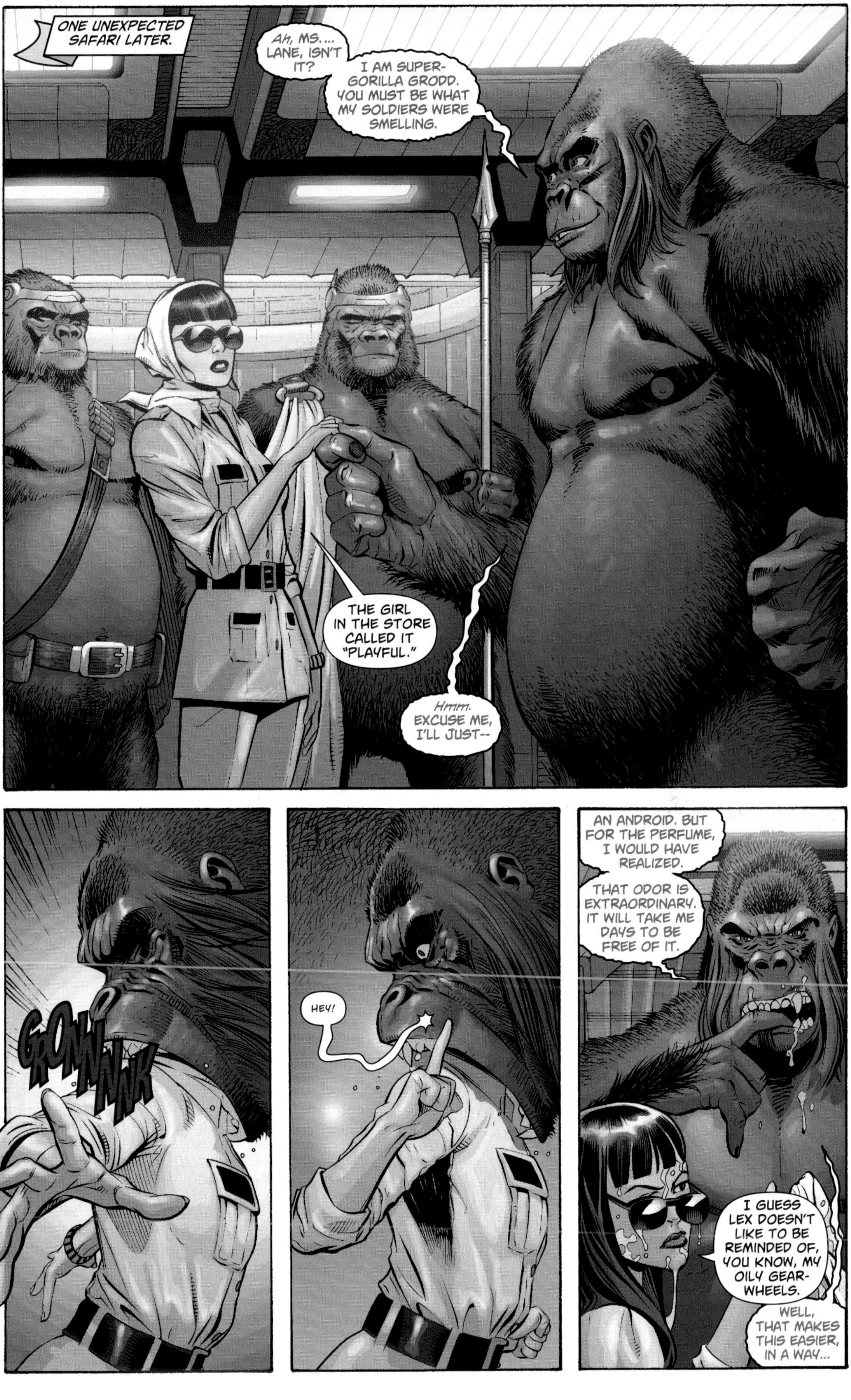
ONE UNEXPECTED SAFARI LATER.
Ah, MS.... LANE, ISN'T IT?
I AM SUPER-GORILLA GRODD. YOU MUST BE WHAT MY SOLDIERS WERE SMELLING.
THE GIRL IN THE STORE CALLED IT "PLAYFUL."
Hmm. EXCUSE ME, I'LL JUST--
GRONNNNNK
HEY!
AN ANDROID. BUT FOR THE PERFUME, I WOULD HAVE REALIZED.
THAT ODOR IS EXTRAORDINARY. IT WILL TAKE ME DAYS TO BE FREE OF IT.
I GUESS LEX DOESN'T LIKE TO BE REMINDED OF, YOU KNOW, MY OILY GEAR-WHEELS.
WELL, THAT MAKES THIS EASIER, IN A WAY...

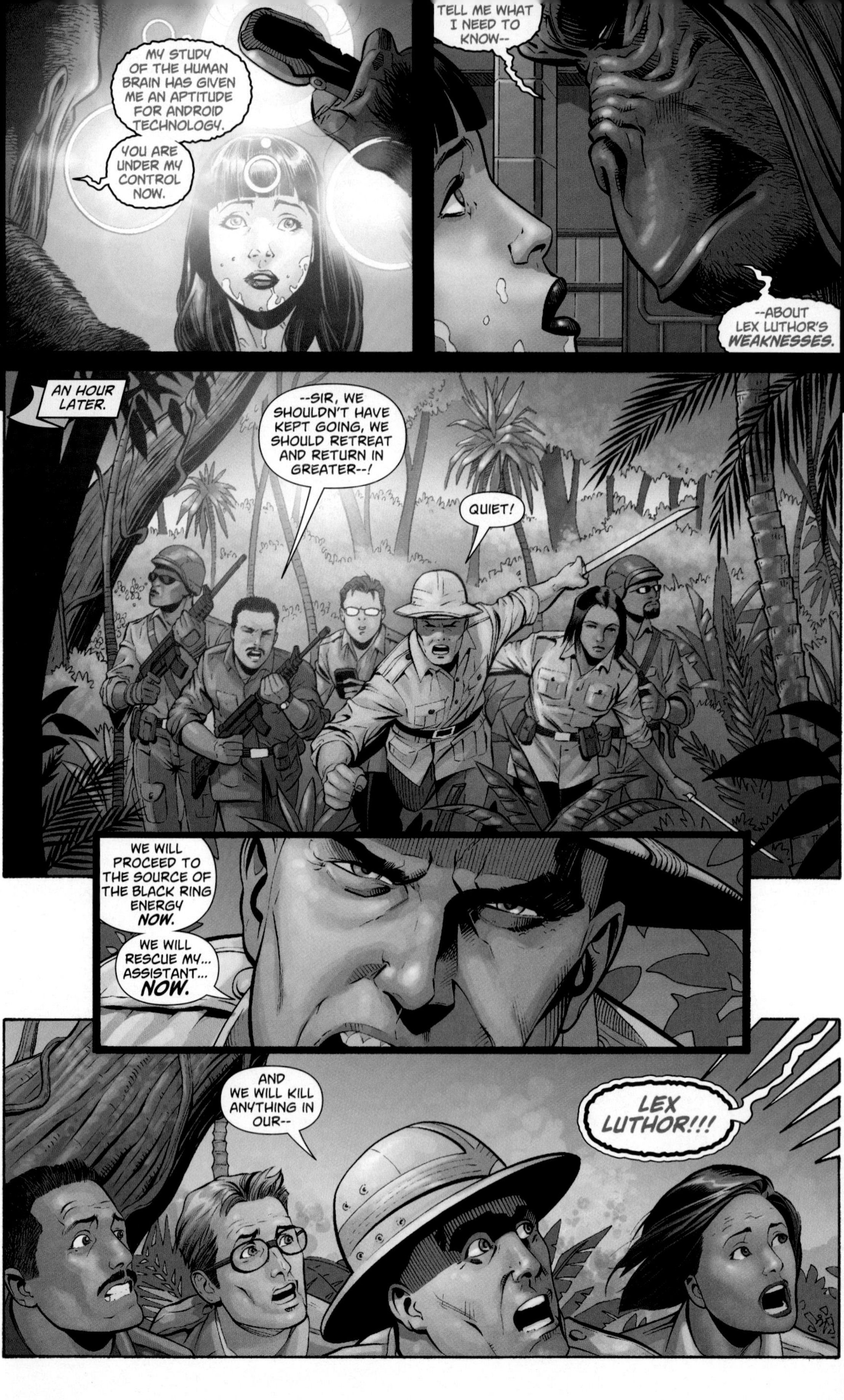
MY STUDY OF THE HUMAN BRAIN HAS GIVEN ME AN APTITUDE FOR ANDROID TECHNOLOGY.
YOU ARE UNDER MY CONTROL NOW.
TELL ME WHAT I NEED TO KNOW--
--ABOUT LEX LUTHOR'S WEAKNESSES.
AN HOUR LATER.
--SIR, WE SHOULDN'T HAVE KEPT GOING, WE SHOULD RETREAT AND RETURN IN GREATER--!
QUIET!
WE WILL PROCEED TO THE SOURCE OF THE BLACK RING ENERGY NOW.
WE WILL RESCUE MY... ASSISTANT... NOW.
AND WE WILL KILL ANYTHING IN OUR--
LEX LUTHOR!!!

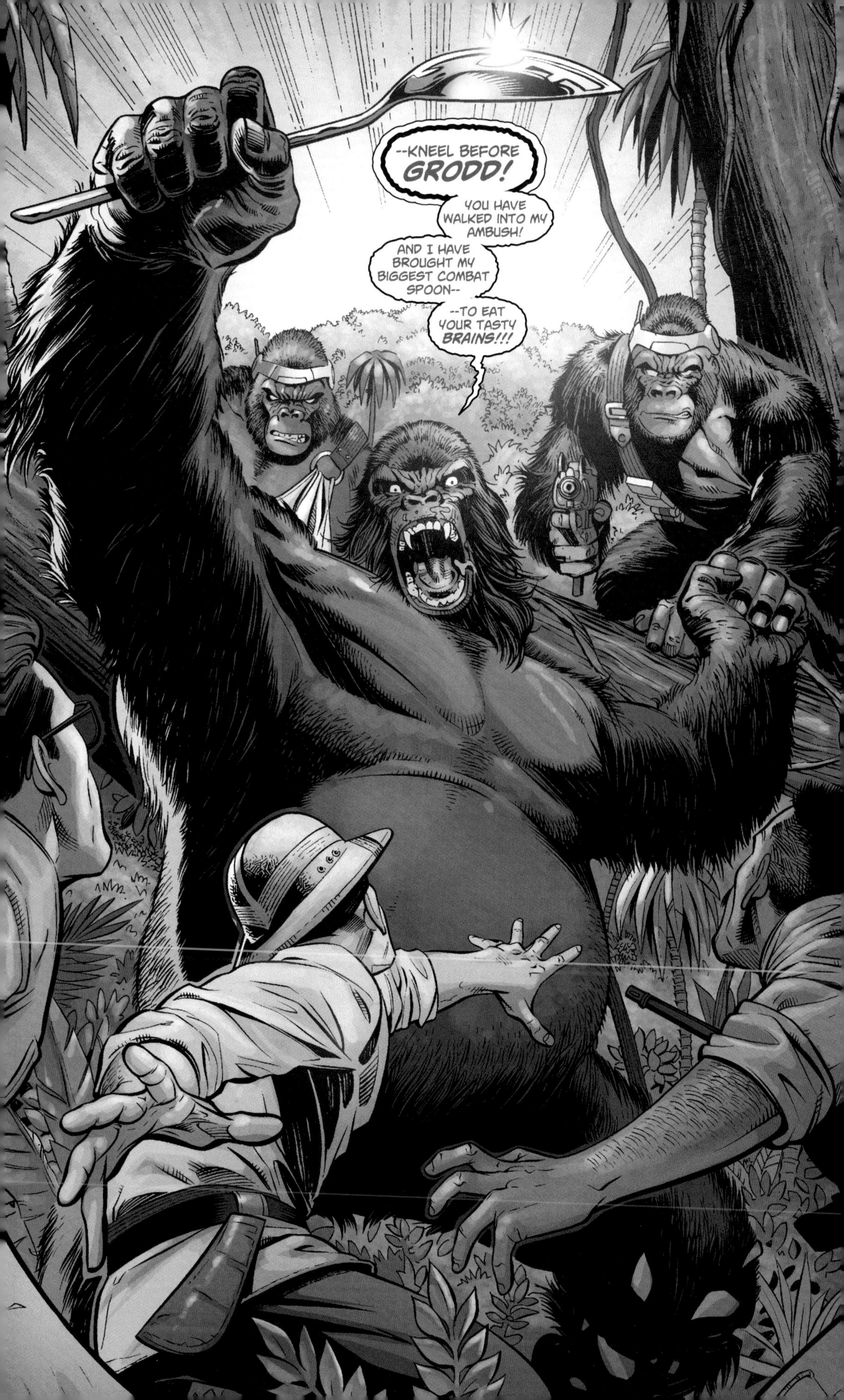
--KNEEL BEFORE GRODD!
YOU HAVE WALKED INTO MY AMBUSH!
AND I HAVE BROUGHT MY BIGGEST COMBAT SPOON--
--TO EAT YOUR TASTY BRAINS!!!

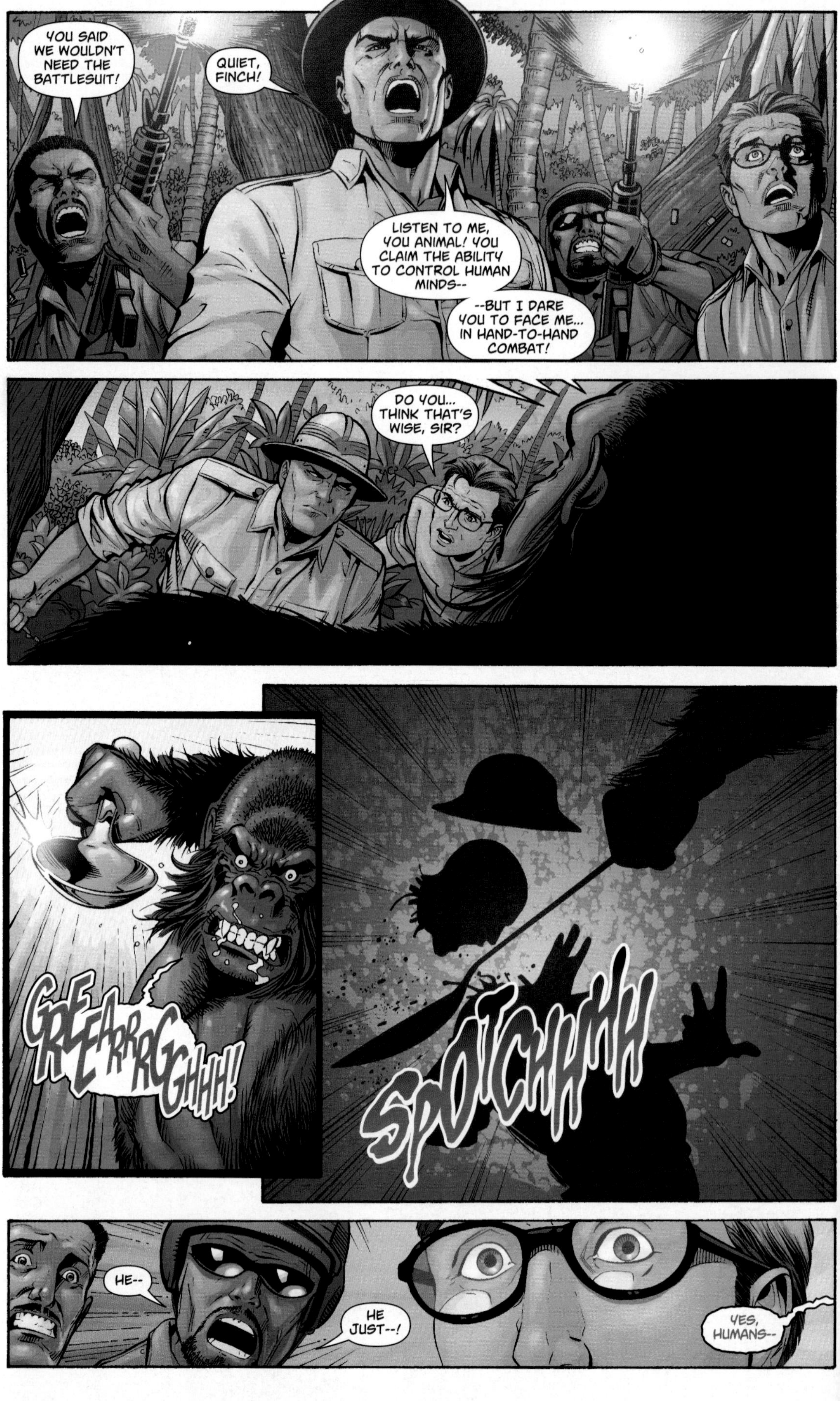

YOU SAID WE WOULDN'T NEED THE BATTLESUIT!
QUIET, FINCH!
LISTEN TO ME, YOU ANIMAL! YOU CLAIM THE ABILITY TO CONTROL HUMAN MINDS--
--BUT I DARE YOU TO FACE ME... IN HAND-TO-HAND COMBAT!
DO YOU... THINK THAT'S WISE, SIR?
GREEARRRRGHHH!
SPOTCHHHH
HE--
HE JUST--!
YES, HUMANS--

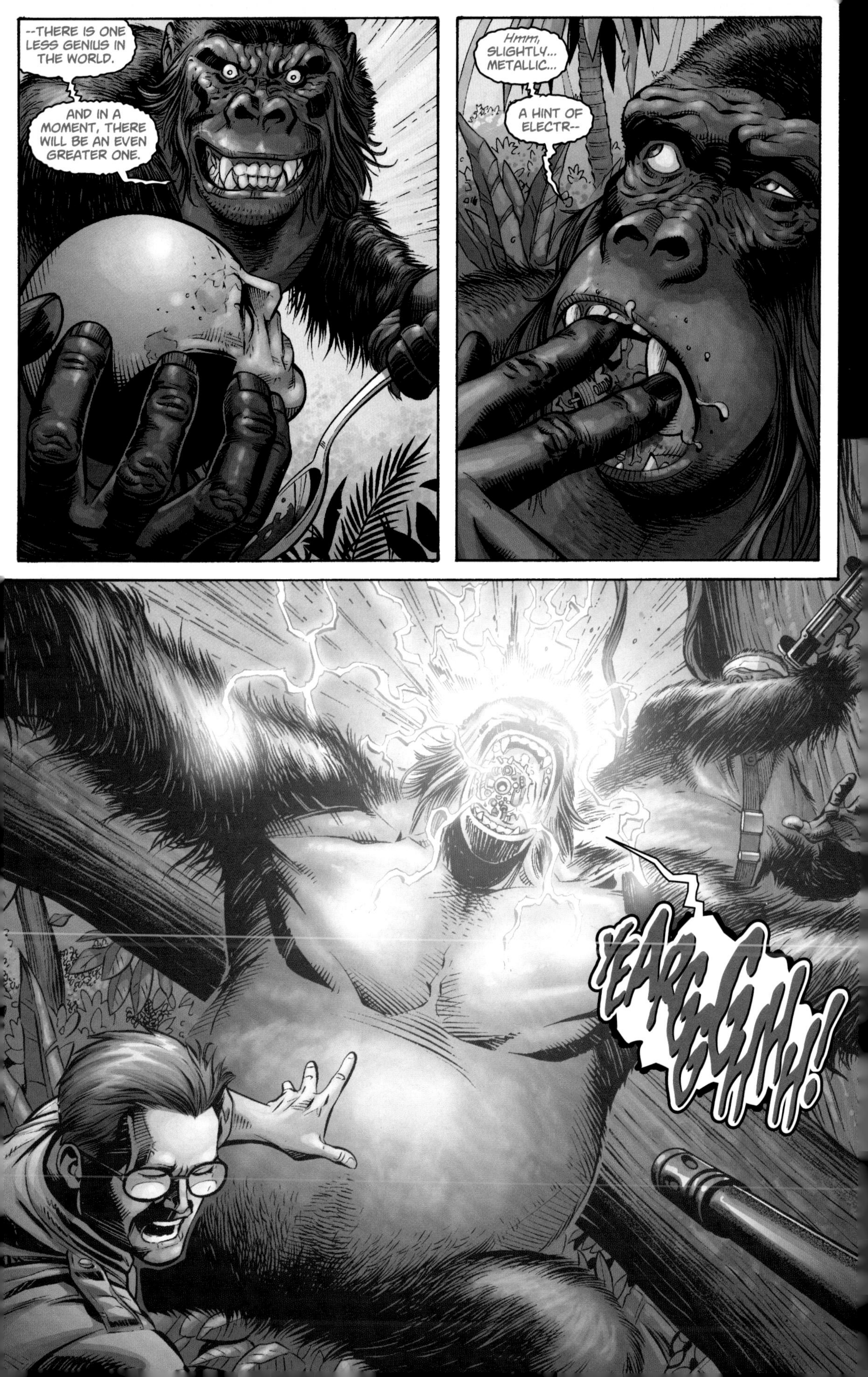
--THERE IS ONE LESS GENIUS IN THE WORLD.
AND IN A MOMENT, THERE WILL BE AN EVEN GREATER ONE.
Hmm, SLIGHTLY... METALLIC...
A HINT OF ELECTR--
YEARGGGHH!

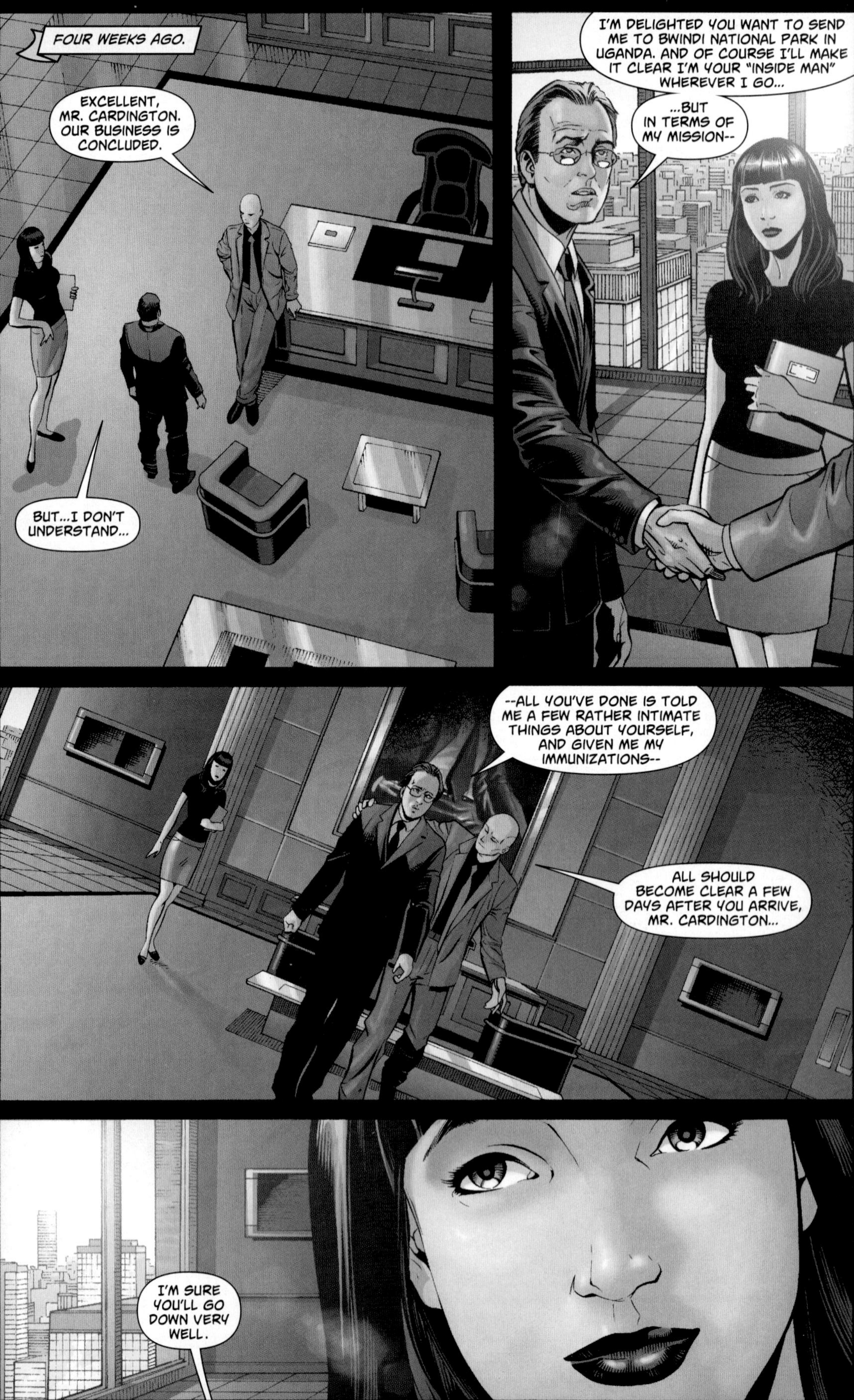
FOUR WEEKS AGO.
EXCELLENT, MR. CARDINGTON. OUR BUSINESS IS CONCLUDED.
BUT...I DON'T UNDERSTAND...
I'M DELIGHTED YOU WANT TO SEND ME TO BWINDI NATIONAL PARK IN UGANDA. AND OF COURSE I'LL MAKE IT CLEAR I'M YOUR "INSIDE MAN" WHEREVER I GO...
...BUT IN TERMS OF MY MISSION--
--ALL YOU'VE DONE IS TOLD ME A FEW RATHER INTIMATE THINGS ABOUT YOURSELF, AND GIVEN ME MY IMMUNIZATIONS--
ALL SHOULD BECOME CLEAR A FEW DAYS AFTER YOU ARRIVE, MR. CARDINGTON...
I'M SURE YOU'LL GO DOWN VERY WELL.

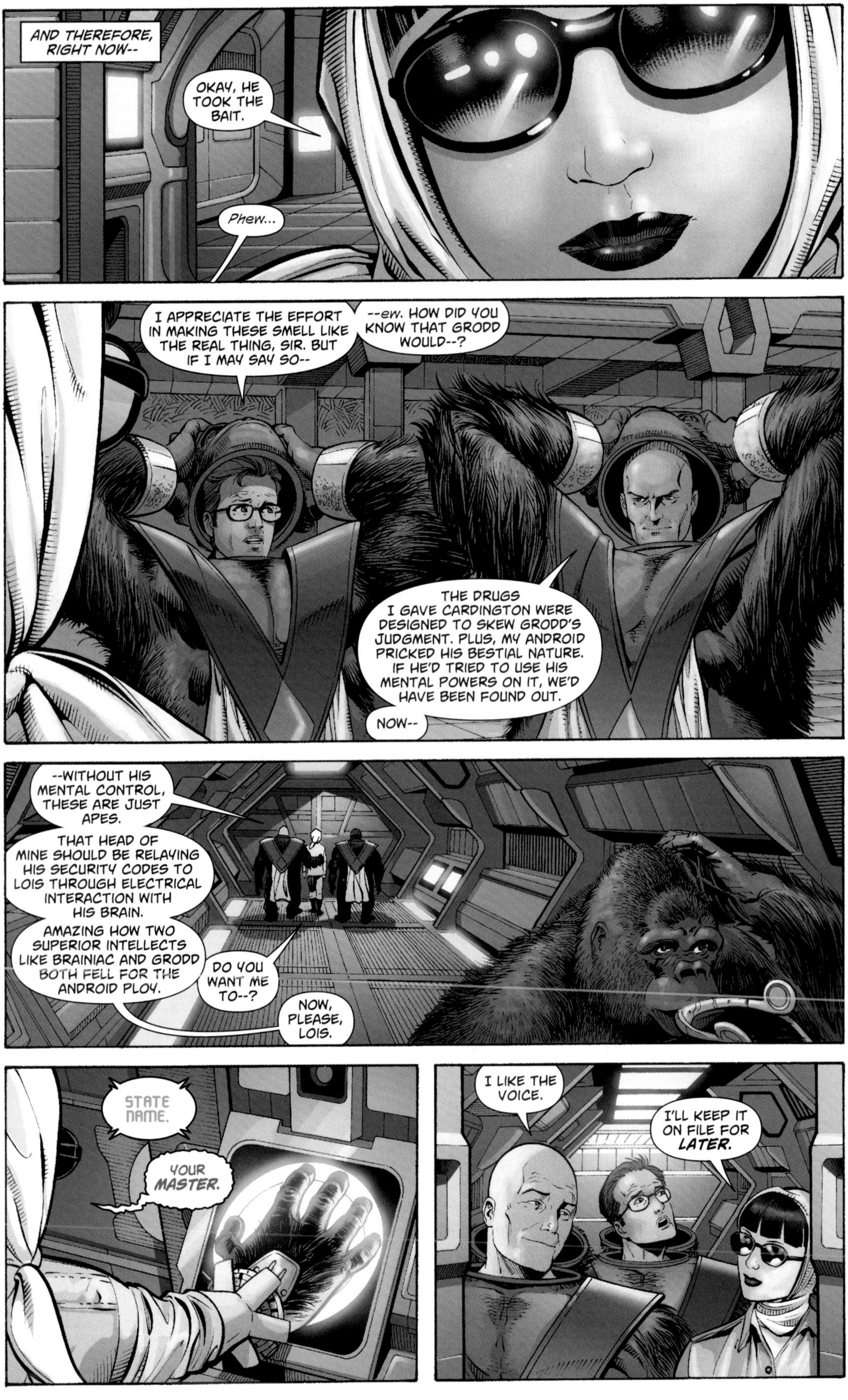
AND THEREFORE, RIGHT NOW--
OKAY, HE TOOK THE BAIT.
Phew...
I APPRECIATE THE EFFORT IN MAKING THESE SMELL LIKE THE REAL THING, SIR. BUT IF I MAY SAY SO--
--ew. HOW DID YOU KNOW THAT GRODD WOULD--?
THE DRUGS I GAVE CARDINGTON WERE DESIGNED TO SKEW GRODD'S JUDGMENT. PLUS, MY ANDROID PRICKED HIS BESTIAL NATURE. IF HE'D TRIED TO USE HIS MENTAL POWERS ON IT, WE'D HAVE BEEN FOUND OUT.
NOW--
--WITHOUT HIS MENTAL CONTROL, THESE ARE JUST APES.
THAT HEAD OF MINE SHOULD BE RELAYING HIS SECURITY CODES TO LOIS THROUGH ELECTRICAL INTERACTION WITH HIS BRAIN.
AMAZING HOW TWO SUPERIOR INTELLECTS LIKE BRAINIAC AND GRODD BOTH FELL FOR THE ANDROID PLOY.
DO YOU WANT ME TO--?
NOW, PLEASE, LOIS.
STATE NAME.
YOUR MASTER.
I LIKE THE VOICE.
I'LL KEEP IT ON FILE FOR LATER.

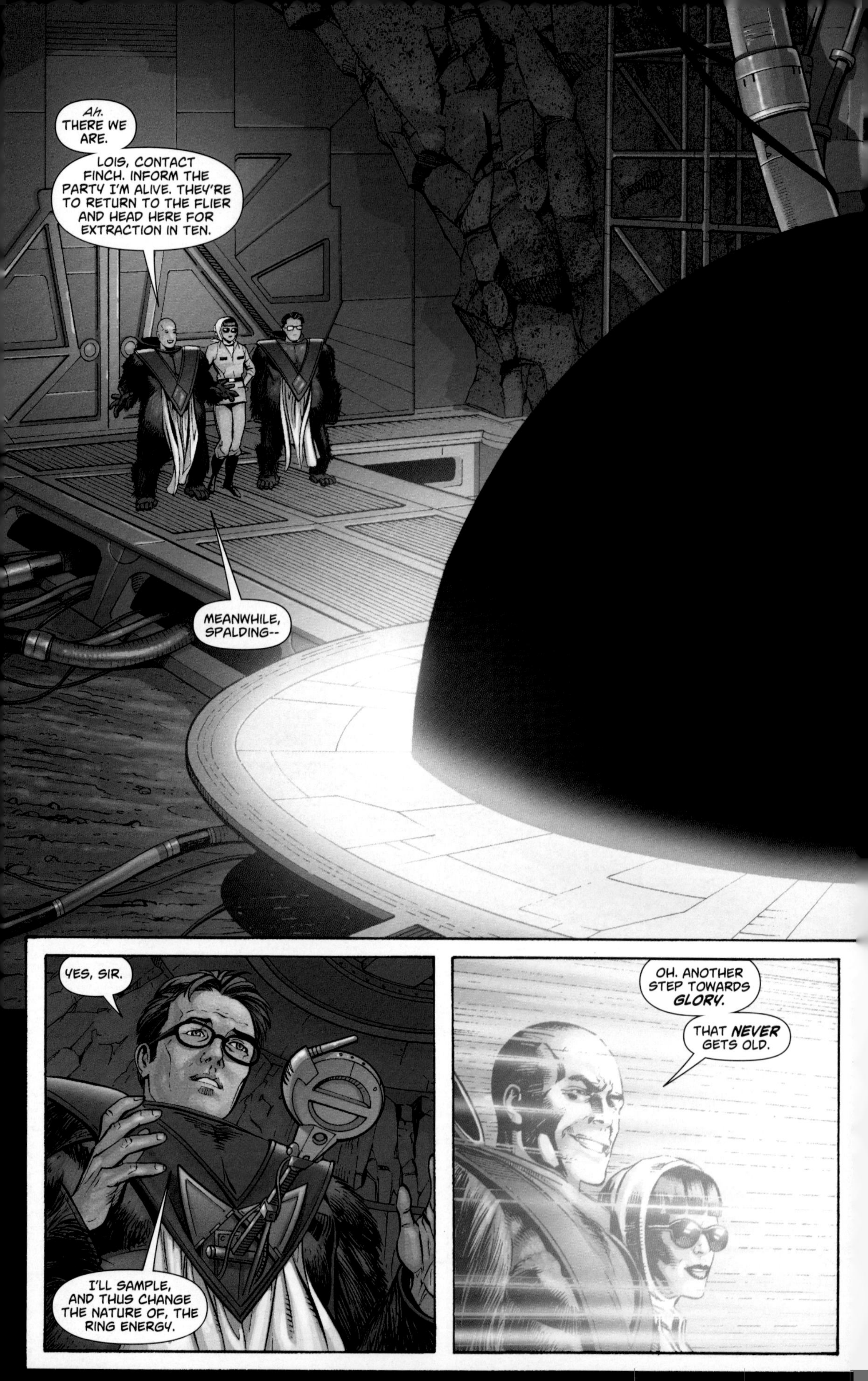
AH. THERE WE ARE.
LOIS, CONTACT FINCH. INFORM THE PARTY I'M ALIVE. THEY'RE TO RETURN TO THE FLIER AND HEAD HERE FOR EXTRACTION IN TEN.
MEANWHILE, SPALDING--
YES, SIR.
I'LL SAMPLE, AND THUS CHANGE THE NATURE OF, THE RING ENERGY.
OH. ANOTHER STEP TOWARDS GLORY.
THAT NEVER GETS OLD.

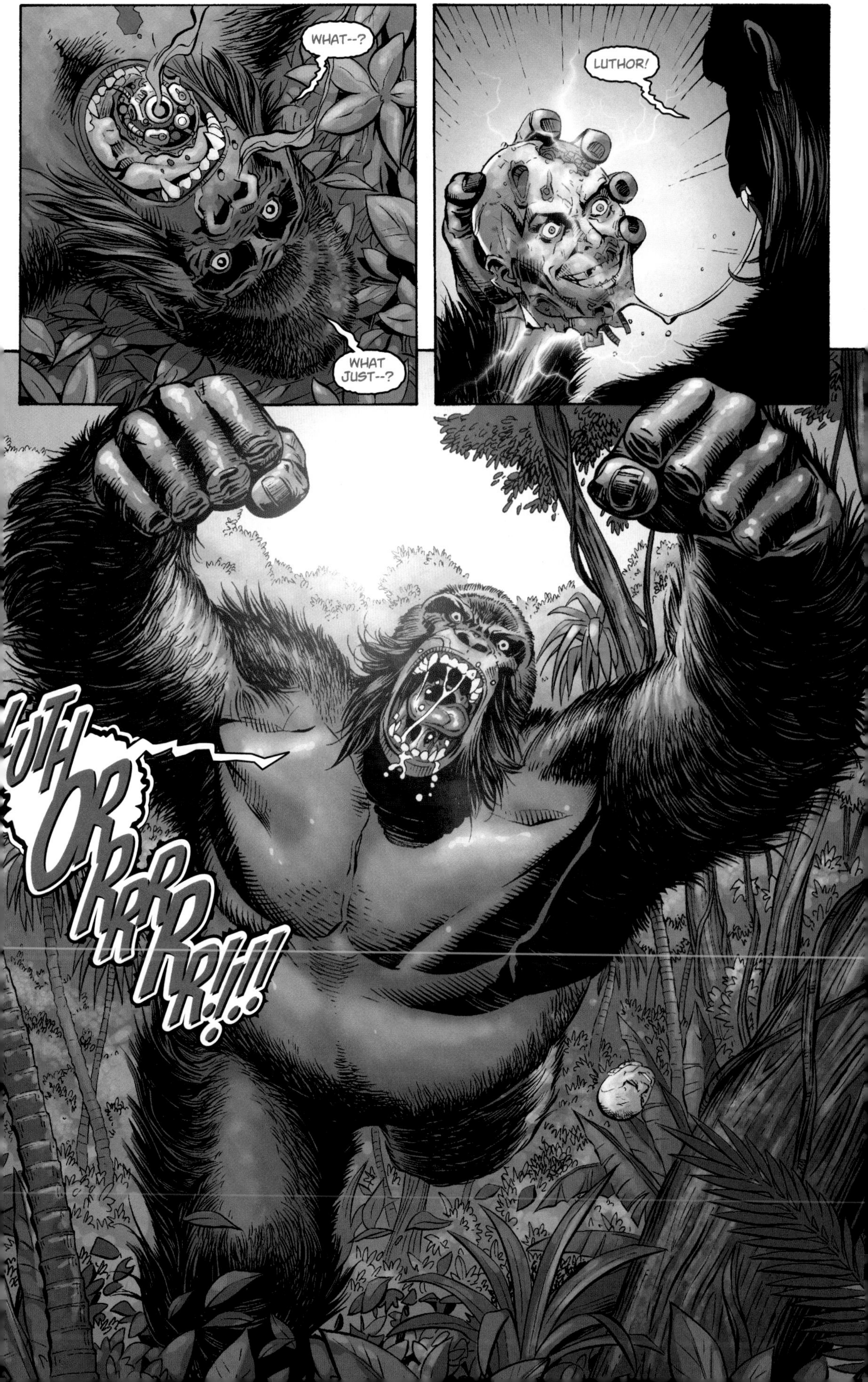
WHAT--?
WHAT JUST--?
LUTHOR!
LUTHORRRRRRR!!!

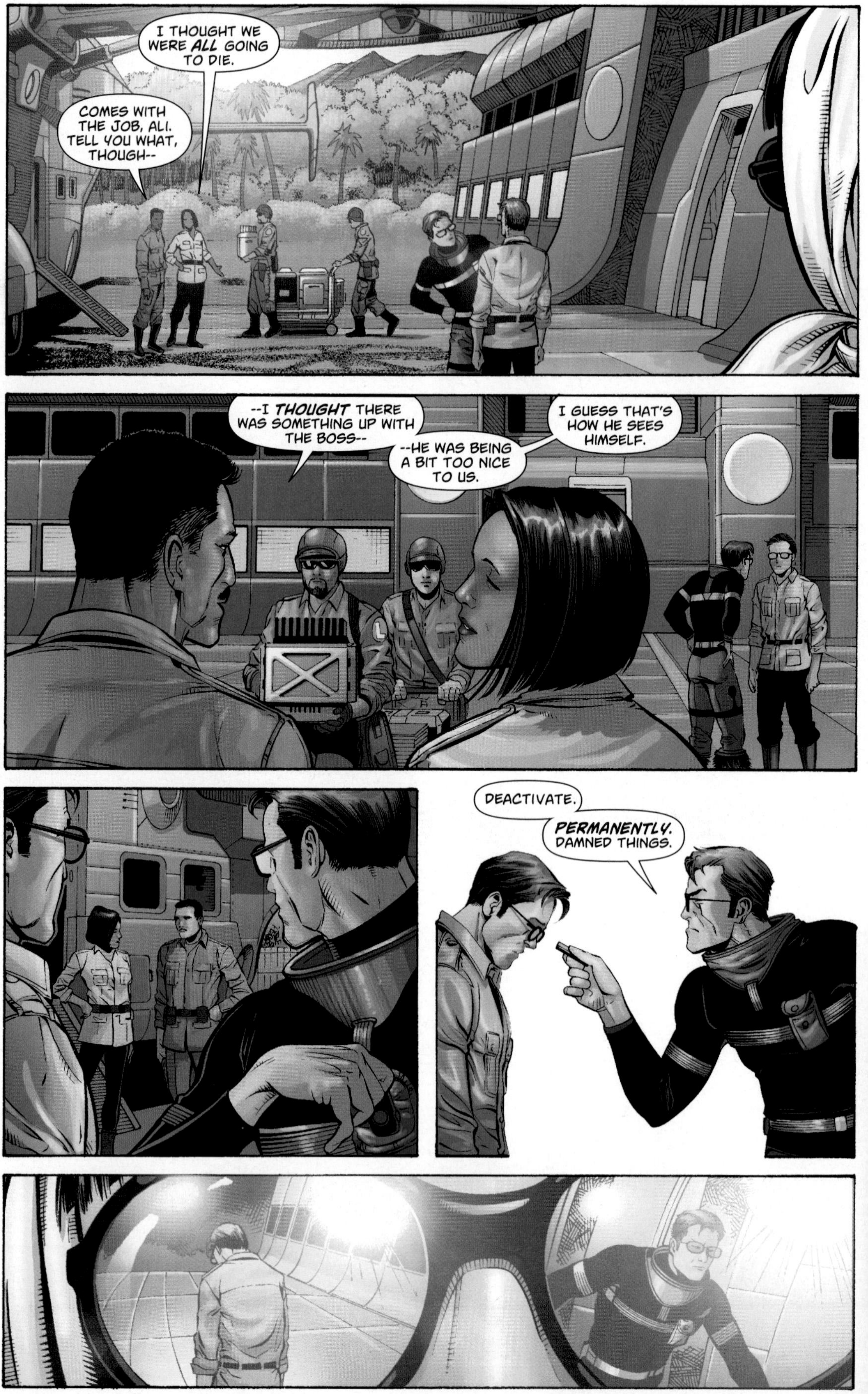
I THOUGHT WE WERE ALL GOING TO DIE.
COMES WITH THE JOB, ALI. TELL YOU WHAT, THOUGH--
--I THOUGHT THERE WAS SOMETHING UP WITH THE BOSS--
--HE WAS BEING A BIT TOO NICE TO US.
I GUESS THAT'S HOW HE SEES HIMSELF.
DEACTIVATE.
PERMANENTLY. DAMNED THINGS.

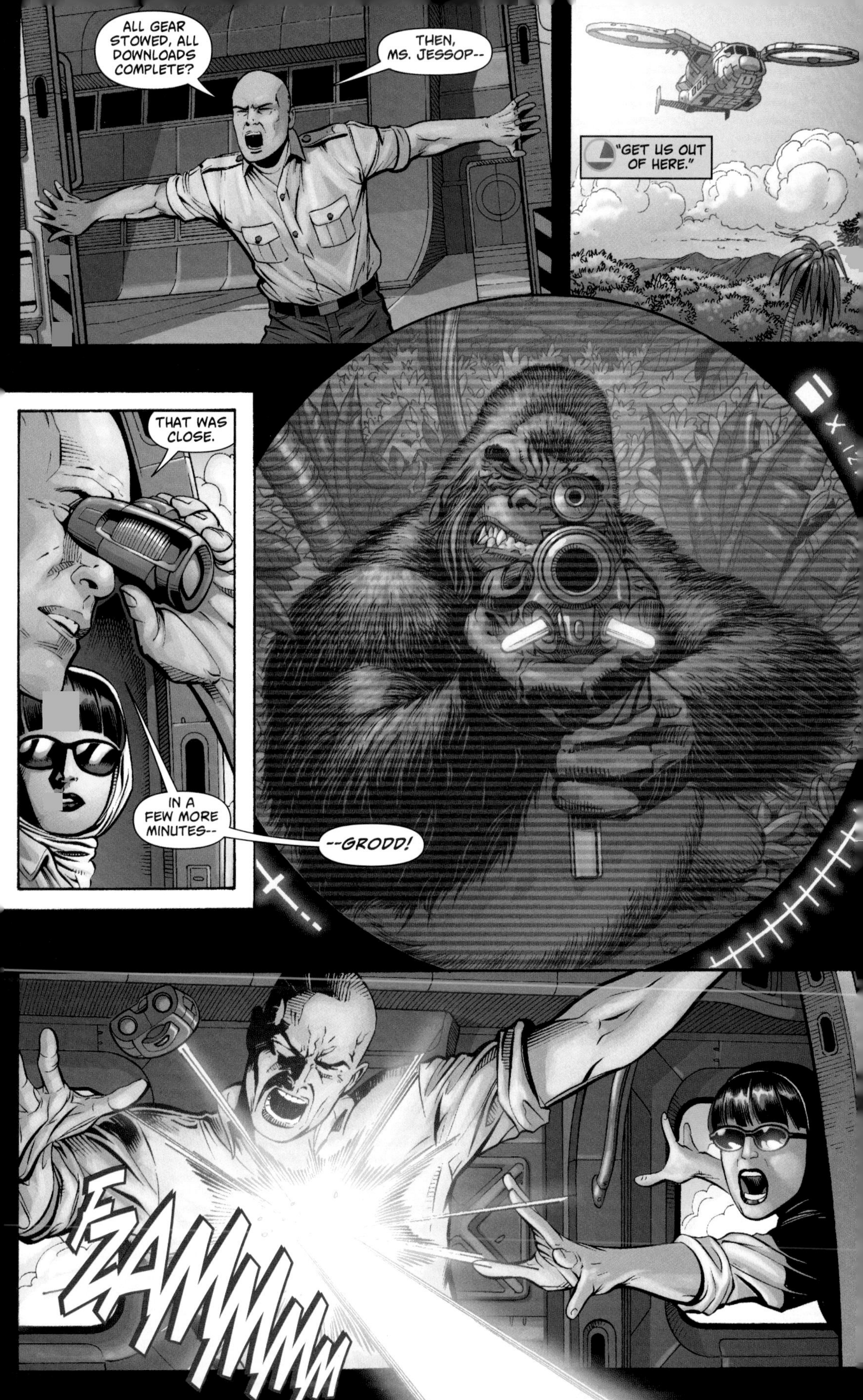
ALL GEAR STOWED, ALL DOWNLOADS COMPLETE?
THEN, MS. JESSOP--
"GET US OUT OF HERE."
THAT WAS CLOSE.
IN A FEW MORE MINUTES--
--GRODD!
FZAMMMMM

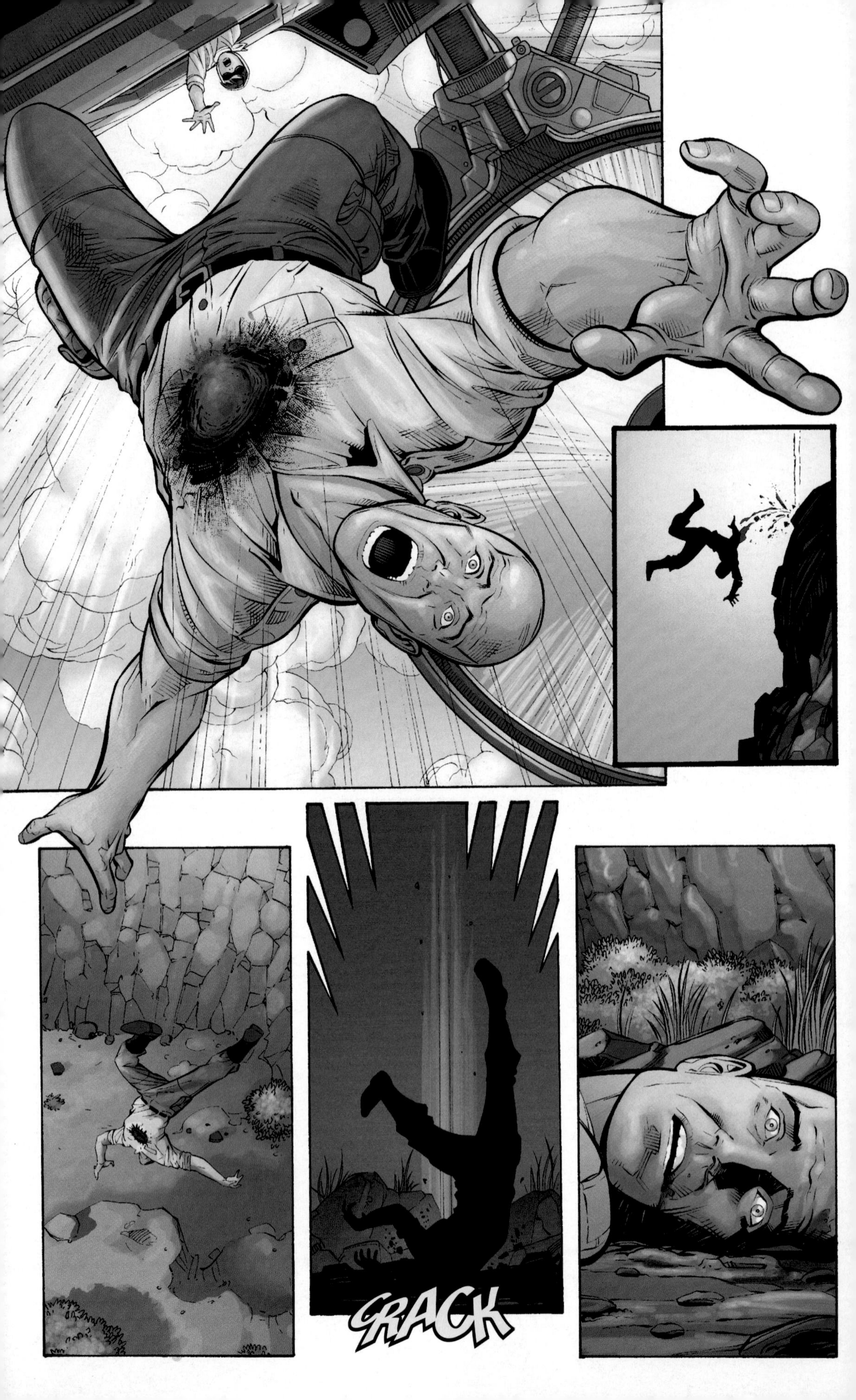
CRACK

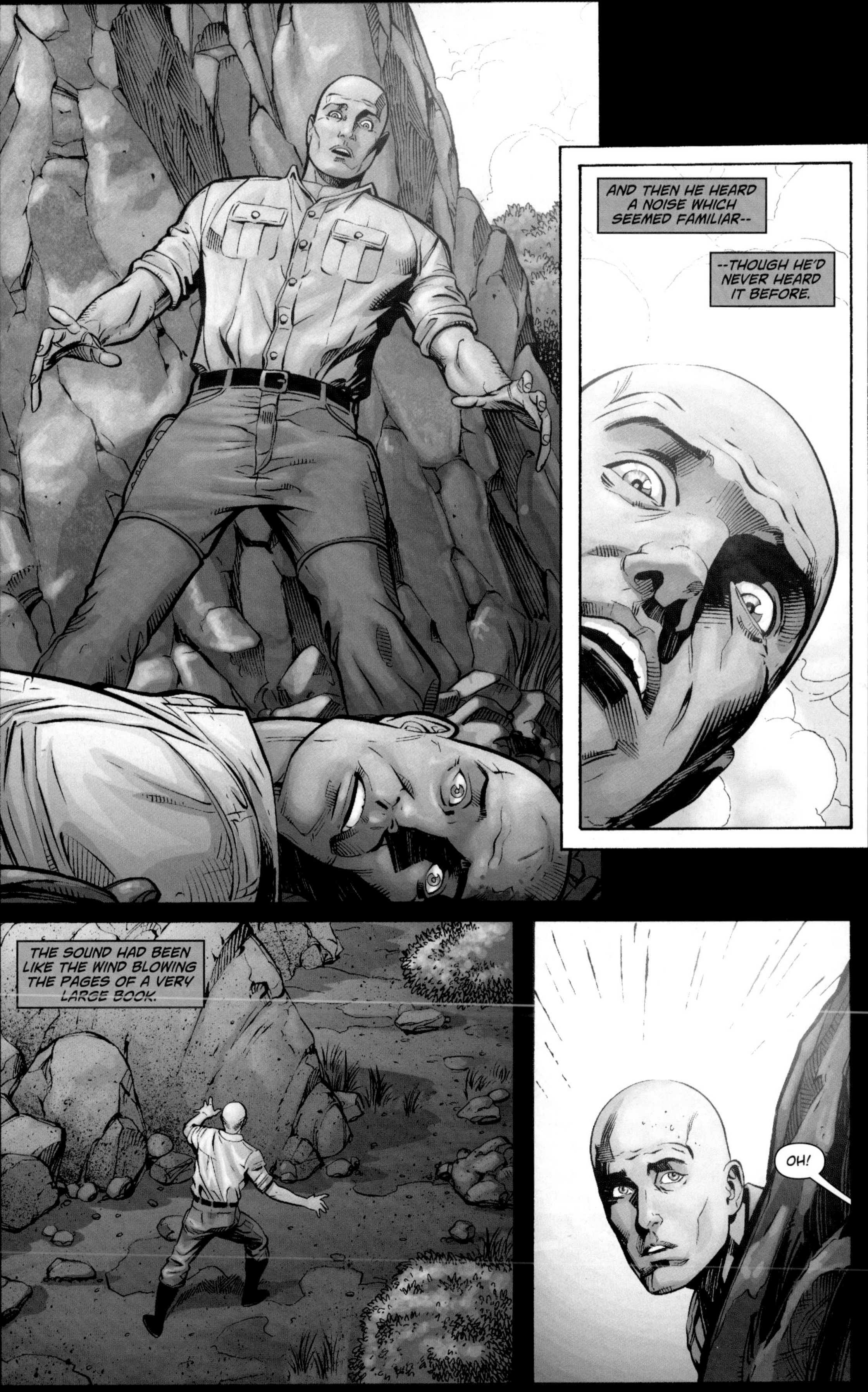
AND THEN HE HEARD A NOISE WHICH SEEMED FAMILIAR--
--THOUGH HE'D NEVER HEARD IT BEFORE.
THE SOUND HAD BEEN LIKE THE WIND BLOWING THE PAGES OF A VERY LARGE BOOK.
OH!

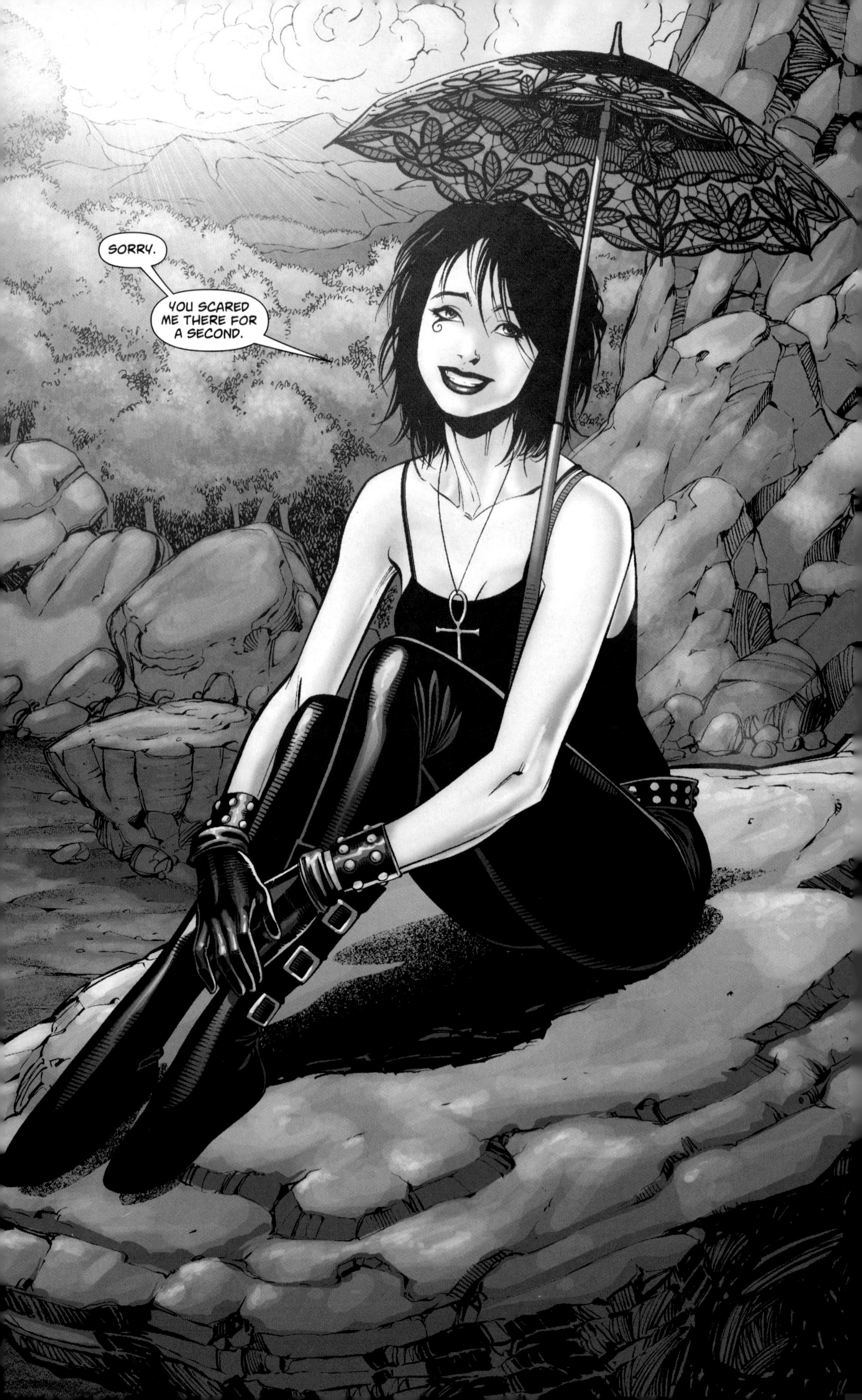
SORRY.
YOU SCARED ME THERE FOR A SECOND.

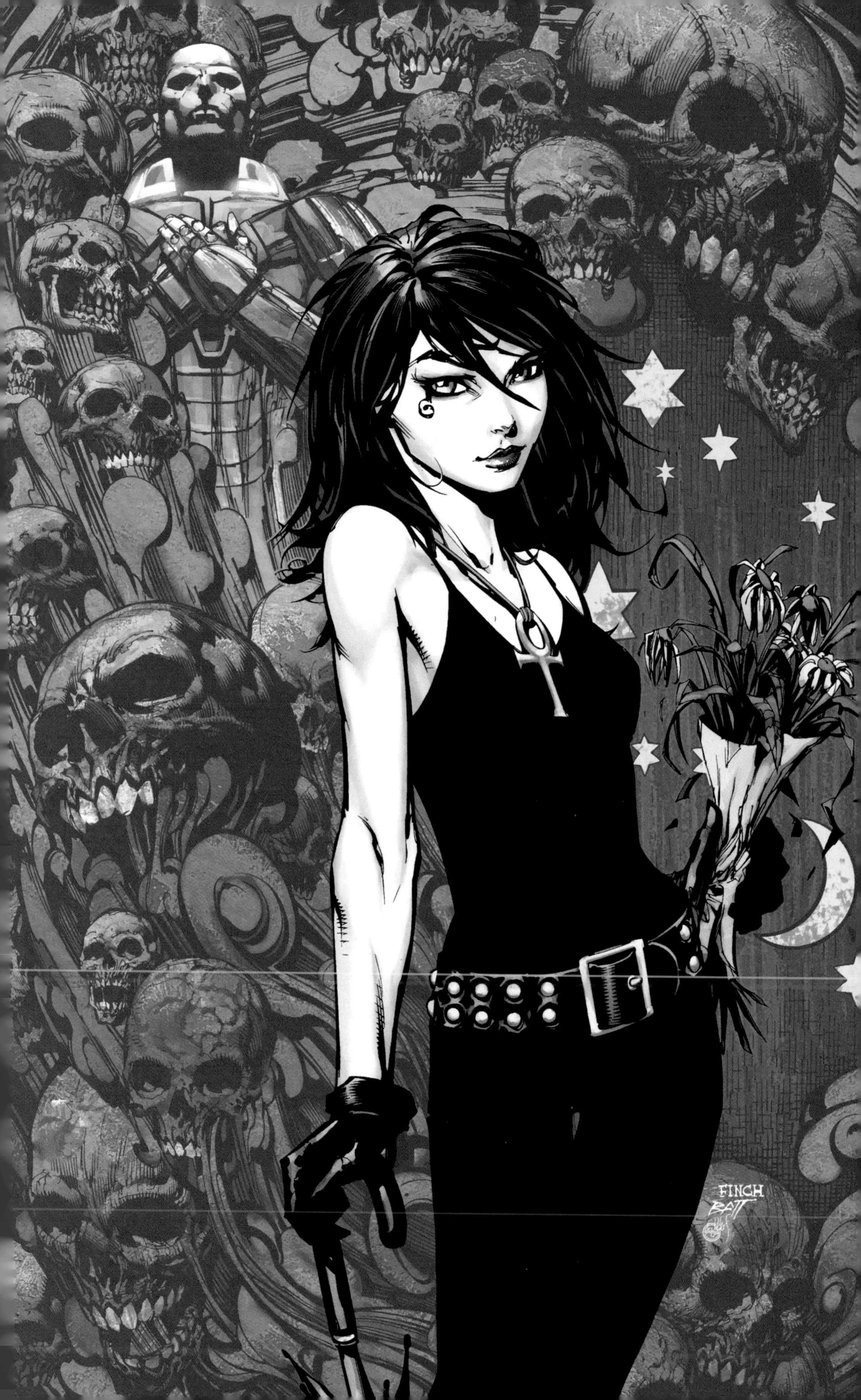
FINCH
BATT

THE BLACK RING
part five

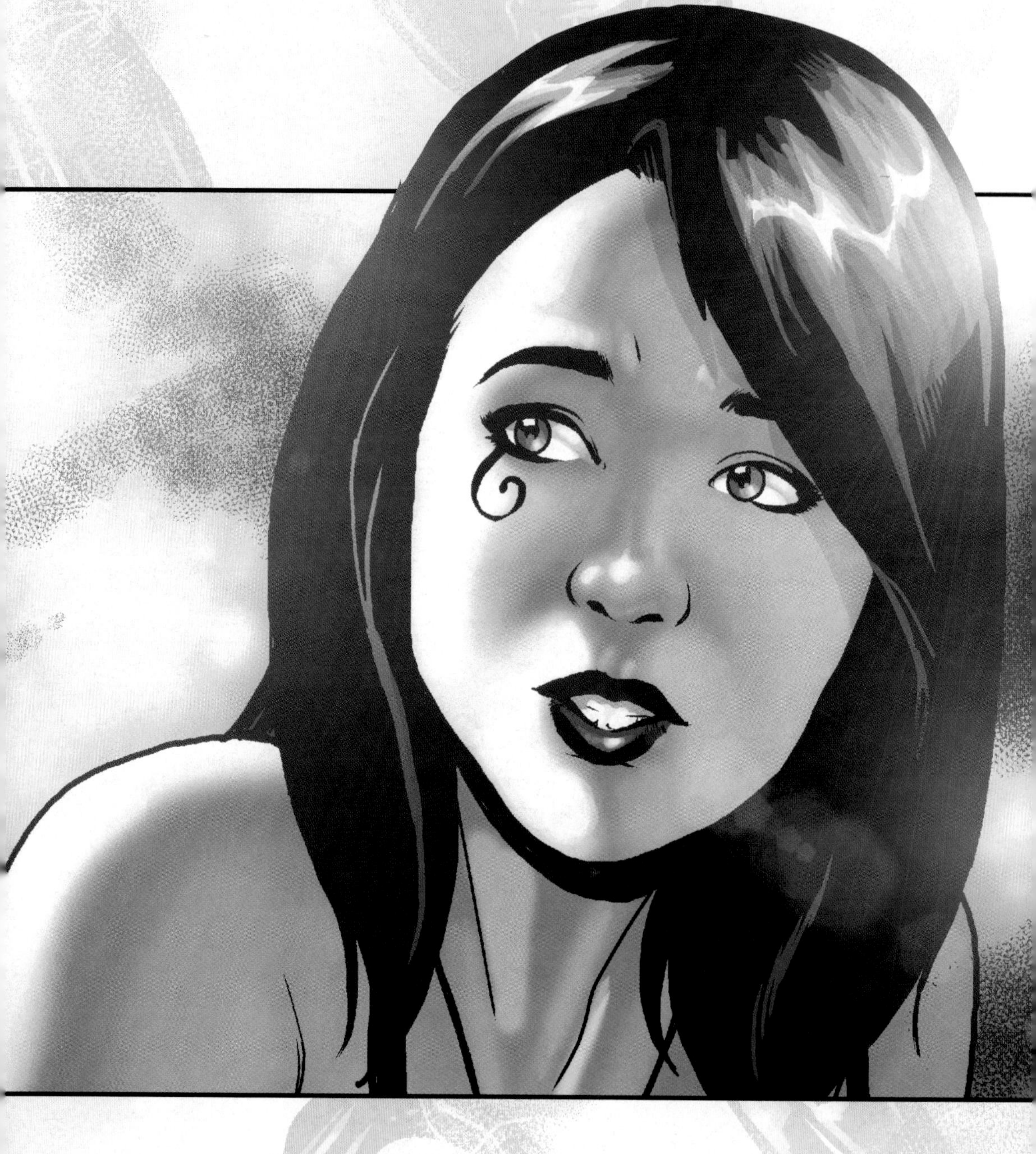

cover by
DAVID **FINCH**, **BATT** & PETER **STEIGERWALD**

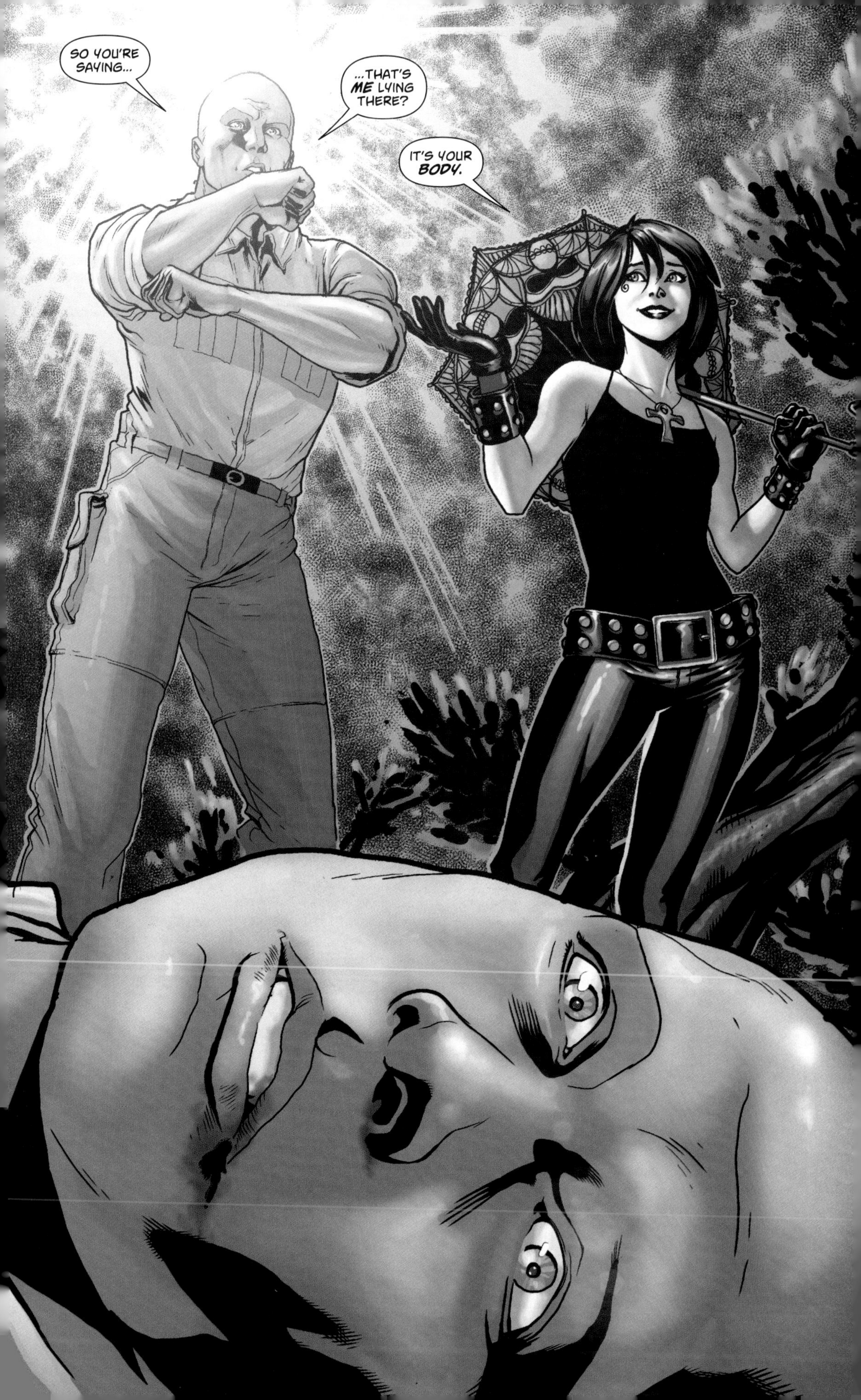
SO YOU'RE SAYING...
...THAT'S ME LYING THERE?
IT'S YOUR BODY.

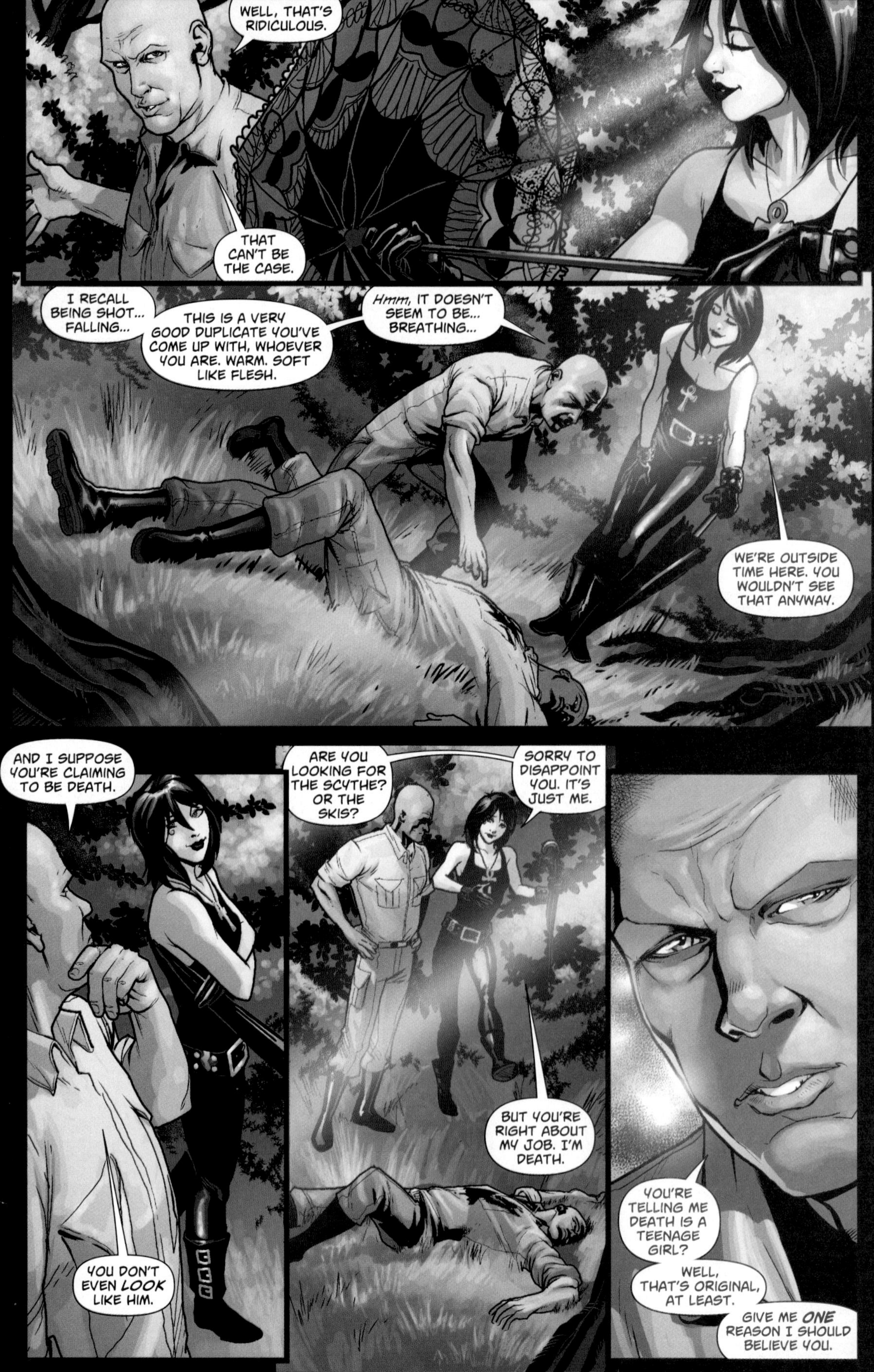
WELL, THAT'S RIDICULOUS.
THAT CAN'T BE THE CASE.
I RECALL BEING SHOT... FALLING...
THIS IS A VERY GOOD DUPLICATE YOU'VE COME UP WITH, WHOEVER YOU ARE. WARM. SOFT LIKE FLESH.
Hmm, IT DOESN'T SEEM TO BE... BREATHING...
WE'RE OUTSIDE TIME HERE. YOU WOULDN'T SEE THAT ANYWAY.
AND I SUPPOSE YOU'RE CLAIMING TO BE DEATH.
YOU DON'T EVEN *LOOK* LIKE HIM.
ARE YOU LOOKING FOR THE SCYTHE? OR THE SKIS?
SORRY TO DISAPPOINT YOU. IT'S JUST ME.
BUT YOU'RE RIGHT ABOUT MY JOB. I'M DEATH.
YOU'RE TELLING ME DEATH IS A TEENAGE GIRL?
WELL, THAT'S ORIGINAL, AT LEAST.
GIVE ME *ONE* REASON I SHOULD BELIEVE YOU.

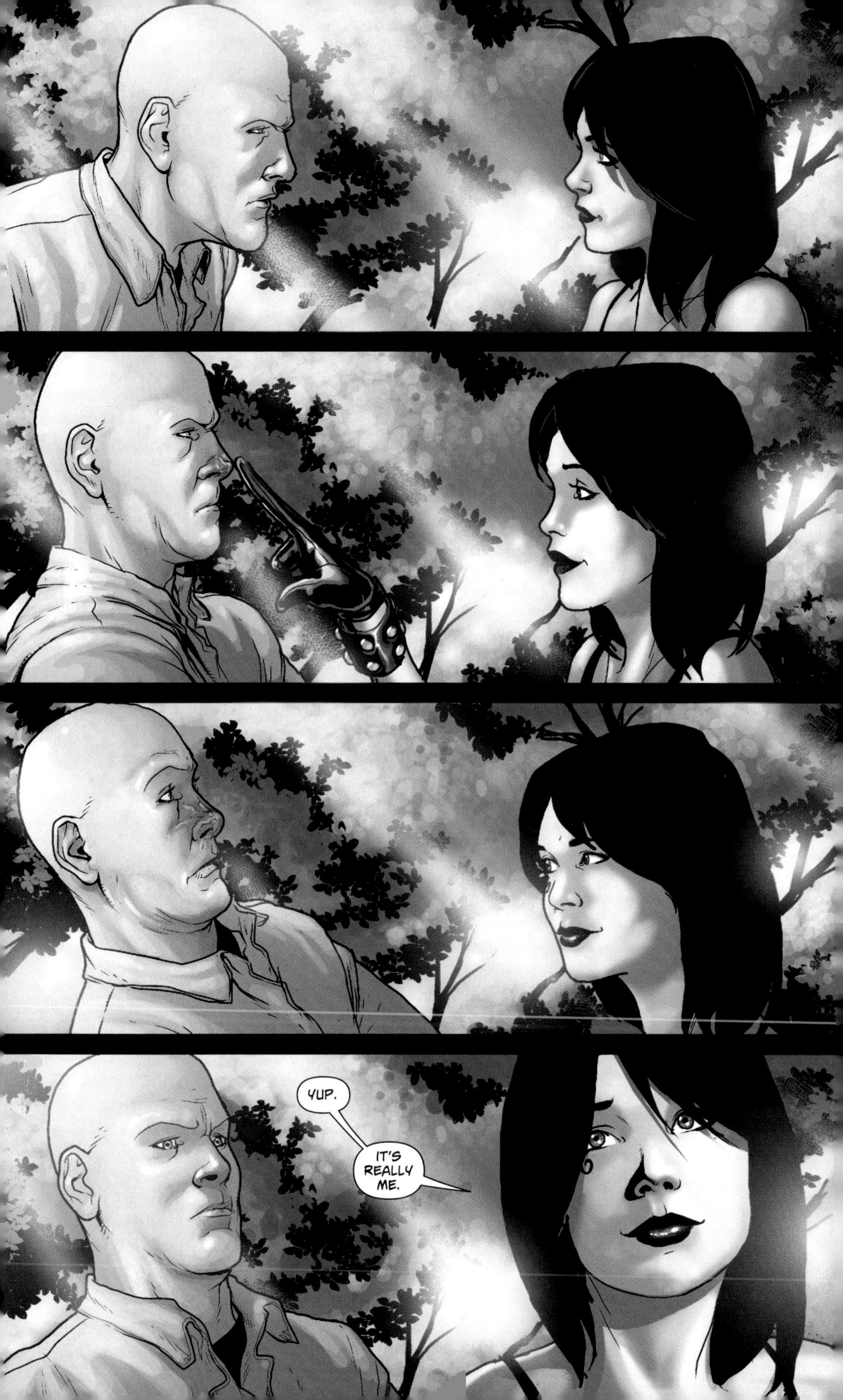
YUP.
IT'S REALLY ME.

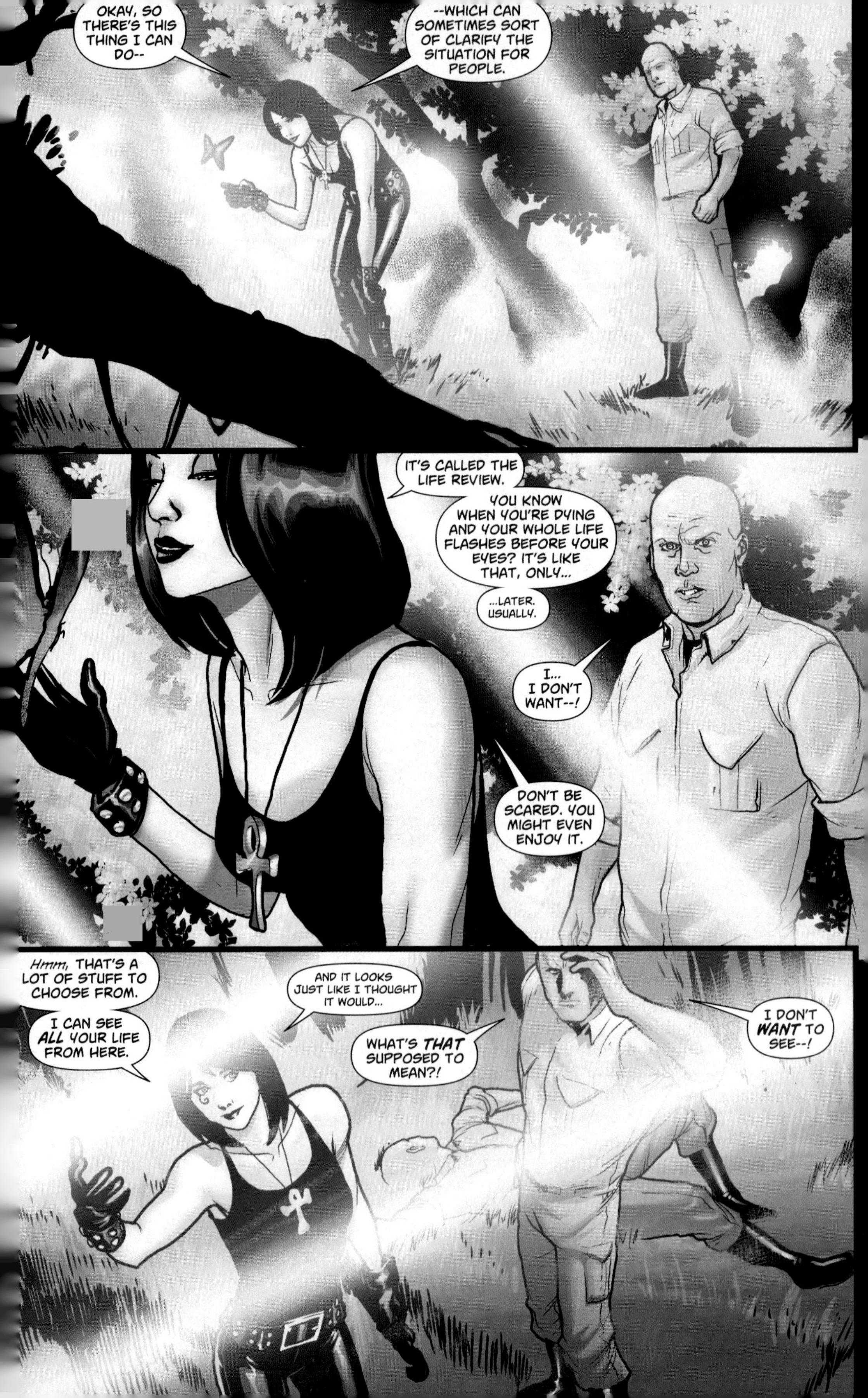
OKAY, SO THERE'S THIS THING I CAN DO--
--WHICH CAN SOMETIMES SORT OF CLARIFY THE SITUATION FOR PEOPLE.
IT'S CALLED THE LIFE REVIEW.
YOU KNOW WHEN YOU'RE DYING AND YOUR WHOLE LIFE FLASHES BEFORE YOUR EYES? IT'S LIKE THAT, ONLY...
...LATER. USUALLY.
I... I DON'T WANT--!
DON'T BE SCARED. YOU MIGHT EVEN ENJOY IT.
Hmm, THAT'S A LOT OF STUFF TO CHOOSE FROM.
I CAN SEE ***ALL*** YOUR LIFE FROM HERE.
AND IT LOOKS JUST LIKE I THOUGHT IT WOULD...
WHAT'S ***THAT*** SUPPOSED TO MEAN?!
I DON'T ***WANT*** TO SEE--!

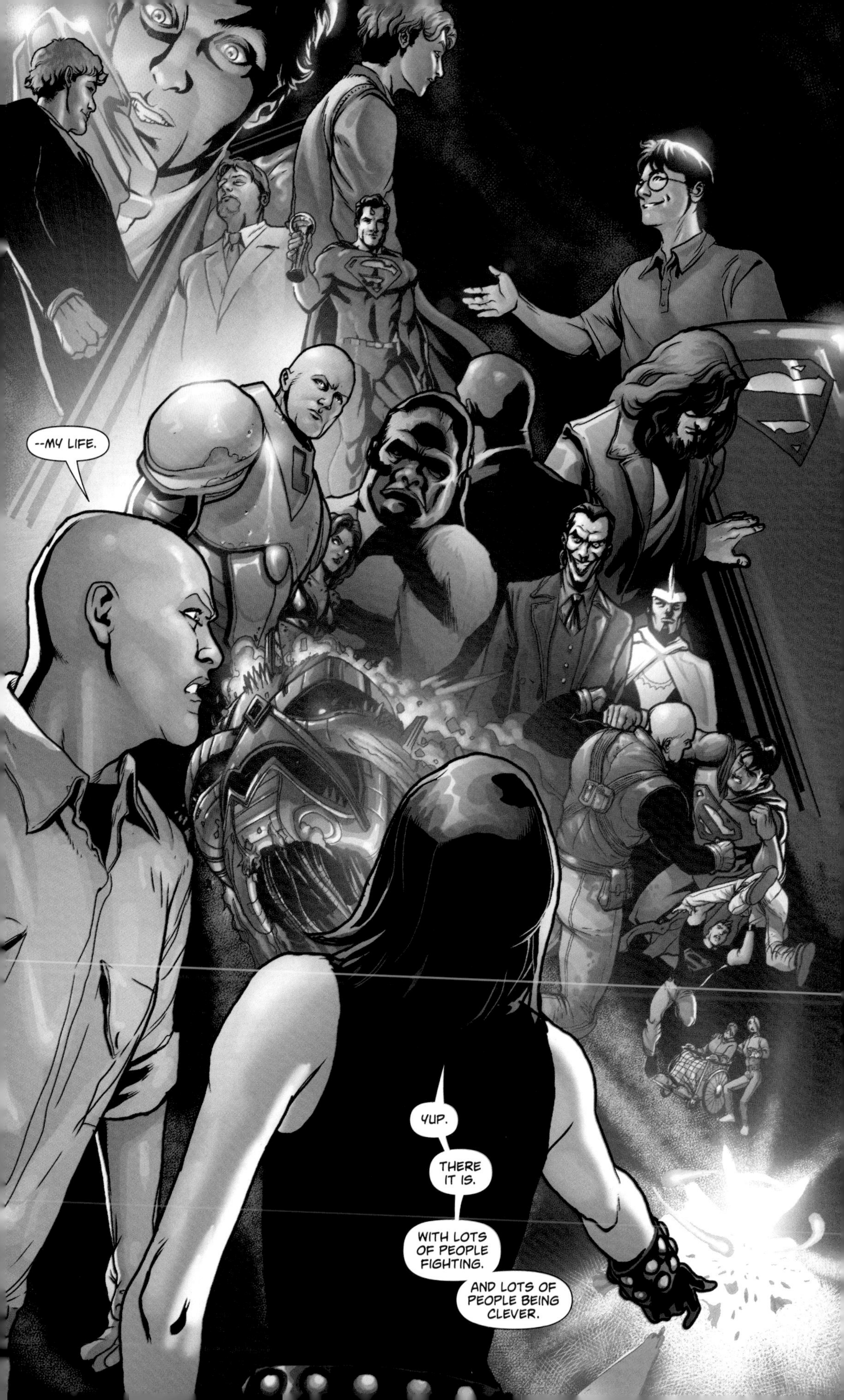
--MY LIFE.
YUP.
THERE IT IS.
WITH LOTS OF PEOPLE FIGHTING.
AND LOTS OF PEOPLE BEING CLEVER.

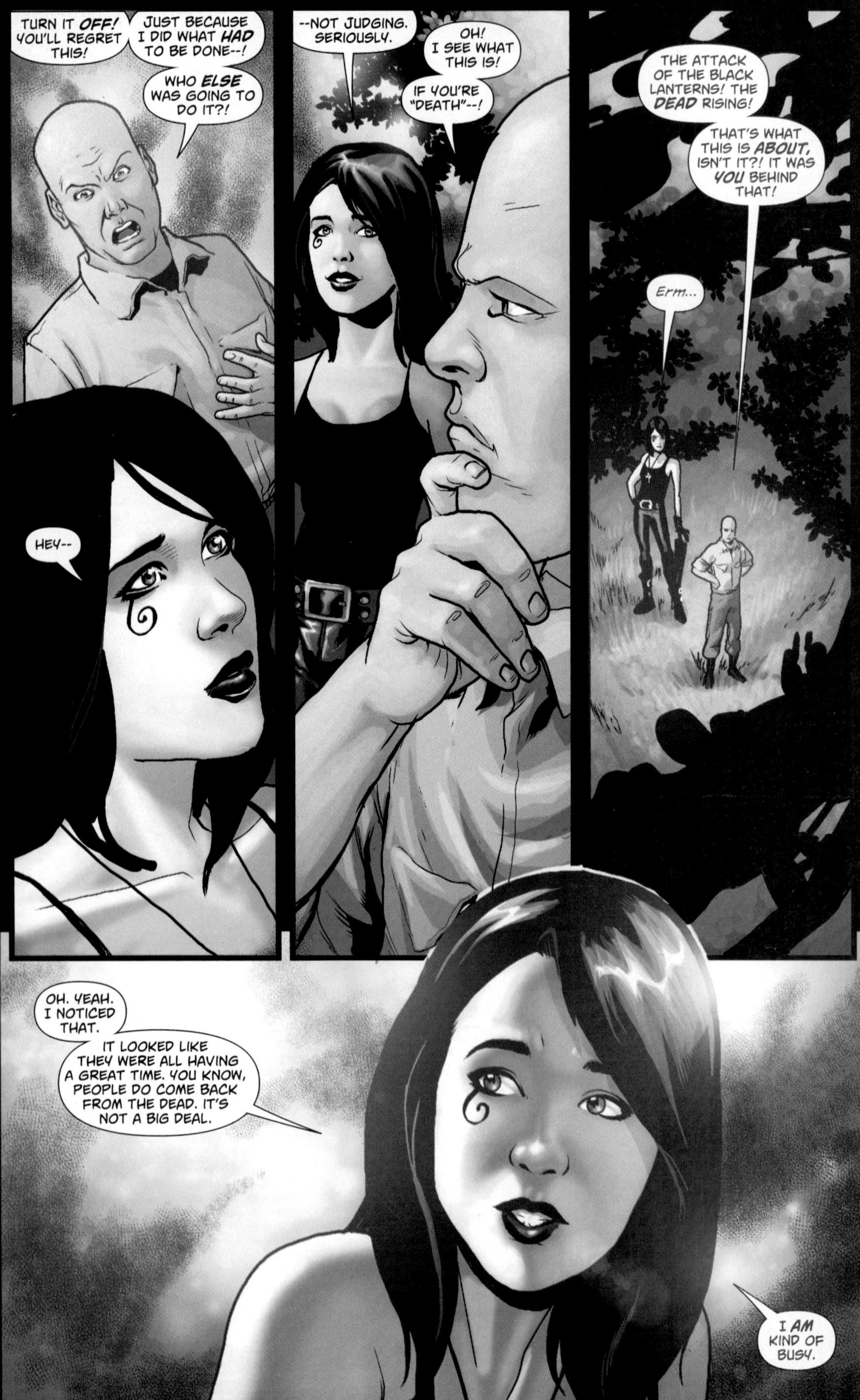

TURN IT OFF! YOU'LL REGRET THIS!
JUST BECAUSE I DID WHAT HAD TO BE DONE--!
WHO ELSE WAS GOING TO DO IT?!
HEY--
--NOT JUDGING. SERIOUSLY.
OH! I SEE WHAT THIS IS!
IF YOU'RE "DEATH"--!
THE ATTACK OF THE BLACK LANTERNS! THE DEAD RISING!
THAT'S WHAT THIS IS ABOUT, ISN'T IT?! IT WAS YOU BEHIND THAT!
Erm...
OH. YEAH. I NOTICED THAT.
IT LOOKED LIKE THEY WERE ALL HAVING A GREAT TIME. YOU KNOW, PEOPLE DO COME BACK FROM THE DEAD. IT'S NOT A BIG DEAL.
I AM KIND OF BUSY.

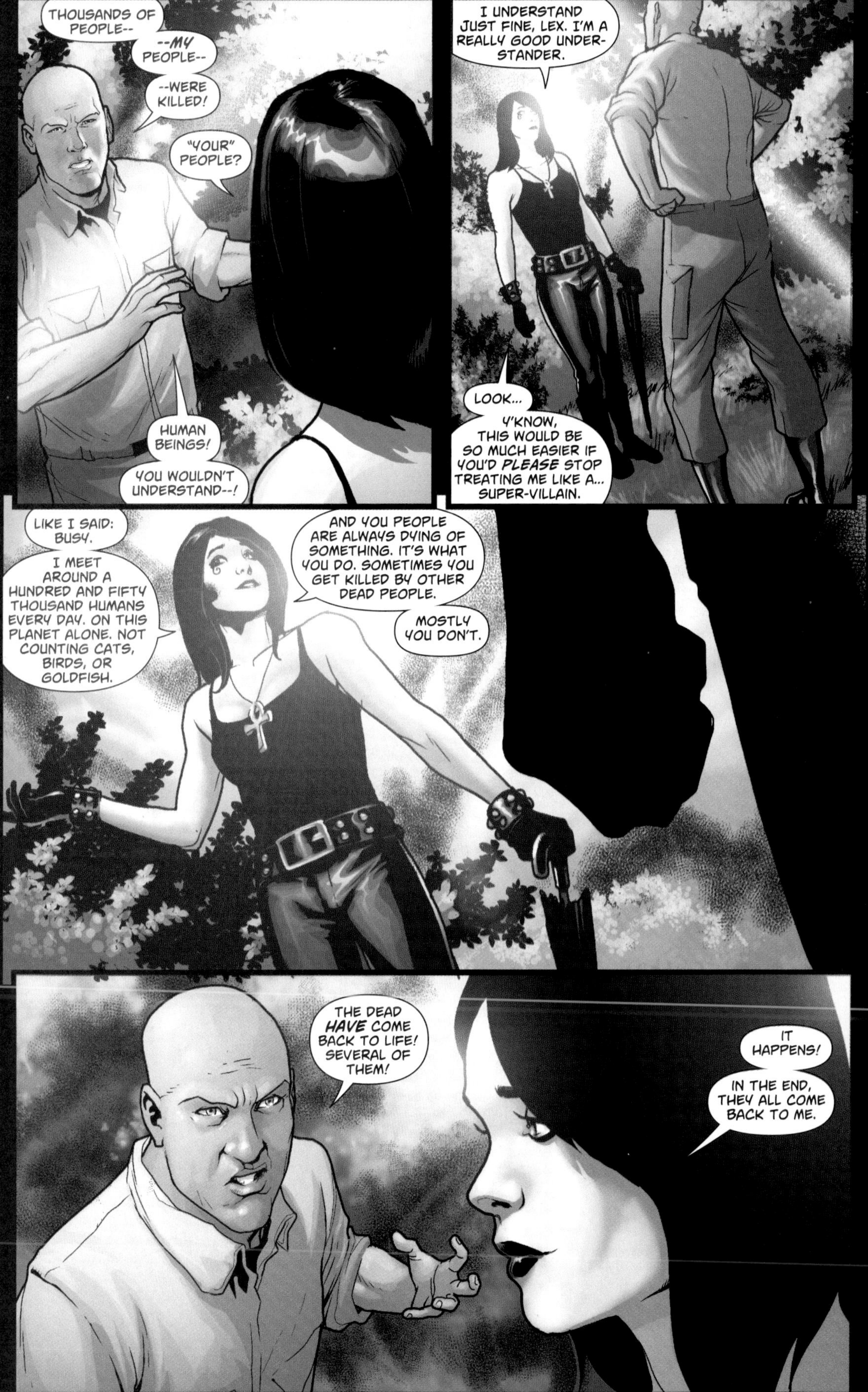
THOUSANDS OF PEOPLE--
--MY PEOPLE--
--WERE KILLED!
"YOUR" PEOPLE?
HUMAN BEINGS!
YOU WOULDN'T UNDERSTAND--!
I UNDERSTAND JUST FINE, LEX. I'M A REALLY GOOD UNDER-STANDER.
LOOK...
Y'KNOW, THIS WOULD BE SO MUCH EASIER IF YOU'D PLEASE STOP TREATING ME LIKE A... SUPER-VILLAIN.
LIKE I SAID: BUSY.
I MEET AROUND A HUNDRED AND FIFTY THOUSAND HUMANS EVERY DAY. ON THIS PLANET ALONE. NOT COUNTING CATS, BIRDS, OR GOLDFISH.
AND YOU PEOPLE ARE ALWAYS DYING OF SOMETHING. IT'S WHAT YOU DO. SOMETIMES YOU GET KILLED BY OTHER DEAD PEOPLE.
MOSTLY YOU DON'T.
THE DEAD HAVE COME BACK TO LIFE! SEVERAL OF THEM!
IT HAPPENS!
IN THE END, THEY ALL COME BACK TO ME.

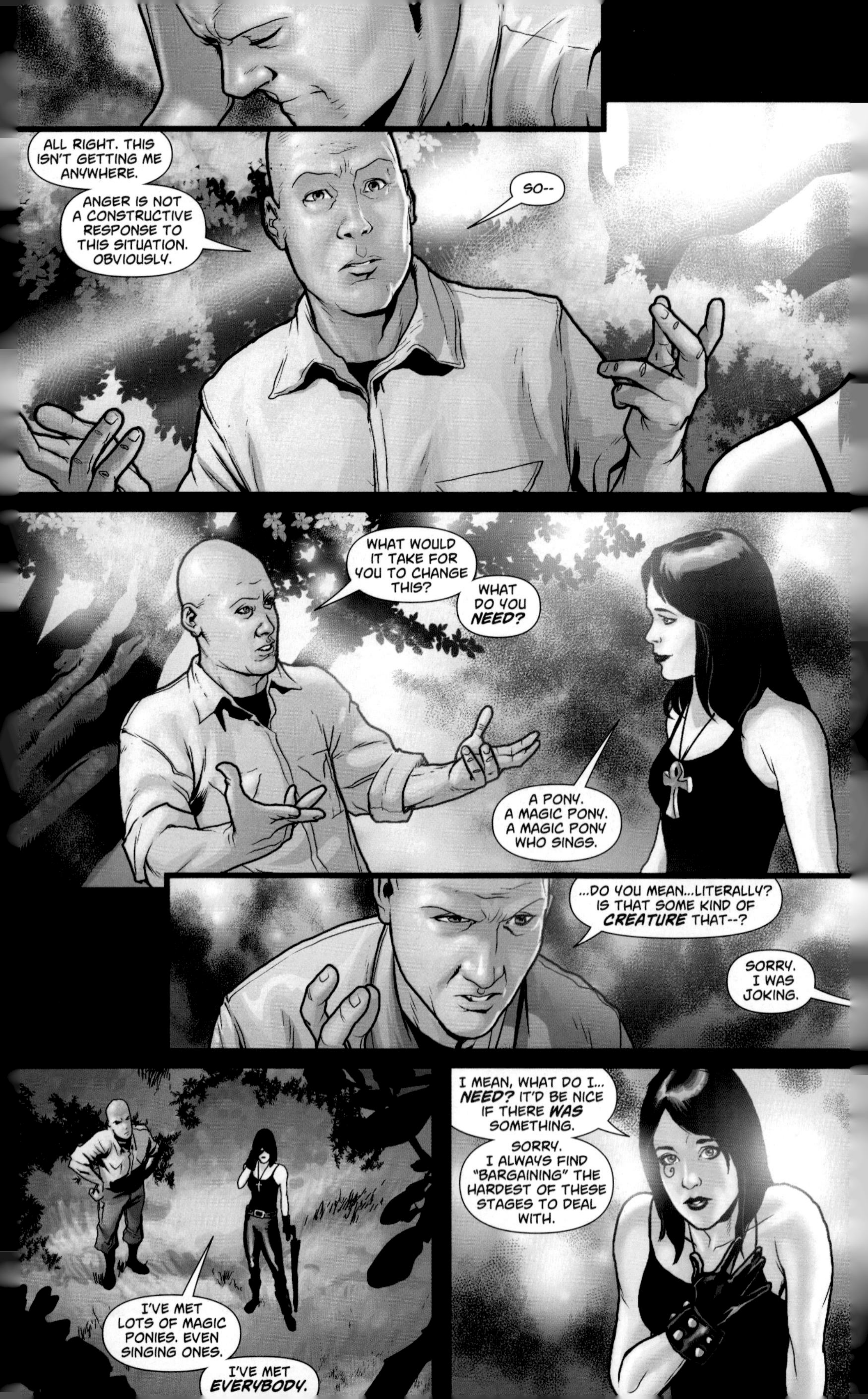
ALL RIGHT. THIS ISN'T GETTING ME ANYWHERE.
ANGER IS NOT A CONSTRUCTIVE RESPONSE TO THIS SITUATION. OBVIOUSLY.
SO--
WHAT WOULD IT TAKE FOR YOU TO CHANGE THIS?
WHAT DO YOU NEED?
A PONY. A MAGIC PONY. A MAGIC PONY WHO SINGS.
...DO YOU MEAN...LITERALLY? IS THAT SOME KIND OF CREATURE THAT--?
SORRY. I WAS JOKING.
I'VE MET LOTS OF MAGIC PONIES. EVEN SINGING ONES.
I'VE MET EVERYBODY.
I MEAN, WHAT DO I... NEED? IT'D BE NICE IF THERE WAS SOMETHING.
SORRY. I ALWAYS FIND "BARGAINING" THE HARDEST OF THESE STAGES TO DEAL WITH.

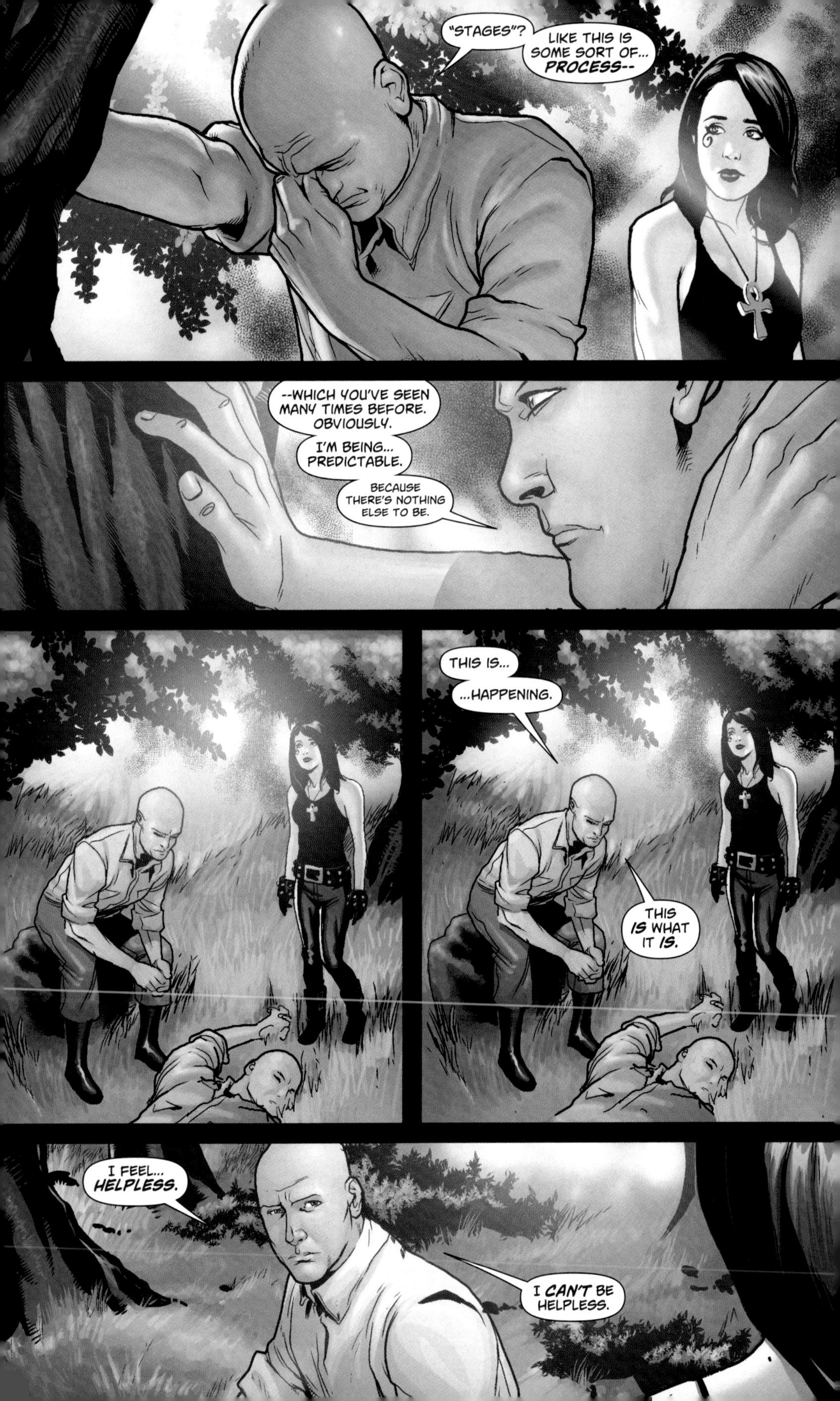
"STAGES"?
LIKE THIS IS SOME SORT OF... PROCESS--
--WHICH YOU'VE SEEN MANY TIMES BEFORE. OBVIOUSLY.
I'M BEING... PREDICTABLE.
BECAUSE THERE'S NOTHING ELSE TO BE.
THIS IS...
...HAPPENING.
THIS IS WHAT IT IS.
I FEEL... HELPLESS.
I CAN'T BE HELPLESS.

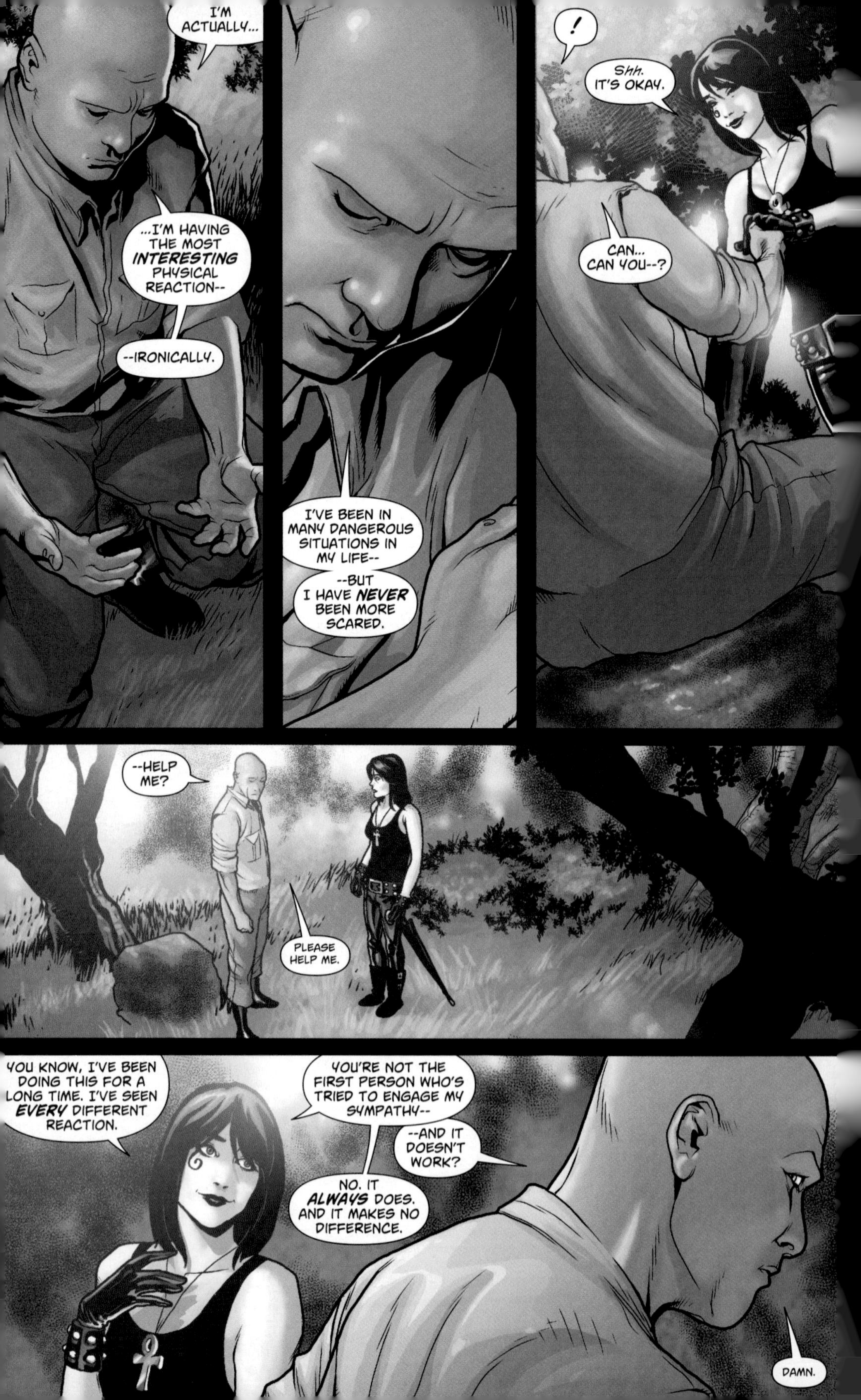
I'M ACTUALLY...
...I'M HAVING THE MOST *INTERESTING* PHYSICAL REACTION--
--IRONICALLY.
I'VE BEEN IN MANY DANGEROUS SITUATIONS IN MY LIFE--
--BUT I HAVE *NEVER* BEEN MORE SCARED.
!
Shh. IT'S OKAY.
CAN... CAN YOU--?
--HELP ME?
PLEASE HELP ME.
YOU KNOW, I'VE BEEN DOING THIS FOR A LONG TIME. I'VE SEEN *EVERY* DIFFERENT REACTION.
YOU'RE NOT THE FIRST PERSON WHO'S TRIED TO ENGAGE MY SYMPATHY--
--AND IT DOESN'T WORK?
NO. IT *ALWAYS* DOES. AND IT MAKES NO DIFFERENCE.
DAMN.

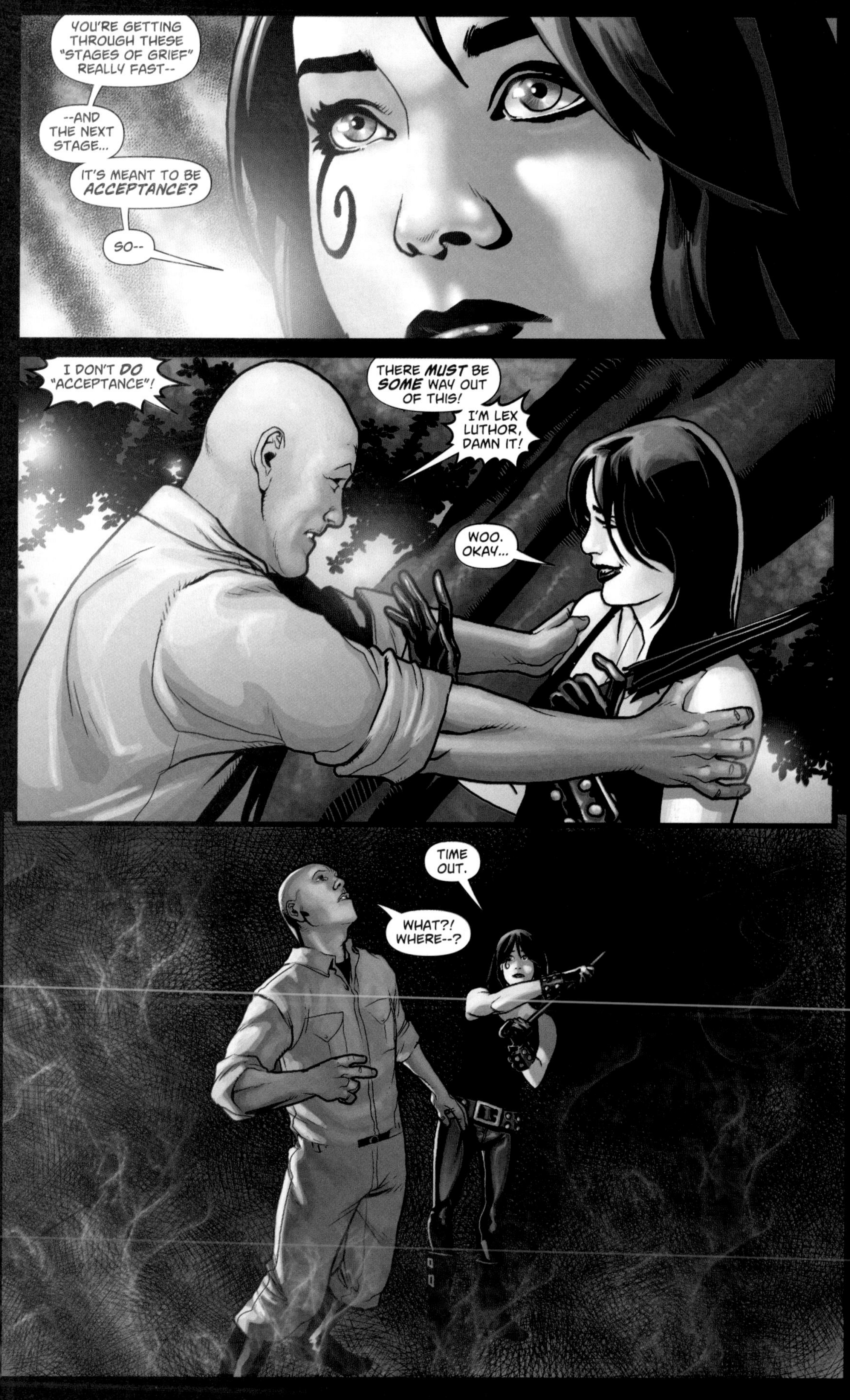
YOU'RE GETTING THROUGH THESE "STAGES OF GRIEF" REALLY FAST--
--AND THE NEXT STAGE...
IT'S MEANT TO BE ACCEPTANCE?
SO--
I DON'T DO "ACCEPTANCE"!
THERE MUST BE SOME WAY OUT OF THIS!
I'M LEX LUTHOR, DAMN IT!
WOO. OKAY...
TIME OUT.
WHAT?! WHERE--?

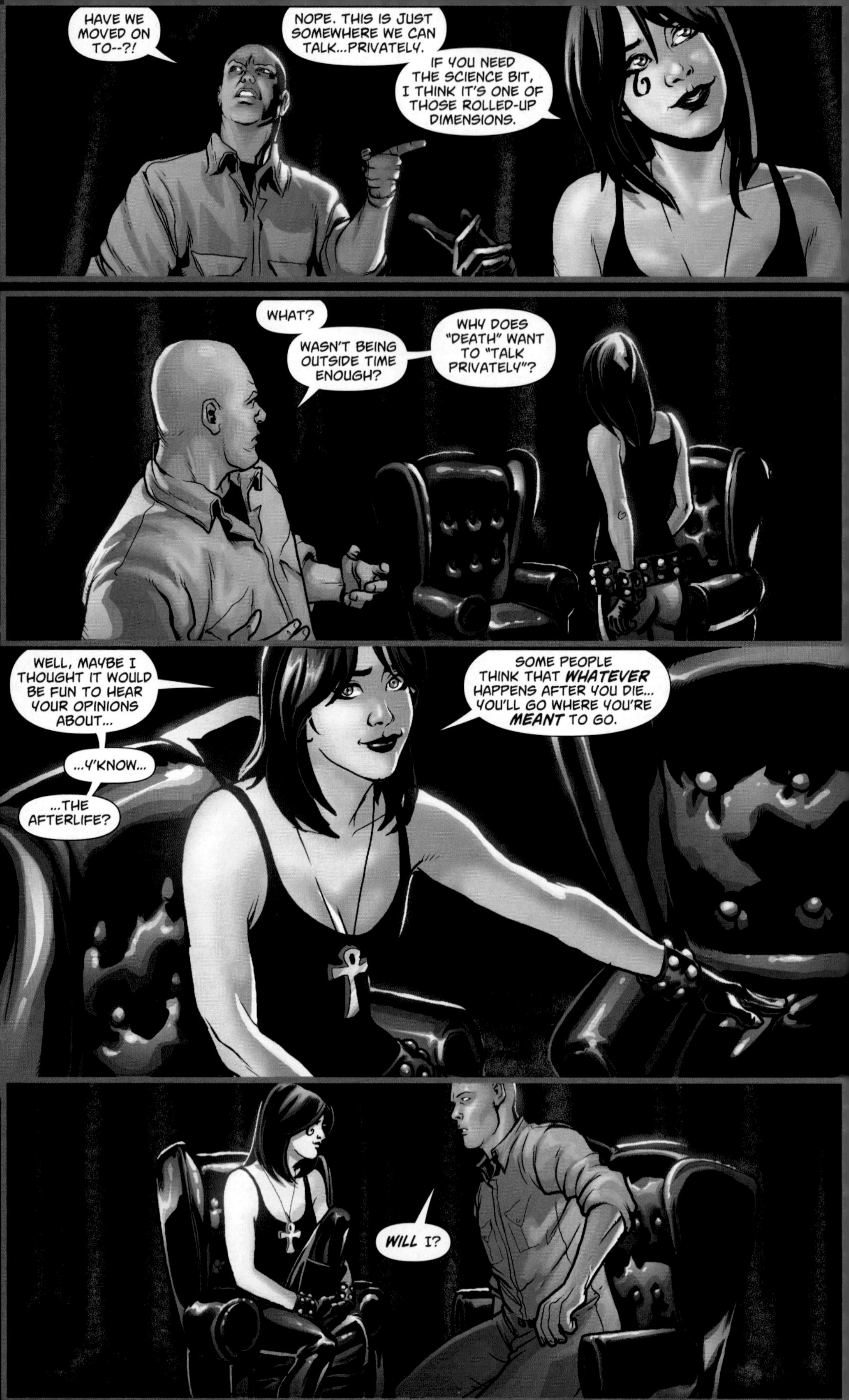

HAVE WE MOVED ON TO--?!
NOPE. THIS IS JUST SOMEWHERE WE CAN TALK...PRIVATELY.
IF YOU NEED THE SCIENCE BIT, I THINK IT'S ONE OF THOSE ROLLED-UP DIMENSIONS.
WHAT?
WASN'T BEING OUTSIDE TIME ENOUGH?
WHY DOES "DEATH" WANT TO "TALK PRIVATELY"?
WELL, MAYBE I THOUGHT IT WOULD BE FUN TO HEAR YOUR OPINIONS ABOUT...
...Y'KNOW...
...THE AFTERLIFE?
SOME PEOPLE THINK THAT WHATEVER HAPPENS AFTER YOU DIE... YOU'LL GO WHERE YOU'RE MEANT TO GO.
WILL I?

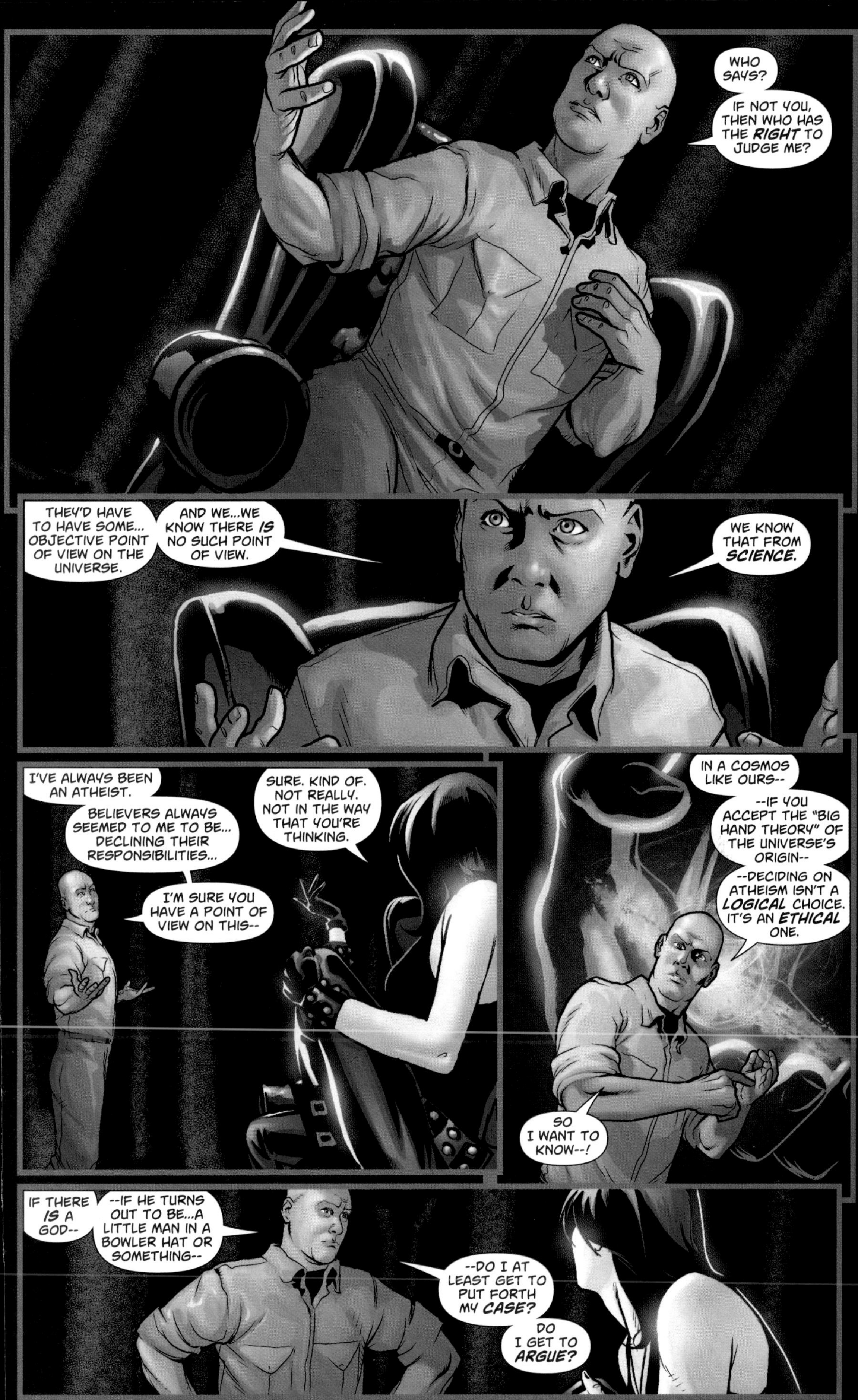
WHO SAYS?
IF NOT YOU, THEN WHO HAS THE **RIGHT** TO JUDGE ME?
THEY'D HAVE TO HAVE SOME... OBJECTIVE POINT OF VIEW ON THE UNIVERSE.
AND WE...WE KNOW THERE ***IS*** NO SUCH POINT OF VIEW.
WE KNOW THAT FROM **SCIENCE.**
I'VE ALWAYS BEEN AN ATHEIST.
BELIEVERS ALWAYS SEEMED TO ME TO BE... DECLINING THEIR RESPONSIBILITIES...
I'M SURE YOU HAVE A POINT OF VIEW ON THIS--
SURE. KIND OF. NOT REALLY. NOT IN THE WAY THAT YOU'RE THINKING.
IN A COSMOS LIKE OURS--
--IF YOU ACCEPT THE "BIG HAND THEORY" OF THE UNIVERSE'S ORIGIN--
--DECIDING ON ATHEISM ISN'T A ***LOGICAL*** CHOICE. IT'S AN ***ETHICAL*** ONE.
SO I WANT TO KNOW--!
IF THERE ***IS*** A GOD--
--IF HE TURNS OUT TO BE...A LITTLE MAN IN A BOWLER HAT OR SOMETHING--
--DO I AT LEAST GET TO PUT FORTH MY ***CASE?***
DO I GET TO ***ARGUE?***

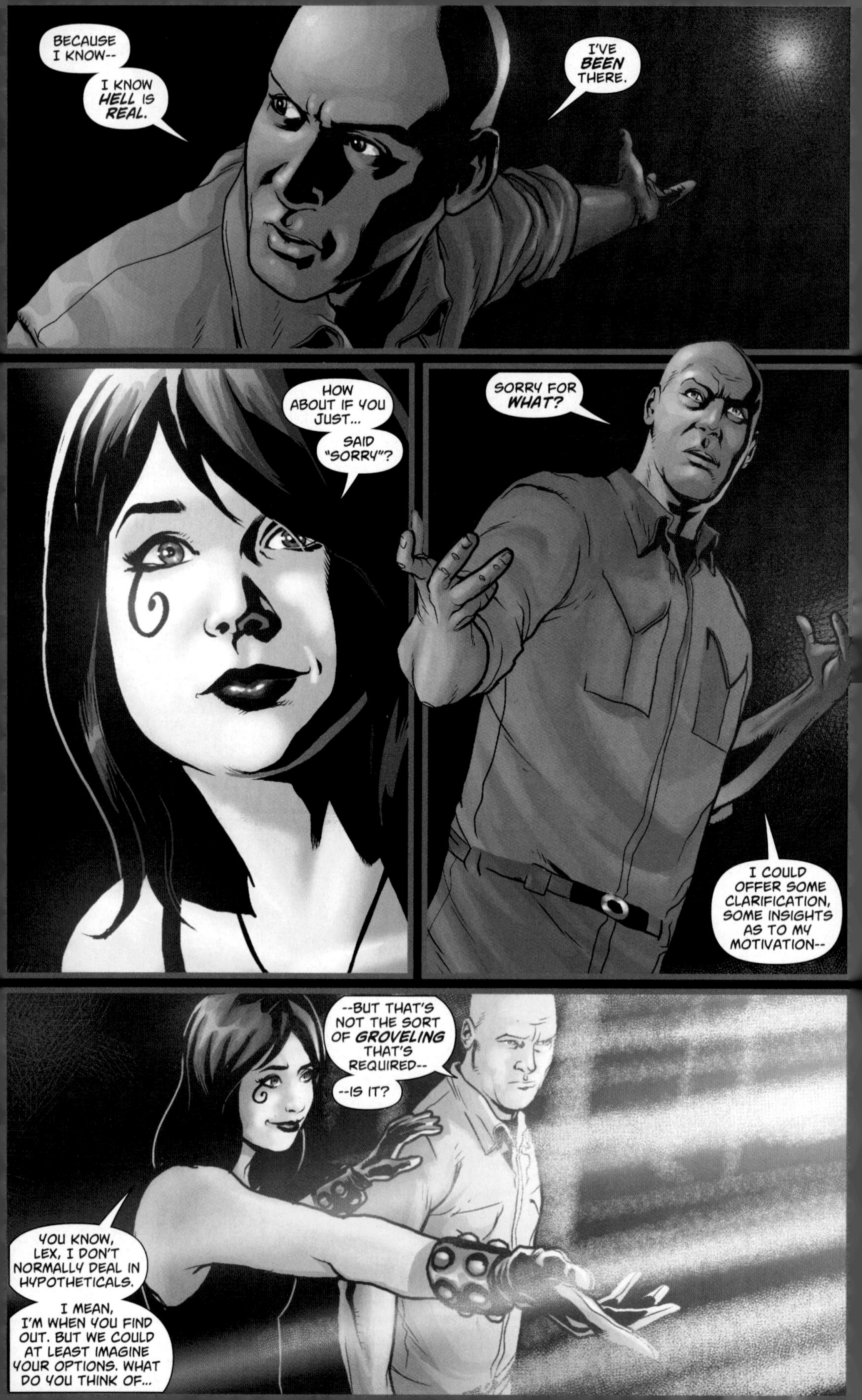
BECAUSE I KNOW--
I KNOW HELL IS REAL.
I'VE BEEN THERE.
HOW ABOUT IF YOU JUST...
SAID "SORRY"?
SORRY FOR WHAT?
I COULD OFFER SOME CLARIFICATION, SOME INSIGHTS AS TO MY MOTIVATION--
--BUT THAT'S NOT THE SORT OF GROVELING THAT'S REQUIRED--
--IS IT?
YOU KNOW, LEX, I DON'T NORMALLY DEAL IN HYPOTHETICALS.
I MEAN, I'M WHEN YOU FIND OUT. BUT WE COULD AT LEAST IMAGINE YOUR OPTIONS. WHAT DO YOU THINK OF...

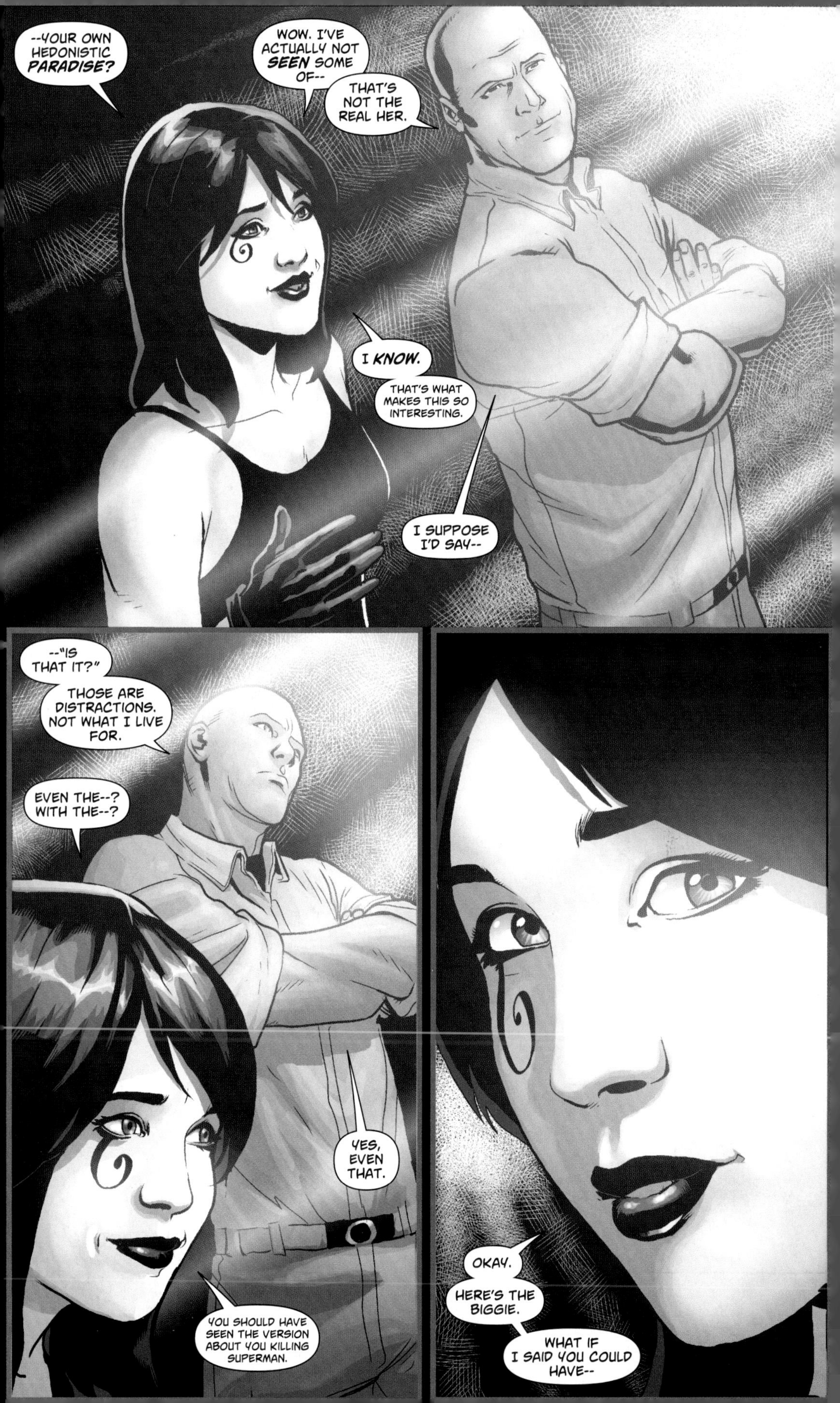
--YOUR OWN HEDONISTIC PARADISE?
WOW. I'VE ACTUALLY NOT SEEN SOME OF--
THAT'S NOT THE REAL HER.
I KNOW.
THAT'S WHAT MAKES THIS SO INTERESTING.
I SUPPOSE I'D SAY--
--"IS THAT IT?"
THOSE ARE DISTRACTIONS. NOT WHAT I LIVE FOR.
EVEN THE--? WITH THE--?
YES, EVEN THAT.
YOU SHOULD HAVE SEEN THE VERSION ABOUT YOU KILLING SUPERMAN.
OKAY.
HERE'S THE BIGGIE.
WHAT IF I SAID YOU COULD HAVE--

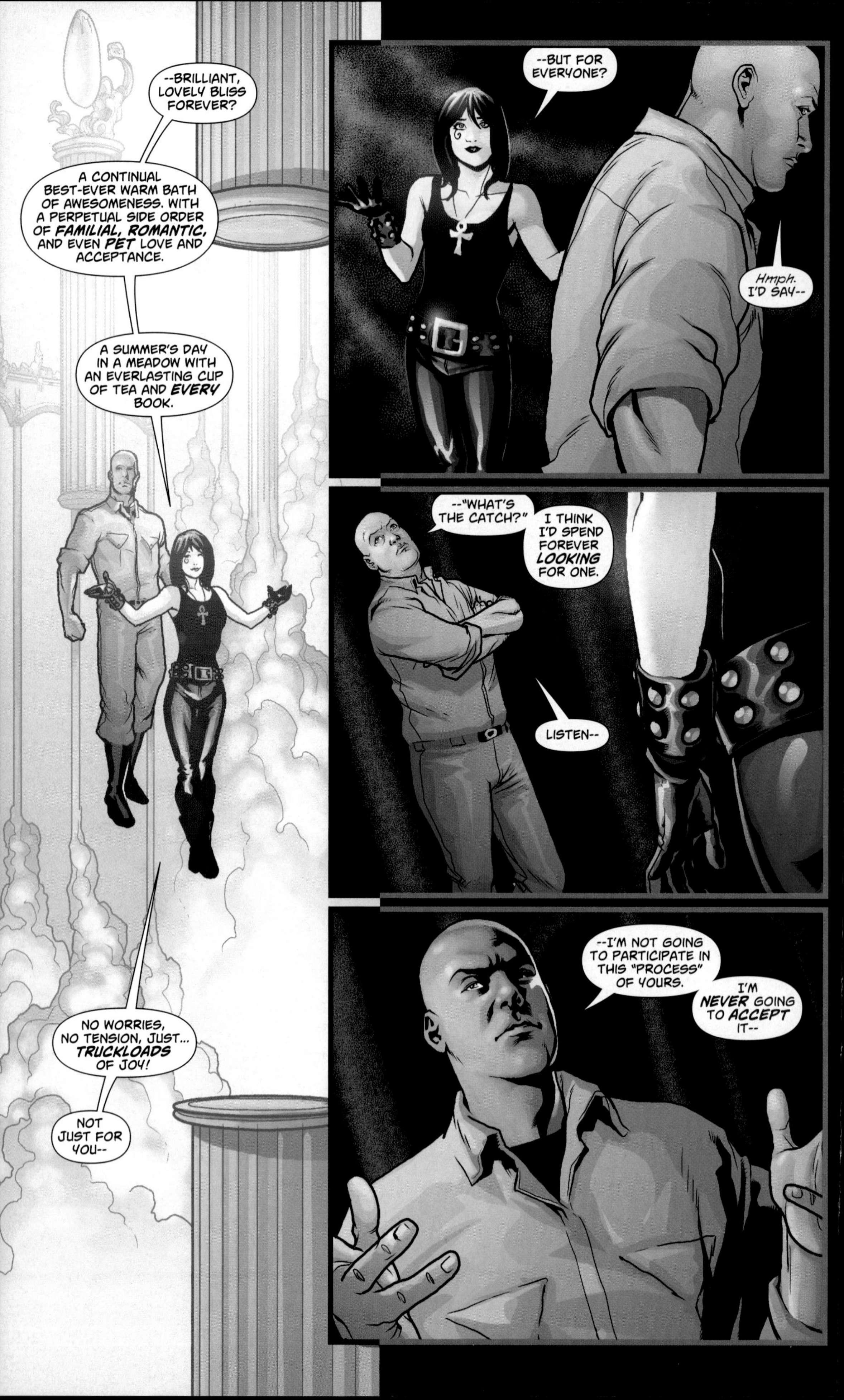
--BRILLIANT, LOVELY BLISS FOREVER?
A CONTINUAL BEST-EVER WARM BATH OF AWESOMENESS. WITH A PERPETUAL SIDE ORDER OF FAMILIAL, ROMANTIC, AND EVEN PET LOVE AND ACCEPTANCE.
A SUMMER'S DAY IN A MEADOW WITH AN EVERLASTING CUP OF TEA AND EVERY BOOK.
NO WORRIES, NO TENSION, JUST... TRUCKLOADS OF JOY!
NOT JUST FOR YOU--
--BUT FOR EVERYONE?
Hmph. I'D SAY--
--"WHAT'S THE CATCH?"
I THINK I'D SPEND FOREVER LOOKING FOR ONE.
LISTEN--
--I'M NOT GOING TO PARTICIPATE IN THIS "PROCESS" OF YOURS.
I'M NEVER GOING TO ACCEPT IT--

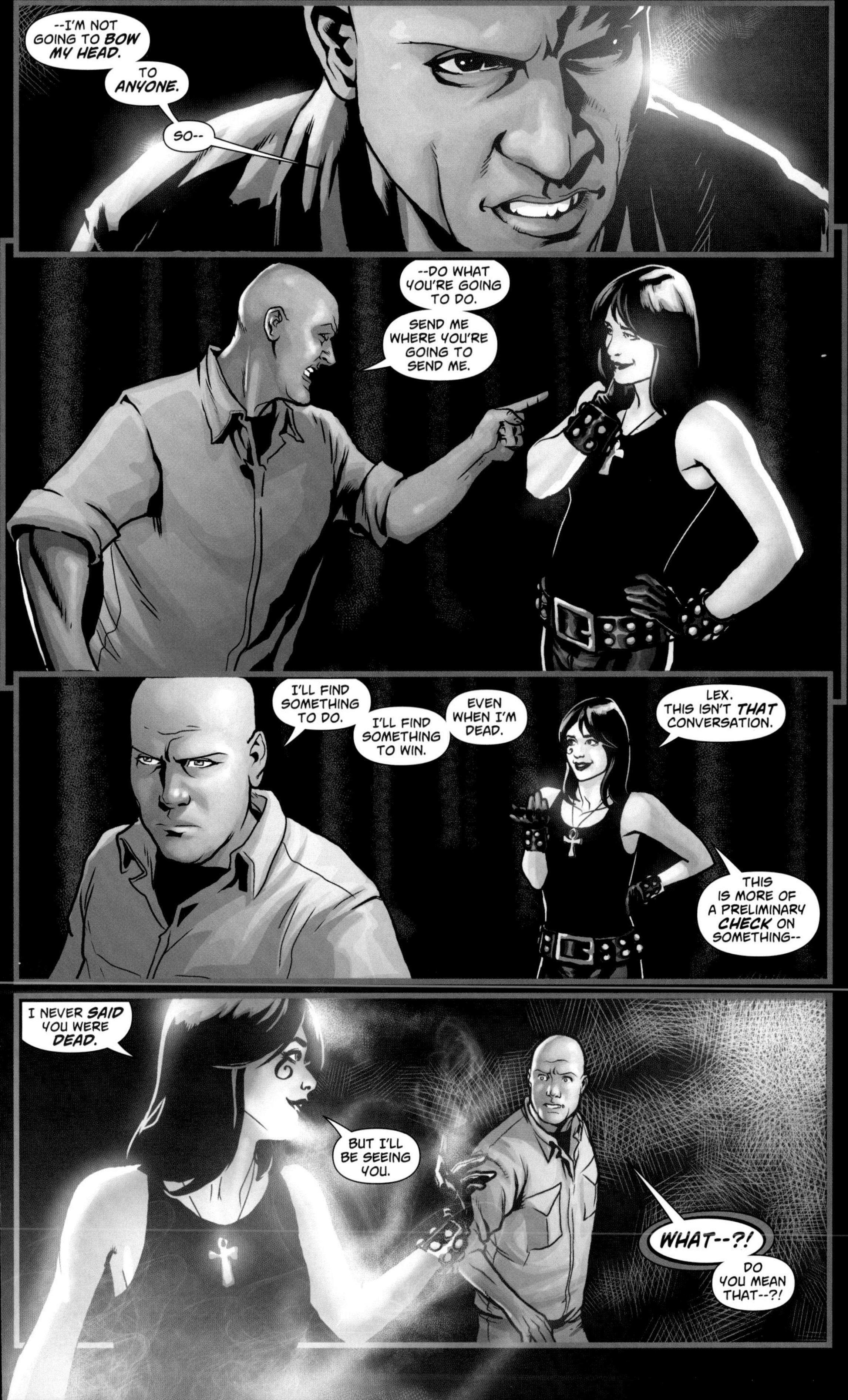
--I'M NOT GOING TO BOW MY HEAD.
TO ANYONE.
SO--
--DO WHAT YOU'RE GOING TO DO.
SEND ME WHERE YOU'RE GOING TO SEND ME.
I'LL FIND SOMETHING TO DO.
I'LL FIND SOMETHING TO WIN.
EVEN WHEN I'M DEAD.
LEX. THIS ISN'T THAT CONVERSATION.
THIS IS MORE OF A PRELIMINARY CHECK ON SOMETHING--
I NEVER SAID YOU WERE DEAD.
BUT I'LL BE SEEING YOU.
WHAT--?!
DO YOU MEAN THAT--?!

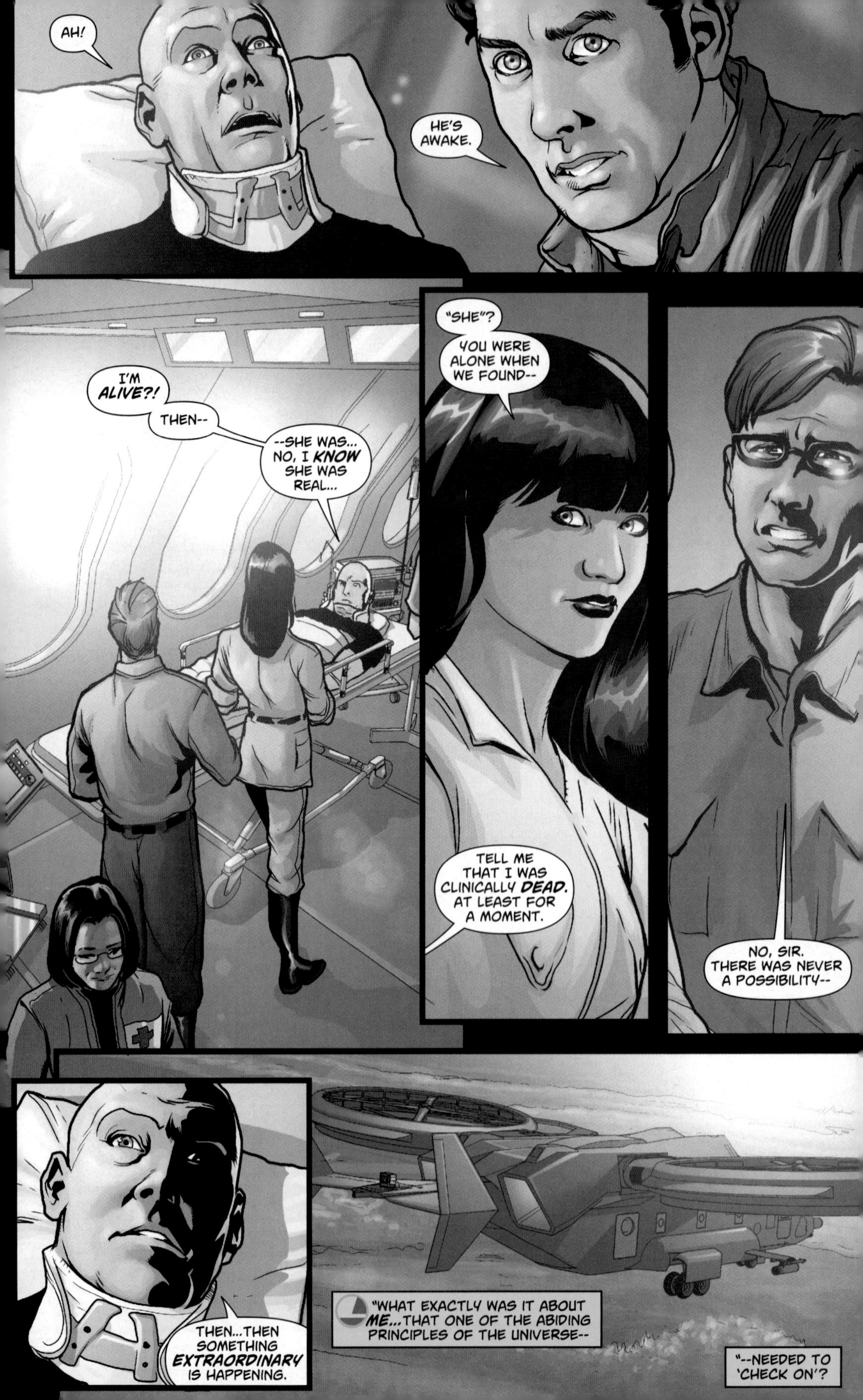
AH!
HE'S AWAKE.
I'M *ALIVE?!*
THEN--
--SHE WAS... NO, I *KNOW* SHE WAS REAL...
"SHE"?
YOU WERE ALONE WHEN WE FOUND--
TELL ME THAT I WAS CLINICALLY *DEAD.* AT LEAST FOR A MOMENT.
NO, SIR. THERE WAS NEVER A POSSIBILITY--
THEN...THEN SOMETHING *EXTRAORDINARY* IS HAPPENING.
"WHAT EXACTLY WAS IT ABOUT *ME...*THAT ONE OF THE ABIDING PRINCIPLES OF THE UNIVERSE--
"--NEEDED TO 'CHECK ON'?

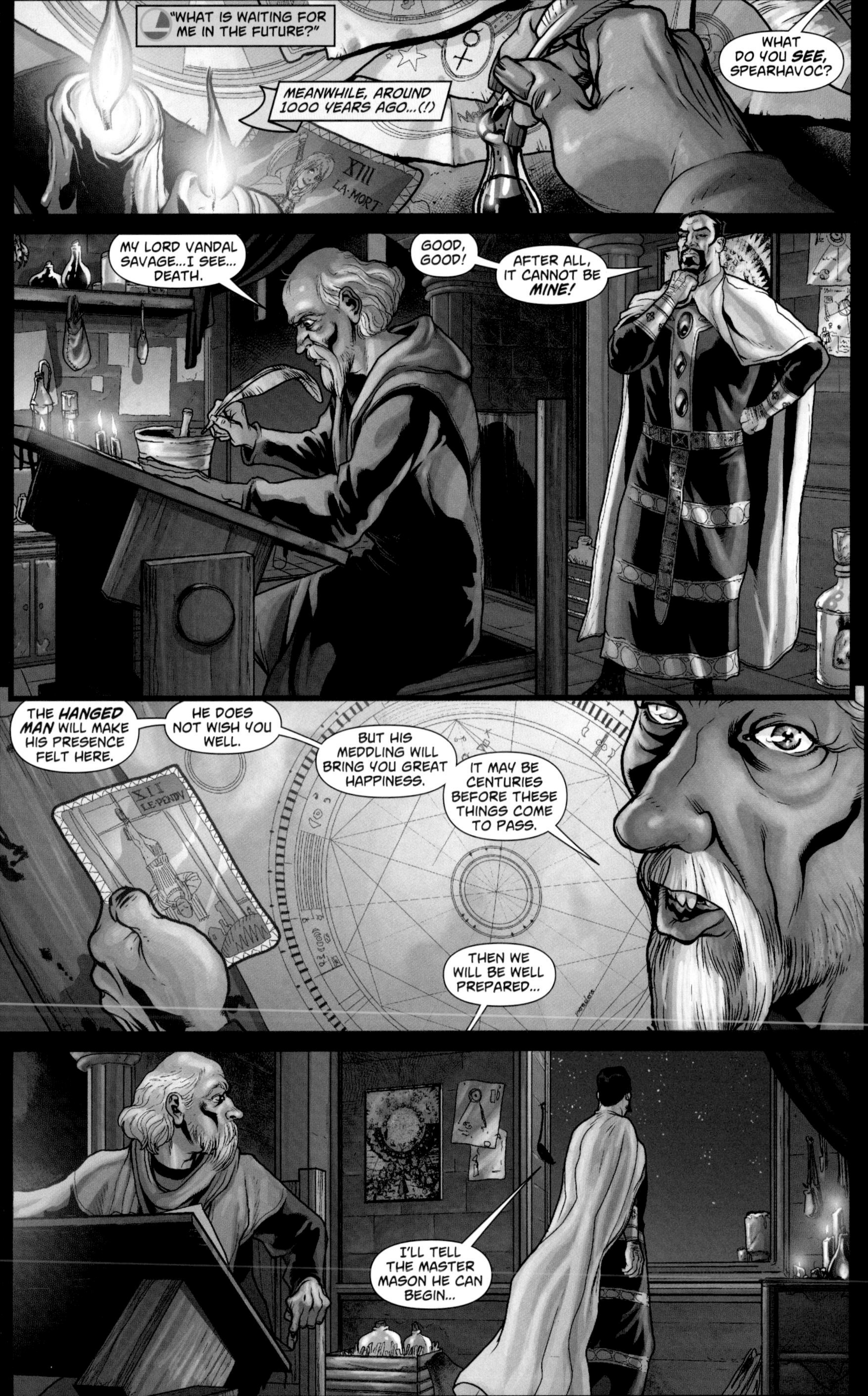
"WHAT IS WAITING FOR ME IN THE FUTURE?"
WHAT DO YOU **SEE,** SPEARHAVOC?
MEANWHILE, AROUND 1000 YEARS AGO...(!)
XIII LA·MORT
MY LORD VANDAL SAVAGE...I SEE... DEATH.
GOOD, GOOD!
AFTER ALL, IT CANNOT BE ***MINE!***
THE ***HANGED MAN*** WILL MAKE HIS PRESENCE FELT HERE.
HE DOES NOT WISH YOU WELL.
BUT HIS MEDDLING WILL BRING YOU GREAT HAPPINESS.
IT MAY BE CENTURIES BEFORE THESE THINGS COME TO PASS.
XII LE·PENDV
THEN WE WILL BE WELL PREPARED...
I'LL TELL THE MASTER MASON HE CAN BEGIN...

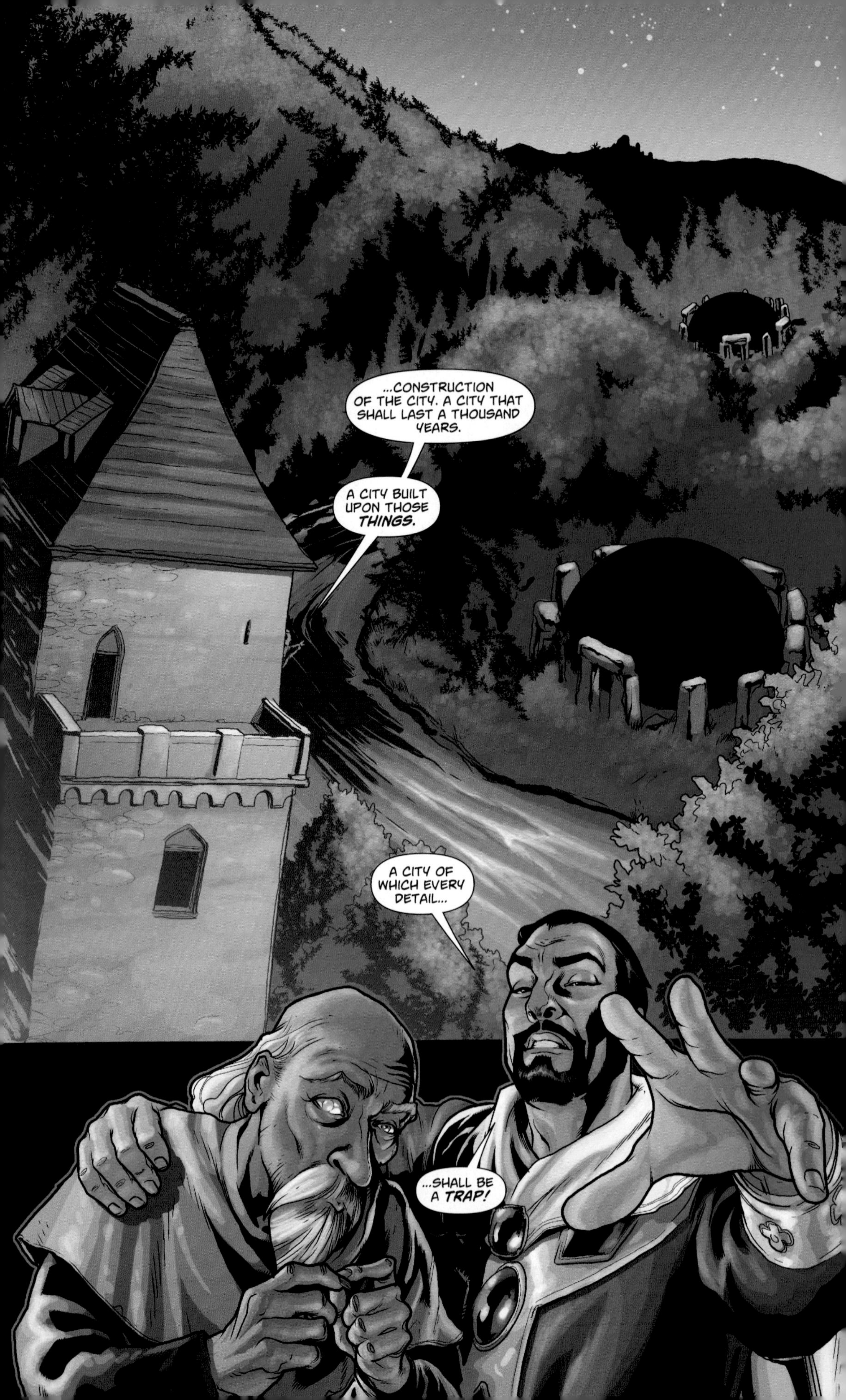
...CONSTRUCTION OF THE CITY. A CITY THAT SHALL LAST A THOUSAND YEARS.
A CITY BUILT UPON THOSE *THINGS.*
A CITY OF WHICH EVERY DETAIL...
...SHALL BE A *TRAP!*

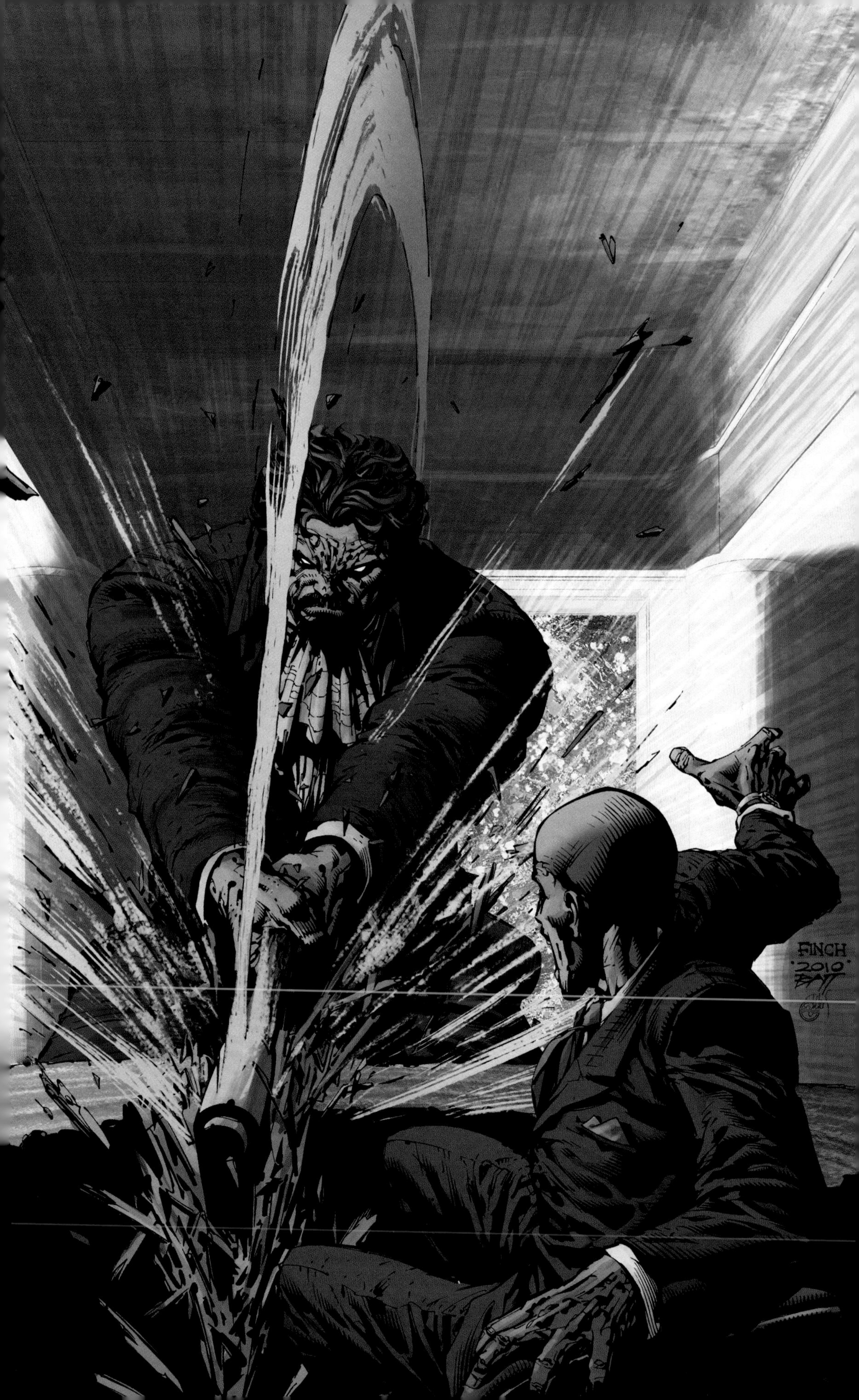
FINCH
2010
BATT

THE BLACK RING
part six

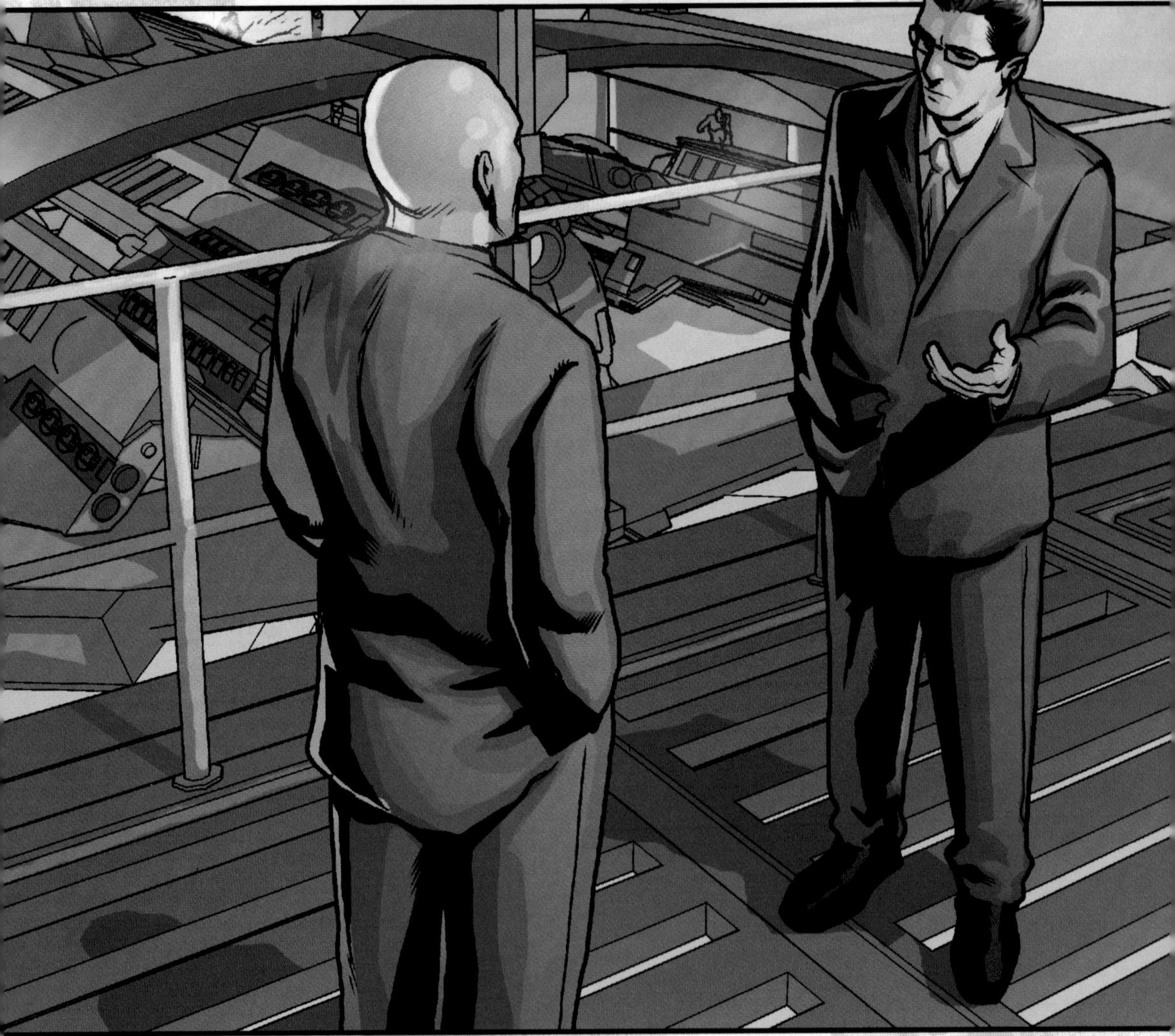

cover by
DAVID **FINCH, BATT** & PETER **STEIGERWALD**

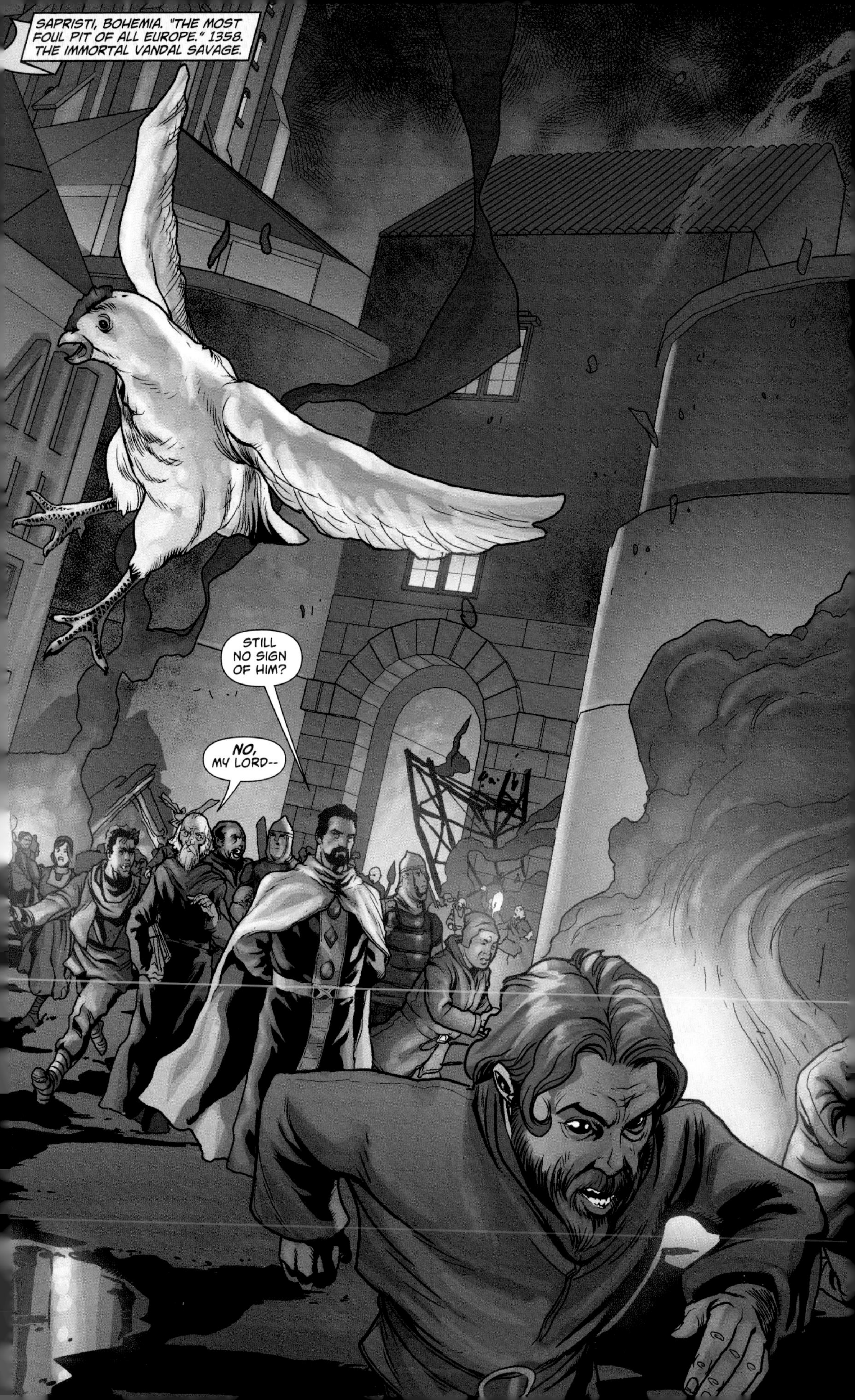

SAPRISTI, BOHEMIA. "THE MOST FOUL PIT OF ALL EUROPE." 1358. THE IMMORTAL VANDAL SAVAGE.
STILL NO SIGN OF HIM?
NO, MY LORD--

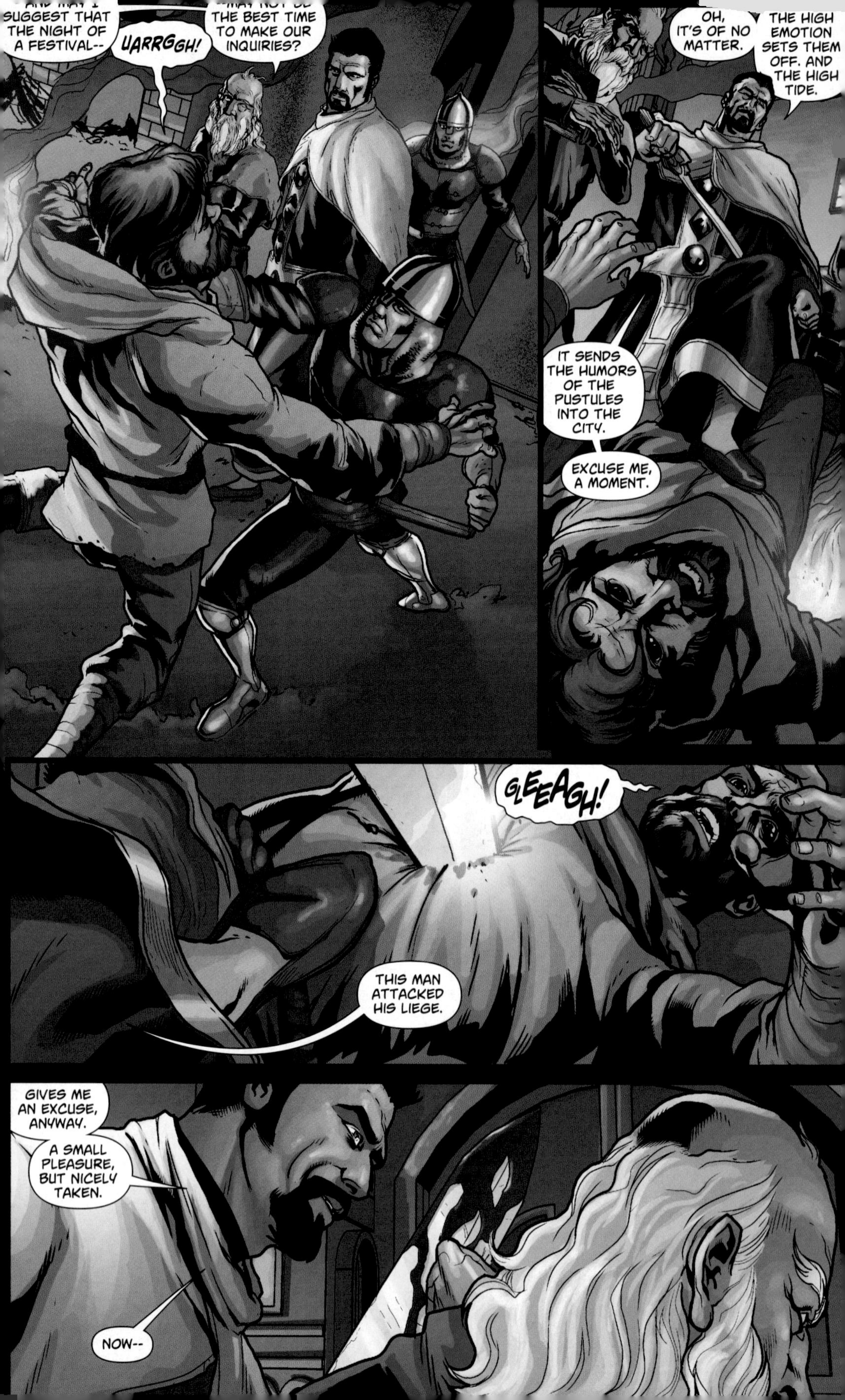
SUGGEST THAT THE NIGHT OF A FESTIVAL--
UARRGGH!
THE BEST TIME TO MAKE OUR INQUIRIES?
OH, IT'S OF NO MATTER.
THE HIGH EMOTION SETS THEM OFF. AND THE HIGH TIDE.
IT SENDS THE HUMORS OF THE PUSTULES INTO THE CITY.
EXCUSE ME, A MOMENT.
GLEEAGH!
THIS MAN ATTACKED HIS LIEGE.
GIVES ME AN EXCUSE, ANYWAY.
A SMALL PLEASURE, BUT NICELY TAKEN.
NOW--

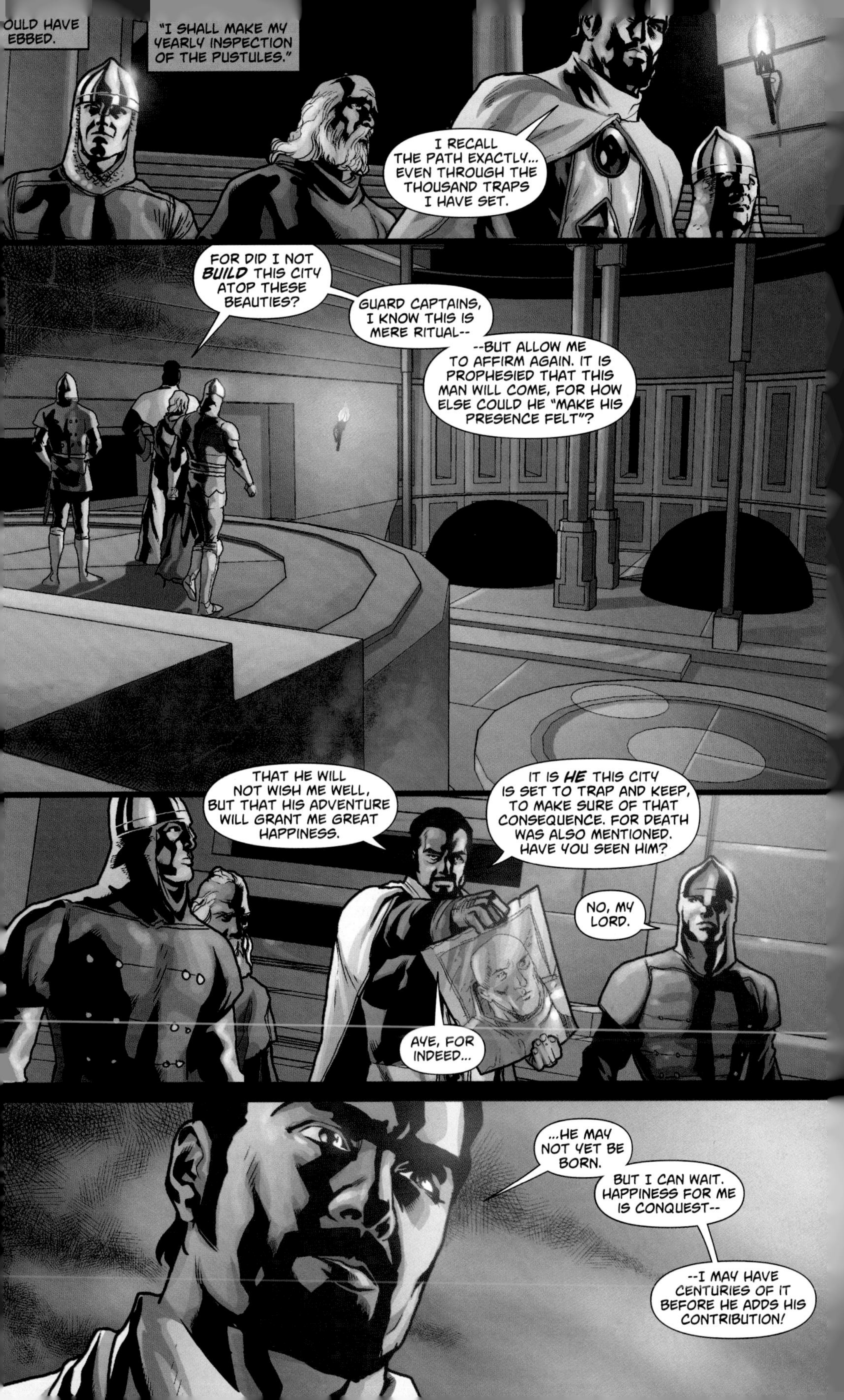
OULD HAVE EBBED.
"I SHALL MAKE MY YEARLY INSPECTION OF THE PUSTULES."
I RECALL THE PATH EXACTLY... EVEN THROUGH THE THOUSAND TRAPS I HAVE SET.
FOR DID I NOT BUILD THIS CITY ATOP THESE BEAUTIES?
GUARD CAPTAINS, I KNOW THIS IS MERE RITUAL--
--BUT ALLOW ME TO AFFIRM AGAIN. IT IS PROPHESIED THAT THIS MAN WILL COME, FOR HOW ELSE COULD HE "MAKE HIS PRESENCE FELT"?
THAT HE WILL NOT WISH ME WELL, BUT THAT HIS ADVENTURE WILL GRANT ME GREAT HAPPINESS.
IT IS HE THIS CITY IS SET TO TRAP AND KEEP, TO MAKE SURE OF THAT CONSEQUENCE. FOR DEATH WAS ALSO MENTIONED. HAVE YOU SEEN HIM?
NO, MY LORD.
AYE, FOR INDEED...
...HE MAY NOT YET BE BORN.
BUT I CAN WAIT. HAPPINESS FOR ME IS CONQUEST--
--I MAY HAVE CENTURIES OF IT BEFORE HE ADDS HIS CONTRIBUTION!

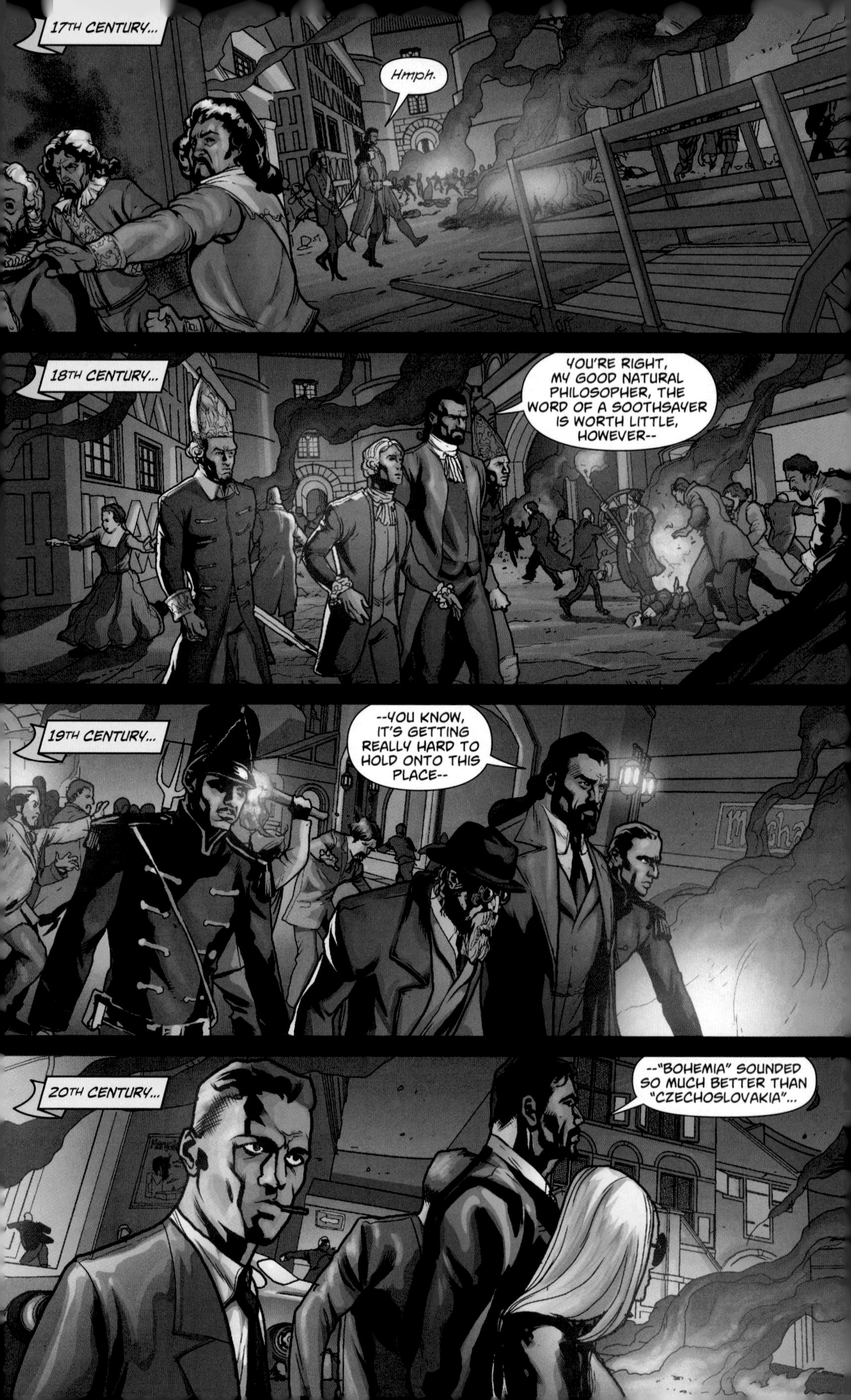
17TH CENTURY...
Hmph.
18TH CENTURY...
YOU'RE RIGHT, MY GOOD NATURAL PHILOSOPHER, THE WORD OF A SOOTHSAYER IS WORTH LITTLE, HOWEVER--
19TH CENTURY...
--YOU KNOW, IT'S GETTING REALLY HARD TO HOLD ONTO THIS PLACE--
20TH CENTURY...
--"BOHEMIA" SOUNDED SO MUCH BETTER THAN "CZECHOSLOVAKIA"...

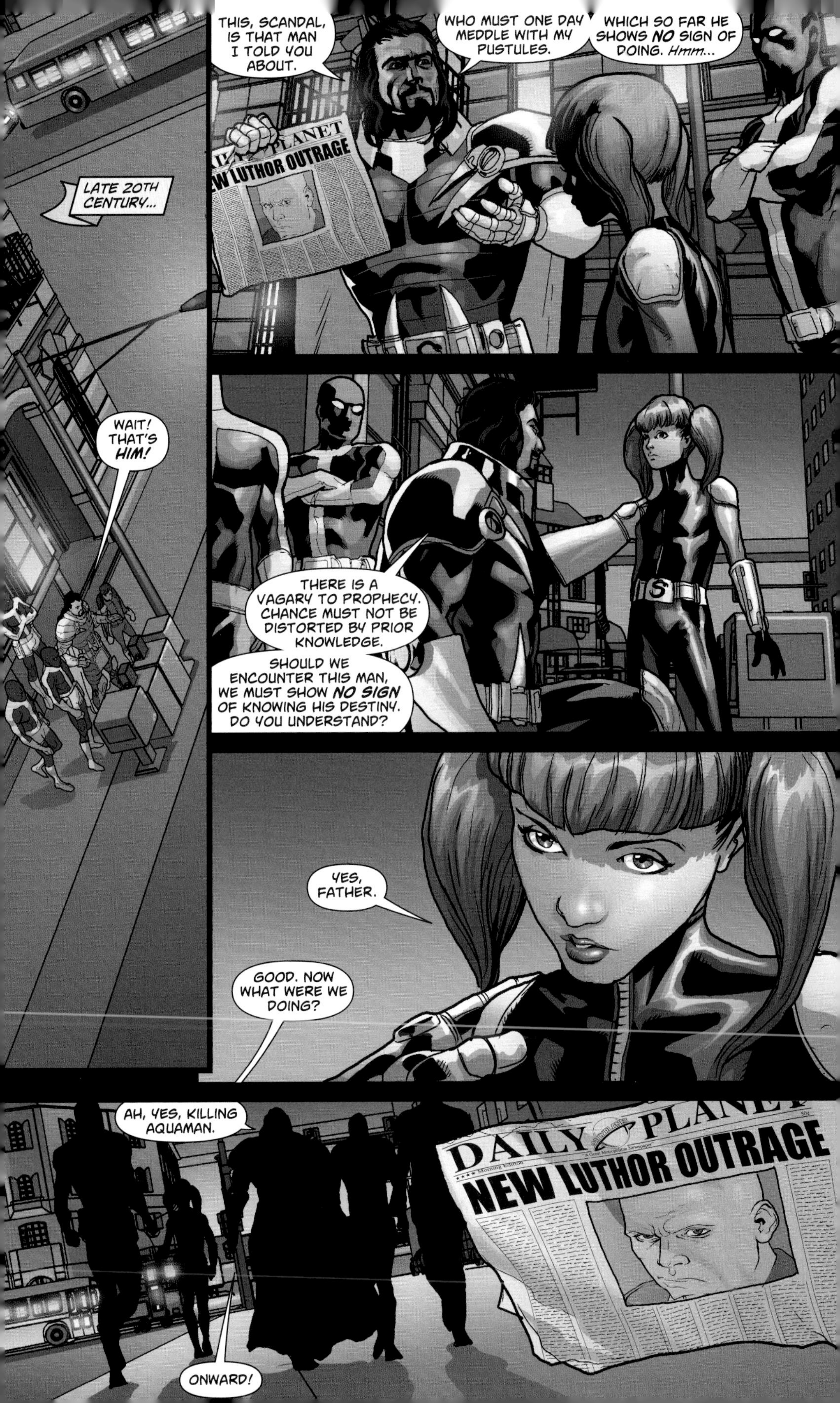
LATE 20TH CENTURY...
THIS, SCANDAL, IS THAT MAN I TOLD YOU ABOUT.
WHO MUST ONE DAY MEDDLE WITH MY PUSTULES.
WHICH SO FAR HE SHOWS NO SIGN OF DOING. Hmm...
NEW LUTHOR OUTRAGE
WAIT! THAT'S HIM!
THERE IS A VAGARY TO PROPHECY. CHANCE MUST NOT BE DISTORTED BY PRIOR KNOWLEDGE.
SHOULD WE ENCOUNTER THIS MAN, WE MUST SHOW NO SIGN OF KNOWING HIS DESTINY. DO YOU UNDERSTAND?
YES, FATHER.
GOOD. NOW WHAT WERE WE DOING?
AH, YES, KILLING AQUAMAN.
DAILY PLANET
NEW LUTHOR OUTRAGE
ONWARD!

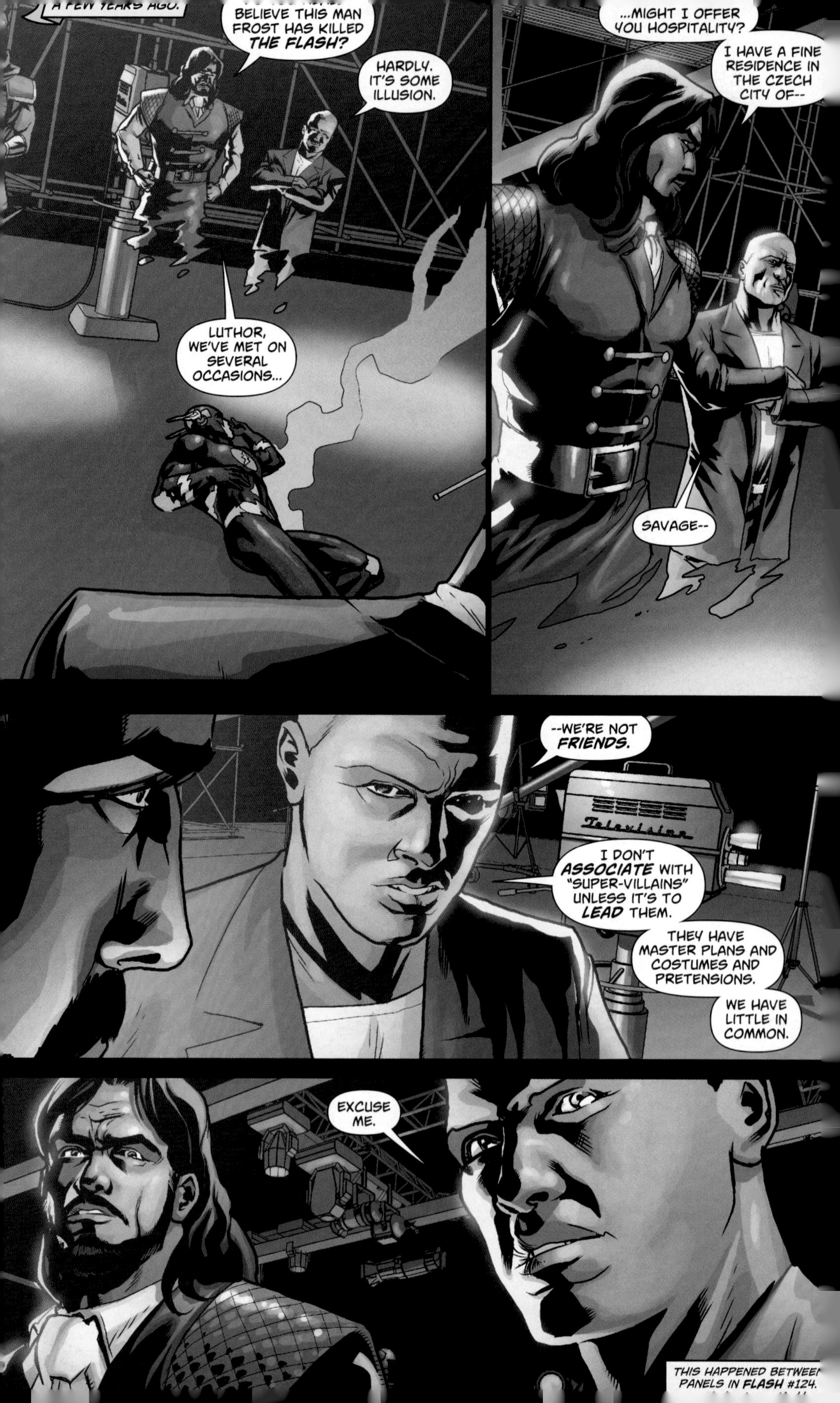
A FEW YEARS AGO.
BELIEVE THIS MAN FROST HAS KILLED THE FLASH?
HARDLY. IT'S SOME ILLUSION.
LUTHOR, WE'VE MET ON SEVERAL OCCASIONS...
...MIGHT I OFFER YOU HOSPITALITY?
I HAVE A FINE RESIDENCE IN THE CZECH CITY OF--
SAVAGE--
--WE'RE NOT FRIENDS.
Television
I DON'T ASSOCIATE WITH "SUPER-VILLAINS" UNLESS IT'S TO LEAD THEM.
THEY HAVE MASTER PLANS AND COSTUMES AND PRETENSIONS.
WE HAVE LITTLE IN COMMON.
EXCUSE ME.
THIS HAPPENED BETWEEN PANELS IN FLASH #124.

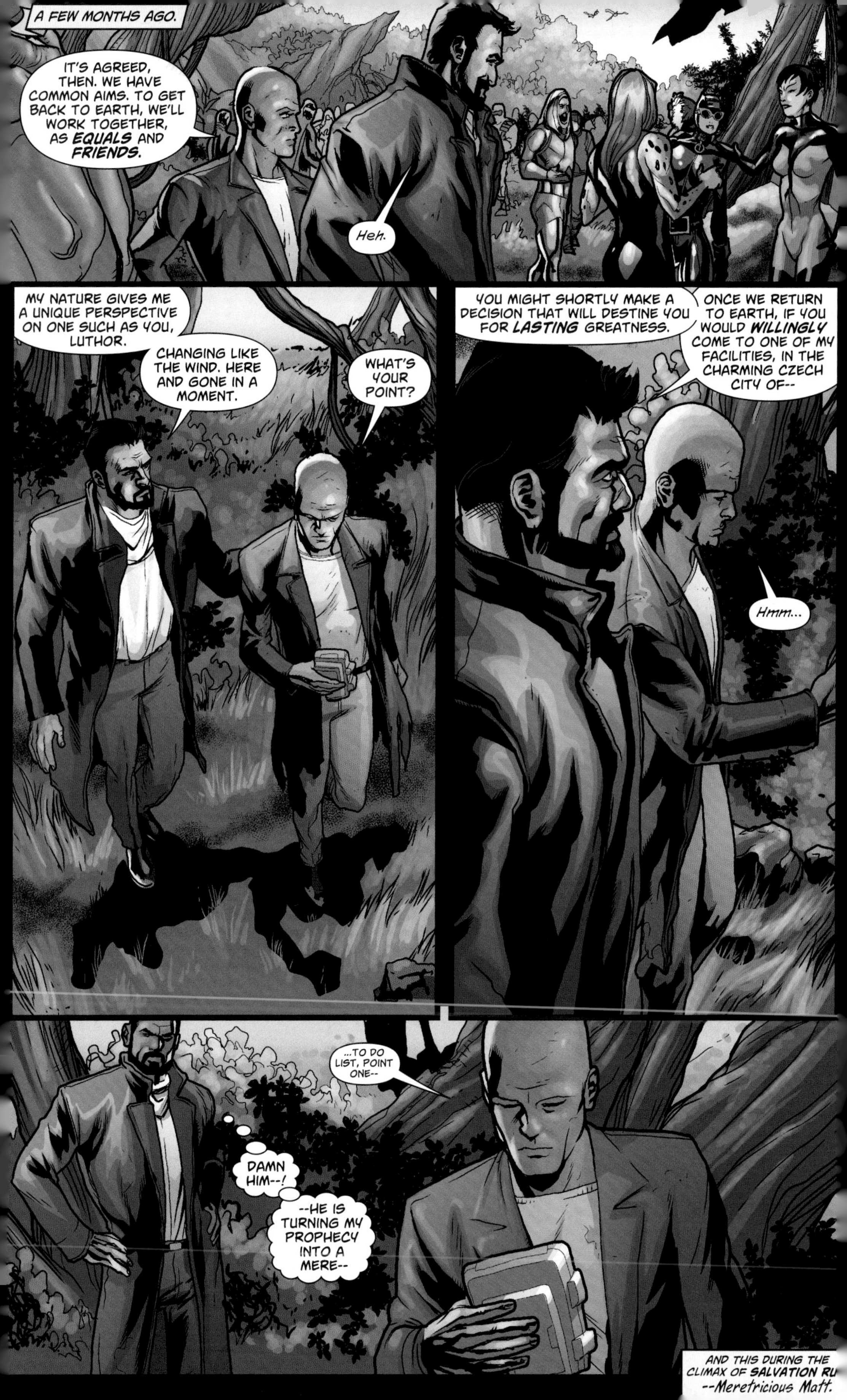

A FEW MONTHS AGO.
IT'S AGREED, THEN. WE HAVE COMMON AIMS. TO GET BACK TO EARTH, WE'LL WORK TOGETHER, AS **EQUALS** AND **FRIENDS**.
Heh.
MY NATURE GIVES ME A UNIQUE PERSPECTIVE ON ONE SUCH AS YOU, LUTHOR.
CHANGING LIKE THE WIND. HERE AND GONE IN A MOMENT.
WHAT'S YOUR POINT?
YOU MIGHT SHORTLY MAKE A DECISION THAT WILL DESTINE YOU FOR **LASTING** GREATNESS.
ONCE WE RETURN TO EARTH, IF YOU WOULD **WILLINGLY** COME TO ONE OF MY FACILITIES, IN THE CHARMING CZECH CITY OF--
Hmm...
...TO DO LIST, POINT ONE--
DAMN HIM--!
--HE IS TURNING MY PROPHECY INTO A MERE--
AND THIS DURING THE CLIMAX OF **SALVATION RU**
--Meretricious Matt.

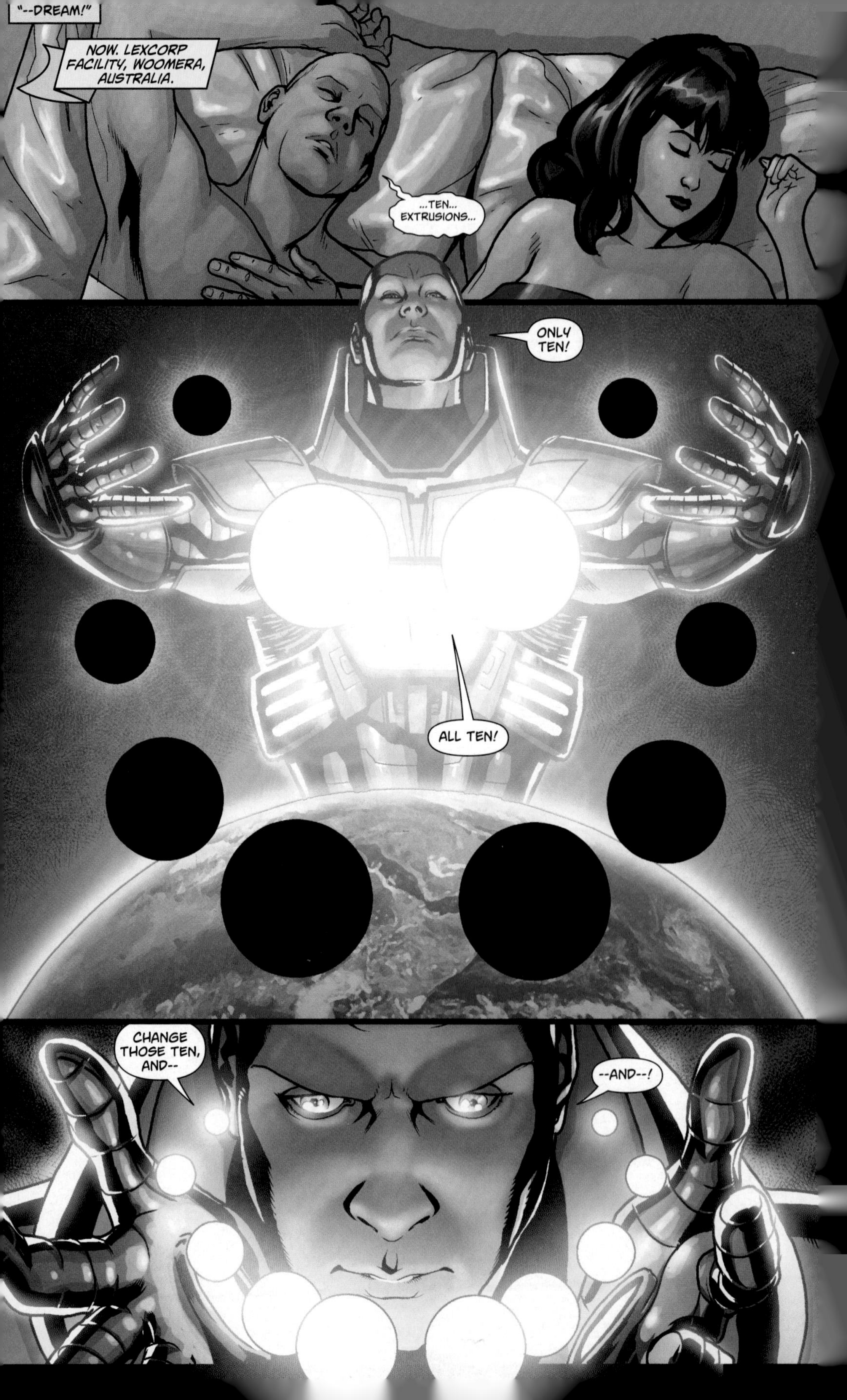
"--DREAM!"
NOW. LEXCORP FACILITY, WOOMERA, AUSTRALIA.
...TEN... EXTRUSIONS...
ONLY TEN!
ALL TEN!
CHANGE THOSE TEN, AND--
--AND--!

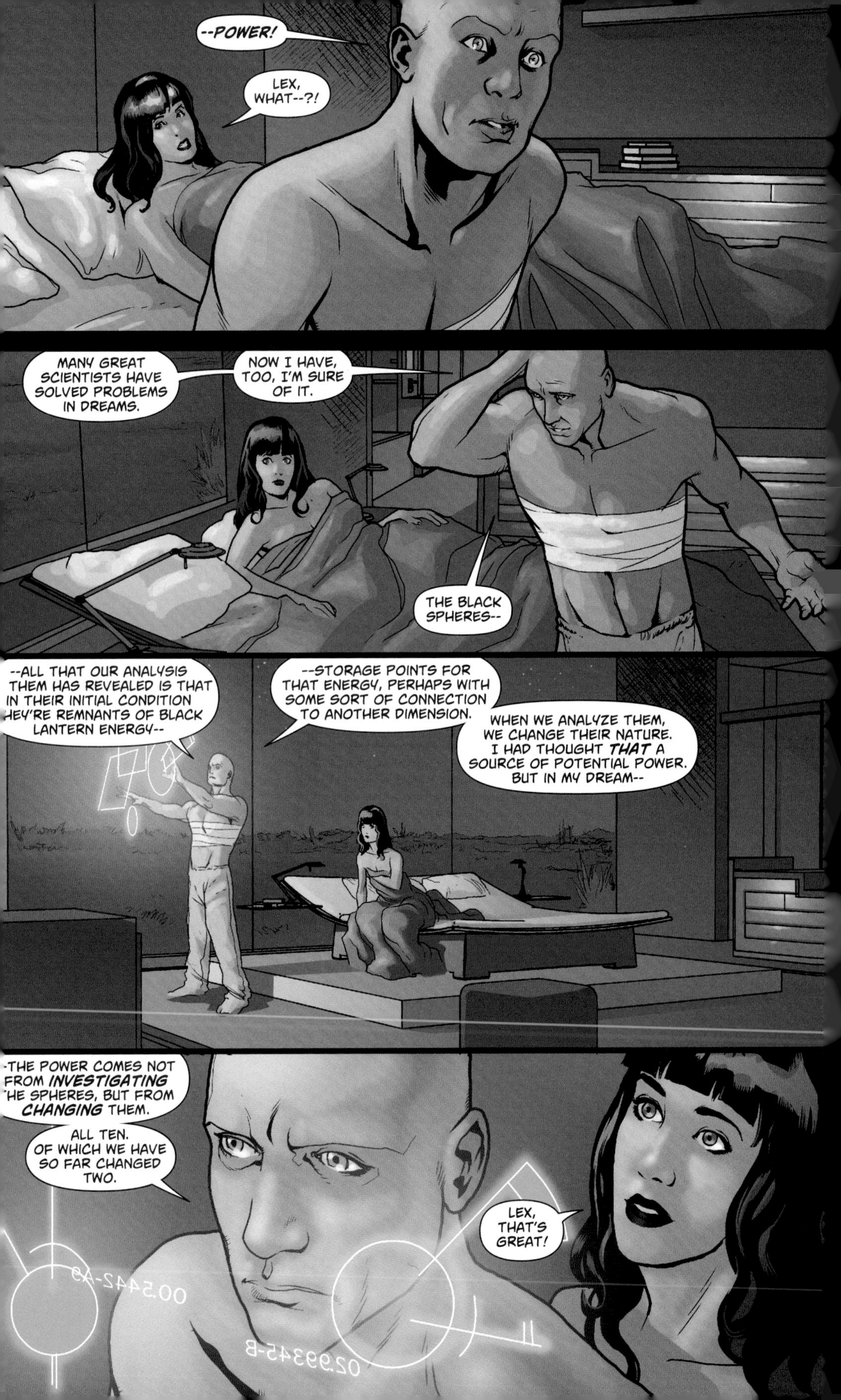
--POWER!
LEX, WHAT--?!
MANY GREAT SCIENTISTS HAVE SOLVED PROBLEMS IN DREAMS.
NOW I HAVE, TOO, I'M SURE OF IT.
THE BLACK SPHERES--
--ALL THAT OUR ANALYSIS THEM HAS REVEALED IS THAT IN THEIR INITIAL CONDITION HEY'RE REMNANTS OF BLACK LANTERN ENERGY--
--STORAGE POINTS FOR THAT ENERGY, PERHAPS WITH SOME SORT OF CONNECTION TO ANOTHER DIMENSION.
WHEN WE ANALYZE THEM, WE CHANGE THEIR NATURE. I HAD THOUGHT THAT A SOURCE OF POTENTIAL POWER. BUT IN MY DREAM--
-THE POWER COMES NOT FROM INVESTIGATING 'HE SPHERES, BUT FROM CHANGING THEM.
ALL TEN. OF WHICH WE HAVE SO FAR CHANGED TWO.
LEX, THAT'S GREAT!

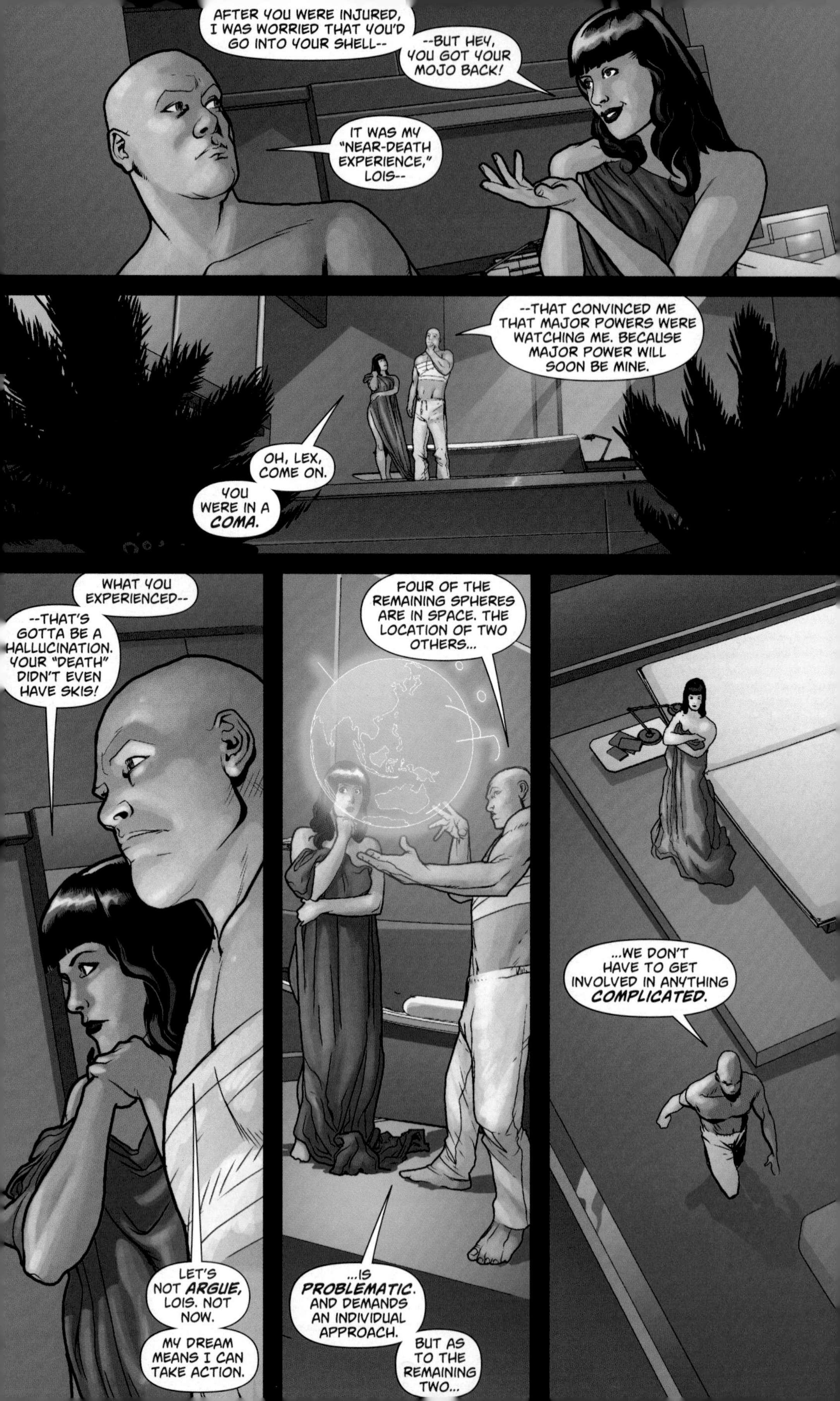
AFTER YOU WERE INJURED, I WAS WORRIED THAT YOU'D GO INTO YOUR SHELL--
--BUT HEY, YOU GOT YOUR MOJO BACK!
IT WAS MY "NEAR-DEATH EXPERIENCE," LOIS--
--THAT CONVINCED ME THAT MAJOR POWERS WERE WATCHING ME. BECAUSE MAJOR POWER WILL SOON BE MINE.
OH, LEX, COME ON.
YOU WERE IN A *COMA.*
WHAT YOU EXPERIENCED--
--THAT'S GOTTA BE A HALLUCINATION. YOUR "DEATH" DIDN'T EVEN HAVE SKIS!
LET'S NOT *ARGUE,* LOIS. NOT NOW.
MY DREAM MEANS I CAN TAKE ACTION.
FOUR OF THE REMAINING SPHERES ARE IN SPACE. THE LOCATION OF TWO OTHERS...
...IS *PROBLEMATIC*. AND DEMANDS AN INDIVIDUAL APPROACH.
BUT AS TO THE REMAINING TWO...
...WE DON'T HAVE TO GET INVOLVED IN ANYTHING *COMPLICATED.*

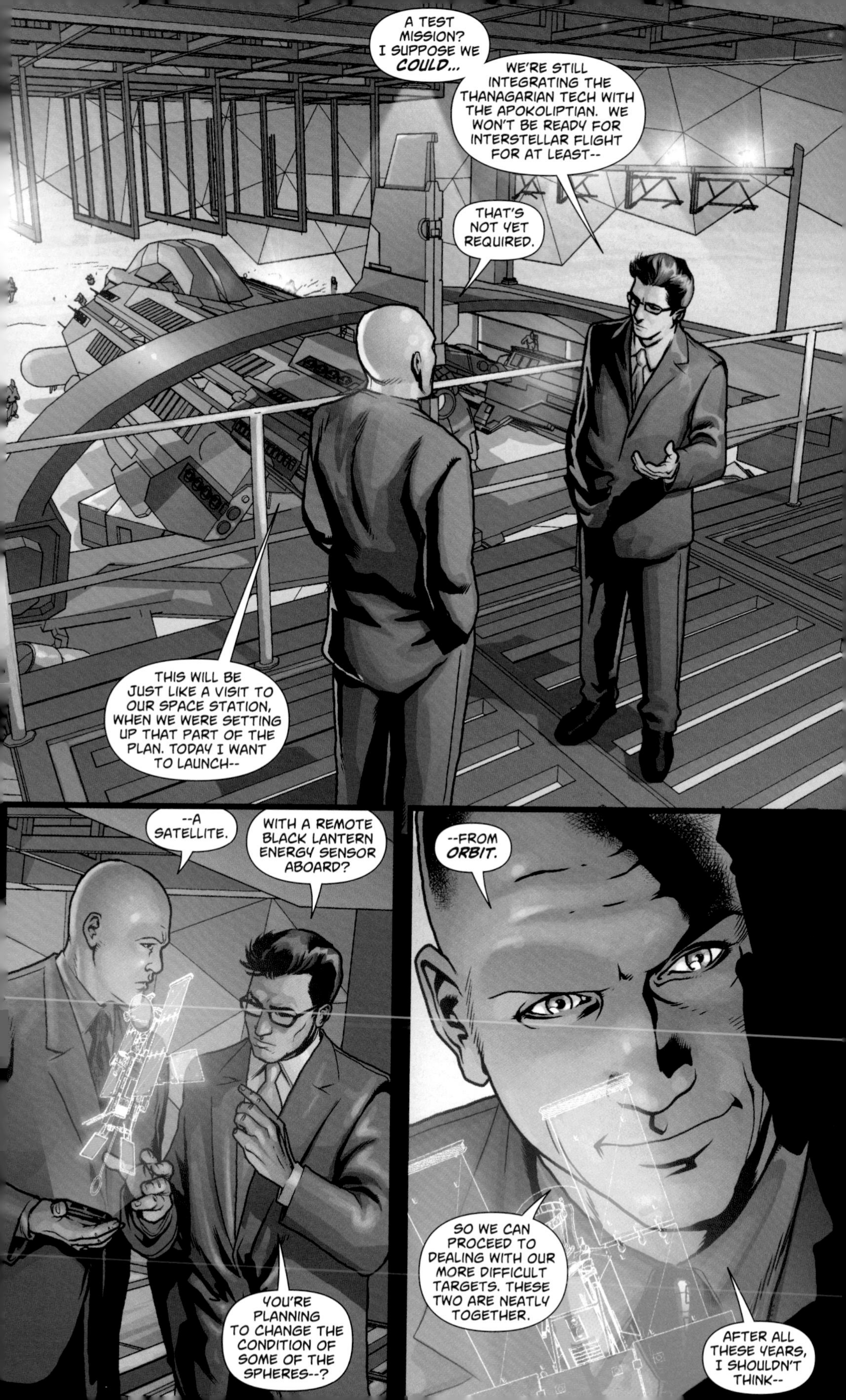

A TEST MISSION? I SUPPOSE WE *COULD...*
WE'RE STILL INTEGRATING THE THANAGARIAN TECH WITH THE APOKOLIPTIAN. WE WON'T BE READY FOR INTERSTELLAR FLIGHT FOR AT LEAST--
THAT'S NOT YET REQUIRED.
THIS WILL BE JUST LIKE A VISIT TO OUR SPACE STATION, WHEN WE WERE SETTING UP THAT PART OF THE PLAN. TODAY I WANT TO LAUNCH--
--A SATELLITE.
WITH A REMOTE BLACK LANTERN ENERGY SENSOR ABOARD?
YOU'RE PLANNING TO CHANGE THE CONDITION OF SOME OF THE SPHERES--?
--FROM *ORBIT.*
SO WE CAN PROCEED TO DEALING WITH OUR MORE DIFFICULT TARGETS. THESE TWO ARE NEATLY TOGETHER.
AFTER ALL THESE YEARS, I SHOULDN'T THINK--

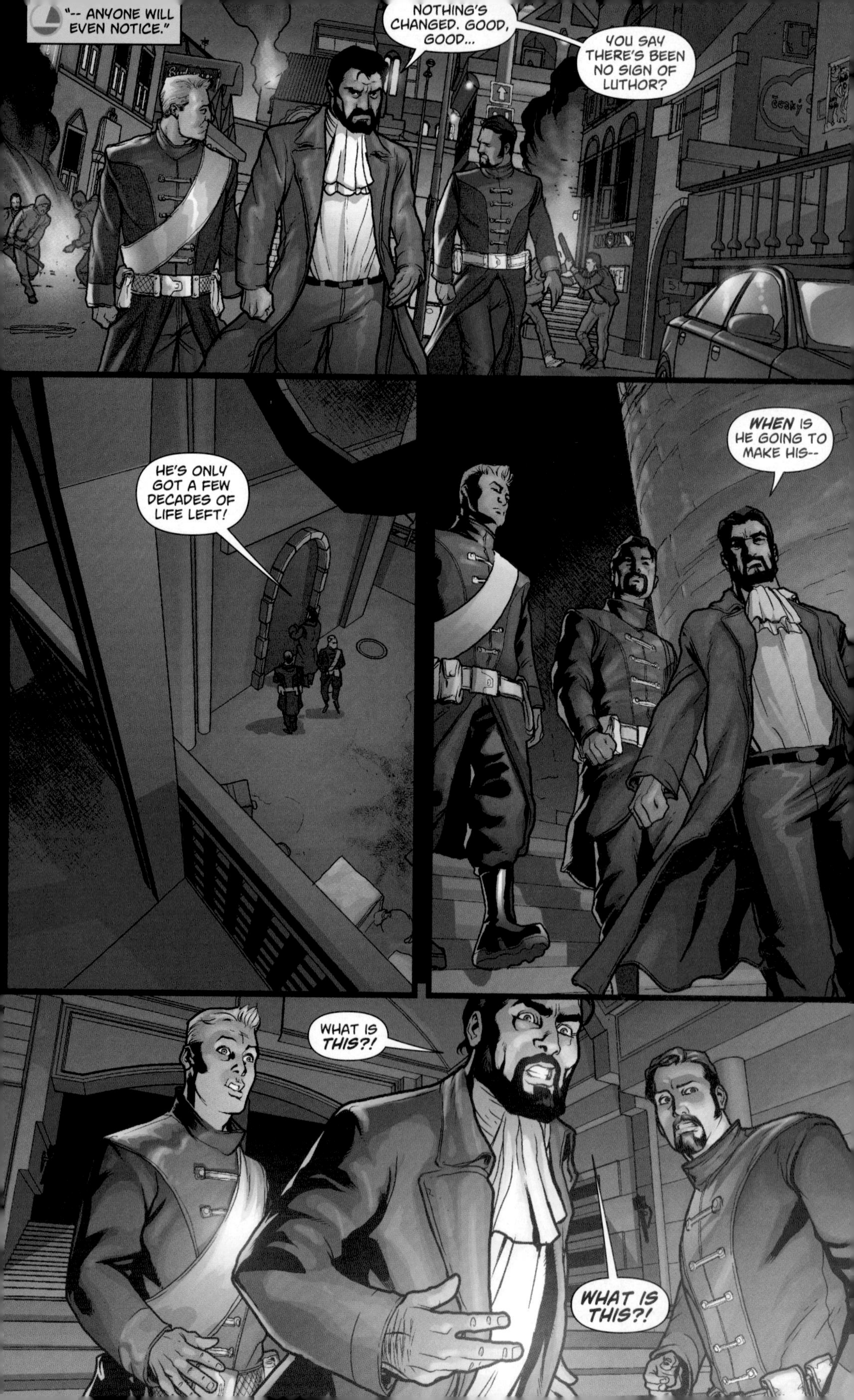
"-- ANYONE WILL EVEN NOTICE."
NOTHING'S CHANGED. GOOD, GOOD...
YOU SAY THERE'S BEEN NO SIGN OF LUTHOR?
HE'S ONLY GOT A FEW DECADES OF LIFE LEFT!
WHEN IS HE GOING TO MAKE HIS--
WHAT IS THIS?!
WHAT IS THIS?!

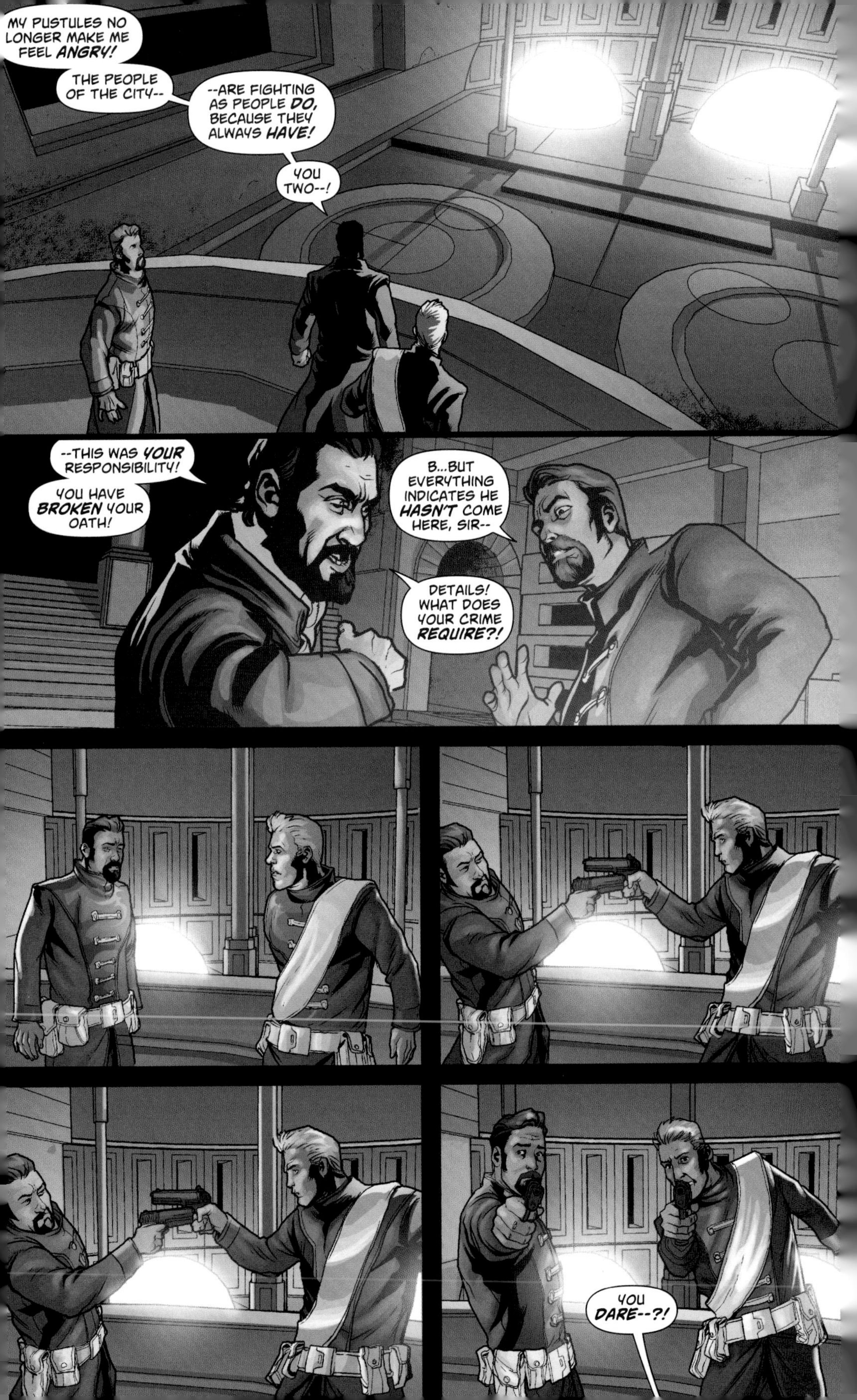
MY PUSTULES NO LONGER MAKE ME FEEL ANGRY!
THE PEOPLE OF THE CITY--
--ARE FIGHTING AS PEOPLE DO, BECAUSE THEY ALWAYS HAVE!
YOU TWO--!
--THIS WAS YOUR RESPONSIBILITY!
YOU HAVE BROKEN YOUR OATH!
B...BUT EVERYTHING INDICATES HE HASN'T COME HERE, SIR--
DETAILS! WHAT DOES YOUR CRIME REQUIRE?!
YOU DARE--?!

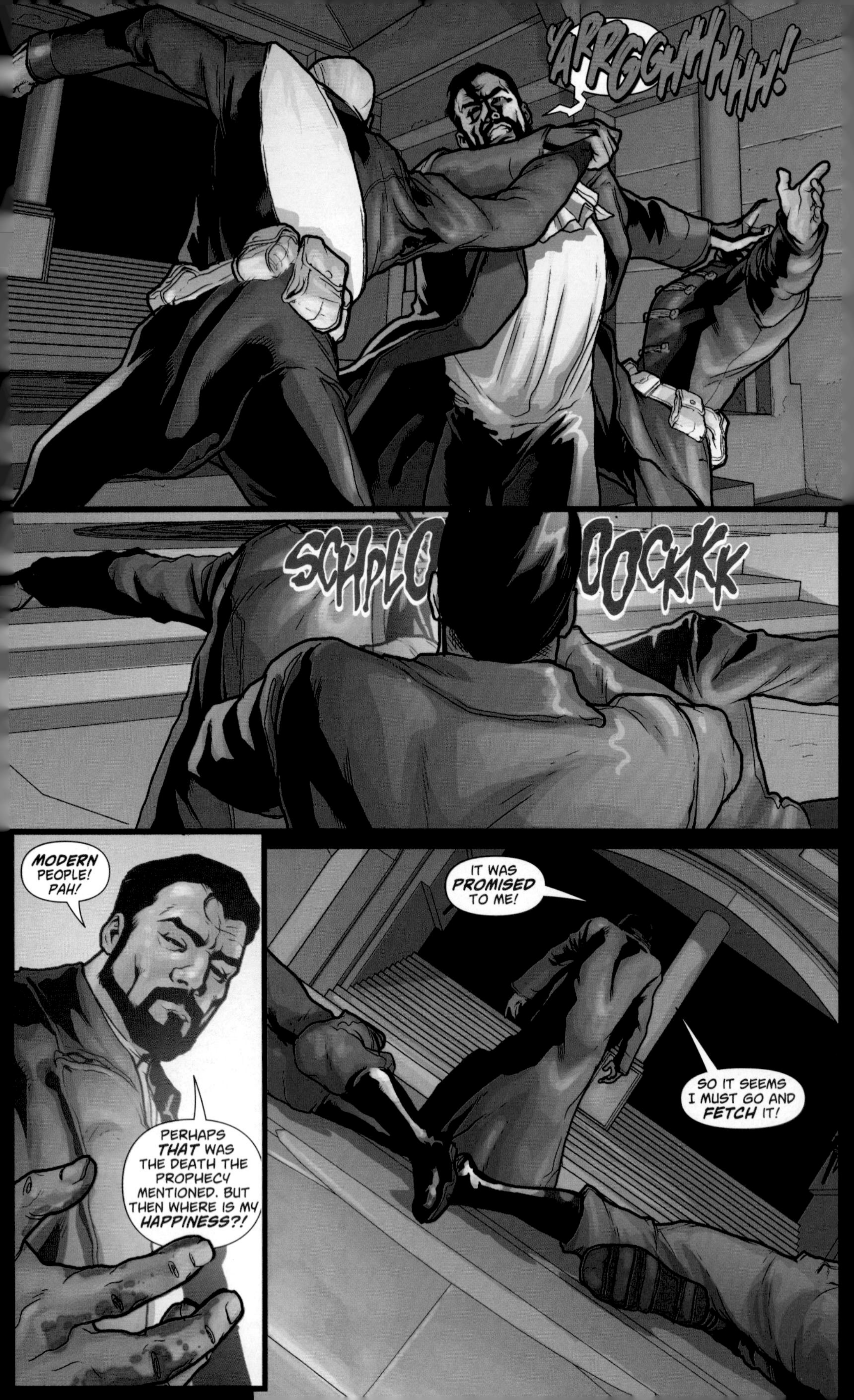
YARRGGHHHHH!
SCHPLO OOCKKK
MODERN PEOPLE! PAH!
PERHAPS THAT WAS THE DEATH THE PROPHECY MENTIONED. BUT THEN WHERE IS MY HAPPINESS?!
IT WAS PROMISED TO ME!
SO IT SEEMS I MUST GO AND FETCH IT!

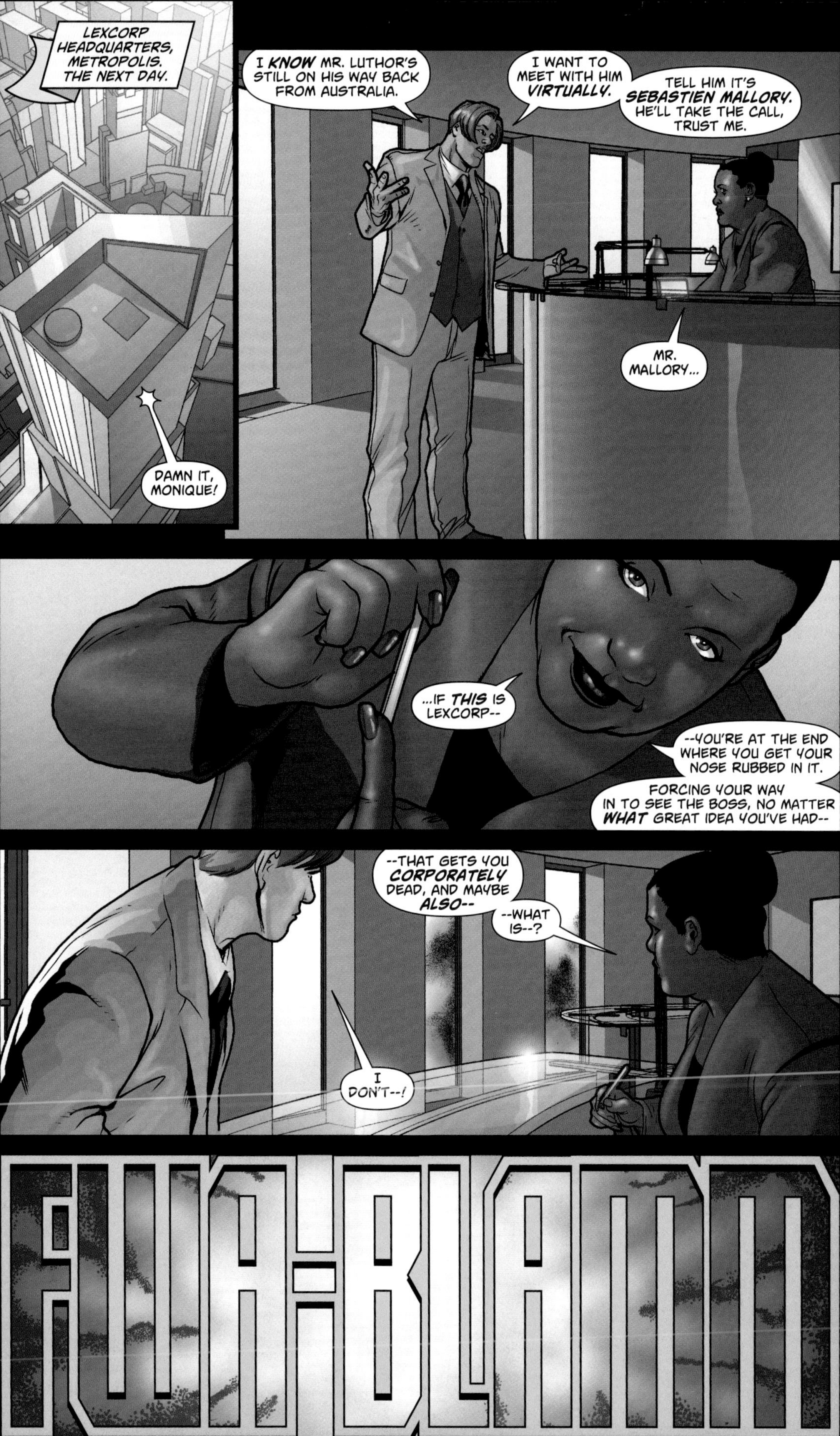
LEXCORP HEADQUARTERS, METROPOLIS. THE NEXT DAY.
DAMN IT, MONIQUE!
I KNOW MR. LUTHOR'S STILL ON HIS WAY BACK FROM AUSTRALIA.
I WANT TO MEET WITH HIM VIRTUALLY.
TELL HIM IT'S SEBASTIEN MALLORY. HE'LL TAKE THE CALL, TRUST ME.
MR. MALLORY...
...IF THIS IS LEXCORP--
--YOU'RE AT THE END WHERE YOU GET YOUR NOSE RUBBED IN IT.
FORCING YOUR WAY IN TO SEE THE BOSS, NO MATTER WHAT GREAT IDEA YOU'VE HAD--
--THAT GETS YOU CORPORATELY DEAD, AND MAYBE ALSO--
--WHAT IS--?
I DON'T--!
FWA-BLAM

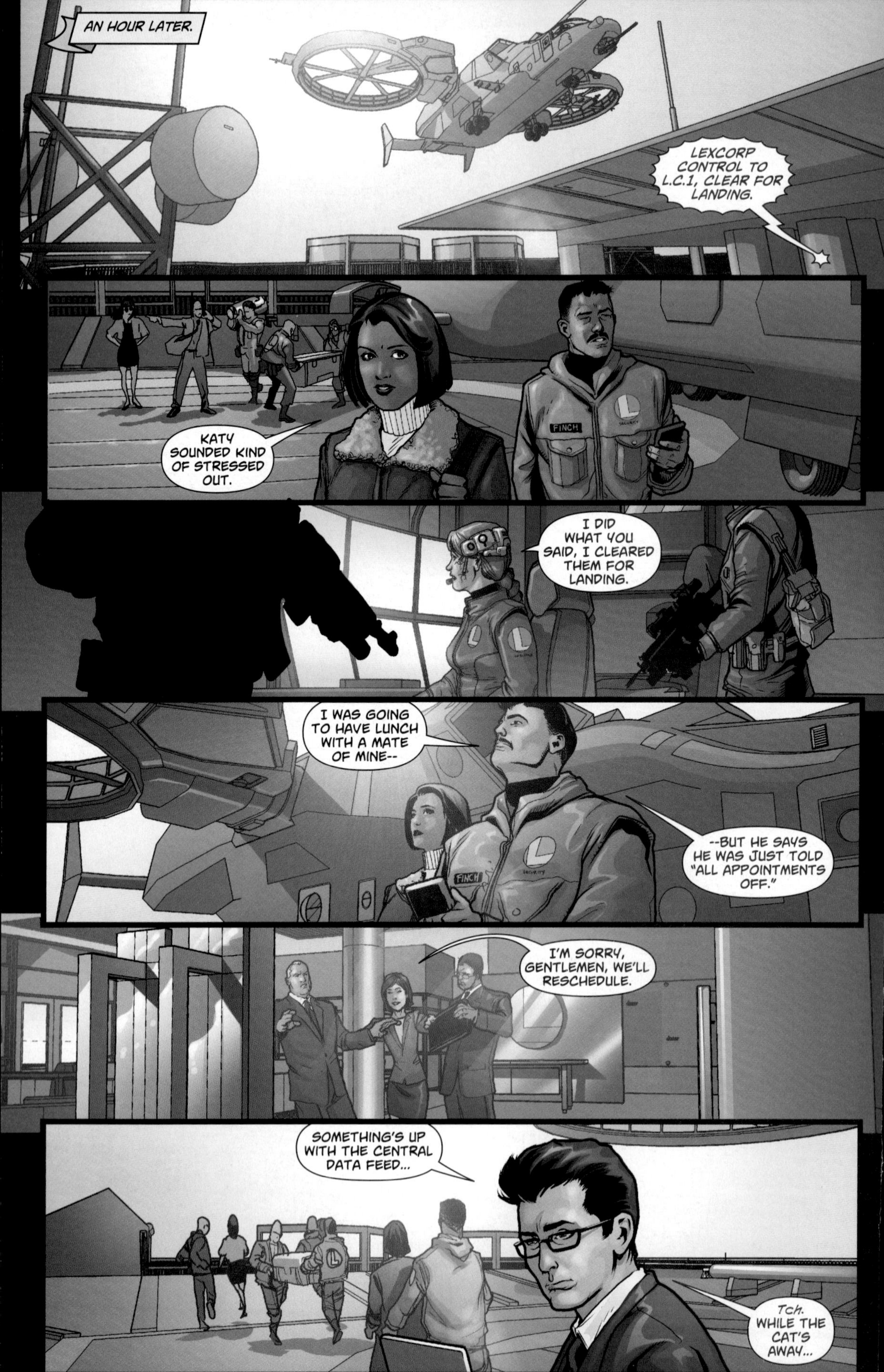
AN HOUR LATER.
LEXCORP CONTROL TO L.C.1, CLEAR FOR LANDING.
KATY SOUNDED KIND OF STRESSED OUT.
FINCH
I DID WHAT YOU SAID, I CLEARED THEM FOR LANDING.
I WAS GOING TO HAVE LUNCH WITH A MATE OF MINE--
FINCH
--BUT HE SAYS HE WAS JUST TOLD "ALL APPOINTMENTS OFF."
I'M SORRY, GENTLEMEN, WE'LL RESCHEDULE.
SOMETHING'S UP WITH THE CENTRAL DATA FEED...
Tch. WHILE THE CAT'S AWAY...

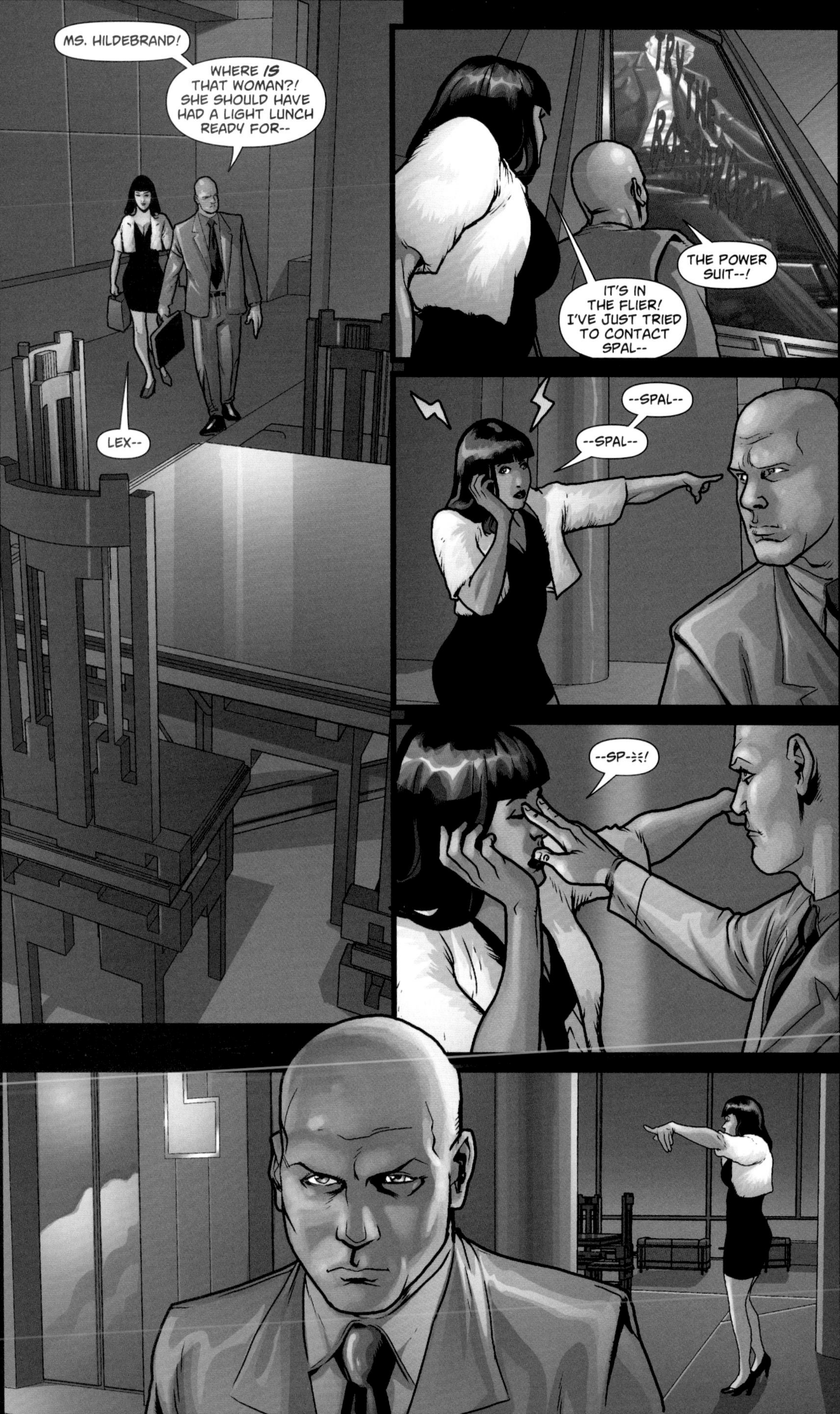
MS. HILDEBRAND!
WHERE *IS* THAT WOMAN?! SHE SHOULD HAVE HAD A LIGHT LUNCH READY FOR--
LEX--
THE POWER SUIT--!
IT'S IN THE FLIER! I'VE JUST TRIED TO CONTACT SPAL--
--SPAL--
--SPAL--
--SP-*!

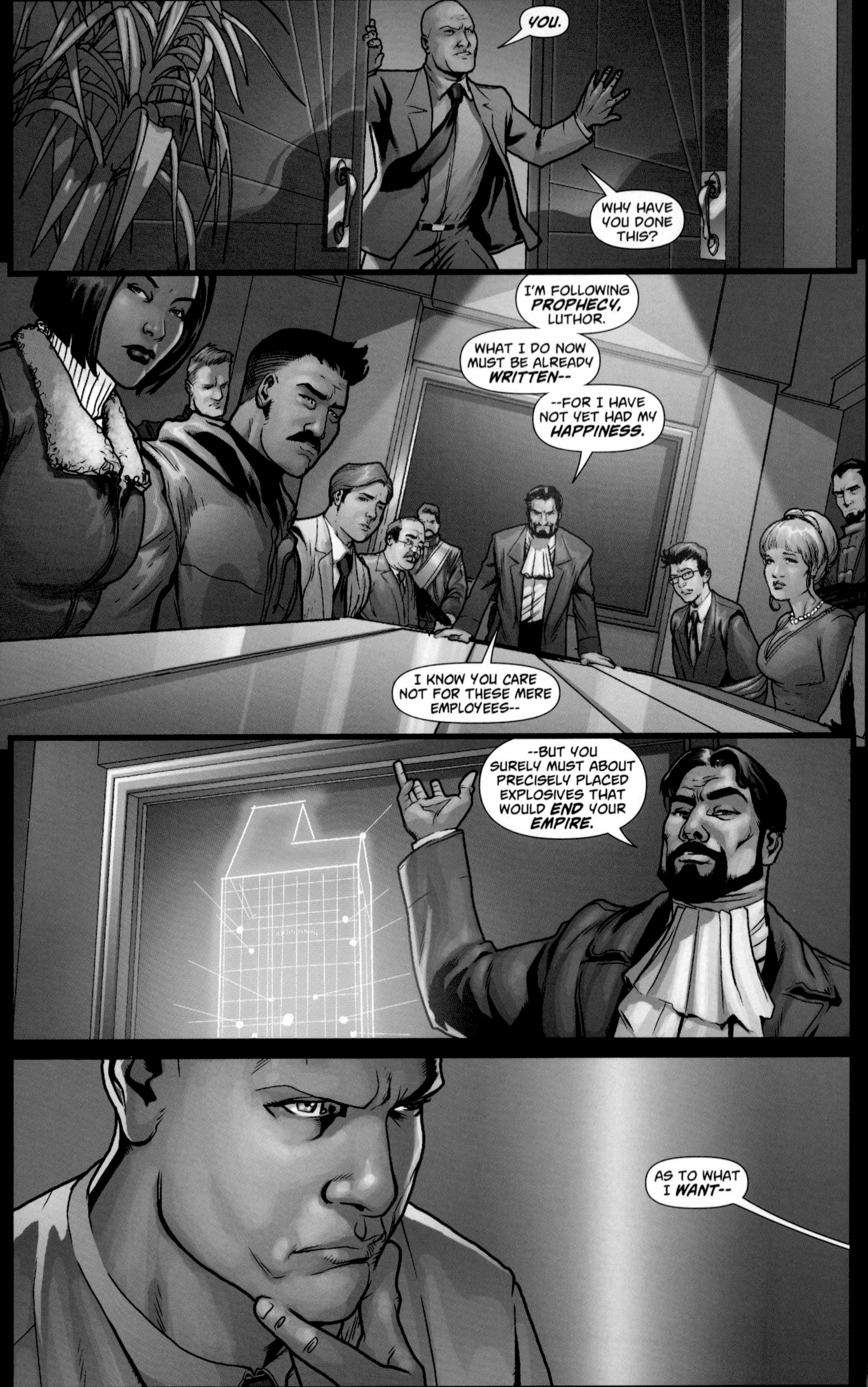
YOU.
WHY HAVE YOU DONE THIS?
I'M FOLLOWING PROPHECY, LUTHOR.
WHAT I DO NOW MUST BE ALREADY WRITTEN--
--FOR I HAVE NOT YET HAD MY HAPPINESS.
I KNOW YOU CARE NOT FOR THESE MERE EMPLOYEES--
--BUT YOU SURELY MUST ABOUT PRECISELY PLACED EXPLOSIVES THAT WOULD END YOUR EMPIRE.
AS TO WHAT I WANT--

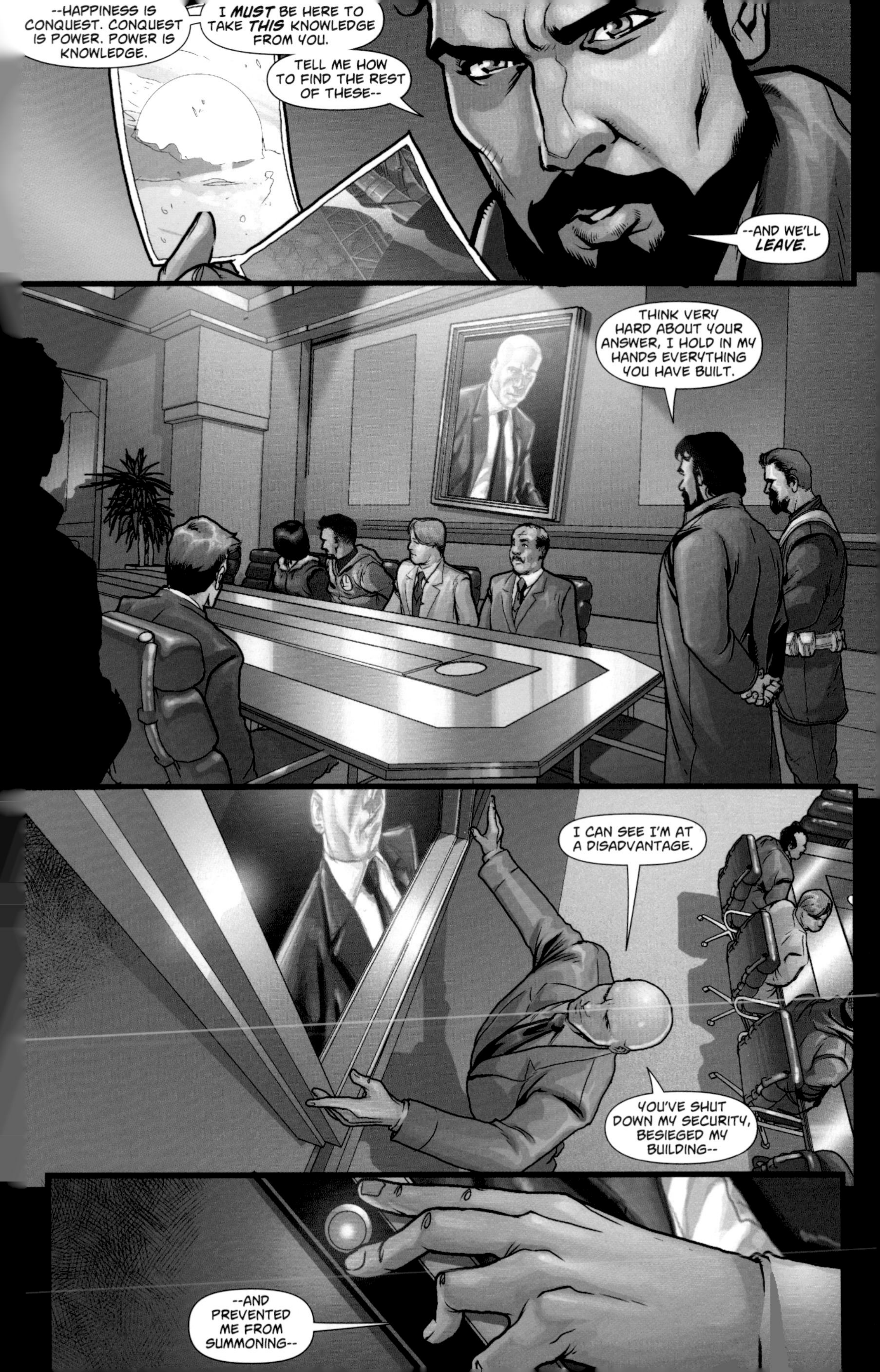
--HAPPINESS IS CONQUEST. CONQUEST IS POWER. POWER IS KNOWLEDGE.
I **MUST** BE HERE TO TAKE **THIS** KNOWLEDGE FROM YOU.
TELL ME HOW TO FIND THE REST OF THESE--
--AND WE'LL **LEAVE.**
THINK VERY HARD ABOUT YOUR ANSWER, I HOLD IN MY HANDS EVERYTHING YOU HAVE BUILT.
I CAN SEE I'M AT A DISADVANTAGE.
YOU'VE SHUT DOWN MY SECURITY, BESIEGED MY BUILDING--
--AND PREVENTED ME FROM SUMMONING--

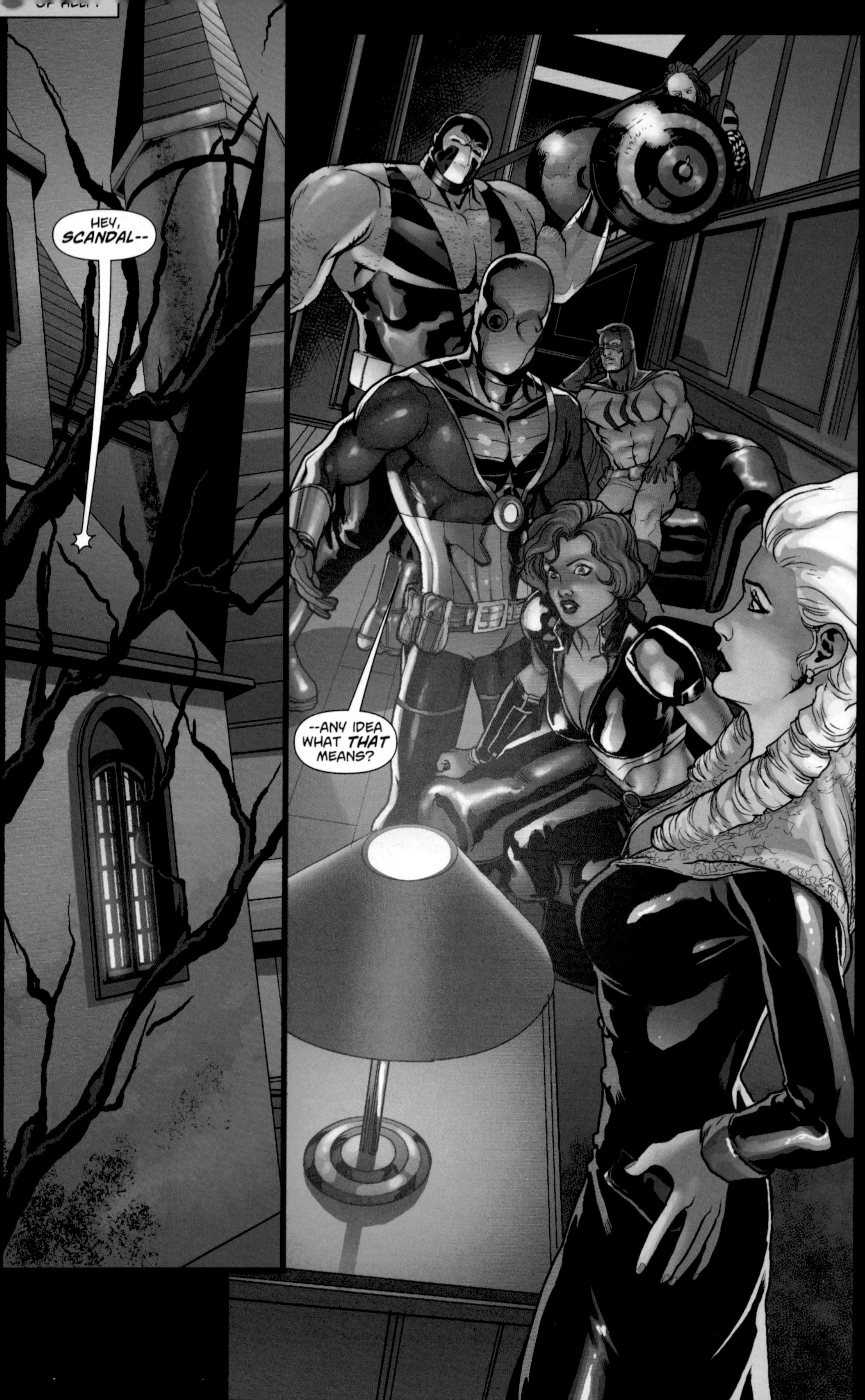
HEY, SCANDAL--
--ANY IDEA WHAT THAT MEANS?

ACTION COMICS 890 variant by
DAVID FINCH & PETER STEIGERWALD

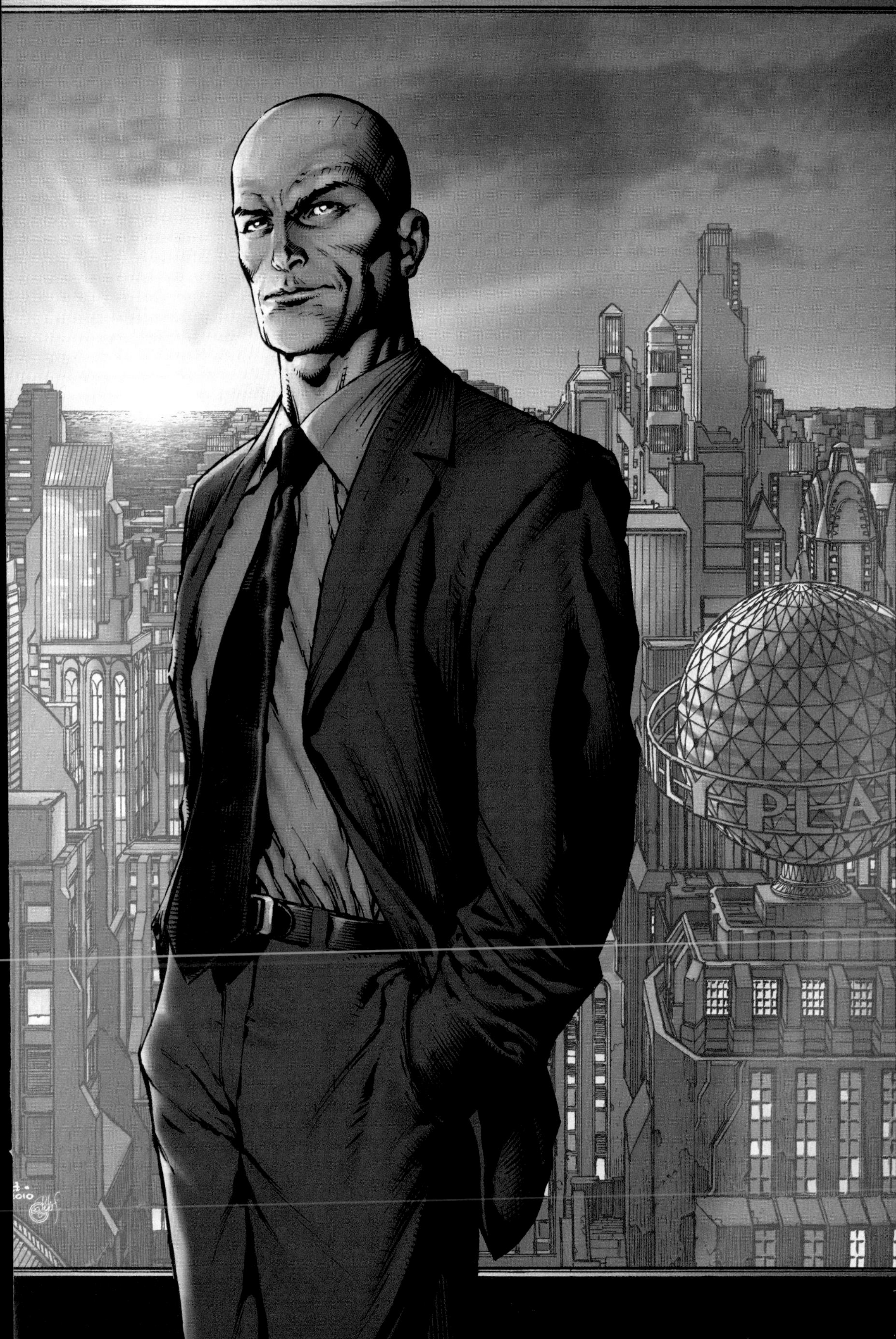

PLA

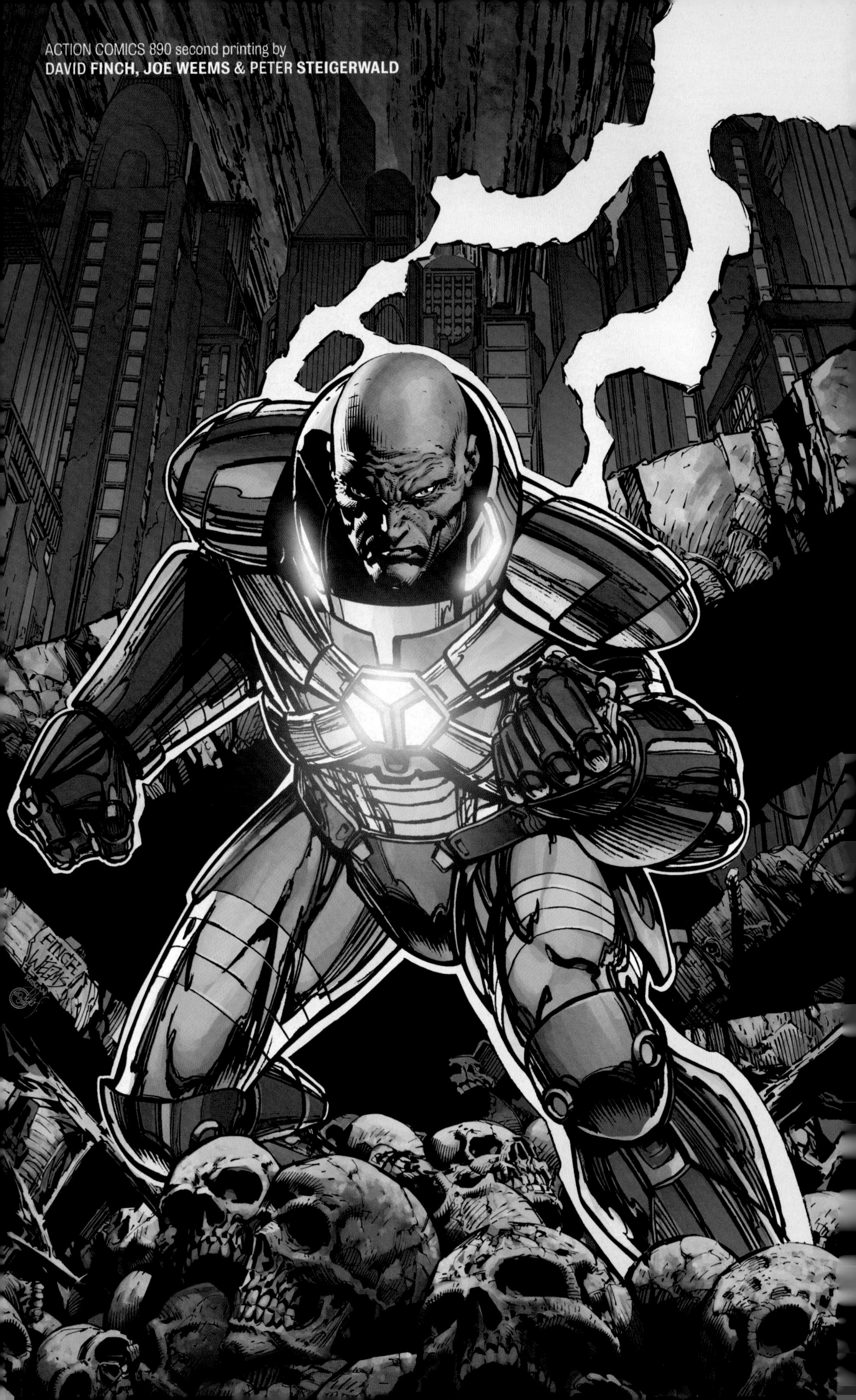

ACTION COMICS 890 second printing by
DAVID FINCH, JOE WEEMS & PETER STEIGERWALD

ACTION COMICS 892 variant by
IVAN REIS, OCLIAR **ALBERT** & ALEX **SINCLAIR** AFTER CARMINE INFANTINO & MURPHY ANDERSON

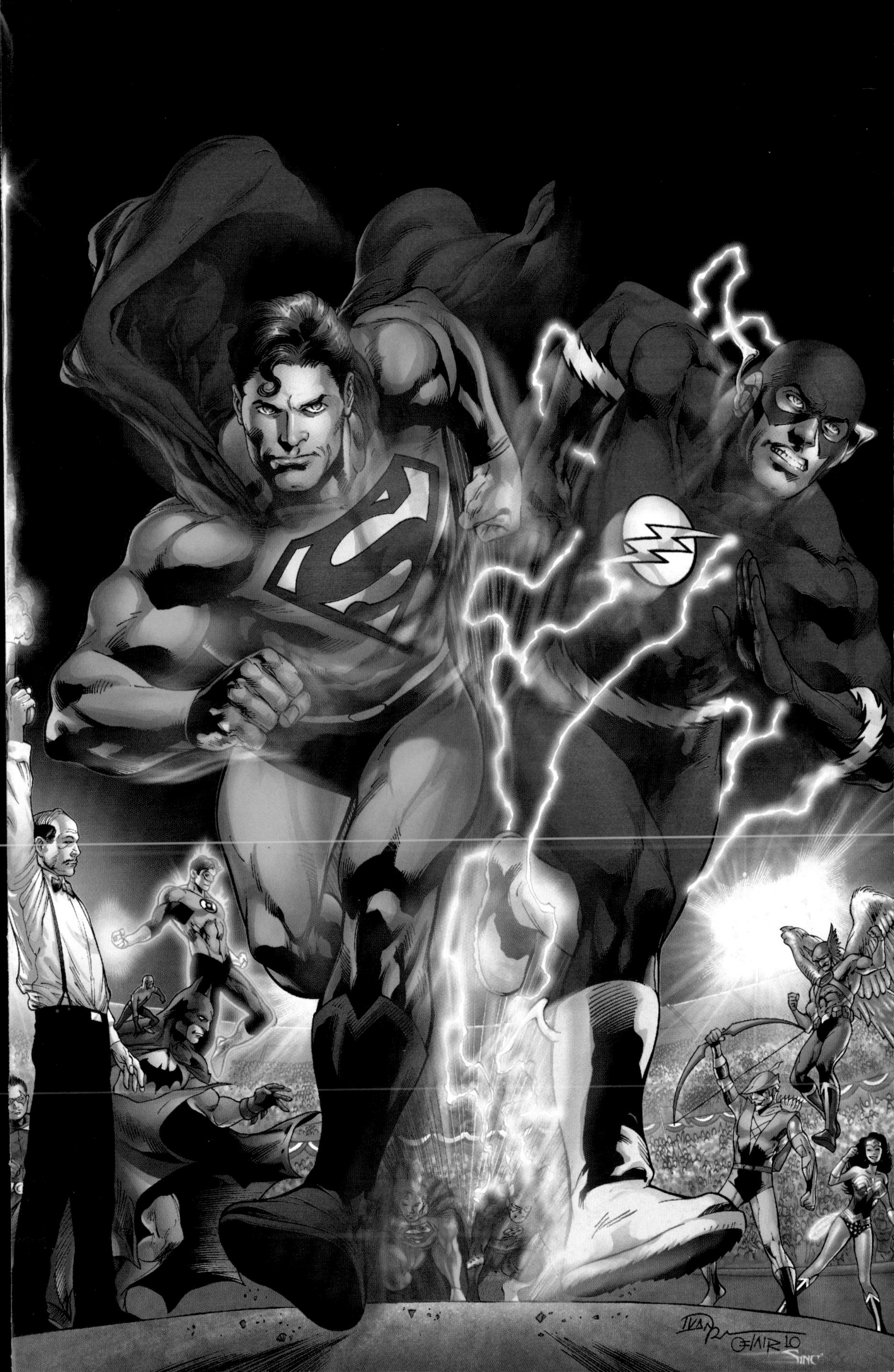

ACTION COMICS 894 variant by
P. CRAIG RUSSELL

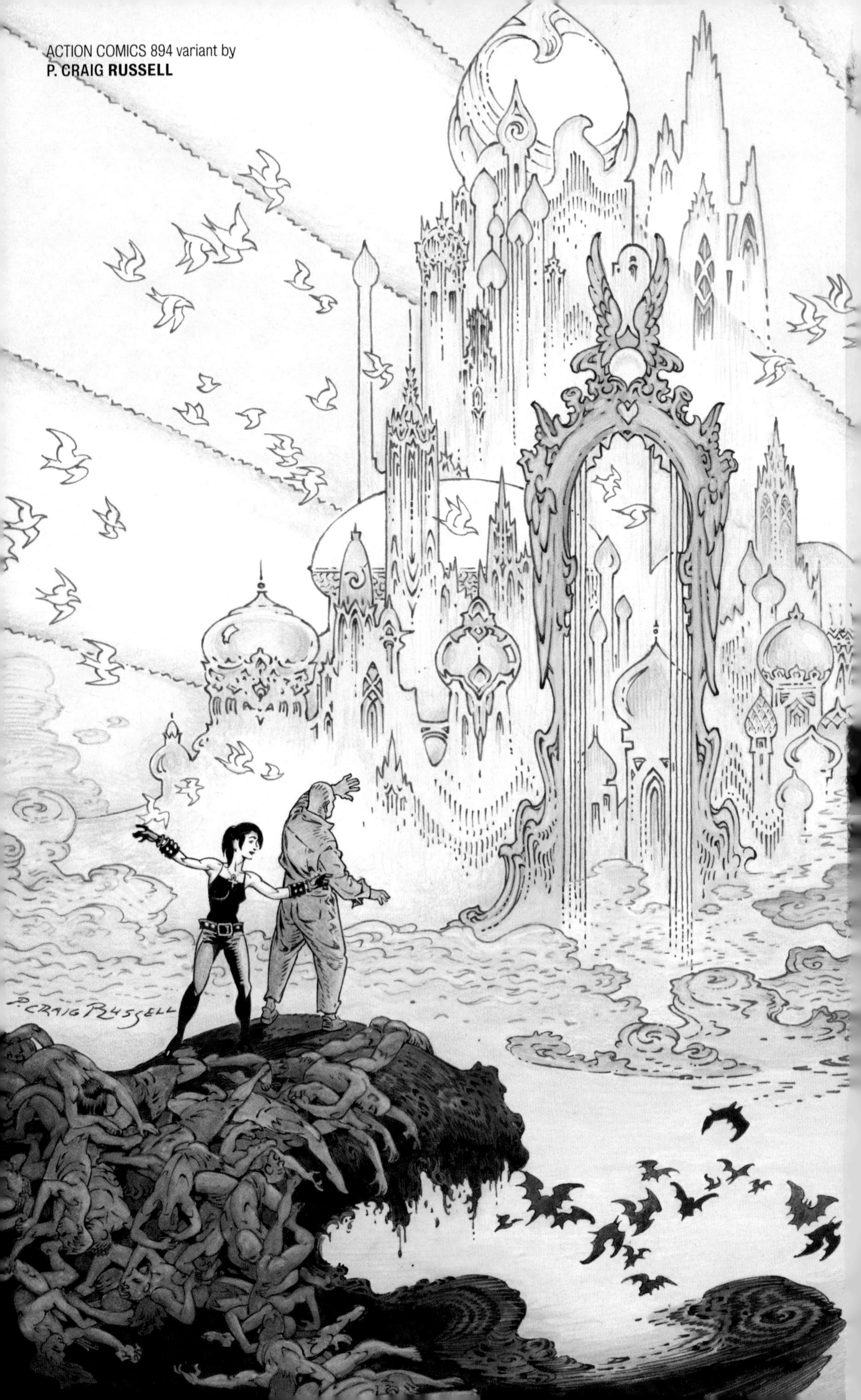
P. CRAIG RUSSELL